# Circles of Freedom

ALSO BY T.C.A. RAGHAVAN

*Attendant Lords: Bairam Khan and Abdur Rahim – Courtiers and Poets in Mughal India*

*The People Next Door: The Curious History of India's Relations with Pakistan*

*History Men: Jadunath Sarkar, G.S. Sardesai, Raghubir Sinh and Their Quest For India's Past*

# Circles of Freedom

## Friendship, Love and Loyalty in the Indian National Struggle

T.C.A. Raghavan

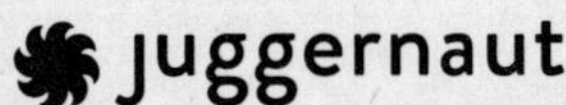

JUGGERNAUT BOOKS
C-I-128, First Floor, Sangam Vihar, Near Holi Chowk,
New Delhi 110080, India

First published by Juggernaut Books 2024



10 9 8 7 6 5 4 3 2 1

P-ISBN: 9789353457952
E-ISBN: 9789353456276



Typeset in Adobe Caslon Pro by
R. Ajith Kumar, Noida

Printed at Thomson Press India Ltd

*For Ranjana*

# Contents

# Introduction

*I was also a note in this grand orchestration of human aspiration.*

– Asaf Ali

The first half of the twentieth century in India is identified with a group of individuals who have dominated its narration long after they were gone: Mohandas Gandhi, Jawaharlal Nehru, Vallabhbhai Patel, Subhas Chandra Bose, M.A. Jinnah, V.D. Savarkar, B.R. Ambedkar. Some may argue that this list tilts towards the later decades of the first half of the century. B.G. Tilak and G.K. Gokhale would restore that balance. If such a list privileges the political class, then the addition of Rabindranath Tagore, Aurobindo Ghosh and Muhammad Iqbal provides some counterweight. These towering figures, these stalwarts, these founding fathers, are habitually invoked by their respective followers whenever India's struggle for freedom comes up for discussion. They provide a kind of history through biography of that tumultuous period when nationalism clashed with imperialism and in the process two nations emerged.

Alongside this gallery is a set of events that are invoked, encompassing an interface between imperialism and nationalism and between the divisions within nationalism. Certain milestones are a standard part of this narrative: the partition of Bengal in 1905; the Morley–Minto reforms of 1909; the pact between the Muslim League and the Congress in Lucknow in 1916; the limited self-government or 'dyarchy' introduced by the 1919 Montagu–Chelmsford reforms; the Motilal Nehru and Sir John Simon reports of 1928 and 1930 respectively; the Government of India Act of 1935; and finally the Independence of India Act of 1947. Constitutional and legislative changes accompanied every stage of the national movement and the manner in which these came about provide another lens to view that half decade. Major protests such as the Khilafat and Non-cooperation movements in the aftermath of World War I, Civil Disobedience in the early 1930s and the Quit India movement of the early 1940s impart to the time its well-known characteristic of struggle, sacrifice, discipline and high endeavour. The constitutional and the agitational modes each had within them a darker underside – in the form of sectional and communal pressures. The period as a whole was therefore not a binary between nationalism and imperialism or between freedom and colonial status but a triangle with communalism and subsequently separatism. August 1947 was, tragically but perhaps fittingly enough, the culmination of each of these trends. The agitations for freedom led to the departure of the British, and India and Pakistan emerged as different entities amidst a communal bloodbath that has left a legacy of suspicion and mistrust as enduring as the ideas of freedom that the first half of the twentieth century fostered.

As the attainment of freedom itself passed its fourth and fifth decades, new schools of historiography posed alternative retellings of the Indian national movement. Emphasis shifted away from the idea of history and politics being driven by great leaders or, in other readings, by constitutional and legal change. In the more powerful of these new explanations, real history was made not by leaders or by institutions undergoing change, but by more subaltern communities and grassroots movements whose contributions had gone unrecognized by the mainstream historical record. Giving them a voice and understanding their agency required reading conventional historical sources and evidence differently – or even against the grain, so to say.

These different perspectives – whether of great leaders leading popular agitation and struggling to keep their flock together, while simultaneously wrestling with constitutional and legal issues; or masses of anonymous subalterns retaining purpose and agency – crowd our perspective and leave little room for other stories. But the Indian national movement was a vast stream made up of numerous and frequently contrarian little rivulets. Millions participated in it and there were many, many representatives, even leaders, all well known in their time or location but who become invisible in the dazzle of Gandhi, Nehru, Patel and others who monopolize the soundtrack of India's struggle for freedom. Bringing them centre stage is not an act of displacement of iconic individuals nor even one of simply reading against the grain the standard narratives they dominate. Rather, it is one of entering more deeply the same grain, and finding and reading in it other, lesser known, stories.

This book is about the veteran freedom fighter Asaf Ali (1888–1953) and also about the circle he was embedded in: those with whom he associated himself at various points of his life and for different reasons. It is reasonable to ask: why Asaf Ali? He was not someone who left behind a large corpus of private papers that would enable future intruders into his life story to construct a thick portrait. While he was a figure who would have been recognizable in an all-India context from the mid-1930s, this would only be to audiences knowledgeable about public affairs and those active in public life. Before that, in the 1920s and earlier, his arena was a smaller one. Delhi was the capital of British India from 1911 but largely a backwater compared to major intellectual and political centres such as Calcutta, Bombay, Madras, Lahore and Allahabad, among others. In Delhi, his territory, he was, through the 1920s, largely in the nature of another important lieutenant, someone in the inner circles of the leaders – almost a subaltern figure in some senses if some liberties are permitted in the use of the term. However, Asaf figured in some of the seminal moments of the freedom struggle and his perspective provides much more than a tangential view to mainstream narratives.

At different stages of Asaf's life we find him juxtaposed against two major figures of the first half of the twentieth century: Mohammad Ali (1878–1931) and the better known Muhammad Ali Jinnah. The former has retreated from our everyday consciousness but a century ago his infectious energy and crusading zeal for Islamist causes in India and abroad made him a model for many. Both came to provide ballast to the contrarian trend to secular and civic nationalism with which Asaf came to identify himself. Their certainties and convictions throw Asaf's frailties and doubts into relief, as also his moderation in a divided and polarized period of our history. These very qualities also bring him closer to us and to our own times even as his period retreats further into the past. At the other end of the spectrum and perhaps closest to him in his thinking is the figure of Abul Kalam Azad (1888–1958). As Muslims, Asaf and Azad strove to situate themselves in the mainstream of the freedom struggle through the Indian National Congress and also constantly struggled against the reality that views such as those of a Mohammad Ali or a Jinnah were easier than their own moderate positions.

And then as a Muslim in the Congress married to a Hindu, Asaf's was an unusual perch to view the different meanings of partition and independence in the subcontinent and the processes by which these end states were arrived at. His marriage itself moreover comprised other dimensions than the obvious Hindu–Muslim axis which made it so singular almost a century ago, much as it does now. Asaf, from quite early in his political career, marked himself as a moderate, a lawyer bent on securing his objectives through force of argument, and a gradualist on matters concerning political change. His wife Aruna (1909–96) came to chart much of her own course as a radical voice within the national movement. Hers was also a critique, a radical critique in fact, both of Gandhian nationalism and also of the incremental political change that her husband consciously adhered to. 'You are the State, I am the Revolution,' she once said to Asaf, quoting Lenin humorously but with considerable accuracy.[1] Both these diametrically opposed impulses within the marriage provide their own dramatic force to any narrative of their lives.

Yet, all of this – the tumultuous times, an unusual marriage and an even more unusual wife, and being a Muslim disagreeing with the need for a separate homeland – bestow on Asaf Ali a certain privileged position from which to view the collision of different ideas and principles by which nationhood both came to be forged and partitioned. Perhaps given the polarities of our own times, Asaf Ali's figure is instructive in other ways too. He is the archetypical attendant lord or a somewhat peripheral figure in a drama packed with larger-than-life characters, but also one who saw with clarity the dilemmas of his time and the need for moderation and compromise but was too incidental to influence the course of events.

Asaf is, however, not the only focus here, for this story is also about a circle of his particular friends. Living at a time when life was more than a search for personal happiness, fulfilment and stability, for them politics, ideology, dissent, great struggle and sacrifice contextualized the more human but equally important acts of friendship, love and loyalty. Asaf Ali was not the 'leader' of this group; nor was this a set of persons who acted together as a unit. But the lives of those in this circle – Sarojini Naidu (1879–1949), Syud Hossain (1888–1949), Syed Mahmud (1889–1971) and finally Aruna Asaf Ali – deeply touched Asaf Ali's at different times and at different stages. And, as is common in many friendships, their relationships did not remain unchanged, evolving over time, as did their personalities and their circumstances.

This small circle, however, acquires its meaning only because of the larger circle of the freedom movement: their relationships with each other were consciously embedded in that larger enterprise. They were not always a group, that is, a set of friends who regularly met; their connection, sometimes intense, sometimes dormant for years, was with each other individually. Each was also part of other informal 'circles' of freedom: Asaf Ali was often in the company of Dr Ansari, Hakim Ajmal Khan, the Ali Brothers, at certain points of time, for instance. At the same time all were part of a larger circle which was dominated by the pantheon of the major figures mentioned earlier.

What this portrayal of Asaf Ali and his circle attempts is to see events through their eyes – a certain peripheral view, if you will, of familiar milestones. It tracks the idea of India's freedom from its small nascent beginnings to its becoming an anti-colonial struggle, an organized mass movement which successfully achieved its goal. Above all, this is an attempt to understand how the huge, unwieldy enterprise that was the freedom struggle articulated its many joints and tentacles. It is not always a ringside view, but what did it look like to people, all very talented, thinking and significant individuals in their own right, just beyond the ring so to speak? What did it feel like to be engaged in this grand project, simultaneously a success and a failure, that engulfed two generations and with which we are still preoccupied seven decades later?

# 1

# London, 1913–1914

Mohammad Asaf Ali never forgot the day he first met Sarojini Naidu. It was in London sometime in mid-1913. Writing about it some three decades later, he recalled being 'full of excitement' as he accompanied Gunnu – Mrinalini Chattopadhyay, Sarojini's younger sister – to the house of an English friend with whom Sarojini was staying. Asaf was introduced as 'Bhai' and 'a member of the family, a full-fledged Barrister, and a poet'. Sarojini 'held out her hand, smiled a bewitching smile, and a cascade of words followed'. Asaf wrote, 'I was a bit flustered and said something to disclaim the last title by which I had been introduced.' Sarojini was 'Akka', or older sister, to Gunnu and 'Akka' she would remain to Asaf too for the rest of their lives.[1]

Asaf, then twenty-five years old, was in London ostensibly to follow up on a case in the Privy Council, the highest court of appeal in the British Empire and therefore the ultimate decision-making body for all legal disputes in India too. But the case was an excuse. He had qualified as a barrister in London barely a year earlier, returned to Delhi but found himself 'homesick' for London where he had spent about three years studying law: 'England lay in my memory like a mountain of lodestone.' A 'hopeless brief' but with a client who could afford the fees of a Privy Council appeal became the means of returning, which felt 'like coming home'. Apart from his legal work, he hoped to start an Urdu literary magazine out of London and already had a title in mind: *Taj*. Some of his own poems were ready for its first issue, and he had persuaded friends for others. He was also spending time in the British Museum collecting samples of Urdu poetry by English writers of an earlier generation. These efforts promised to be 'greatly stimulated' by Sarojini Naidu's presence in London. She was after all a poet who had already received some acclaim in England, and consequently even more in India, with her collections, *The Golden Threshold* (1905) and the recently published *The Bird of Time* (1912). The former in particular had made Sarojini into a celebrity in both England and India. In one assessment, 'never had a book of poems by an Indian caused such a stir abroad'.[2] It pre-dated Tagore's *Geetanjali*, published in 1910, by some years. The English translation came in 1912.

Sarojini's brother had been a friend of Asaf's since 1908 when Asaf had first arrived in London as a student. Virendranath Chattopadhyaya (1880–1937), or Chatto or Binnie, was the first member of Sarojini's family to become friends with Asaf, and even at the time of their initial meeting Chatto was already on the path to becoming the Indian revolutionary and dissident in permanent exile in Europe. To Asaf he was 'affectionate, brimming with humour . . . moved by lofty idealism' but also 'sentimental to a fault' and with endless 'amorous tangles'. Asaf met Chatto's younger sister Gunnu during his second sojourn in London and in the process discovered that the Chattopadhyays were an 'amazing family'. They made friends for life but there was 'a kind of rivalry among themselves in several matters including friendships'. Moreover, with friends they discussed their brothers and sisters with remarkable frankness. He had soon been enlightened about Gunnu's and Chatto's current views of Sarojini, their oldest sibling: she was 'a little too self-centred, a sort of Narcissus', he was told.

His reading of her poetry and her siblings' descriptions had led him to expect 'a wisp of a women, given to dreamy silences and observant by side glances only'. But meeting Sarojini he found wispy she was not; she was 'full figured, picturesquely dressed, heavily bejewelled'- she 'falsified my mental picture of her in every single detail'. Sarojini Naidu was, to Asaf's fascinated eyes, 'radiant and restless, full of sparkling life and laughter'. Nobody would have believed that this sophisticated woman – she was then thirty-three or thirty-four – 'so full of youthfulness' was the mother of four, of whom the oldest was already a teenager. Sarojini was in England for an extended stay, away from her children and devoted husband, a successful physician in Hyderabad. She was in London for rest and treatment which involved surgery but her personality and her energy belied any of this. Ill health was not something Sarojini would allow to affect her. That she came from an established, even affluent background in Hyderabad was evident from the circles in which she moved in England. With her 'ceaseless stream of words', the dazzled Asaf found her to be 'all life and light, vibrant and brilliant by the mere fact of being'.

Not surprisingly, for the rest of his stay in London he was part of the court that surrounded her. The group soon included Syud Hossain, another friend of Asaf from his days in London as a student. Syud was also in London to study law but Asaf had soon guessed the Bar was no more than 'the second string to his bow'; he wanted to be a journalist. On qualifying for the Bar Asaf had returned to India but Syud, having discarded any pretensions about the Bar, stayed on, in and out of debt, in love with a married Englishwoman and working as a freelance journalist.[3]

'Sarojini, Syud and I,' wrote Asaf, 'soon became a trio.' They were 'invariably together', whether at poetry readings or lectures, visits to clubs, or travelling to Oxford and Cambridge, barring those times when Sarojini 'with her much wider and higher connections was rocketed into what appeared to us was the stratosphere'. Sarojini in her letters to her children referred to Asaf and Syud as part of her 'special group of friends'.[4] She, having studied in England earlier, was in territory familiar to her. To English-educated Indians generally, London was a world capital as well as the first city of Empire. For upper-class Indians and those who aspired to that status, to travel to and stay in England was important. Apart from its obvious political significance, it was here that social, intellectual and literary recognition was generally bestowed.

When Rabindranath Tagore halted in England in April 1913, on the return leg of his voyage back from the United States, the Indian residents in London organized a reception in his honour to which Asaf and Sarojini were invited.[5] Tagore had visited England earlier, from June to September 1912, on his way to the US, but had then been relatively unknown, except to a small set of poets and writers. But that stay led to the English translation of the *Geetanjali,* which came out in November 1912 after his arrival in the US, and his reputation as a poet had preceded him across the Atlantic. By the time he returned to London in April 1913 to take the ship back to India, 'he had become a sensation and a curiosity'.[6] During his earlier visit of 1912, the *Times of India* had commented, derisive as always given its predictably British view of India and Indians: 'Mr Tagore is discovering we fancy that Indian poets are likely to receive more honour in London than in their own country and we cannot blame him for going to a place where he will find himself not without honour and much petted.'[7]

At the reception itself, when the crowd had thinned, Sarojini took the young Asaf to the great man and introduced him as a 'fellow poet'. Asaf was a lifelong admirer of Tagore, but found a series of lectures later delivered by the poet on sadhana, or his philosophy of life, falling 'flat'. He and Syud had purchased the highly priced tickets for the event; Sarojini was probably a special invitee. Asaf thought Tagore's 'fascinating face and saintly personality' a great asset but that his voice, 'shrill, pitched in a high key and almost metallic was a disadvantage; it belied the gravity and calm of his personality'. Sarojini agreed, 'a poet should not stand forth as a philosopher in prose', and was also at odds with Ananda Coomaraswamy's position at a talk he gave at the London Indian Association. The lecture of this famous Ceylonese metaphysician and historian of Indian art was on the 'History of Hindu Art' which all three attended. In it, after a survey of Buddhist and Hindu art, Coomaraswamy 'suggested with regret that elements of true art inspiration were wanting in modern Indian activities and thought'.[8] He also said, 'The *Bande Matrum* was a war cry rather than an art inspiration and so too were other songs of Bharata.' A report mentions Sarojini disagreeing: 'she felt that India was coming in for a new art life of which even Dr Coomaraswami [*sic*] would sing the praise [of], and which would add to the lustre and towering grandeur of the past'.[9]

Sarojini had been associated with the Indian national movement for some years, had addressed nationalist public meetings and ably demonstrated her powers of oratory. To her, India's emergent nationalism was a renaissance of the nation to be, no less.

Being in Sarojini's inner circle therefore went beyond the literary and the aesthetic. In particular, this led to a closer acquaintance with another star of the Indian diaspora in England who was also already a leading figure in India, Muhammad Ali Jinnah. Asaf had first met Jinnah at around this time in 1913 or early 1914 at the National Liberal Club, a favourite haunt of both. Asaf later recalled that Jinnah's reserve then was 'not a thousandth part as freezing as it has now become. He was a stickler for principles, transparently honourable and genial.'

Jinnah was already friends with Sarojini, an 'enviably close friendship', Asaf called it. They had met in 1906 at the Calcutta session of the Indian National Congress which had as its backdrop the 1905 partition of Bengal that revived the organization but also led to its first great split. Sarojini was to describe Jinnah as being then 'a rising lawyer and a coming politician' and one who, fired by 'virile patriotism', had long been part of the National Congress and regularly attended its annual gatherings.[10] Perhaps Asaf saw Jinnah then, as no doubt many other young men would have, as a model for a career path. Jinnah was at home in both England and India; he was a polished speaker, someone with a formidable reputation at the Bar; he was a liberal, not wedded to religious dogma and above the Hindu–Muslim compartments into which many others divided their public lives. Finally, he was someone who spoke his mind without equivocation.

While Jinnah and Syud were important in Asaf's life at this point, Sarojini was more significant. Asaf Ali had never met a woman like her before and nothing in his social experience in Delhi or London had prepared him for the encounter. His life in Delhi was socially restricted when it came to interacting with women not closely related. London was obviously different but here the novelty was to occasionally meet young Englishwomen. An Indian woman at ease with the opposite sex – both among her compatriots and the English – was something new and unusual. Moreover, if Sarojini also realized how very unusual she was, she carried this knowledge lightly.

Sarojini, Asaf wrote, 'quoted your favourite poets for you in her lyrical voice and with a tilt and rhythm which sounded pleasant to the ear even if somewhat un-English'. She was like 'a breathing anthology . . . Anecdotes and humorous stories dovetailed into one another . . .' Sarojini was moreover more than just a literary person. She was active in public life in India; she had a large circle of friends and acquaintances, and finally, she was genuinely interested in him as a person. These were reactions she evoked through most of her life in most people she came in contact with.

Syud, Sarojini, Jinnah and Asaf sometimes formed a quartet. In the recollection of a younger contemporary, Hosain Ali Khan, a student in Oxford from Hyderabad and therefore well known to Sarojini, the four would meet at the National Liberal Club and then 'would go for an aperitif to the Café Royal, and thence to the Monico nearby but more usually to some Soho restaurant for dinner . . .' These evenings would end at 'either Syud Hossain's rooms at Holborn or Asaf Ali's in West Kensington talking till the small hours of the morning'.[11]

Sarojini was at the centre of such gatherings and she certainly liked being surrounded by a court. The picture that emerges of the young Asaf is of someone trying hard to fit into the cosmopolitan set he found himself in, a universe away from the Old Delhi haveli he grew up in. He was trying to be at ease in a set to which he aspired but in which he still felt he was an outsider. Perhaps meeting Sarojini gave him the first sense of life on a larger stage. But others saw it differently. On one occasion Sarojini was invited to Oxford, and Syud and Asaf went with her. Hosain Ali Khan as a student of the university was tasked to show them around and he remembered being embarrassed as a young undergraduate 'walking the streets of Oxford with two sophisticated gentlemen from London, dressed in the height of fashion – well cut, well pressed lounge suits, fancy waistcoats, butterfly collars, foulard bow ties and bandana silk handkerchiefs shyly peeping out of breast pockets'.[12]

*Asaf Ali as a young man in London*

Asaf was so grateful for all the horizons Sarojini had opened up for him in London that he decided to hold a reception in her honour, organizing it with the help of Syud and others. Needing a main speaker, he wrote to a number of prominent British poets. W.B. Yeats agreed and after that it was plain sailing. Including the Indian guests, 'covers were laid for more than 250', he noted happily. Asaf's only disappointment was the meagre coverage in the mainstream British press, which he attributed to not enough champagne being served to the journalists present. Nevertheless, for him, 'the flashlight photograph of the dinner, our table plan and menu with the toast list and the letters and autographs of literary personalities of the day are among my treasure of mementos'.

Sarojini's health was always a factor through her stay; she was soon run down given the hectic pace she maintained. Admitted to a nursing home, in no time she was receiving her countless friends, and Asaf found the 'nurses on a verge of a breakdown, carrying flowers sent or brought by friends, guiding visitors, finding vases for flowers and looking after them no less than their ungovernable patient'. Her room, noted Asaf, was like a florist's shop, with the same strong scents, and the 'doctor's instructions had been flouted to extinction'.

But literary soirees and frantic socializing were not the only aspects of Asaf's life in London that were galvanized by Sarojini's presence.

Inevitably, perhaps, Asaf's bachelor status would crop up and he writes about how a 'potentially big event of my life suddenly crystallized out of the transparent air like mountain dew'. Sarojini announced the arrival of Liaq, a beautiful girl from one of the elite families of her home town, Hyderabad, who was in London under her chaperonage and on the lookout for a possible groom. 'Sarojini was full of praises of the girl's looks, training and family background and told me that she had a receptive mind still awaiting formation. Why should I not take my chance, if I was not wedded to bachelorhood?'

The idea of Liaq as a potential bride 'was a stimulating suggestion'. This was as romantic as he could hope for, 'if I was to marry an Indian girl; in the Muslim society of that time in India I could not hope even to catch sight of one prior to marriage'. His family's background in Kucha Chelan in Darya Ganj in Old Delhi would certainly rule out even the remote possibility of meeting and getting to know someone before a marriage was contemplated. Other suitors for Liaq (or so some of her relatives hoped) also included M.A. Jinnah. The formidable Sarojini would engineer a meeting with Jinnah as well, although, in Asaf's recollection, she did not think that Jinnah's being interested in Liaq was a feasible idea.

A meeting between Asaf and Liaq was arranged. The occasion was to be a large gathering but Asaf was to have opportunity for conversation both before the other guests arrived and afterwards. Sarojini was 'dressed to kill' but it was Gunnu who would adroitly 'manoeuvre' Liaq and Asaf into sitting next to each other. Sarojini was of course the star of the party with all the conversation in her hands. 'She sparkled and drew ripples of admiring laughter all round, coaxing some, bullying others, and generally radiating dazzling brightness.' Liaq, who had just arrived in London, was daunted. Asaf, sensitive to her insecurity, noted it was 'a new experience for poor unsophisticated Liaq'. Jinnah, 'too high and aloof in his dignity', ruled himself out, and Asaf found that his 'neighbour found in me a natural refuge' amidst the wit and sophistication of the evening which had clearly overwhelmed her.

The initial meeting went well and others arranged by Gunnu followed. Thereafter, Asaf sent a formal proposal to Liaq's parents in Hyderabad along with 'Mrs Naidu's recommendation in words of which I can be proud'. He wrote to Liaq regularly during her stay in England. 'I wrote letters in my perfervid style' till Gunnu advised him, 'You are frightening that child out of her wits with your poetry and intellectual stuff.'

By mid-1914 as war, which would become a world war, broke out in Europe Asaf was a changed young man in at least two significant ways. First, the desire to live in England, once so overwhelming, had evaporated. For one, he was now certain that he would never marry an Englishwoman because if 'one married in England one must stay there'. When the possibility of marrying Liaq was broached, he had closely examined his feelings and found he had had enough of England, his 'maturing mind now turning homeward'. This was a complete reversal for someone who had felt 'homesick' for England, had sought the company of English people in India and even manufactured a brief to come to London. It was almost as if the second stay in England had been an exorcism. One day Asaf found that the 'the fragrance of a jasmine flower . . . wrung from the depth of my heart a paroxysm of nostalgia'. Now eager to go back to India and to Delhi, he therefore 'plucked this emblem of purity of its stalk and put it into my button hole as a symbol of the new life'.

As his world view with regard to England shifted, India came to the fore. Amidst all the hectic social activity and his own budding romance, Asaf was conscious of all that was happening around him. Both during his student life in Delhi and even more so after arriving in London as a law student, he had been exposed to the different nationalist currents then at work. But he had hitherto been more an interested observer than a committed participant. What perhaps triggered a change was the outbreak of war between Britain and the Ottoman empire as part of the general breakdown of the European security order that heralded the start of World War I. This catalyzed a latent sympathy and admiration for the embattled Muslim Ottoman empire into something more definite.

That it was so is not surprising. A young Asaf growing up in the alleys of Old Delhi where the spirit of the great Mughals still ruled – although they and their power were long gone – would have been inclined to identify with the Ottoman empire of the Turks centred in Istanbul. Through the nineteenth century a consciousness among Muslim intellectuals in India had grown that the Ottomans were the last empire standing of the trio of great Islamic powers, with the Mughals in India and the Safavids in Persia weakening and disintegrating amidst an expansion of British power. With the final disappearance of the Mughals in India after 1857, an overwhelming sense of loss spread amongst many Muslim clerics, intellectuals and public figures, and this fed a growing sentimental attachment to the Ottomans as the leader of the Islamic world.

Over the second half of the nineteenth century and in the first decade of the twentieth, the increasing fragility of the Ottomans and their shrinking footprint was evident as their former subjects – the Serbs, the Greeks and the Bulgarians – progressively gained independence. During 1912–13 the Italians, keen to found their own empire in Africa, found the Ottoman territories in present-day Libya a convenient area to expand into. In most of these conflicts Britain had not formally been a player, and sympathy and support for the Ottomans did not mean disloyalty to the British for Muslims in India. There remained a sense of unease, and sometimes more, for many Muslims in India that an alliance of Christian powers – the Russians, the Italians, the Greeks, the new Balkan states of Serbia and Bulgaria – were in concert to weaken and erode the Ottomans.

By the beginning of the second decade of the twentieth century, however, the European balance of power system was in flux: Britain was tied to Russia and France in alliance, and the Ottomans were in concert with Germany. As World War I broke out it was a matter of time before the Ottomans would become a party to it on Germany's side and ranged against Britain. The outbreak of the Ottoman–British war in November 1914 made Asaf realize that he 'was more pro Turkey than I knew' and that his 'home influence of sentimental attachment to the Turks sprang into the saddle of my reason'.

This leap in political consciousness and anti-British feeling resulted in action on a more personal matter that had been weighing on young Asaf's conscience for some time. It related to a friend of the family, a former colleague of his father, someone he does not name and only identifies as 'Uncle'. Not for the only time in Asaf's life, the personal and the political would be indistinguishable. As a fatherless boy Asaf had tried to trace his father's old colleagues in the police to learn more about his parent and perhaps seek guidance and help for his own future: 'These friends had been at the same level as my father but had risen high in the police force in the years since his death.' 'Uncle' in particular stood out and Asaf had made his acquaintance in his last year of school in 1906: 'A fine, dignified person with a powerful but kindly presence.' Towards the end of his second year in St Stephen's College in Delhi around 1908, 'Uncle' had encouraged Asaf to write to him regularly about public meetings and other gatherings he attended and what transpired at these; he was also told to keep these letters secret and confine himself to stating facts and not his opinions. In return 'Uncle' paid him an allowance which was gradually increased, and in fact his studies in England, to some extent at least, were financed from this source.

Gradually Asaf had discovered 'Uncle's' real identity as a senior officer of the Government of India's intelligence department who was keeping tabs on dissident and nationalist opinion, and he correctly surmised he was therefore a source. 'This came', he recollected later, 'as a shock to my awakening conscience' but he was also 'hypnotized by "Uncle", who had become an awe inspiring father figure' and breaking with him 'seemed (like) all but suicide'. Asaf writes that through his college days in Delhi, then later as a law student in London, he squared this role as an informant with his conscience by deciding 'as a compromise to be no more than a journalist reporting events and speeches. Only such persons as were known to hold certain views would be identified in my correspondence . . .'

But the truth could not be sugar-coated. Undeniably, in this formative period of some five years of Asaf's life, he was a part-time but paid police informant reporting on such nationalist activity as he encountered amongst other students, and later amongst friends and associates.

This 'nightmare' – as Asaf later termed the clandestine reporting of nationalism-related activity – ended with the dramatic turnaround in the evolution of his political consciousness, the British–Ottoman Turkey war providing the obvious tipping point. His anguish over the fate of the Ottomans was inseparable from his opposition to British rule in India. But this was perhaps part of a longer incremental process, including moving in a circle such as Sarojini's, that uplifted him, making him conscious of public life alongside the personal. It made him begin, he was later to write, 'the reclamation of my soul, redeeming it by serving the cause of the country's freedom'. He sent a telegram to 'Uncle' terminating the arrangement. For the young but now politically conscious Asaf, this cable to 'Uncle' was, as he later wrote, 'an act of noncooperation at a time when it was not yet known by that name in India'. But if the young Asaf imagined this was the end of the matter, he was mistaken.

# 2

# Delhi at the Turn of the Century and London, 1908–1912

Growing up in Delhi in the 1890s and as a teenager in the early 1900s, Asaf lived in an environment where the events of 1857 and their aftermath still dominated the city's mental mindscapes. This was true for a great many Delhi families, Muslim families in particular, and it was so with added intensity in Asaf's case. The haveli he was born in, in Kucha Chelan, deep in the by-lanes of the old city, had been purchased by his maternal grandfather post 1857 in an auction of confiscated properties of those who had – or were believed to have – participated in the uprising. The house, in the old Darya Ganj quarter and within walking distance of the Red Fort and the Jama Masjid, had been the site of a massacre in 1857 carried out by avenging British troops after they retook the city and such resistance as remained was brutally stamped out. Asaf, recalling the stories that dominated his childhood, wrote, 'no less than two hundred persons of the locality who had taken shelter in the house were put to the sword in the spacious halls and courtyards of this house'. Their memory 'haunted the house every time the word *ghadar* was mentioned'. In fact the Kucha Chelan massacre had been of an even larger scale and one history of the events of 1857 estimates that as many as 1,400 were massacred in the locality as a field gun 'blew the haveli apart'. Kucha Chelan had been famous as the city's 'most intellectual *mohalla*', and among the dead were the most talented poets and artists of the time.[1]

Asaf's grandmother came from one of the many upper-class Muslim families closely connected to the erstwhile Mughal court. They were driven out of Delhi after 1857 and on return found a devastated, unrecognizable cityscape. She was later married to Irtiza Khan, the one who purchased the Kucha Chelan haveli. Their daughter Akbari Begum was married to Ahsan Ali, a police official, from a family from Nagina, Bijnor, in the United Provinces and their son Mohammad Asaf Ali was born in May 1888. Ahsan Ali was to marry at least once more – possibly an Anglo-Indian or a Christian woman – and there were children from that marriage. Asaf's mother, incensed at this and possibly also at her husband's general philandering, returned to her father's house in Kucha Chelan. They never reconciled because Ahsan Ali died soon after and Asaf's mother found herself a widow at the age of twenty-two.

Asaf was therefore brought up in his mother's family home, a largely matriarchal household with his grandmother and mother as the dominant influences. Both were avid readers. His mother, Asaf was later to recall, spoke the fine Urdu of the best Delhi families, had 'a keen ear for music and knew a great deal about it'; she also 'had a refined taste for things aesthetic'. Most importantly she understood the value of education, and in Asaf's recollection, 'I was barely four when my mother began to talk of engaging a tutor for me.' He soon had more than one including one for English. Tuition at home ended with admission first to a neighbourhood primary school, and then to the famous Anglo Arabic School of Delhi in Ajmeri Gate.

Asaf's life in Delhi was interspersed with occasional visits to his father's family home in Nagina where his paternal grandmother now lived. For his mother this connection remained important, for financial help from her husband's ancestral holdings was essential both to prevent a descent beyond the genteel poverty they managed to live in, and also in particular to pay for Asaf's education. The first and subsequent visits to the ancestral village in Nagina Tahsil retained for Asaf a magical, almost mythical quality. The trip itself was 'exhilarating . . . rivers, Ganges included, and the great canals which had to be crossed. The bridges, the landscape with a distant view of the hills, the wayside stations, towns and villages were to me the revelation of a new world. No conqueror could have felt happier than I did . . .'

After school Asaf joined St Stephen's College in Delhi. He had wanted to do so from the time he was a schoolboy. 'Every time I passed the gates of St Stephen's College in Kashmere Gate, I yearned to pass inside them as an alumnus. They seemed to me to be the portal for understanding the mystery of the universe and of life.' And yet when the time came to join college, there was a tussle between it and the Muhammadan Anglo-Oriental College in Aligarh. The choice proved difficult and was important enough for Asaf and a friend on the horns of the same dilemma to visit Aligarh and see for themselves. They did so but 'our first contact with some of the alumni of Aligarh, who were our hosts for the solitary day we passed there, left so distasteful an impression on our young minds – and I may say unsullied minds – that we caught the first train back to Delhi'. Asaf does not reveal what so repelled him except that 'The place seemed to reek of levity and vulgarity.' Writing later, he concedes that the senior students they met may have been exceptions but also that 'the encounter was sufficient warning for us'. We could speculate that the idea of living in hostels with its possibility of homosexual encounters may have repelled Asaf – a theme to which we will revert with Asaf in London as a law student.

Growing up in Delhi had meant coming of age in a political backwater, which is what the former capital of the Mughals was following 1857, and especially when compared to cities such as Calcutta and Bombay or older Mughal cities such as Lahore and Allahabad, which had acquired a fresh lease of life as provincial capitals. But even in Delhi external political influences on Asaf were not entirely absent. When he was about seventeen years old and in the final year of school, a friend returned from a visit to Calcutta with news of the ferment in Bengal after its partition in 1905 and how strongly Bengalis had rallied around the nationalist slogan of 'Vande Mataram'. Asaf recalled later, 'We did not read newspapers in those days, there being no local paper and the *Pioneer* from Allahabad [was] forbiddingly costly.' Yet the Bengal news was of sufficient interest for him to subscribe to a Calcutta weekly to keep abreast of happenings there. Also interesting was a friend's tutor who was an accomplished speaker and would hold forth at 'a spot on the Rajghat overlooking the Jamuna River'; Asaf much enjoyed his 'diatribes against the foreigners'.

In St Stephen's College he had at least a few teachers who delivered 'frankly nationalist lectures'. In his recollection, 'step by step, the meaning of alien rule was slowly sinking into our minds'. The ambition of becoming an Indian Civil Service (ICS) officer – the highest level of the bureaucracy in India – was, however, also very strong, as it would have been for many young men of his background at the time. Writing in prison some three and a half decades later, he saw a contradiction in his younger self: 'How this incipient political consciousness could be reconciled with the role of a prospective candidate for the Indian Civil Service was a riddle which, at that time of immature mental development it did not even occur to me to think about.' But this was a judgement in retrospect: in the first decade of the twentieth century, nationalism was still an incipient force, perhaps no more than a strong sense of grievance against alien rulers or a feeling of unjust exclusion from the decisions being taken about their own country. Or perhaps there was the first stirring of that question critical to all anti-colonial movements: how are the British better than us?

But he had no complaints against St Stephen's College. He selected what he termed as an 'odd group' of courses, combining science and philosophy with English and Persian. S.K. Rudra, its first Indian principal, and C.F. Andrews, the Anglican priest who identified with the political aspirations of his Indian colleagues and students, legends even then, were the teachers who left the greatest impression. Studying law was the other possibility. Travelling to England seemed to be the best way to address both sets of options: the ICS and the law. The fact that a friend had received a scholarship to study in England further spurred Asaf. His mother was opposed to the idea: he was an only child after all and Asaf was also worried about his grandmother's health. He consulted Hakim Ajmal Khan, a famed Unani physician, one of Delhi's most prominent and respected residents, who was known to his family; he received sound advice: 'By staying here you cannot save her if she must go, but she won't, and you can go with an easy conscience.' How this extended stay in England could be paid for was of course another question.

This was when 'Uncle', the friend and police colleague of his late father, stepped in and 'offered to make it possible for me to go to England and study for the Bar or the ICS'. Asaf subsequently realized the arrangement was more transactional than a purely generous way of helping a former colleague's only son. But at the time, he was simply 'overjoyed'.

Once Asaf stepped ashore at Marseilles sometime in 1909, he was transported into a different universe. His thoughts were: 'Europe is all light, uniformity, mechanism, bustle and the freedom of women.' He decided, 'I liked the change' and 'subconsciously began to fall in step with Europe'. The next stop was Paris where a guide took him to a *maison* where he was 'reduced to a nonplus by the hospitality of half nude women' and beat a 'hasty and cowardly retreat'. Discovering Paris was an experience in itself: 'I went from place to place with the insatiable curiosity of a virgin mind and the unbounded joy, at every step, of an impressionable and observant child.' But even as he was 'drinking up everything in deep draughts', some things jarred. 'The nude statues (I was yet to see the wealth of erotic Indian sculpture), the seminude actresses and the freedom with which wine was consumed – in fact as a substitute for water – shocked me.' There were also 'certain habits of the western civilized world' in matters of personal hygiene 'which appeared barbaric': 'the absence of ablutionary arrangements in the water closet, and the wallowing in bath tubs in preference to bathing with fresh water'.

In time and once settled in London, Asaf reflected more on the East–West disjunctions he had encountered. Although he was to pen these reflections some three decades after his first actual experience of England and Europe, we get a sense of this young man's thinking at the time. Such ruminations were probably common to young people from India visiting the great imperial capitals of the era such as London and Paris.

> There was much in Western culture and its scientific spirit which left the worn out and fatigued East leagues behind. But surely our decline was a natural turn in the ineluctable processes of nature. No morning, no spring, no majestic pageant of the starry night could last longer than its appointed period in the Book of Time. We had reached the summit of our destiny and gone to sleep exhausted by the exertion.

Settling down in London meant becoming an interested spectator and participant of Indian and India-related public life, including diasporic dissident activity and nationalism in London. The first city of the empire drew Indians from a cross-section of society beginning from the maharajas and the fabulously rich to the aspirants who included Indian students from wealthy and the best-established families as well as those from the struggling middle class – all with eyes on the coveted ICS or the Bar. The Indians in London spanned the ideological spectrum from those entirely and blindly loyal to the British Raj and to those who tempered their loyalty with seeking slow and orderly representation in its governance and administration. The elements of British society they were most in touch with comprised former civil servants or army officers who had served in India and were either diehard imperialists or reformists sympathetic to Indian aspirations.

Amongst the Indians there were also a handful of revolutionaries seeking 'freedom' in all its undefined and multiple meanings. The militant nationalists and the revolutionaries were of obvious and pressing interest to British intelligence and the police, and dissident opinion from nationalist young Indians was closely monitored and tracked. During the early part of his stay in London Asaf appears to have gravitated to just this set. To an extent this was because a friend and travelling companion from Delhi was in England on account of a scholarship provided by Shyamji Krishan Varma (1857–1930), almost a one-man institution for Indian nationalists in England and in Europe in the early twentieth century. Varma had instituted six scholarships, named in memory of Shivaji and other Indian greats from history, for Indians to study in Europe. He had also in 1905 started a weekly journal, *The Indian Sociologist*, which had as its motto the following sentences from the work of the English scholar and thinker Herbert Spencer:

> Everyman is free to do what he wants provided he infringes not the equal freedom of any man.
>
> Resistance to aggression is not simply justifiable but imperative. Non Resistance hurts both altruism and egoism.[2]

Varma had also established a hostel for Indian students, India House, in London in 1905. On his first arrival in May 1909, Asaf and his friends from Delhi had stayed there for a few days. It was a regular haunt of Indian students and visitors, and, in his words, 'a rendezvous for politically minded Indian youths, and a training ground for prospective public men and revolutionaries'. Varma had by now shifted to Paris: British intelligence had kept a close watch on him and he feared arrest for sedition if he remained in England. Thereafter, V.D. Savarkar, also a recipient of one of Varma's scholarships, was in charge of managing India House on behalf of Varma. Asaf on arrival had found 'Savarkar to be its "presiding deity"' and one who despite his 'careless English' was so evidently sincere that a 'memorable impact on the audience' was inevitable.

The stay in India House was brief, with food that 'defied description' driving Asaf away to seek other lodgings. In his recollection the food 'was called Indian, but Indian is such an imprecise label where food, language and manners were concerned. And here there were Madrasis, Maharattas and Punjabis, each so far apart in tastes.' He also grumbled – young, impatient and unaware of the part that politics would play in his life – that 'the atmosphere in India House, surcharged with politics, got on my nerves'.

But however apolitical he deemed himself, the seeds of awareness were awakening. He remained a regular at India House's Sunday get-togethers which were occasions for patriotic themes to be discussed and debated.

Savarkar would occasionally read out excerpts from his recently published history of 1857, *The Indian War of Independence*, already banned in India as seditious. It was at one such gathering that Asaf met Virendranath Chattopadhyaya or Chatto, who soon became a close friend. Clearly, Asaf was something of a regular at the meetings in the weeks after his first arrival in England, for in late June 1909 he was asked to chair a session. He was, he recollected, 'secretly flattered' but also 'really raw and exceptionally shy'.

That afternoon, Niranjan Pal, son of the famous nationalist Bipin Chandra Pal – prominent in the 'extremist' wing of the Indian National Congress – had as part of the proceedings sung a patriotic song, but the occasion was otherwise uneventful. Writing over three decades later, Asaf was unable to recollect the precise theme of the evening's discussion. He did, however, recall a 'taciturn' Madan Lal Dhingra, whom he had earlier encountered at India House, requesting more patriotic songs at the end of the evening. Since Niranjan could not sing in Urdu, Asaf sang and played a thumri and a ghazal on the organ. Dhingra went into 'a transport of joy'. This seemed to Asaf 'rather extravagant' but he explained that 'Dhingra was a most rare bird – a wistful uncommunicative person who gave you the impression of being cross with life'.

Dhingra was a regular in these weekly gatherings but never spoke 'and was seldom noticed by anybody'. He was from a well-known Amritsar family. One of seven brothers, he was the odd one out amongst them, the others all well established in medicine, business or the Bar. Their father, something of an autocrat, was an eminent doctor and had held the post of civil surgeon. This was a family that prided itself on its high social standing, which was further cemented by personal connections with British officialdom in India. Madan Lal did not quite fit in into this ensemble. He had run away from home on one occasion and worked as a seaman for several months. Possibly this youthful rebellion had followed his father's unsuccessful efforts to settle him in a stable job. His brothers managed to persuade their father that higher studies in England would provide the stability Madan Lal needed, and this was how he found himself in London, where, much to his family's disapproval and apprehension, he decided to stay at India House. This was quite possibly his way of coping with homesickness in a foreign country; in India House the nineteen-year-old Madan Lal had attached himself to the admiring circle around Savarkar.

Some three days after his chairing of an India House Sunday session, on 1 July 1909, Asaf was 'horrified' when informed by a fellow boarder that an Indian had killed a high-ranking British official. He was then, he said, 'nearly stupefied' to find that the assassin was Dhingra who had shot dead Sir Curzon Wyllie at a reception. The assassination took place at an 'At Home', or a reception, in Jahangir Hall of the Imperial Institute in South Kensington which was hosted by a group loyal to the British Raj: the Indian National Association. Asaf himself had intended to attend the event but did not go in the end because he 'had not yet got an evening dress'. Dhingra himself is described as being 'smartly turned out in a lounge suit and a blue turban'.[3] He was immediately apprehended after the shooting, summarily tried and executed. His defence was that the British were responsible for countless atrocities and deaths in India, and that it was his patriotic duty to fight them in any way he could. Savarkar was suspected of being involved in the assassination plot and also of being the author of a written statement that was found in Dhingra's pocket when he was apprehended immediately after the killing.[4]

There were many unusual aspects to the Wyllie assassination. For one thing, the speed with which things proceeded after the event was unprecedented. Curzon Wyllie was killed on 1 July, and the trial was completed and Madan Lal executed by 17 August. In one account the legal proceedings took just over an hour and a half because no real defence was offered. Dhingra maintained that he had carried out the assassination and had intended to kill his target. During the trial he made a statement that was published in a London newspaper a day before his execution. One part of it struck Asaf in particular and he was to remember it over three decades later: 'I believe that a nation held in bondage . . . with the help of foreign bayonets is in a perpetual state of war. Since open battle is rendered impossible to a disarmed race, I attacked by surprise.'

Madan Lal's family in India was horror-struck on learning the news and went to great lengths to clarify to the government that they shared none of his views on British rule in India. Their sense of shame was as sincere as their sentiments of loyalty to the British. They ascribed Madan Lal's act to mental instability. This last point failed to convince the government which otherwise showed considerable sympathy to the family's predicament.

Sir Curzon Wyllie was a senior aide to the secretary of state for India, Sir John Morley. It appears that Madan Lal had really wanted to assassinate either Morley or former Viceroy Lord Curzon. A postcard with Curzon's picture and 'Heathen Dog' pencilled across it was found in Dhingra's belongings. It is possible that Dhingra shot Curzon Wyllie because the opportunity to target these bigger fish was just not available. Nevertheless, the choice was not without its curious elements. Curzon Wyllie had spent many years in India and knew the Dhingra family well. Madan Lal's father had in fact written to Curzon Wyllie asking him to keep an eye on his son as he was worried about his staying in India House and the company he was keeping. Curzon Wyllie had tried to contact Madan Lal and had written to him some weeks previously wanting to fix a meeting. It is also possible that Madan Lal's difficult relationship with his family had something to do with the final choice of his target as well.

Savarkar was to be arrested later but on a different charge; he was transported back to India and thereafter sentenced in 1910 to two terms of life imprisonment in the Andaman Islands that would have amounted to fifty years in jail. In the process he became a household name in India. In 1921 he was brought over to a jail in the mainland before being released with various conditionalities relating to refraining from any form of political activity. Savarkar was a prolific writer and with his writings on history and politics he gave to a different trajectory in Indian politics its intellectual and ideological ballast. In his view Christians and

Muslims could not be true Indians since their faith was of a non-Indian origin. Therefore, the freedom struggle against the British, while no doubt important, was only a subset of an older millennium-long struggle against foreign domination of Hindus. Uniting Hindus against Muslims, reforming Hindu society to strengthen its defences against Christian and Islamic proselytizing activity were among the defining characteristics of his thought. Complete freedom from government restrictions came in 1937 after which he joined the Hindu Mahasabha and served as its president a number of times.

But in his London days Savarkar clearly had some influence on the young Asaf and the impact of his *The Indian War of Independence* was considerable. We get a sense of this from the fact that Asaf was to introduce his young wife Aruna to it even some two decades later. Many years later, Savarkar was a suspect in the conspiracy behind the assassination of Mahatma Gandhi. After Gandhi's killing, at one point, Savarkar's house was attacked by an angry mob and he had to be rescued by the police. Asaf noted wryly in 1948: 'How the wheel of destiny has turned in the opposite direction today.' Asaf does not say so, but we may surmise that he was also thinking of the transformation in Savarkar's political thought over the four decades since they first met.

For Asaf, like many others, *The Indian War of Independence* was a foundational text for reasons other than the fact that it was seen as incendiary by the authorities and banned. What would have had most impact was one of the young Savarkar's central arguments: that the eruption of 1857 was a joint Hindu–Muslim enterprise and it remained as such to the very end. The contrast between this and the Savarkar of the 1930s and 1940s is possibly also what was uppermost in Asaf's mind when he wrote about the 'wheel of destiny'.[5] When he wrote these lines, it is possible another similar transition was in his mind too: Jinnah from being the principal protagonist of Hindu–Muslim unity in the first two decades of the century to its principal opponent in later years. The 'wheel of destiny' certainly moved mysteriously through the freedom struggle.

After Wyllie's assassination the weekly gatherings at India House came to an end. Asaf had 'presided' over the last of them. If all this meant an uneasy settling in for Asaf in London there were soon other preoccupations. For his law degree he joined Lincoln's Inn because some friends recommended it: its 'dining hall was the best for the quality of food . . . wine was free, even a bottle of champagne or hock on guest nights'. Oxford had been considered but was rejected after a brief visit for much the same reason as Aligarh had perhaps been earlier: 'because I ran into the wrong type of its alumni'. It is unclear what happened there to explain this dismissal of Oxford but there are no markers left. Perhaps Asaf then had an excessively puritanical streak and encountering a homosexual relationship in Oxford may have repelled him. Sometime later, during his second stint in London, a friend commented on Asaf's attending the notorious trial of the author Oscar Wilde. Wilde had been charged with homosexuality and this thoroughly 'disgusted' Asaf, as also that present in the court were 'some overdressed . . . slightly painted effeminate youths – pansies in modern, picturesque parlance'. Returning to his chamber he tore to pieces a portrait of Wilde whom he had admired earlier. The friend was to comment, 'I understand that there was the strain of the Puritan in him' and he would not brook any variation from 'strict normality'.[6]

In London as a student Asaf appears to have used his time to read widely and he read what pleased him: 'poetry, literature, history, philosophy, anything but law'. The ICS idea was soon abandoned, 'mainly from a repugnance to industry'. Clearly, he was having too exhilarating a time to embark on the monastic existence that studying for the ICS examination would have entailed. He nurtured ambitions now 'of releasing my soul in poetry and plays'. He writes that for relaxation, 'we often visited the theatres, which along with newspapers, struck me as informal and interesting sources of liberal education'. He learned to roller-skate and was soon so skilled that he was 'never in much want of partners for dancing on the rink because I made a good partner'. There was also a new friendship and it proved to be a close one – someone like him but also different.

# 3

# Syud and Asaf in India and in England: Muslims and Modernity

Asaf had met Syud Hossain soon after his arrival in London. Syud was also at Lincoln's Inn and already had, Asaf says, 'the reputation of a prodigy'. Syud's real passion, however, was not law but journalism. His was a well-established Muslim family of Bengal, tracing its lineage back to the Mughals. Major landlords at one time, the family had lost out over time in financial terms but took enormous pride in their Mughal and Persian origins. Living in Bengal and in Calcutta they did speak Bengali, but Urdu and Persian were the languages they preferred and appreciated the most. Their women lived in cloistered spaces, were schooled at home, and were steeped in notions of family honour and tradition. Syud's father, Nawab Syud Mohammad Azad, was a civil servant who had risen up the ranks of the lower provincial bureaucracy to the extent possible in colonial Bengal. His was a traditionalist view of the world, and in the words of a granddaughter, he 'lived by the values of a vanished world'.[1] Nevertheless, change in adapting to the needs of knowing English and having a modern education was inescapable.

Syud grew up in Calcutta, and on finishing school from the then famous Calcutta Madrassa joined the Muhammadan Anglo-Oriental College in Aligarh after having failed to get admission into Calcutta University. Clearly, his academic performance at school did not give an accurate picture of his abilities and talents. One of the recommendations that led to his admission in Aligarh was from Denison Ross, highly regarded in British India as a historian and an orientalist and his principal at the Calcutta Madrasa, who wrote in 1907:

> I have no hesitation in saying that the applicant's knowledge of English is as good as any graduate in India. In fact, I don't know more than half a dozen Indian gentlemen who possess a better command of the language . . . his failures in repeated attempts to pass the Entrance [to Calcutta University] was due solely to the fact that he has a non-mathematical mind.[2]

The Muhammadan Anglo-Oriental College in Aligarh was itself the outcome of the growing realization on the part of a traditionalist Muslim elite that the changes the British had brought about were inescapable. Sir Syed Ahmed Khan had established the institution in 1877, essentially to educate a younger generation of Muslims in English and in the modern sciences. To him the Muslim elite had borne the burden of the events of 1857 and needed a fresh start, beginning with reassuring the British authorities of their loyalty and reversing the suspicion and distrust that 1857 had engendered in the official mind about his co-religionists. To the protagonists of the Aligarh initiative, their efforts were as much directed towards bridging the gulf between Indian Muslims and the Raj as they were towards bridging the gulf between traditional Islam and modern education.

To many Muslim intellectuals in India at the time, both these were matters of the highest concern and vital to their fate as a minority in India. It was clear that modern education was essential to secure adequate representation in government bureaucracy, this being the principal means to hold on to such residual power and status that remained with them. The differential rates at which Hindus and Muslims had accessed government service and educational institutions – with the latter believed to be lagging far behind – had worried Muslim intellectuals and public figures for a long time and was one of the impulses behind the founding of the college in Aligarh. To a considerable degree, British recognition of the depth and validity of this concern and the Muslim elite's pervasive fear of marginalization was the basis of the Raj's policy of divide and rule as it confronted an emergent nationalism in India.

The fear of marginalization also stemmed from a keenly felt loss of power and status with the fading of Mughal glory in India; but equally it was also the more universal phenomena of the decline of Islamic influence and the encroachment of Western power and civilization amidst the erosion of Ottoman power and the end of the Persian empire. This sense of loss was most strongly articulated by an associate of Syed Ahmed Khan, the poet Altaf Hussain Hali. Hali wrote a long elegy in the 1870s on the rise and fall of Islam and Islamic dynasties, and this work, known as the 'Musaddas', became a popular expression of Islam's past glory and the need to restore it. This was a classic statement of Indian Muslim nostalgia for the age long past when Islam was a prominent force in the world and a depiction of the depths to which it had apparently then fallen. To the young Muslim undergraduates in Aligarh and more generally across India where Urdu poetry was appreciated, recitals from the 'Musaddas' became both an elegiac expression of the loss of self-esteem amongst Muslims alongside a loss of prestige and real power, and a call to regain and restore these. These recitations would frequently leave audiences in tears, steeped in the nostalgia for a lost past. Alongside 'an outspoken loyalism to the British Empire',[3] the 'Musaddas' 'awakened generations of Indian Muslims to the decline of their political power'.[4]

There was therefore a potential gulf always looming between this perspective and that of an emergent Indian nationalism represented by the establishment of the Indian National Congress in 1885 as an instrument to seek concessions towards more representative government from the colonial authorities. More representative government would have appeared to many Muslim intellectuals to be a government less representative of Muslims, given their numerical minority in large parts of India and the fact that Hindus had turned to Western education and government jobs earlier and with greater rapidity.

In Aligarh, Syud showed promise as a debater and also as a writer. On completing his intermediate degree he returned to Calcutta and found employment in the provincial civil service in 1909, a subordinate hierarchy to the ICS but nevertheless promising a steady job and a career. During this brief stint as a junior bureaucrat, he wrote in the *Statesman* and in the *Englishman*, both popular amongst the British and English-educated Indians. His writing abilities were noted by his British superiors who advised his father to send him to England to acquire a law degree. How this venture was paid for is not very clear. Possibly it was a family enterprise bolstered by the expectation that it would be a good investment in the long term.

Syud's experience of growing up in Calcutta and the later experience of Aligarh were pivotal to the choices he made later. The first decade of the twentieth century was a time of ferment all over India but particularly in Calcutta and in Bengal. The military victory in 1905 of Japan over Russia confirmed to many that Western belief in its superiority over Asian civilizations was wrong. This added momentum to an emergent nationalist sentiment outraged by the partition of Bengal in 1905 into two provinces of East and West Bengal largely on religious grounds; it was done principally to divide Indian opinion and weaken it, as the partition meant different things to the Hindus and the Muslims of Bengal. The decision to partition the province was strongly opposed in Bengal, where the geographical and territorial division meant the vivisection of the Bengali people united by a common history and equally by a common language and culture. Opposition to the step began with protest meetings and petitions but soon extended to efforts to promote self-reliance through home-grown industry and education – in a word, Swadeshi. Some traction also developed around boycotts of British-made products, government education institutions and even social boycotts of those considered Raj loyalists. The news spread. It also strengthened the nascent idea that agitation and pressure on the government was needed, rather than piteous appeals to the better judgement of the British – a position taken up by the 'extremists' in the Congress.

Yet it was undeniable that opposition to the partition came principally from among Hindus. A new Muslim-majority province of East Bengal meant new opportunities for Bengali Muslims, in particular those who were educated and sought government jobs. A Hindu–Muslim divergence on the partition was therefore as evident as the outrage with which the decision was greeted by many in India.

Although we know little of Syud's political views and inclinations at the time, since he came from a family that identified itself with the Bengal Muslim aristocracy it could be reasonably assumed he would have opposed the protagonists of the Swadeshi movement that unified those protesting the division of Bengal. For families such as Syud's – members of a declining aristocracy, which saw government service as a means of retaining some status and position – the partition offered hope and greater opportunity. Amidst the persistent criticism of the partition decision, a delegation of Muslim notables, encouraged by the principal of the Aligarh college and some senior British officials, famously called on Viceroy Minto in October 1906, expressing support for the partition of Bengal in view of the opportunities it created for Bengal's Muslims. They also pleaded to a sympathetic viceroy on behalf of the Muslims that 'under any system of representation extended or limited, a community in itself more numerous than the population of any first class European power except Russia, may justly lay claim to adequate recognition as an important factor in the State'.[5]

To the nationalists in the Congress and many others, this was a command performance staged by the government to deflect the pressure and criticism the Bengal partition had engendered. But to many Muslims – both those who were products of modern institutions such as Aligarh and those who represented the landed aristocrats who had lost out under the British – the points made by the deputation to the viceroy were just and reasonable. Underwriting this was a more subterranean concern: the Muslims were not simply a minority; they were the former *rulers* of India and this should be a factor in any consideration of the future governance architecture of India. In the words of the deputation to the viceroy, the position accorded to the Muslims should 'be commensurate, not merely with their political strength, but also with their political importance'.[6] This meant therefore consideration being given to the 'position which they occupied in India, a little more than a hundred years ago and of which the traditions have naturally not faded from their minds'.[7]

The deputation to the viceroy soon evolved into the formation of the Muslim League which was formally established in Dacca in December 1906. For many who joined, it was not a radical change in political direction away from the umbrella cover the Congress provided: at the time it was only one more organization focusing on a specific constituency. In any case we can assume that the young Syud Hossain would have been in general agreement with the sentiments being expressed by the deputationists about the need for greater opportunities for Muslims to be created. Soon after joining government service as a junior civil servant, he wrote a series of articles on Dacca's history, interspersed occasionally with his own family's. *Echoes from Old Dacca* was published in 1909 as a separate pamphlet of about thirty-five pages – essentially a compilation of three articles. He was then only twenty or so and writing for a wider public for the first time but displayed an ability to write engagingly and with style. *Echoes* had no political content as such but the introductory and closing sentences certainly do suggest that the young Syud saw the emergence of a new provincial capital as something to be celebrated. The booklet began: 'After the lapse of over 200 years Dacca has once more been restored to its ancient dignity of a capital town.'[8]

This language does not suggest Syud saw the partition of Bengal as a tragedy or as a malign British ploy to divide Muslims and Hindus and weaken the spirit of nationalism, which was the view of many contemporary Hindus. It is possible too that he would have agreed largely with the prevailing view that the fate of the Muslims in India depended largely on the goodwill of the government and therefore loyalty to the empire was essential. This was, at its core, the view of Syed Ahmed Khan, the founder of the Aligarh institution, and in many ways represented the consensus view then of Muslim modernity in South Asia.

Yet, through Syud's time in Aligarh, there was also a contrarian current visible that had its roots in anxieties over the fate of Islam in a world dominated by the West. The decline of the Ottomans in Turkey was symptomatic to many of the more general loss of power that Muslims the world over had experienced including in India. Alongside were the stirrings of Indian nationalism and the questioning of British colonial policies, akin to the reaction of the other side, the Hindus, to the partition of Bengal. In Aligarh, howsoever faintly, there was also the emergence of the question whether loyalty to the British was still the best means of securing the interests of their community. In 1905 the principal of the college was shocked to find the students' union voting in favour of the Swadeshi movement in Bengal. This need not be given an exaggerated importance, but it does suggest an instinctive desire to support those criticizing alien rule.

A contemporary of Syud in Aligarh recalled a meeting of the Muslim League in Aligarh in 1908 that Muslim notables from across the country attended. The students decided to hold a debate 'in order to give them a bit of their mind'. The subject chosen was 'The hopes of the Muslims are centred on the All India Muslim League'. He remembered the role of Syud Hossain who spoke against the motion:

> He was a very good speaker even in his student days. His English was extremely good. He could write and speak English nearly as well as his own mother tongue. He made a vehement speech accusing the Muslim leaders of selling the country for a morsel, a few services and there was great shouting. All the leaders had to try and soothe our feelings saying that the Muslim community was not yet prepared to take this extreme step ... [and] tried to dissuade the students but it was given out that we had revolted against this policy ... It greatly embarrassed and puzzled the Muslim leaders of those days.[9]

How does this square with Syud's life once back in Calcutta where he clearly tended towards seeing the new province of East Bengal in positive terms? Perhaps we cannot fully understand and ought not to try to do so. He was a young man full of contradictory ideas and impulses, much as Asaf himself: aspiring for the ICS yet also swayed by the nationalist stirrings of the time.

It was inevitable that Asaf and Syud, both having recently arrived in London and being students together at Lincoln's Inn, would become friends. At that point neither had more than a distant interest in nationalist politics or politics of any kind for that matter. They were young and, for both, life in London was fun. Asaf had some aspirations at the time to be considered a poet in English. Some verses that he wrote, a poem entitled 'Destroyer of the Soul', won praise from Chatto. Syud was also impressed and asked John Squire, an upcoming name in English poetry circles and literary editor of the newly established *New Statesman*, for his opinion. Squire sent the verses back with the comment that they 'read like a good parody' of John Mansfield, a noted poet of the time. For Asaf this left-handed compliment, if it was even that, was clear enough and he saw it as a reminder of his Indian identity. 'I plucked off the half-opened bud. It was no use hoping to blossom on an alien stock. Urdu was my mother tongue and in Urdu alone I would seek my refuge and the medium of expression.'

In any case life as a law student meant that there were other preoccupations and numerous pleasant distractions. He had eclectic enthusiasms:

> The common room of Lincoln's Inn gave us free stationery, cheap but good lunches and teas, and we could invite friends to meet us there. It became our rendezvous and club. Some of us who were deeply interested in literature and art formed our own group. I came to be looked upon, in this group as a sort of specialist of the 'decadents' – Walter Pater, Oscar Wilde, Ibsen and so on.

Studying for the Bar meant being a 'gentlemen at large' with the only compulsory requirement being 'dining in' at the selected 'Hall of the Inn' for a certain number of dinners each term and 'taking one's own time to pass the prescribed examinations whenever it suited one'. A friend or fellow student entered his name for the Roman Law examination as a joke. Asaf knew nothing about the subject but put in a week's hard work – and passed! 'This exhilarating experience had the effect of making me treat the remaining examinations lightly.' In this way Asaf qualified as a lawyer by

January 1912. 'It was a red-letter day. With what pride I ordered my wig and gown and with elation I "sat" for my photograph.'

It was time now to return to India. In the two and a half years in England, interest in politics was on the whole a relatively minor factor in Asaf's life, but it was never entirely absent. There was the early exposure to India House, Savarkar and Madan Lal Dhingra. Then there was a close association with Chatto, en route himself to being fully immersed in the European revolutionary movement – so much so that he never returned to India, spending the next quarter-century in different parts of Europe; he would be executed in Moscow in one of Stalin's purges in 1937. Asaf became a vice president of the London Majlis, a gathering of Indian students of which the 'extremist' Bipin Chandra Pal was the president. So, clearly, Asaf's commitment to nationalist politics had been awakened even if he did not yet see himself being politically active.

Asaf stopped in Turkey while returning to India and, in Istanbul, he happened to be present at the Aya Ayubia mosque just as the Ottoman sultan arrived to pray. The sultan looked to Asaf 'a fat, somewhat bent old man with a pointed white beard, in every respect a European except for his tarboosh'. Despite this unprepossessing appearance the scene left Asaf very moved, and his recall of that moment three decades later spoke of his profound emotion: 'It was an impressive scene. I confess that all the emotions nurtured by my early upbringing in a Muslim home, and all the sentiments associated with this last vestige of Muslim freedom and greatness welled up in me – in spite of my rationalism – and my eyes were moist . . .'

# 4

# Delhi: 1912–1913

Once back in India, Asaf seemed to take no real interest in the politics of the time. During his absence in England, Delhi's formal status had changed; it was now the new colonial capital. Along with the annulment of the partition of Bengal, the shift of the capital from Calcutta to Delhi had been announced by George V, the king-emperor, in December 1911 at a grand durbar in Delhi.[1] If the change in Delhi's stature was immense, its actual impact would be felt only gradually and incrementally. Delhi at this point was more quiescent in a political sense than it had been during Asaf's college years. At that time the spirit of Swadeshi, charged up by the Bengal partition, had led to ripples of political activity amongst some students, including those in St Stephen's College, and a few politically conscious Delhi residents. By 1912 things were far more placid. A bomb attack in December 1912 on Viceroy Lord Hardinge during his procession through Chandni Chowk may suggest otherwise, but the involvement of Delhi itself in this act was negligible. The city was certainly on the cusp of transformation, but at that moment it was the sleepy administrative and political backwater it had been since the cataclysmic drama of 1857.

After the hectic activity and exhilaration of London, settling back in Delhi proved to be more difficult than Asaf had anticipated and his complaints began from the time his ship docked in Bombay. Boarding a train back to Delhi 'the sights and sounds at Victoria Terminus jarred' and his revulsion with everything around extended to the hawker from whom he purchased bedding for the night on the train: 'The cushions and pillows were loud with riotously flowered chintz . . .' The train itself was 'suffocating and the railway station's odours unpleasant'; in Delhi 'everything looked squalid. The road was unswept and dusty . . .'

At home, the old haveli in Kucha Chelan, a crowd of relatives waited to welcome him, and he was obviously happy to meet his mother and favourite relations. But he could not like 'their incongruous and gaudy dresses, the unrestrained expression of emotion and loud talk'. The gathering, apart from near and distant relatives, also included neighbours, singers and musicians, beggars and servants including those specially hired for the occasion. The house had been freshly whitewashed and the street outside decorated. For Asaf all this suddenly seemed too much:

> My nerves were giving way, and I suddenly begged my mother to shut off the musicians and to cut short the ceremonies. I fear this shocked everyone and confirmed their fear that I had become a foreigner in spirit. There was a murmur all round, but my mother saw my point and I was allowed to go upstairs to my newly prepared quarters – a study-sitting room and bedroom.

Asaf wrote that he felt like a shower:

> but there was only the old bath with a metal tub, and it was downstairs so that I would have to go through the courtyard with the throng of guests watching. There was nothing odd about this in our Indian way of life in those days, but I was overcome by irritation.

This hypercritical mood did not in fact lift and extended to other aspects of his life in Delhi. As a lawyer Asaf was in the relatively privileged position of being an England-qualified barrister and therefore the subject of some hostility and sneers. Barristers were ranked higher than other lawyers with qualifications gained in India. At the time in Delhi there were only six barristers and the rest of the Bar were pleaders with Indian qualifications who were jealous of the England-returned youngster. He admitted being 'blank about practical procedure' and that it was this 'ignorance of Indian law and court procedure . . . and the irony of the most junior of barristers being senior to the most experienced and able among Indian lawyers of Indian qualification, which had created the atmosphere of hostility'. In the courts the Bar Room was 'poorly furnished and had a depressing atmosphere', kindling nostalgia for the Lincoln's Inn common room.

A number of relationships that were to play an important role in Asaf's life and career were forged soon after his return from England. The first was with Dr M.A. Ansari (1880–1936), some eight to nine years older than Asaf, a skilled physician and surgeon with qualifications superior to the English civil surgeon and seniormost government doctor in Delhi 'who was taken aback to see an Indian in private practice charging the highest fee which had hitherto been his prerogative'. Asaf met Ansari in connection with an illness in the family, after which both cultivated each other 'for both of us felt lonely'. They found that they were excluded from Delhi clubs – all-white premises that they were – and therefore joined a new set-up established by friends and acquaintances in similar positions. This was the Orient Club, which stipulated 'no white man was to be admitted as a member'.[2]

Dr Ansari was one of the earliest among Muslims to opt to study modern medicine in Europe rather than the traditional Unani Tibb. His two elder brothers were famed hakims. After his medical studies in Edinburgh, Ansari had worked in a London hospital for some years, returning to India in 1910 to set up what would become a flourishing medical practice in Delhi.[3] He had spent about a decade in Britain. That he would have much in common with Asaf was to be expected. In Asaf's recollection, 'Ansari had brought with him a new professional atmosphere and ethics'. In his practice a certain number of hours were set aside for the poor but he also had amongst his patients the wealthiest in the country. Till his death in 1936 Ansari was to be the go-to physician for many leaders of the national movement.

When Asaf first met him, Ansari lived near the walls of the old city at Mori Gate. His house 'Behisht', or Paradise, was the location of many significant meetings of the Congress and the Khilafat movement and also where many important leaders stayed when visiting Delhi. In 1928 he moved to an elegant building by the old city walls in Darya Ganj, a few minutes' walk from Asaf's house in Kucha Chelan, which he named Dar e Salaam – Abode of Peace. It quickly became an even more prominent centre for the Congress and for nationalist activity in Delhi, and it was, in the words of one historian, 'a counterpoint of Motilal Nehru's Allahabad residence Anand Bhavan'.[4] In later years Ansari's flourishing medical practice underwrote a lot of Congress activity, especially when it came to meeting election expenses of numerous Congressmen.

Someone else of significance he got to know well at that time was Mohammad Ali who turned up at Asaf's house one day to introduce himself, dressed 'in morning coat, striped pants, white spats and a sky-blue hat'. He said he was 'generally known as Mohammad Ali Oxon'. Mohammad Ali[5] was a graduate of the Aligarh college, who had then with his family's support reached Oxford. He attempted and failed the ICS examination during his stay in England. On his return in 1902 he held administrative posts in the princely states of Rampur (briefly) and then Baroda for seven or eight years till 1910. The experience of being a subordinate civil servant in Baroda outside his more familiar north Indian milieu left him frustrated. As one historian summed up:

> Activity and companionship were the drugs he craved. He yearned for the *Mushairas*, which was his passion from the college days, and the mehfils where he could transmit the flame of his intellectual excitement to others. The drab and routine work as a civil servant combined with the unfamiliar cultural milieu and the hostility of his colleagues could offer no solace to the buoyant and exuberant Mohammad Ali.[6]

A career in journalism thus seemed the best option and he did very well in it after resigning the Baroda job. Journalism catapulted him to the limelight he sought. The transfer of the imperial capital to Delhi made that city the ideal place to establish his newspapers: *Comrade* in English and *Hamdard* in Urdu. For Mohammad Ali it was the world of Islam, no less, that beckoned and its state that most concerned him. His writings soon 'performed the important role of providing a framework for the uneasiness and dissatisfaction of the Muslim educated elite'. One particular concern that he attached himself to with considerable passion was the Ottomans: 'The *Comrade* of the early years testifies to its vigorous and passionate interest in the Turkish cause.'[7]

Asaf already knew Mohammad Ali by reputation: copies of the *Comrade* had reached London when Asaf was a student. The press he was setting up in Delhi and the house he was furnishing were both near Asaf's own home. 'During this period, he divided his time between supervising the work in the neighbouring premises and virtually staying with me.' Asaf's bachelor 'quarter' within the Kucha Chelan house had its advantages: 'A stairway led directly to it from the *deohri* or outer entrance, so that it was altogether separate from the zenana or women's part of the house.' Mohammad Ali was about ten years older than Asaf, already a well-known figure, and joined the circle around Dr Ansari. Shaukat Ali (1873–1938), Mohammad Ali's brother, was soon also part of the group, and in Asaf's recollection, both were delightful company, 'each capping the other's jokes or even smutty stories'. The brothers combined a deep piety, Islamism and passionate devotion to the Ottoman cause with an enthusiastic attitude to the good things of life, including good food. 'They would decline paan when smoking their cigar' citing an Islamic injunction, 'No marriage with two sisters at the same time!' The paan therefore had to follow the cigar! Ansari and the Ali brothers were older than Asaf but clearly they all enjoyed each other's company.

On one of these evenings at a dinner in Mohammad Ali's house, Asaf met someone closer to him in age, in fact some months younger. Maulana Abul Kalam Azad, Asaf recalled, was a 'slim, handsome person ... with a head wrap after the style of the Arabs' and one 'who talked brilliantly and with confidence'. The Maulana already had an impressive reputation and Asaf was dazzled: 'Applying his mental powers akin to genius, to an incredible store of learning, he sparkled and dazzled, and only Mohammad

Ali whose intellectual keenness was matched by witty volubility, could keep pace with him.'

Abul Kalam was a name familiar to many on account of his scholarship as well as for his journalism and activism. Born to an Arab mother and a father who was a Sufi teacher with a considerable reputation and following, the early intellectual influences on him were traditional and he grew up in an environment that grounded him in Persian and Arabic, in Islamic philosophy and practice. Growing up in an age when the world of Islam was in a state of ferment both over the loss of political power to European colonialism and in the interface with Western modernity, the young Azad was strongly influenced by Sir Syed Ahmed Khan, the most significant figure of Islamic modernity in India quite apart from being the founder of the Muhammadan Anglo-Oriental College in Aligarh. This influence enabled a more critical and objective perspective on the classical grounding of his knowledge. Perhaps this process also strengthened – or even led to – what was a characteristic feature of Abul Kalam: an open-mindedness and spirit of toleration that made him stand out amongst the leading Islamist ideologues and intellectuals of his generation. His Arab roots and his immersion in the world of Islam meant also a deep-seated connection with West Asia. Iran, Iraq, Arab nationalism and Egypt, Turkey and the Ottomans all formed part of his mental world.[8]

Abul Kalam's impact on his contemporaries can be specifically traced to his editorship of *Al-Hilal* from 1912. The newspaper provided a platform to project his views on the kind of polity that Muslims should aspire to in India and his writings suggested how much he was already impacted by the nationalist impulse then emergent in India. Simultaneously the fate of the Ottomans in Turkey provided another plank. Both these sets of ideas really emerged from the general issue of how Muslims should deal with the fact of European domination so evident in their societies. While the tone of *Al-Hilal* was religious, the political takeaways it provided were evident to its growing readership. Its publication largely coincided with the appearance of Mohammad Ali's *Hamdard* in Delhi. Both publications would ultimately contribute significantly to a changed political atmosphere – but that was still in the future.

It may not have been fully evident as yet but Maulana Abul Kalam and Mohammad Ali represented a new generation of Muslim leaders from the traditionalist and largely loyalist elite that had hitherto dominated the community. One assessment held that between them they 'mirrored the two most powerful strands amongst Indian Muslims – pan Islamism and sympathy for nationalist forces'.[9] Both situated themselves almost exclusively within the mainstream Islamic tradition and addressed Muslim audiences in their public advocacy. While, at this early stage, it would be anachronistic to apply categories such as 'secular' or 'communal' to characterize or distinguish them, there were differences of approach that would have been evident to Asaf even then. Maulana Azad was a scholar, an ideologue, even a theorist. Mohammad Ali was a crusader concerned not about the accuracy or the sophistication of his arguments but about their emotional impact.[10] Perhaps Abul Kalam, given the scholarship he had steeped himself in, had a more nuanced and contingent understanding of his times than Mohammad Ali with his more combative and black-and-white positions.

Asaf himself appears clearly at ease both with the liberal Abul Kalam Azad and the more doctrinaire Mohammad Ali – both possessing an Islamic world view yet progressively deriving different conclusions from it. Azad was intellectually inclined towards the ideological position that Muslims must realign themselves to ally with the Congress, and he found Quranic and scriptural authority to underline the need for common cause with Hindus against the British. His role, it appeared to him, was to allay his community's fears of Hindu domination. In his thinking these fears and apprehensions could be easily traced to British policy to consolidate Muslim support for their rule in India. Mohammad Ali generally agreed with this, but his overall approach was more tactical and even transactional, rather than derived from rigorous study and reflection. According to one one assessment 'he acted where others doubted or reasoned' and in addition 'he possessed to the full the resources of traditional oratory – its repertoire of tricks'.[11] At this stage he was hardly a declared critic of British rule in India but was certainly not one of the dutiful loyalists who dominated Muslim politics in general and the Muslim League in particular. It was the predicament of global Islam and the Ottoman Turks in particular that drew his attention and his passion. Amidst these strong and magnetic personalities, Asaf would probably have been broadly in agreement at the time, listening and participating in their intense discussions and debates. Possibly the young Asaf, curious about everything, felt most comfortable in a Westernized set quite regardless of its religious texture or indeed its political opinion.

The Maulana's and Mohammad Ali's brilliance cast a spell on Asaf's circle but a very different influence was another larger-than-life personality, Hakim Ajmal Khan, who was well known to Asaf's family, as indeed to many of the old residents of Delhi.[12] It was to Ajmal Khan that Asaf's family had gone for advice when the question of his first travelling to England had come up and the health of his grandmother was a concern. The hakim was possibly Delhi's most prominent citizen in the first two decades of the twentieth century and a mentor to the city's intellectuals. He came from a family that had been physicians to the Mughal court and this aristocratic background was certainly a factor in the esteem he and his family were held in the city. The revival of indigenous medical treatments, his family profession, was his great passion and as a Unani practitioner he was 'renowned for seemingly miraculous cures'. His aim was the creation of a formal teaching institution in Unani medicine and the foundation of Tibbia College in Delhi was the realization of that ambition.

The hakim was also a strong protagonist of communal harmony, and this was also in line with a professional commitment to developing cooperation between the Unani and Ayurvedic systems of traditional medicine. Through the first decade and a half of the century he was close to the British and actively courted their support on numerous issues. In 1906 he was part of the delegation of Muslim notables that had called on the viceroy in support of the decision to partition Bengal. This position of strong loyalty to the British would gradually change, as it did for many other prominent Muslims later in the second decade of the twentieth century, but that too was still in the future.

We get a flavour of Asaf's life in Delhi when, at Dr Ansari's insistence sometime in October or November 1912, he was asked to arrange an 'Indian' evening with music. 'My bachelor digs', Asaf wrote, was deemed most appropriate for this. The reason was the famous British writer E.M. Forster's presence in Delhi. Forster's escort was Ross Masood, a grandson of Syed Ahmed Khan who had recently returned to India with a degree from Oxford; both were house guests of Ansari at Bashisht. His hosts had decided that 'the music of Delhi's professional singers should be part of the experiences that Forster was amassing'. The gathering was arranged in the open on the terrace as it was peak summer. In Asaf's recollection the evening was not the greatest of successes. 'All of us squatted on the floor, for the most part in obvious discomfort. I was on pins and needles.' He had been given very little notice and 'the singer was not the best'. Also, in Asaf's recollection, Forster's regard for the truth 'did not allow him to disguise the fact that he found the music incomprehensible'. It was in any case, he felt, not possible for a Westerner to relate to Indian music for music 'brings out the essential difference between peoples'.

While Asaf is brief about this evening at his house we can tease out some more details from others. Forster wrote that the evening came about because Ansari 'insisted on treating me to a *nautch*'.[13] He was, Forster wrote, not very keen 'partly because of the expense, partly because I was a little nervous at the exact degree of festivity'. If he thought he was going to be part of an oriental orgy he needed to have no such fears. There was nothing else planned other than traditional entertainment of music and dance for a guest. There were aspects of the evening he liked. He described the venue as being in the middle of the old city: 'a most romantic place – on the roof of a house belonging to one of his friends'. Forster's description of the evening, however, does confirm Asaf's worst fears: 'The noise was often excruciating – the musicians seemed out of tune and playing in different keys . . . and the ladies voices went into my ears like battering rams.' Nevertheless, 'the dresses and gestures were so lovely, and the singing was clearly so emotional that I did get a great deal of pleasure from it'.

Forster writes that there were nine or ten others present and that he knew all of them. Who they were, apart from Ansari, Asaf and

Ross Masood, we do not know but one somewhat unwilling guest was Asaf's neighbour Mohammad Ali. He had been in his newspaper office contemplating suicide, he said, as he had just read a Reuters report that the Bulgarian forces were a mere twenty-five miles from Constantinople, 'a name that had for five centuries been sacred to every Muslim as the Centre of his highest hopes'.[14] His acute depression about the course the Balkans wars had taken and the losses the Ottomans faced was interrupted by Ross Masood who

> insisted on my company, and hard as I pleaded the excuse of a busy editor and still harder the state of my feelings after that last message of Reuters my friend would not take any denial and almost bodily lifted me from the Editorial sanctum and carried me by main force to the private nautch party next door.[15]

And so it was that 'instead of being a horror of broken bones and bleeding body' that would have followed his jumping from the third storey of his house, he ended up instead at the nautch. Some weeks later Mohammad Ali 'blurted out something of my mental torture that night' to an English journalist. He was to find to his great discomfiture that a story thereafter appeared in the London *Times* of how a leading Muslim agitator had spent the eve of Turkey's defeat indulging in an 'orgy'![16]

Asaf's circle on his return to Delhi then was made up of a Westernized upper-middle class – at least in terms of exposure and aspirations – of young Muslims. External politics certainly figured in their situation, but only as one factor and then too very unevenly. The experience of living in England certainly seems to have been the more relevant binding factor. In time politics would come to predominate and to a great extent consume those in it. Delhi may have still been a political backwater but it was embedded in a larger context of political change, and in gatherings of educated and aware Muslims, such as Asaf found himself in, there would have been much to discuss.

The passage of the Indian Councils Act of 1909 by the British parliament had been a conscious effort by the government to win back moderate political opinion in the country, deeply alienated by the partition decision. It conceded, in principle at least, the representation of Indians in legislative bodies at the central and provincial levels. In the Imperial Legislative Council, the government majority was maintained but the number of seats by election for Indians was increased. In the provinces, non official majorities became possible. Most significant had been the decision providing for separate electorates for Muslims. For Muslims meeting the income and property qualifications, separate electorates had meant that a wider avenue was now open for them to enter public life insulated from competition from Hindu politicians. While this had been a huge plus as far as Muslim public opinion was concerned, the revocation two years later, in 1911, of the partition of Bengal was a shock to many of them. Certainly, it would have appeared to them to vindicate the agitational technique adopted to oppose it by the majority community. The revocation was, as noted earlier, announced simultaneously with the shift of capital to Delhi. The shift was intended to mollify Muslims upset over the annulment of the Bengal decision by projecting it as a recollection of past Mughal glory centred in Delhi. It was also a sop to those disturbed over the plight of Turkey and the Ottomans. The real motive was also evident: the imperial capital in a quiet Delhi was infinitely better than its current location in politically supercharged Calcutta.

That summer – the summer of 1913 – the Delhi heat drove Asaf to Simla where he soon found himself in an anglicized group with which he had much in common. The group included the law minister of the princely state of Patiala, Chaman Lal. This set may have consciously sought to keep politics and nationalism at a distance from their lives but they were nevertheless deeply affected by it. Chaman Lal was in fact a brother of Madan Lal Dhingra, the assassin of Curzon Wyllie, whom Asaf had met in London. Asaf noted that the family had dropped the surname 'Dhingra' and also that Mrs Chaman Lal was a granddaughter of the great Bengal reformer Keshub Chandra Sen and a protagonist herself of inter-caste and interregional marriage. This again was a set into which Asaf found that he fitted easily seeing it as a simulacrum of modernity:

> I was schooled in the etiquette and tastes of the better type of anglicized Indian society. This appeared to be a good blend, into which Europeans could fit without difficulty. All spoke English and in all but ladies' dress and a preference for Indian cuisine, approximated to the western way of life.

While in Simla Asaf soon made the acquaintance of an attractive young Englishwoman and 'she and I aroused much envy by pairing together much of the time, at the Rink especially for we made the best dancing and skating couple'. News of this travelled and we have Dr Ansari somewhat uncharacteristically writing from Delhi: 'You lucky dog! Who is this great beauty . . .?' On the whole, politics was a distant factor here, and in company such as Asaf encountered in Simla, it was possible to live a somewhat Western way of life – including the occasional trophy Englishwoman – in which the few Indian elements were dress and cuisine. Nonetheless Asaf noted that the group's 'criticism of certain Western ways was scathing': cleanliness was superficial, they felt, and did not include personal hygiene.

Asaf was seeking to find his feet in India and locating himself in what he felt was a like-minded group socially and intellectually. That he spent over three months in Simla suggests just how congenial he found them.

On his return, Asaf found his friends in Delhi agitated about the war in the Balkans which Bulgaria, Serbia and Montenegro were waging with Russian support against their former overlords in Turkey and which seemed to be driving one more nail into the coffin of the tottering Ottomans. In tandem, Greece announced the formal annexation of the former Ottoman territory of Crete. Amongst the more pious, there was growing concern over the Turkish-controlled Islamic holy sites of Arabia. With the heavy losses the Ottomans had faced in the Balkans there was growing apprehension that European encroachment into its territories in the Arab world was next.

From these concerns emerged the Anjuman-i-Khuddam-i-Kaaba, or the Society of the Servants of Kaaba, Islam's holiest shrine. Its many ambitions remained largely on paper but it received at the time an enormous amount of attention in the Urdu media, becoming the centre of much propaganda and rhetoric. The Ali brothers, Shaukat and Mohammad, and Dr Ansari were certainly energized and there was much talk about raising an Indian contingent for an 'International Islamic Brigade' to defend and safeguard the holy sites. Asaf wrote: 'The plight of the Turks had gripped the minds of the Musalmans.' The fiery rhetoric associated with the Anjuman's protagonists, however, also put many off and in particular those who feared the government's displeasure.

The more practical idea to emerge was of a medical mission to help Turkey in the midst of war. Dr Ansari readily organized and led this initiative. The medical mission idea received an overwhelming response. The Government of India was not opposed to this initiative in support of Turkey and in fact encouraged it; Britain was not a party to the Balkan wars, so this was not dissident activity in a political sense and many in the Muslim elite and upper class were supportive. Popular support was soon massive. In Delhi a procession of 15,000 Muslims accompanied the mission all the way from Jama Masjid to the railway station to bid them farewell.[17] The seven-month-long mission, from December 1912 to July 1913, led to the consolidation of the public reputations of Dr Ansari and even more so of Mohammad Ali, the former for leading the mission and the latter for publicizing its Turkey activities in India. The story of the mission came alive to many in India through the pages of the *Comrade* which regularly published Dr Ansari's letters on its daily activities.[18]

While Asaf also had a sentimental attachment to the idea of the Ottomans – as was evident when he saw the sultan in Constantinople – he appears to have been somewhat detached from the activity around him, as indeed from other political developments in India at the time. His engagement, such as it was, with the medical mission scheme appears more an outcome of his knowing Ansari and Mohammad Ali rather than as a newfound commitment.

Barring the Simla interlude and the friendships with the Ali brothers and Dr Ansari, Asaf had on the whole a somewhat miserable time in the months after his return. Being a London-qualified barrister would have meant a head start in establishing a practice in the subordinate courts of Delhi, in time extending to the high court in Lahore and elsewhere. As a natural fit into the circle of upper-class Westernized Indians, seeking to establish and grow his legal practice to become in time a permanent member of that set, would have seemed the natural career progression for him. Yet this does not appear uppermost in his mind for, quite simply, he yearned to be back in London and England. His initial reactions to the dirt, the dust, the shabbiness and the chaos of things did not evaporate but only grew stronger.

So jarring, he says, was the Delhi experience that within a few months he would have grasped at any straw that would take him back to England. Asaf therefore looked for a way out and when a slight opportunity presented itself, he seized it. 'I was dreaming of practice at the Privy Council bar' – in other words setting up a practice dealing with Indian cases making their way to the Privy Council as the highest court of appeal, establishing a home in England, and then sending for his mother to live with him. It was, he wrote later, 'a silly delusion for it was sheer folly to expect that my mother would ever go to England'. His friends were sceptical and mocked the whole enterprise. Mohammad Ali, in particular, 'who had become quite intimate, while not probing into my Privy Council brief, poked much fun, according to his wont, at my quest after the English lady of Simla or other manifestation of the eternal woman'.

Asaf's second stint in London – when he spent so much time with Sarojini, Syud and others – however, cured him of his England fever. He was no longer the impressionable youth who had arrived in England marvelling at the light. The reasons were also possibly more than personal – such as his engagement to Liaq so assiduously brought about by Sarojini. Asaf does not refer specifically in any detail to the outbreak of World War I in his recollections of this period but it provided an obvious backdrop to his own evolution. One reason for this was that the Ottomans were soon to be on the side of the Germans and ranged against the British and their allies. This would expand the war beyond Europe and bring it to areas geographically and psychologically closer to India.

Alongside, all the political influences and sentiments that he had experienced – and which he had seemed indifferent to – were now coming to the fore. The memories of the mutiny massacre in his house in Kucha Chelan, the encounter with Madan Lal Dhingra, the sympathy for the fading Ottomans were all different impulses that were fusing and crystallizing together. Friendship with Ansari and Mohammad Ali widened his horizons and the time with Sarojini in London opened these up even further. Perhaps Sarojini's own career and profile showed him the reasons to participate in public life at such a moment in India's history. All this had led to his break with 'Uncle' and the ending of the arrangement in which he had been reporting on his fellows and acting as an informant to the colonial intelligence services.

This return voyage was therefore very different from the first time he had bid goodbye to England when leaving his life in London had been a terrible wrench. This time, as the ship crossed the Straits of Gibraltar (the stretch of water separating Morocco and Spain, and the Atlantic Ocean and Mediterranean Sea), Asaf paced its deck and 'there came before my mind's eye the invasion of Spain by Tariq, the Arab general who has been immortalized by the name Gibraltar – Tariq's rock'. In his state of mind at that point, Gibraltar immediately evoked memories of the first century of Arab expansion and the name of the Arab general, Tariq bin Ziyad, who led that expansion into Spain and Portugal, and from whose name the Spanish derivation of Gibraltar – Jabel Tariq, literally Jabel's Mountain – is derived.

He found that the other returning Anglo-Indians were 'a standoffish lot'. As the ship sailed into Port Said in Egypt he found the harbour decked out colourfully and cannons being fired in celebration. War with the Ottomans had led Britain to declare Egypt a protectorate. An English fellow passenger rather tauntingly asked him whether he liked the new arrangement, and he responded angrily, 'No more than would the owner of a house, whose home has been burgled by brigands …' Asaf's recollection of his mindset at that time was that: 'Incident after incident was thus laying the foundations in my mind for the assertion of personal self-respect which, in the circumstances, was bound up with India's political status.' His tryst with nationalism had begun.

This transition – from an enthusiastically Westernized, even Anglophile, carefree young man maturing into a committed nationalist – seems an almost inevitable progression and an outcome of the changing national and international political environment. The break with 'Uncle' and ending of the role as an informant appears to be a natural consequence. Perhaps his friendship with Dr Ansari, the Ali brothers, meeting Abul Kalam and thereafter Sarojini Naidu and Syud Hossain increasingly made this double role impossible to sustain and also pointed to a life fully immersed in public affairs as the preferred option. The way forward for his life and career now seemed quite different. He had been moving towards becoming a member of India's upper-class, Anglophile set secure in their professions in the Bar, the army or civil service, or in corporate employment as a boxwallah. But now a more turbulent, unpredictable life appeared far more likely for him.

Was Asaf actually more invested in the role as informer than he later revealed? And did this, in turn, make his ending the arrangement more than an overdue termination of a practice he had long ceased to carry out seriously? In other words, was it more than just the rite of passage he described it as? The question arises as one reads his recollections. Possibly yes, and we can speculate that his drifting to India House soon after his arrival in London may well have been a path laid down by 'Uncle' himself. India House at the time was watched closely by British intelligence and there were in it a number of informers.[19] Asaf himself tried to mitigate his unease by saying the information he gave was known and he was reporting more like a journalist than a spy. It's quite possible his information he provided had little intrinsic value, but any information coming from a source from within an adversarial situation acquires value in an intelligence bureaucracy. It is clear this entire arrangement weighed heavily on Asaf's mind, and the termination of that relationship may well have been both a personal and a political act that marked the beginnings of a more public personality. To his mind it was an act of redemption.

He had drifted without too much thought into an arrangement that was convenient, and may even have appeared natural, as a still immature young boy but it was to cause him much pain and mental agony as a young man. Years later, when Asaf reflected on this phase of his early life, he was not harsh on 'Uncle' who was doing him what he thought, 'from his perverted point of view', a great favour. An education in England was obviously 'a big opening' but it was a 'paradise [which was to] soon turn into hell'. Asaf was honest enough not to blame 'Uncle' for he 'knew no better'. But by the same token he was not unduly harsh on the younger Asaf, 'a youngster who himself knew no better'. A century and more later, it is possible to view this less judgementally; to understand the pressures behind the choices Asaf made; to factor in his youthful ignorance of the implications. In any event his rejection of the arrangement with 'Uncle' was not the end of the matter.

# 5

# Sarojini and Hyderabad

On disembarking in Bombay, Asaf did not go straight to Delhi. His first stop was Hyderabad, 'to see Liaq and her people, and of course Sarojini'. Note the 'of course' and the fact he seemed equally enthusiastic about seeing both. Sarojini 'was an ideal hostess' and she organized a reception 'at which Hyderabad's elite were present'. Sarojini also arranged an outing to Golconda and her husband took Asaf to a Masonic function.

At the time of Asaf's visit in January 1915, Sarojini Naidu's house, named the Golden Threshold after her first poetry collection, was a spacious bungalow with a well-maintained garden. She had only recently returned after two and a half years in England, and she was at thirty-six in her familiar surroundings, with her husband, four children aged between eleven and fourteen, and numerous friends around her. It was a gracious upper-middle-class lifestyle made distinctive by Sarojini's own gregarious personality and commitment to being as inclusive as possible. In a letter to Gopal Krishna Gokhale, at the time possibly the leading Indian public figure and with whom she had been corresponding for at least a decade, she described 'just one average day':

> Between 9 and 12 when I do not happen to have any committee meetings on, I hold my morning durbar to which everyone in Hyderabad comes without distinction of class. Nawabs and officials, fashionable England returned men and poor students, without shoes on their feet but full of fire in their hearts. Maulvis with long beards, pundits with bare bodies

and shawls, poets chanting Persian and Sanskrit, Telugu, Tamil and Urdu verses. Men in motors, men on elephants, men on palanquins – and I sit in a big Chinese chair and talk to each after his kind, and learn a great deal of old lore and wisdom from this medieval habit of mine of holding morning receptions and mine of course is a home which is at the centre of the Hindu–Mohammadan unity in its fullest sense.

In the afternoon 'Ladies, Hindu and Mohammadan alike find it convenient to come' and made for a fresh set of conversations. 'At 4 I go for my bath and when I return, I usually find a fresh row of ladies sitting on my bed quite unabashed!' Every day 'is very full because underlying it is the same purpose, the unifying of emotions of conflicting sets and communities'.[1]

How much of this was real and how much imagined and aspirational is hard to say, but certainly the picture of an active and sociable personality that had so impressed Asaf in London is reinforced. It is also evident that Sarojini consciously imagined herself as a person surrounded by Indian diversity in all its meanings and sought to act as a very real bridge across different divides.

The Irish writer and suffragette Margaret Cousins, a house guest in mid-1916, wrote about the 'delightful sense of coolness and culture' of Sarojini's home where the 'perfection of artistic taste' had combined 'Eastern colour in carpets and crafts' with the 'comfort of Western lounges and modern conveniences'. Cousins, who later established the All-India Women's Conference (to become a premier Indian non-governmental organization), wrote admiringly of the ' tall vases or wide bowls full of the most beautiful white lotuses I had ever seen'. Most of their conversations took place in Sarojini's bedroom since Sarojini was weak from a recent bout of sickness, and here, for Cousins, the effect was of a 'brilliant French salon at the height of France's glory. The silver ornaments on her dressing table of the French empire design, the gestures she so often uses, slight mannerisms akin to pose, the foreign nuance in her accent, and her wit and vivacity, caused one to speculate romantically about her last incarnation ...'

Cousins noted the minor affectations, but appreciated Naidu's highly developed sense of dress and its impact. For a call on E.S. Montague, the secretary of state for India, on a visit to India to hand over a representation on behalf of Indian women, '[Naidu] had chosen her sari with care that day so that its effect might be like the gleaming of the silver moonlight in the dark blue vault of the heavens – the woman, the poetess and the stage manager aiding and abetting the demand for justice and equality.'

Cousins gives us a sense of the person Sarojini wished to project herself as:

> I have called her a peace maker and it is one of the names she loves . . . It is one of her dearest desires to link with the bonds of love and mutual interests and understanding the great Moslem and Hindu sections of Indian life . . . The circumstances of her life have caused her to be a living epitome of what she seeks. Hindu by birth, brought up in constant touch with Mohammadens in a Mohammaden city . . .[2]

Sarojini was the eldest of eight children born to Aghorenath Chattopadhyaya and Varada Sundari. It was a family that gave high priority to learning and culture. Aghorenath was of a scholarly bent. He studied in Calcutta University and went to do a PhD in chemistry in Edinburgh in 1877.[3] He was also a scholar of Sanskrit and employed by the Hyderabad state in its education department, playing an important role in establishing a modern education system there. In addition, he was interested in women's education and nationalism. Sarojini's siblings also showed distinctive character traits. Virendranath Chattopadhyaya or Chatto who had so impressed Asaf in London, was a revolutionary who spent most of his adult life in Europe. Mrinalini or Gunnu, who introduced Asaf to Sarojini, became the principal of the Sir Ganga Ram Training College for Women in Lahore.[4] The youngest brother, Harindranath, was a poet, a dramatist and an actor.

An assessment of Sarojini's growing-up years puts it thus: 'it was an interesting, talented and diverse family that occupied a home that was one of the centres of every kind of intellectual adventurism and free thinking in Hyderabad.'[5] Harindranath was born just a little before Sarojini got married and set up her own home but his description of the parental home as 'something of a cross between a museum and a zoo' is evocative of the diversity in her background. He recalled: 'Mother spoke to father in Bengali, to us in Hindustani and to the servants in Telugu. Though we heard the Bengali tongue spoken in our house we never spoke it.'[6]

This was the unusual diasporic Bengali home Sarojini grew up in. The connection with Calcutta was, however, always present: her father on one occasion, when turfed out of the nizam's Hyderabad for undesirable political activity, lived in Calcutta for some time before being restored to the good graces of the state authorities. On retirement Aghorenath chose not to live in Hyderabad and moved back to Calcutta, but for Sarojini Hyderabad was home. As a young girl she was something of a prodigy and clearly was precocious by any standard. By the time she was twelve, in 1891, she had passed the Madras matriculation exam in the first class, and was already composing long poems – one as long as 1,300 lines.

By the time she was fourteen she had fallen in love with Dr M. Govindarajulu Naidu. He had just returned with a degree in medicine from Edinburgh and had joined the nizam's government service as a doctor. But clearly all this emotional activity took a toll on Sarojini, and as she put it: 'My health broke down permanently about this time and my regular studies being stopped, I read voraciously. I suppose the greater part of my reading was done between fourteen and sixteen. I wrote a novel; I wrote fat volumes of journals. I took myself very seriously in those days.' Sarojini would be plagued by illness all her life – the health issues are not specified anywhere – but she seldom let this interfere with her plans, travels and ambitions.

Her feelings for Dr Naidu were, however, strong enough to alarm her father. Sarojini's contemporaries must have known the reasons for his objections. Her biographers certainly have speculated about them. In other families that Dr Naidu was from a different caste and region would have been a factor, but the general consensus is that Aghorenath was more concerned that Sarojini at fourteen was too young to think of marriage.

A nizam's fellowship to study in England in 1895 offered a way out and Sarojini spent the next three years there. She did not complete a formal course but attended many lectures at King's College in London and Girton College in Cambridge. In one assessment 'she spent most of her time reading and writing poetry' and also meeting other poets, some of whom advised her about the quality and depth of her writings.[7]

A number of her letters from England to Dr Naidu have survived and these love letters also bring out her initial homesickness, her efforts with her poetry, and her gradual familiarity with the environment she was in. Poetry certainly occupied a large space of her life at this time, and the correspondence and friendship with then well-established names – such as the poets Arthur Symons and Edmond Gosse – suggest the direction of her aspirations. These formative years in England gave to her the confidence and the vocabulary to navigate with ease the interface with the Western world in which she was to display so much versatility later and which was obviously very useful in a colonial society.

The relationship between her and Govindarajulu proved a durable one and they were married on her return around December 1898 with her parents' approval. This was an inter-caste, interregional marriage which was rare at the turn of the century. But both belonged to a similar social set and even at that time this was a clinching factor. The early years of married life followed a largely conventional pattern and by 1904 she was a mother of four. But clearly for her a settled upper-middle-class existence came to have its limitations.

In 1905 her collection of poems, *The Golden Threshold*, was published in London. Her mentor-cum-friend Arthur Symons played a major role in the publication of this book, generally described as Sarojini's 'finest collection' and which established her reputation as an up-and-coming Indian woman of letters. It received favourable reviews in the British press, including in established journals and newspapers. A kind of celebrity status followed; she was twenty-six, a mother of four, a published poet and quite ready to take on an active role in the wider world.

The nationalist ferment in India following the partition of Bengal meant that a larger stage was coming into being and it promised to be one that would gradually dwarf the world of poetry. Her biographers describe Sarojini as being in Calcutta in 1905 and as having 'plunged into politics'. She spoke at the 1906 session of the Indian National Congress that was held in Calcutta. By then, she was apparently already a popular speaker and in one assessment 'she and her audiences quickly discovered her innate gift for oratory'.[8] Speaking engagements soon expanded into a larger interface with India.

Her letters suggest frequent travels out of Hyderabad and in 1908 or 1909 she was awarded the Kaiser-i-Hind medal by the colonial government for her famine relief work. She was corresponding and meeting with the best-known figures in public life in India and by 1910 the list already included R.C. Dutt, G.K. Gokhale, Madan Mohan Malaviya, C.P. Ramaswami Aiyar and others. Two other collections of poems, *The Bird of Time* and *The Broken Wing*, were published from London, so poetry remained important but it is very clear that her interests were now much wider. In one assessment of Sarojini, 'her reputation as a poet was at its height from 1905 to 1907 and then there was a steady decline afterward'.[9] Clearly public affairs and politics were now becoming the principal drivers of her interests.

Soon after *The Bird of Time* was published in May 1912, Sarojini left for England because of her ill health and that is when Asaf Ali and Syud Hossain came to know her. She would return to India some two years later in October 1914 and henceforth she would be fully in the vortex of Indian politics, becoming in time one of its principal figures.

The end of the first decade of the twentieth century, that is before her departure for England, is a good time to take stock of the personality of this feisty and gifted woman as she turned thirty in 1909. She was evidently a young woman of tremendous drive and energy, despite her constant ill health, and had no qualms about investing in the causes she believed in. Inevitably this meant that she became the target of questions that would rarely have been addressed to her male contemporaries or peers, most relating to how her husband and family reacted to her life as a public figure.

The first generation of her biographers saw her as a woman driven strongly by the desire to change India's colonial status as also its internal inequities especially with regard to women's rights. Khwaja Ahmad Abbas, in a short biography published on the centenary of her birth, wrote in a chapter entitled 'From Mother-to-Mother India':

> her first incursion in public life was on the issue of women's emancipation. The women's movement was just beginning in India. And so, she was invited to meetings everywhere as the fame of her oratory spread from one corner of the country to another. Dr Naidu never once stood in her way – he was himself an ardent advocate of women's emancipation and he practiced what he preached. To keep the one woman with her fiery tongue, who could set the whole country on fire, locked up in her house would be treachery to the cause.[10]

When Sarojini left for England in May 1912, Jaisoorya, her eldest offspring, was about eleven and Leilamani, the youngest, eight. Her letters to each of them bring out a mother who is connected and also conscious of the toll her long absences may take. Writing to the eleven-year-old Randheera in February 1914 she said:

> You know a family is like a piece of machinery. Each separate part must be in good order and do its own work satisfactorily for the machinery to keep going . . . Nearly 12 years old and I am sure you have already begun to think of sensible things, and your own share in making our home a place of happiness and well being.

She was scheduled to return to India around this time but was asked to extend her stay on health grounds. A week later, her letter to Randheera said, 'So you are fearfully disappointed that I am not returning till September.' At this time to the thirteen- or fourteen-year-old Jaisoorya she wrote:

> I am greatly touched by your brave and manly letter on hearing the doctor's orders for my continued stay in England . . . This separation is a great trial and a great test for all of us and it will depend on our individual worth if we come out of it finer than before.[11]

In general, we get the picture of Sarojini as a fond and devoted mother and wife and, at the same time, someone who took it as a given that she was going to play more than these roles in her life. She was therefore more modern a century ago than we are ourselves conditioned to accept. Finally, there is a veil that makes family and personal life opaque for both the contemporary observer and also the historical excavator, and since neither she nor Dr Naidu discussed it publicly, we may never know. What gives her choices their significance is the wider context of the nationalist movement. Her own public awakening coincides with its earliest stirrings, and the maturing and consolidation of her public persona overlaps and converges almost completely with it.

A cause she was to tirelessly champion was Hindu–Muslim unity. It is useful to recall that while ritual obeisance to the concept was widespread, her unwavering focus was unusual. She consciously went about making this central not just to her politics and her poetry but most of all in her personal life in terms of the importance she accorded to her large number of Muslim friends. Her admiration of Jinnah is well known and around it many stories grew with the passage of time, including that they were lovers. There is little evidence for this; Makarand Paranjape for instance notes that Sarojini was 'fond of Jinnah but there is no evidence of her having been in love with him'.[12] During the London years – 1912–14 – when they were together a great deal, Asaf had noted that Sarojini's admiration for Jinnah was deep and that they had an 'enviably close friendship'. She was perfectly open and unselfconscious about her admiration, which makes a clandestine relationship that much less likely.

Jinnah was closer to Sarojini in age than many of her own reverential admirers such as Asaf or Syud with whom she surrounded herself. Most traces of the Asaf–Sarojini friendship have been lost with time; their letters, of which there must have been a considerable number as they were regular and frequent correspondents, were not preserved at either end and what has survived is limited to Asaf's autobiographical jottings, references to him in Sarojini's letters to others, and Aruna Asaf Ali's stray comments on his devotion to Sarojini. She was always 'Akka' or 'elder sister' to him and initially the relationship was an almost consciously hierarchical one – affection and fondness on both sides but also deference on his part, given the ten years or so between them. Asaf was supported, motivated, counselled and occasionally admonished by Sarojini; he would bring to her his dilemmas, often complain about the world, and always be devoted. In time the age difference would matter less and the hierarchical element reduce as each went on their different paths, but the affection forged during the early years in London would remain a bedrock in their lives.

# 6

# Sarojini, Syed Mahmud and Syud Hossain

This elder sister–younger brother model was replicated in Sarojini's association with another young man but with some pronounced differences. Syed Mahmud was the same age as Asaf and Syud Hossain, and although in England at about the same time was not part of the court around Sarojini. Nor can we say for certain that he met Asaf during the time both were in England. Mahmud certainly was in touch with Syud in London, and on more than one occasion Syud had written to him for a small loan to settle his rent. They knew each other from their student days in Aligarh.

Syed Mahmud was from a family of prosperous landlords of Rae Bareli in the United Provinces. He spent about seven years in Aligarh, from 1901 to 1908. Notwithstanding the conservative Islamic orientation he inherited, Mahmud was drawn to the national movement quite early: he is described as having attended a Congress session in Benares in 1905 when still just sixteen or seventeen years old. Even as a young man he represented in many ways these two divergent trends: concern about loss of Islamic power and prestige and the future of Muslims in India on the one hand, and the great draw of a budding nationalism that would unite all Indians, regardless of religion, against a foreign empire.

Mahmud had been among the students in Aligarh in the first decade of the twentieth century who had opposed the pro-government inclinations of the faculty and found the feudal grandees at the helm of the League too servile to the British. He was thus part of the small group in Aligarh that 'sought to integrate Muslim politics with the wider search for Indian national identity, represented by the Indian National Congress. This group rejected those leaders of their community who stressed cooperation with the British government and opposition to the Congress and who dominated the All India Muslim League . . .'[1] His campus activism in Aligarh led to his expulsion and by 1908 Syed Mahmud was in England reading for a law degree. His time in England appears to have further strengthened his nationalist sentiments and given them a pan-Islamic dimension – in brief, one deeply concerned about the fate of Islam in a Western-dominated world, and one who saw the disempowerment of Muslims in India as part of wider global malaise.

Alongside his law degree in England Syed Mahmud completed a PhD in history from the University of Munster in Germany. Returning to India in 1913 he started a legal practice in Patna. He remained closely involved with the Home Rule League and the Congress, and also with the Muslim League which, now under pressure of public opinion, was modifying and nuancing its loyalist stances following widespread concern about British policy towards the Ottomans in Turkey.

At this stage, an unexpected event occurred in Mahmud's life in 1915 when he was twenty-six or twenty-seven. Only recently married, he was in Bombay at the end of the year for the Congress and Muslim League sessions where he met Sarojini Naidu. He appears to have fallen headlong in love with her or at the very least was seriously attracted to her. This situation is evident in the letters Sarojini wrote to him, some of which were preserved amongst his papers.[2] Sarojini comes across in her letters as a more mature, older woman who, while very fond of Syed, seeks also to divert and temper his infatuation. It is clear that she saw this new friendship also in terms of a larger context in which Hindus and Muslims would connect in bonds which were more than simply political. Within some days of this meeting in December 1915, we find Sarojini, still in Bombay, writing to Mahmud on 6 January 1916 of the 'happy and poignant memories of the few days we spent together in the national week of endeavour to create and establish the Hindu Muslim unity'. And later in the same letter, seemingly as a reminder that they were in the midst of a rising wave of nationalist sentiment and this was as much a driver of her actions as her personal emotions: 'Redeem then your promise to me: and you cannot offer me a sweeter and nobler token of your affection for me than to consecrate yourself to the country's welfare.'

Only Sarojini's letters to Mahmud survive but these certainly do convey a sense of how much he was overwhelmed by her. His letters were, she wrote to him, 'like the cry of a wounded creature in agony'.[3] Evidently Syed Mahmud was smitten and clearly he had never met a woman such as Sarojini before. His letters must have been an outpouring of what we can call calf love – although he was then in his mid-twenties and, as noted, already married. In response to one evidently impassioned missive she referred to the 'upheaval of all your centers of thought and experience' that 'you are so dazed, so resentful, so helpless . . . that you feel lost and paralyzed'. Mahmud's health was a problem even when he was a young man. Sarojini urged him in April 1917 to come to Hyderabad and be treated by her husband: 'he is a skilled physician and a most loyal friend.' Mahmud does in fact make the journey and we have this reference to his stay in Hyderabad in a letter from Sarojini to Syud Hossain in August 1917: 'Mahmud is here. Better in spirit with more control . . . but ill. My husband says European medicine has no cure for his disease but that Unani medicine perhaps has.'[4]

Mahmud's health would plague him through his life, something he had in common with Sarojini. The difference was that she would invariably make light of it. For Mahmud, as we will see, health issues would have consequences for his political life.

We can surmise from these letters that Mahmud remained deeply infatuated for at least two years, and that Sarojini was the stronger and more mature of the two and is equally a very considerate, concerned friend in what is also clearly a relationship of mutual fondness. Yet it is also possible to misrecognize the tenor of these letters as suggesting a relationship that was more than platonic because Sarojini Naidu had always had an extravagant style of writing and expressing herself. Evidently Mahmud had fallen under the same spell, but more deeply so, as Asaf and Syud Hossain had, and as in their case, a friendship of great durability and one anchored in the twists and turns of the national movement ensued. What is also constantly present in Sarojini's letters to Mahmud, besides the larger national cause, are references to his wife and to her own husband and family. There is also a letter from Sarojini's daughter Padmaja written on behalf of her mother: 'She has been so ill since her return from your benighted Behar (I mean enlightened of course but the alliteration is rather pleasing *n'estee* [*sic*] *pas*?) that she wasn't able to get beyond addressing the envelope.'[5]

Sarojini's letters show an older woman sensitively and kindly handling the infatuation of an impressionable, excessively sentimental and highly strung younger man. She did not want to snub him too forcefully or ignore him and clearly did not want to lose the friendship altogether. Makarand

Photo Section, PMML

*Sarojini Naidu in 1919*

Paranjape described it as an 'unequal relationship': 'Not only was Sarojini older and more experienced, she was far stronger emotionally.'[6]

The letters that survive continue up to February 1919. Those from the latter half of 1917 suggest a Mahmud more in control of his emotions than the picture that emerges from Sarojini's letters of 1916 and early 1917. Possibly subsequent letters were not retained; their frequency also reduced over the years as Mahmud steadied himself and the infatuation waned, although the friendship with Sarojini continued as did his own involvement in the freedom struggle. Mahmud's sentimental susceptibility to stronger and attractive personalities would, however remain, and in time we will see a similar pattern with Jawaharlal Nehru. Not calf love of course but an eagerness to defer and be led.

Sarojini had a gift for devoted, committed friendships – from Ruttie Jinnah, Jinnah's wife, to Mahatma Gandhi – which she sustained through lively correspondence, meetings when possible and an intense interest in all the minutiae of her friends' lives. While her letters are filled with generous praise of the person she is writing to, and an obviously genuine interest in the details of his or her life, it is also clear that she craved their admiration; she needed an audience for her thoughts and actions and to feel part of a densely knit wider circle outside her family, outside Hyderabad.

Syud Hossain, Asaf Ali's close friend in London and part of the core of the court that surrounded Sarojini in England in 1913–14, was another such lifelong friend. Although Syud Hossain was the same age as Asaf and Syed Mahmud, he emerges as the friend she had the most equal relationship with. The tenor of his interactions with Sarojini also differs from the deference shown by Asaf, and Mahmud's passionate infatuation that she handles maturely and calmly. There is an equality of need: 'I find that there seems no one else whom I can confide so freely, so frankly,' she writes.[7] Again, only her letters survive since Syud kept them, but we may surmise support and advice flowed in both directions. We get a sense of this from the very first letter in the cache Syud preserved and this is written from onboard the ship SS *Arabia* on 14 October 1914, a few days after she left England. The letter ends: 'I shall look for a letter from you to reach me very soon after I get home . . . I am also a woman with a woman's need of protection – and kindness and where shall I find it?'

Sarojini's letters, which occasionally verge on the coquettish, also reveal the intellectual aspect of the friendship in which appreciation and encouragement are freely given. She wrote in April 1915 from Hyderabad about an article by Syud Hossain on the crisis in the Islamic world: 'Your brilliant and lucid exposition of the Islamic question gave us great pleasure and pride. My husband has been carrying your article along in his surgical bag and reading portions of it aloud to his young friends.'

Many of her letters – to others like Asaf and Syed Mahmud as well – forwarded her own poems, each transcribed by hand, the act of copying ten or fifteen pages of poems itself suggesting how much she valued their feedback. Thus her letter of 8 April 1915 to Syud: 'I am sending you some poems which require your frank criticism. There are actually more of them written down on paper for the first time & will likely call for revision before final publication.'

There is also a good deal of attention to the political but nothing was ever entirely political with Sarojini. We find her writing to Syud on 5 May 1915 about the impending visit of M.K. Gandhi to Hyderabad when he was still a relative unknown in India, but with a growing reputation: 'I had a letter – a beautiful letter from Mr Gandhi in which he tells me that he is coming to Hyderabad soon. Of course, he and his wife Kasturba will stay with us. The children are already mad with excitement.'

Her letters also provide an outlet for feelings difficult to put aside and suggest what often drove her public activities. Since her entry into public life Sarojini had been a devoted admirer of the leading moderate figure in Indian politics G.K. Gokhale, and on his death she wrote to Syud Hossain in April 1915:

> Gokhale's death – I cannot speak of – it has broken something inside me but that somewhat [has] been definitely and deliberately converted into work & such strenuous work which has marked a new and

unexpected epoch in the history of the Nizam's state. The wonderful memorial meeting for him of men that I was chiefly instrumental in getting up and the still more remarkable meeting of 500 women which of course I entirely 'ran' when brilliant speeches were made by them in six languages – English, Urdu, Marathi, Telugu, Tamil and Gujarati – were both perhaps considering the unique circumstances of our internal affairs the most eloquent public testimony placed anywhere in India to Gokhale's all conquering and creative greatness.

Demonstrably, along with her charm and ability to make and keep friends, she enjoyed larger settings and public events, and being at their centre, possibly seeing this as an essential adjunct for someone who wanted to make a significant difference to the world around her. Sarojini's letters to Syud provide a graphic account of her activities, her health and numerous engagements as she carved out a space for herself in the public sphere in India. There is also news about her husband, family and friends and her travels. But never absent in these often very long letters is the personal and the reference to the bond with Syud. In April 1915 after a visit to Calcutta she wrote:

> Do you know our friendship is in the second generation – because I find that your father and mine were at school together forty years ago in Dacca? When I was in Calcutta I wrote and asked your father to come and see me because I claimed some share in you !. . . He stayed with me a long time and we talked chiefly of you . . . but he began by saying 'I have known your name so long and yet I never realized till the other day that you were the daughter of my dear old friend.'

And on her thirty-eighth birthday in February 1917 she wrote to him as standing apart, 'Unchallenged and unchanging among my friends who have won the secret of my inner life'.

From the end of 1916 Syud himself was back in India and based in Bombay, working at the *Bombay Chronicle*. Meetings again become possible and the letters occasionally give a sense of these. She wrote on 9 January

1917, 'I hope to arrive on Tuesday morning and perhaps if you are very nice will lunch with you.' And after detailing some other engagements, she added, 'My evening – after dinner – will be strictly, though need I assert, harmlessly, engaged. So please see that no Committee or Home Rule meetings are fixed for 15th and 16th evenings. I have much work with the Gokhale Mazzini reincarnation.' The latter is evidently a reference to Syud himself, and while obviously a joke it also gives a sense of how she saw him as an exceptional figure, comparing him to the nineteenth-century Italian nationalist Giuseppe Mazzini. The slightly flirtatious tone in the letters to Syud is also characteristic of Sarojini's correspondence with others. There were a number of visits to Bombay for various reasons and the letters to Syud thereafter supplement what we already know about this busy, gregarious woman.

Photo Section, PMML

*Syud Hossain around 1919*

Almost all the approximately fifty letters relate to the period from late 1914, when Sarojini left London, to end 1918; some are undated or without a year, as was often Sarojini's wont, but appear to fall in this period. Possibly the correspondence had continued for some time at least but the letters were not retained for in early 1919 as we shall see, Syud was to move to Allahabad where a dramatic, life-changing event lay in wait for him.

Theirs was obviously then a relationship of fondness, mutual support and admiration – perhaps unusual given the almost ten-year difference in age between Syud, then in his late twenties, and Sarojini in her late thirties. Could it have been more: perhaps a romantic core provided to the relationship its other attributes? The tenor of Sarojini's letters, with their affectionate familiarity and unrestrained quality, could suggest this; but there is otherwise no other basis to think so.

While it is impossible to determine the precise nature of this relationship with Syud, there are more significant and more obvious takeaways. As mentioned earlier, Sarojini's conviction was that strong personal friendships between Hindus and Muslims were the basis on which Indian nationalism could be securely based. We see this clearly in place with all the three young men close to her – Asaf Ali, Syed Mahmud, Syud Hossain – and there were many other Muslim friends. This was quite possibly partly the result of growing up and living in Hyderabad, the capital of a princely state ruled by a Muslim dynasty where the social and intellectual elite had a pronounced Islamic flavour. Through Sarojini's juvenile writings and in her more mature poetry we find an idyllic view of the environment in which she grew up, an enormous admiration for its ruling dynasty, and a highly romanticized perspective of the inter-communal relations in it – this at least was the view of some of her contemporaries.

K.M. Munshi, a senior Congressman and nationalist, stands out in this category given his own connection with Hyderabad as agent of the Government of India to the nizam's government from January 1948 till September 1948. This was when the state acceded to India after the military intervention of Operation Polo, a move by the Government of India to secure Hyderabad's accession to independent India. This was accompanied by a great deal of bloodshed, in part the pattern of the communal bloodletting in the rest of India alongside freedom and partition, but was also a reflection of Hyderabad's own communal fault lines. Munshi's grouse was that Sarojini was oblivious to these fault lines – that she must have known about it but chose not to delve into the issue. In his autobiographical account of this tumultuous nine-month period in Hyderabad, he wrote about Sarojini's relationship with Hyderabad vis-à-vis her poem 'Ode to H.H. the Nizam of Hyderabad'. 'In the beginning of this century Shrimati Sarojini Naidu who was steeped in the traditions of the Muslim aristocracy addressed an ode to the nizam.'[8]

Beneath whose sway concordant dwell
The peoples whom your laws embrace
In brotherhood of diverse creeds
And harmony of diverse race

So may the lustre of your days
Outshine the deeds Firdausi sung
Your name within a nation's prayer
Your music on a nation's tongue

Munshi remarked, 'I did not find any vestige of the concordance so eloquently sung. But it shows how the make-believe of communal harmony with which the nizam surrounded himself could make an impression on the heart of a youthful poetess.' Munshi held a particular position about the nizam and Hyderabad, and there were other views of the nizam and his benevolence – or the lack of it as his detractors insisted.

Sarojini, however, implicitly believed in the truth of the verses she had composed. She had written that the 'Ode to the Nizam' was presented to the nizam in an Urdu translation done by 'a well-known Mohammedan poet' and it was 'something quite novel in the annals of Indian tradition for a woman to present a poem to a sovereign in full durbar'. She mentioned that she would not have dreamt of 'going forth unveiled' for that would be 'the scandal of India'. About the nizam himself – and she was referring here to Mir Mahbub Ali Khan (1866–1911) – she wrote: 'among all the princes of India, you cannot find more picturesque, more brilliant and alas more pathetic.' The latter because he concealed 'the real loneliness of a poet': although 'under happier circumstances of race and opportunity he would have been a leader among men but now he is merely the eastern Hamlet'. At her wedding, she said, ghazals composed by the nizam had been sung when 'her mother had a great reception for Mohammedan ladies'.[9] On the nizam's death in August 1911 she wrote to her publisher William Heinemann: 'I cannot tell you what it means to us who adored him . . . He was our heart's idol, the very light of our eyes . . . We would have given our lives to save him.'[10]

In March 1915, writing to Gandhi asking him to visit Hyderabad, she had described it as: 'The great city which is the true centre of Hindu Muslim unity and brotherhood.'[11] Sarojini's formative years in Hyderabad had led to the internalization of a particular view of India that would confer on her a certain ease in navigating the minefield of communal relations in the first half of twentieth-century. In June 1913 we find her writing to G. Natesan, editor of the then popular *India Review*, on a possible rapprochement between Hindus and Muslims on the issue of separate electorates, which as we will see did lead to an agreement between the Congress and the Muslim League in 1916, and in general on the two communities coming together in dealings with the government:

> You have realized that the Musalmans have definitely held out their hand to the Hindus. Be gracious, be wise, be brave when the Hindus hold out their hands to the Muslmans at the next Congress. Do not analyse motives too closely, but take the proffered hand and hold it fast and so represent truly the Indian world as far as your influence reaches.[12]

The view that Sarojini was blind to the realities of the Hindu–Muslim interface and was steeped in, as Munshi had put it, a world of 'make-believe communal harmony' had possibly wider circulation than is generally acknowledged. Certainly, Sarojini was conscious that her 'pro-Muslim' image had many critics. She wrote to Syud Mahmud in 1917 when a noted Muslim author of the time dedicated a new book to her:

> Have you seen Hassan Nizami's new book with its beautiful and pointed dedication to me – it constitutes another link in the long, long chain of 'evidence against me' as a lover of the Muslim community and culture – such heavy evidence, such long standing and fast accumulating evidence all of which counts in the indictment. Well – che [*sic*] sera, sera as the Italians say. What is the use of bothering? One lives only once and cannot afford to deviate from the principles and devotion of a life time for the sake of personal gain, ease or safety.

This was not perhaps simple naivety or an excessively romanticized view of the world but a pragmatic and thought-through position grounded on emphasizing points of agreement and consensus, and avoiding – for as long as possible – areas of conflict. The expectation was that certain gulfs would be bridged only in time and were in the interim best left alone.

# 7

# A Broken Engagement and Other Clouds

In Hyderabad in January 1915 Asaf's main business was meeting Liaq's family. While her father had approved the match when Asaf wrote to him from London this was, he realized, only a general nod of principle. There were other expectations Asaf had to meet or, at least, generally address. He first called on Liaq's maternal grandfather, the commander-in-chief of the nizam's army and clearly the key figure in the family. There was also a meeting with her father. Liaq thereafter telephoned to apologize for not meeting him – 'it was not done' – even though her family had 'approved' him. The telephone call and the fact that Liaq could not meet him, Asaf wrote, 'chilled me. It began to look more and more like a conventionally arranged match and I was left wondering whether it would succeed.'

Other doubts crept in. Seeing the 'social milieu of Liaq's people, I was more than a little frightened'. Possibly being Sarojini's house guest gave him a foretaste of the upper-class ambience Liaq took for granted and he was apprehensive about 'not [being able to] reproduce these conditions of ease and affluence in Delhi'. Being in England, especially for one who was a London-qualified barrister, was in a sense a great equalizer; back home the realities of the difference in economic status, even if not class per se, asserted themselves. Plus, there was the question of how Laiq would cope if – as he clearly already intended – he embarked on a political life with all its uncertainties.

He returned to Delhi in a pensive mood and prey to doubts, reflected in his reluctance to fix a date for the wedding. Soon enough Sarojini, perceptive as always and with an intuitive insight into Asaf's mind, had a better sense of the state of the relationship. She wrote to Syud on 8 April 1915:

> I get occasional letters really in volumes from Asaf Ali, very characteristic and very full of badly repressed excitement, emotion, discontent, drama etc. He has sent me a long new poem. His love affair has become somewhat lunar in quality (with increasing mildness) and decreasing intensity of devotion . . . on both sides perhaps.[1]

Letters from Liaq to Asaf contained hints of family pressures that a wedding date be fixed quickly. Liaq's father also wrote, supplying in addition the information that there were other offers. Sarojini's tone too became more exasperated than understanding and she gave Syud a fuller picture, hoping no doubt that he too would put his weight behind her advice in his letters to Asaf. While Liaq's parents were open to Asaf's proposal when it was first broached, they had expected him to demonstrate reasonably adequate means to support her. Possibly this only became clear to Asaf in Hyderabad once he met the family and realized this match meant meeting some minimum expectations with respect to Liaq's future lifestyle. To Sarojini this was reasonable but Asaf, she told Syud on 5 May, was 'shillyshallying'. Liaq too was 'getting tired of his vague wondering moods and humours and cannot naturally follow his political vagaries'. To Sarojini it was obvious that Asaf had to make up his mind one way or the other: 'Surely every parent has a right to ask what prospects a would-be son in law has before [giving] their formal consent.'

Liaq also sent a telegram on these lines. A telegram in the second decade of the twentieth century was a statement of significance and to Asaf it now seemed his engagement was reduced 'to an arranged match subject to competition'. His present situation ruled out marriage for a while 'on practical grounds' because it was clear he would not be in a position to maintain Liaq, for at least some time to come, in the style she would expect. He sent a telegram back to Liaq that 'she was released from her promise'. The telegram was worded in a way that left open the possibility that if Liaq were to protest at this, that could 'restore the degree of emotion and sentiment' to 'revitalize the relationship'. Such a reply did not come and the engagement was at an end.

Possibly the most distressed person in this entire affair was Asaf's mother. She felt he had acted hastily because he was upset and resentful at the references to 'other proposals'. She saw the allusions to 'other offers' as natural: 'stones will be cast into a house that has clearly a plum tree'. But Asaf was seeking, he said, 'an affinity of values, not a mere wife'.

If this was not entirely a happy homecoming, Asaf does not appear unduly disturbed by the ending of the engagement and perhaps, as Sarojini appears to have suspected, had been reconciled to this outcome for some time. 'Time proved', Asaf later wrote, 'that my decision was right', meaning that he had come to realize that Liaq was not the wife he wanted. Clearly, he was not interested in a simple and straightforward future whose attributes included a stable and settled life, gradually building up a thriving legal practice, marriage into a family high in Hyderabad's hierarchy, and finally a gradual and steady rise in his own social prestige and standing. But soon after his return to Delhi a darker cloud was to descend on Asaf, much bigger than this broken engagement.

Returning to India Asaf found the change in his political perspective coinciding with a wider change that had occurred in the city of Delhi. While this may have already begun when he returned from England for the first time in 1912, it was far more evident in 1915. Delhi was no longer a sleepy provincial backwater but was the imperial capital. Politics here had a new optical value and symbolic power now. In addition, Muslim intellectual opinion was charged up on account of the Ottoman empire's terminal crisis, its successive military defeats and loss of territory, and most of all by the fact that the British were ranged against it in the world war. In this ferment Asaf's old friends Dr Ansari and the Ali brothers were passionately involved and, as already seen, leaders of public opinion. Abul Kalam Azad, who had so impressed Asaf earlier, was also set on the course to emerge as the person to provide a new kind of leadership to Muslims in India. The contrast between this group and the existing leadership of the Muslim League – politically conservative and desirous above all of being on the right side of the authorities – was unmistakable. While there were numerous other internal factors at play in this process, on the surface it did appear much as Mohammad Ali himself described the situation:

> The attitude of England towards the enemies of Turkey, Persia and Morocco had begun to alienate the sympathies of Indian Musalmans ever since 1911; and this estrangement could not but react on their relations with the British officials in India, who . . . could not help looking askance at Indians daring to criticize an English Government with a candour and courage unusual for a subject race.[2]

Asaf thus on his return to India in January 1915 was not just himself a changed person politically, but also someone who felt a 'marked change in the political atmosphere' with a 'wave of excitement and indignation among the musalmans'. He saw Muslim politics, hitherto 'timid, petty and narrow', taking 'giant strides forward'. Abul Kalam with his publication *Al-Hilal* in Calcutta and Mohammad Ali with *Comrade* and *Hamdard* in Delhi were amongst those voicing this opinion even as 'prayers were commonly said in Mosques for Turkey's victory'. His own frame of mind was simple: 'the atmosphere was electric. I was happy.' To be part of something so much bigger than oneself was intoxicating.

In this politically charged atmosphere there was also a great deal of fun and entertainment. To an extent this was also a continuation of the social life he had plunged into on first returning from England, the difference being that the political undertone now was much stronger. 'Dinners and music performances at Mohammad Ali's, at Ansari's and my houses filled our evenings' even as 'the ferment of agitation' amongst Muslims was increasing.

Mohammad Ali was evidently still the figure who impressed and inspired Asaf the most. Even in London he had debated the respective merits of Mohammad Ali and those of Jinnah with Sarojini. He would later recall: 'On one occasion Sarojini and I debated in the company of Syud at a private dinner, the comparative merits of Mohammad Ali and [Muhammad Ali] Jinnah. My zealous advocacy on behalf of Mohammad Ali evoked Sarojini's retort, now proved true – "My Mohammad Ali will go further than your Mohammad Ali."'

In Delhi in 1915 Asaf found that Mohammad Ali's weekly speech in the Jama Masjid after Friday prayers had become a regular and popular feature:

> Few orators or political journalists among his contemporaries had his combination of qualities: his range of articulate emotions, his capacity for analytical argument, his pathos, fantasy and wit and his power to marshal all these, through his command over the resources of the language, towards ends clearly discerned and passionately desired.

Mohammad Ali's poetic talent and memorizing of a vast collection of verse worked in tandem with the ability to extract just the right verse for a particular context. All this meant was that different elements had 'combined with his fervour and the desperate situation in which Turkey found herself after the war . . . to create in him a feeling of impending martyrdom'.[3] That had also been his sentiment earlier when he had contemplated suicide over the Ottoman defeat in the Balkans conflict but was dragged off instead to the nautch in honour of E.M. Forster at Asaf Ali's house in October–November 1913.

We can imagine Asaf observing, absorbing and also aspiring to these attributes of the politician's craft. But he also soon realized that Mohammad Ali, in his drive to mobilize support for Turkey and the Ottomans, was 'too full of his own zeal to think of any moderating influence as anything but weak-kneed retreat if not treachery'. This extended even to Hakim Ajmal Khan who often suggested moderation in that at least a more temperate tone be employed in references to the British government:

'This jarred on Mohammad Ali's nerves. He even went to the length of suspecting Hakimji as a spy and an agent of the government.' For Asaf Ali, Mohammad Ali was 'not much of a judge of men' and his attitude 'towards Abul Kalam, and even Ansari, was one of patronage'.

His brother Shaukat Ali had his own eccentricities, and at the time 'was in a fanatical mood', or so it appeared to the young Asaf. Those who tried to reason would be turned upon with 'Coward, Coward! A Muslim should fear none but God.' Asaf noted other oddities: 'He would get into a tonga . . . and if the driver was a Muslim he would pat him on the back and say "Keep ready, the time's come."' The 'time' referred to the coming jihad to assist the Turks, or perhaps an imagined Islamic revolution. Yet Asaf also understood that Shaukat 'was capable of wide tolerance and understanding' and therefore 'was a bigger man' than the better-known brother. The larger point, however, was that in the middle of the second decade the Ali brothers 'were fast eclipsing other Muslim leaders'.

But now, in this early phase of his introduction to advocacy politics in Delhi, emerging from his now close friendship with the Ali brothers and Ansari, something occurred that would long blight Asaf. 'It was not uncommon for Mohammad Ali to drop in and send for his dinner from his house next door and stay on talking in my bachelor's quarters.' On one occasion Ansari also joined for dinner, 'a potluck affair'.

In the ensuing conversation Mohammad Ali revealed that a secret coded communication in the form of an invitation had been sent to the emir of Afghanistan to attack the British in India in sympathy for the Turkish cause. Asaf found the idea somewhat improbable but Mohammad Ali was confident that the Afghans would help India regain freedom in return for which the frontier tribal regions would be gifted to them. To Asaf it appeared unlikely 'that a conqueror would go to the length of lavishing the fruits of his victory on a people who could not help themselves'. Asaf 'ventured to say something expressing doubt about the advisability of inviting the Amir's intervention'. There was in any case little point in discussing the issue with Mohammad Ali and it does not appear Asaf was being asked for his advice or his views. Mohammad Ali was at this time being hauled through different courts for his writings in *Comrade* and Asaf was himself on the defence team in appeals in the Lahore High Court. A little later Mohammad Ali heard somewhere that the plan inviting the emir was known to the British and also that Asaf Ali was the source of the betrayal. He, already extremely prone to suspect conspiracies and conspirators, appears to have accepted this at face value and Asaf was soon denounced as a traitor.

For Asaf 'the effect . . . was indescribable: no thunderbolt, no sudden opening of a chasm under my feet could have been worse . . . there I was . . . tarred with a vile lie just when I felt the cleanest'. He had made what he thought was an irrevocable break with the past in ending the reports on nationalist and dissident activity to the authorities and was now a 'reborn soul'. But his juvenile lack of judgement had now come back to haunt him. On reflection Asaf worked out what may have happened. The invitation to the emir was hardly a secret: the plan was not just Mohammad Ali's and had other protagonists as well. Then, also, 'it was difficult for the Ali Brothers to be tightlipped about anything'. The authorities could therefore have got the information from a number of sources. Mohammad Ali's informant who blamed Asaf must somehow have learnt of his earlier connection with the intelligence department through 'Uncle', and concluded that Asaf was the source of the betrayal.

The damage to the young Asaf was considerable. He tried to speak to Mohammad Ali but 'he avoided me like poison'. Shaukat was 'more decent' or perhaps 'diplomatic' and agreed that 'Yes, Mohammad is too ready to lend his ears to others'.' Things, however, did not improve for Asaf. The internment of the Ali brothers – not on account of this issue but for their incendiary writings and speeches – meant that as their stature rose further, his 'reputation sank correspondingly'. He was, he recalled, in a dejected and suicidal mood.

Asaf's letters at this time to Syud, now in Bombay and working for the *Bombay Chronicle*, reveal how devastated this charge left him and how deeply he felt his reputation had been besmirched by it. 'The events of my life,' he wrote on 6 December 1916, 'have taken a most unexpected turn and I am as good as dead. But I am content. Let me retain but only a very few honest and true friends – it is enough for me.'[4] And again a little later, on 9 December: 'My melancholy mood is freezing into an avalanche which might descend on the remainder of my spirit and blot all "life" out of existence. I need nerve tonic that's all.' A few days later, on 16 December, we find him writing, 'I have declined the honour of representing Urdu at the Urdu Conference at Lucknow on behalf of Delhi . . . To be sure I have no desire to appear before a crowd tarred from head to foot.' This was an event possibly held to coincide with the Congress session in Lucknow in December 1916 which the Muslim League was also attending; the two organizations would craft the famous Lucknow Pact and forge what they hoped would be a new chapter of Hindu–Muslim unity. Some two months later his despair had not lifted and we find him quoting in a letter to Syud on 12 February 1917 a stanza from the then very popular 'The Hound of Heaven' by the English poet Frances Thompson, a favourite of Asaf:

> My harness piece by piece
> Thou hast hewn from me
> And smitten me to my knee
> I am defenceless utterly

Asaf's letters also reveal that the psychological stress had triggered physical symptoms, a characteristic that would persist and increase over time. His letter of 12 February to Syud, for instance:

> My life has overflowed the banks. I am suffering from the excess of morbidity. My nerves are like highly stretched fiddles, sensitive even to the passing wind and ready to snap at the slightest touch of human hand. I spend whole days in cloistered silence with 'vigorous music' in my heart, while my 'fingers stray upon a shattered lute' – the lute of my life.

The quotes are from Alice Maynell, another favourite of Asaf's and well known during the time he was in England.

There was clearly public humiliation and perhaps even a social boycott at work here. He wrote to Syud on 9 January: 'The campaign of ruthless vilification against me has caused all doors to be banged in my face.' The public stigma and slur on his reputation also led to an understandable desire in him to just get away from it all and the older desire for living in England occasionally would rekindle, even as a passing fancy: 'My passionate desire is to secure the Readership at the London School of Oriental Studies & failing that the librarianship of some state library.'

As the news spread and grew in strength, we find Asaf turning to Syud and Sarojini for support. The rumour had reached Hyderabad and 'Sarojini wrote . . . most sympathetically refusing to believe it'.[5] Sarojini and Syud certainly conferred on this crisis and the seriousness of the situation was not lost on Sarojini, perhaps much wiser about the way reputations could be tarnished. 'Poor Asaf ruined', she was to write to Syud on 13 February, remembering their time together in faraway London three years earlier. Some weeks later she was in Bombay and Syud persuaded Asaf to also visit at the same time. 'Poor Asaf is in Bombay now,' Sarojini wrote to her oldest daughter, 'to see us both and find some means of helping him out of all his difficulties.' The letter also says: 'you cannot think of what it means to Asaf to find that he had some friends at least who would believe in him.'[6] She was in Delhi a little later staying with Dr Ansari and wrote to Syud on 28 March: 'Asaf I hope is already happier. On Thursday he is to come here for a free talk with Dr Ansari and myself and today I am taking Mrs Ansari to see his mother.'

Essentially Asaf concluded he had to do something concrete and that the only way to wipe out this 'unmerited blot' and 'also the entire past was to make a clean breast' of the whole matter to Dr Ansari and Sarojini – in other words, explain his past relationship with 'Uncle' and how he had terminated it. For: 'If I could not win them with an honest recital of the truth, I must lose them.' He went to Dr Ansari's house:

> Ansari took me into an inner room where Sarojini was. She sat on a bed and I took a chair facing Ansari and her. Ansari sat through my recital with his big, bushy brows arched high, indicating tense but patient

> attention. Sarojini in a similar strained mood, ran her tongue every now and then over her lips as if they were dry. My story was simply, frankly and honestly narrated, perhaps with inevitable emotion. At the end of the interview, Ansari led me out through the zenana apartment to my carriage. Before saying goodbye, he warmly shook my hand and said: 'Asaf, I feel so relieved.'

Asaf also travelled to Simla to meet Jinnah, now back in India, and told him the entire story. 'My faith in him was great and not in vain.' Jinnah's response, accompanied with 'one of his rare, charming, smiles', was: 'Others have their flings in other ways, and you have had your fling in that way.' The accompanying advice was also sound: 'Lie low for some time.'

To Asaf this advice gave 'new strength' and showed that 'the world was not bereft of persons who were prepared to believe me'. He felt a deep sense of indebtedness to Jinnah that remained with him notwithstanding the 'misfortune that in politics' they were later at different ends of the spectrum. But that he should have gone to Simla to meet Jinnah to unburden himself and seek advice is revealing. While they knew each other well in London, Jinnah does not appear to have been a close friend. Possibly Asaf's trip reveals Jinnah's stature in India, and that he would have appeared to Asaf to be a wiser and more experienced man of the world and so his advice would be valuable.

When the opportunity presented itself, Asaf also narrated his story to Abul Kalam. The final exculpation came in 1919 when he was in contact with Gandhi over the Jallianwala Bagh atrocity. When he came to Delhi on one of his periodic visits, Gandhi 'referred laughingly to my past association'. With this Asaf felt grateful and 'absolved'.

The intervening period of about four years was, however, 'the most difficult' that he faced, and each day then had brought 'black moments of despair'. The intensity of the rumour that he was an informer or police spy gradually faded, but it did have a long afterlife and many of those associated with him were conscious of it. A close political acquaintance from Delhi, Jugal Kishore Khanna, recalled it was the local CID (Criminal Investigation Department) that started the rumour that 'while he was a student in England [he] was connected with government intelligence and that he used to pass on information about the visits of Indian leaders and their activities in England'. Khanna recalled that the allegation was made much of even a decade later when Asaf was contesting against a Hindu Mahasabha candidate for the Delhi seat to the Central Legislative Assembly.[7] Asaf, as we shall see, lost that election although the old rumour was not a major factor in the defeat. Even as late as 1934, the allegation would occasionally surface and on one occasion Dr Ansari had to refute the charge in a public meeting.[8] Perhaps, although there is no direct evidence for this, it also had something to do with Asaf's sudden resignation in February 1918 as secretary from the Delhi unit of the Congress which he had helped to found.[9] Sarojini summed up the situation to Syud on 17 February 1918: 'Poor Asaf has written a very doleful as well as soulful letter: he is having a bad time. Wretched boy and how [he] is being literally hounded [for] he is far more capable of fine work than all his hunters.'

Decades later Aruna Asaf Ali was asked about the differences between the Ali brothers and Asaf Ali and she had replied, 'I think it was something personal' and 'They were his enemies'.[10] It is possible she was not aware of the details of the issue, but saw that there was a certain tension between them. Clearly the divergence with the Ali brothers meant a breach that could never be fully bridged although in time, on the surface at least, a minimum courtesy would be restored to the relationship.

In later years Asaf himself did not refer to the charge – at least in public – but as he reflected upon his past while he was in jail in the 1940s, he realized the toll it had taken on him as a young man making his entry into public life in Delhi. But that he was able to put it behind him and move ahead on a political trajectory also points to his staying power and determination.

# 8

# A Larger Stage

After over two years of lying low, over the course of 1917 Asaf was determined to immerse himself in Delhi's public and political life, deciding to rise above the blow to his reputation and peace of mind. Two factors provided a platform for his new activities. First, in February 1917, the formidable Mrs Annie Besant established a branch of the Home Rule League in Delhi and Asaf was one of its early members.

Annie Besant was Irish and had lived in India from the 1890s. She was active in Theosophical circles, a kind of a new religious cult that drew on different religious doctrines and mystical experiences including Hinduism. By the early twentieth century she had become a central figure of the Theosophical Society of which the Adyar branch in Madras had emerged as the international headquarters. From the second decade of the twentieth century Besant's interests had widened to Indian politics and in particular to demanding from the colonial authorities a greater measure of self-government for Indians. The Home Rule League movement was set up by her and B.G. Tilak with branches in Madras and Poona respectively.

The branch in Delhi marked a change for the city. Since Mohammad Ali's internment in May 1915 the city had entered a quiet phase, as if slipping back to its original character as a political backwater despite its new status as the imperial capital. The branch of the Home Rule League in Delhi provided some political activity. Dr M.A. Ansari was an early enthusiast and his reputation on account of the Turkish medical mission drew others in.

Asaf's law practice and activism on issues taken up by the Home Rule League gradually became his principal preoccupation. Asaf says he was choosy about what he did at the Bar and did not opt for 'the steady small work which is the life blood of a junior's practice'; instead, he demanded good fees and accepted only the comparatively well-paid cases. Nevertheless, despite his privileged status as an England qualified barrister, settling down to legal work in what in effect were the district courts in Delhi was not easy. At one stage, soon after he started regularly attending the courts, he wrote to Syud about his colleagues in the Bar and the experience of legal practice in a subordinate court: 'I am more than ever disgusted with this miserable profession and the country in which it flourishes in its lowest form. Only a villain of the deepest dye can succeed in this profession in this part of the world. The members of this learned class actually swindle people.'[1] This was perhaps no more than the fulminations of an idealistic young man frustrated at the reality he confronted in the grind of day-to-day work, and part of the inevitable process of settling into a new profession.

More significantly, his public-speaking skills were starting to attract attention as the growing activism of the Delhi branch of the Home Rule League meant frequent public meetings 'to ventilate grievances and carry on educative political propaganda for self-government'. 'I became,' Asaf wrote, somewhat immodestly, 'the League's star turn.' But perhaps this was also an indication of how fledgling politics was in Delhi at the time, outside of the polemics of the Ali brothers which was entirely addressed to a Muslim audience and centered around the fate of the Ottomans. The Home Rule League believed it was a broader church and also took up local issues accordingly. Asaf tried to develop his own particular speaking style. He would make sure that a speech would have at most four or five principal points, and each would be so developed that it culminated with a carefully chosen Persian or Urdu verse from a well-known master to bring the audience to cheers. This was well suited to Delhi's Urdu-speaking milieu and he recalled: 'Meetings swelled to thousands, sometimes as much as 30,000.' This may have been an exaggeration but to Asaf it certainly appeared that 'a new spirit was released and Delhi was now becoming politically conscious'.

In addition to the Home Rule League activities and his legal practice, Asaf began to write regularly in newspapers and magazines, which added to his profile and supplemented his income. He had been a regular contributor to local Urdu magazines but acquired a larger audience after Syud joined the famous *Bombay Chronicle* on his return to India in end 1916. The *Bombay Chronicle* was then edited by the legendary B.G. Horniman, and Asaf began to write regularly for it in English. Under Horniman it had become the vehicle for conveying news and comments with a nationalist tinge, quite distinct from the official and establishment view usually taken by the *Times of India*. For Asaf, writing in its pages was the ideal way to convey to a larger audience news about what was happening in Delhi in terms of the activities of the Home Rule League, popular and nationalist expectations from the local government and in general voicing the frustrations of its articulate citizens.

At that time the default mode for those in politics or public life meant being circumspect. The general tenor of the times was to be extra cautious about not openly crossing officialdom and taking particular care not to come to the adverse notice of English officials or give them any grounds for offence. Just how sensitive the official establishment could be to transgressions is illustrated by an episode in mid-1917. It relates to a follower of Annie Besant, Leonora Gmeiner, principal of the Indraprastha Girls School, later to become a prestigious women's college of Delhi.

Gmeiner, an Australian, had lived in India since the 1890s and was active in the Home Rule League's activities in Delhi. Her activism soon led to official disapproval and at one stage Malcolm Hailey, the then chief commissioner of Delhi, warned her that she risked losing the government's financial support for her school unless she withdrew from Home Rule League activities. Asaf's journalistic forays in the *Bombay Chronicle* in fact began with this episode – in support of 'the decencies of public life'. The *Bombay Chronicle* editorialized on the issue and, Asaf writes, 'Haileyism was added to the vocabulary of political polemics'. Much of what the

*Bombay Chronicle* published on the issue came from Asaf – acting as both a journalist and an activist in these proceedings. Significantly, with the issue being aired in the media, public financial contributions to the school swelled and the matter acquired local notice and even notoriety.

Shortly afterwards the Delhi government was informed that Asaf had made a speech in which he had reportedly described this particular action of the chief commissioner – of threatening to withdraw government support for Gmeiner's school unless she toed the line – as an 'act of folly'. In Asaf's recollection this phrase 'disregarded the restraints of those days' but 'the audience applauded me to the echo'. Asaf wrote, 'I knew now what was wrong with our public life. It was not the people who lacked the spirit of self-assertion.' He meant that it was leaders who were timid.

A few days later he received an invitation to meet a senior English official who told Asaf that he had 'used some expressions which it was not usual in public controversies to use'. Asaf's speech had been in Urdu and he had used the Urdu term himakat to describe the chief commissioner's action. The plain-clothes police monitoring the event had translated this to the authorities as 'idiocy' or 'dunderheadedness', relaying that the term 'conveyed some impression of contempt'. In the interview Asaf responded, as he informed Syud in a letter, that he had 'not exceeded the limits of parliamentary expressions' since 'himakat' only meant 'unwisdom' and his audience had understood it as such.[2] The officer responded that he 'did not think that in the Parliament anybody ever called a public servant a fool'. Asaf's response was that the meaning being ascribed to the term used was wrong and therefore incorrect information about him was being circulated.

During this 'interview', precedents from the English parliament were discussed, including those set by Winston Churchill and Lloyd George.[3] In Asaf's record of the conversation, his English interlocutor 'admitted that Mr Lloyd George had, when he began his vigorous speeches 10 or 11 years ago, made some startling departures in polemics, but even the expressions he had used were not stronger than the expression I had used in my speech!' Asaf had responded that while 'I could not help being surprised at the flattering comparison', Lloyd George and Winston

Churchill 'had been called a pair of ugly ducklings' and 'foul mouthed tub thumpers', that is, it was not as if British practice was above board.

This exchange, unimportant in itself, is nevertheless revealing of the politics of the time. Such verbal duels and ambivalent speeches were the stuff of the moderate politics of early Indian nationalism. What is significant is how quickly this and also the mood of the times were changing. For Asaf the takeaway from his interview was 'the narrow limits within which public speech making is . . . confined'. If, he wrote, 'fair criticism must stop short at compliments and ambiguous references to the defects of administration, the public must ever remain in the dark'.

Each of these details would be printed in detail in the *Bombay Chronicle* in columns entitled 'Imperial Delhi'. Issues such as the refusal of official permission to hold public meetings, the routes to be taken by Dussehra and Muharram processions, the excessive police and intelligence scrutiny of the Delhi Home Rule League activities, etc., each became vehicles for campaigns in the press against the local authorities and against 'Haileyism'.[4] On the Indraprastha School and Miss Gmeiner issue, the *Bombay Chronicle* editorialized in 'Imperial Delhi': 'the circumstances of the onslaught at that wholly innocuous and admittedly admirable institution . . . [throw] a flood of light on the manners and mentality of those who have the run of India's metropolis, the capital selected by the King Emperor himself . . .'[5]

That issue of the newspaper also carried a long letter from 'Bar At Law' – one of the names Asaf employed for his letters, which in effect were columns, to the *Chronicle*. The lengthy letter covered a wide range of complaints: 'the abnormal activity of CID agents in relation to the Home Rule League'; the exclusion of Indraprastha school girls from a function on the king's birthday that illustrated the 'craven stupidity of the sycophants but also the peevish and childish spirit of the authorities responsible'; that 'more than half of Chandni Chowk has been denuded of trees' – 'one act of blind philistinism has reduced the best street of Delhi to a state of intolerable ugliness'.[6] The last point – the trees being removed from Chandni Chowk – had in particular incensed Asaf, a citizen of Delhi to the core.

This project itself was not a new one and dated back to the 1912 assassination attempt on the then viceroy when he entered Chandni Chowk in a ceremonial procession; the trees were believed to have provided cover to the assassin. The failed attempt had not drawn much support in Delhi and given its overall political dormancy had even shocked most people. Asaf had referred to the attempt as having 'evoked much condemnation'. But the trees being felled now certainly upset him, as he expressed to Syud Hossain on 21 May 1917:

> Oh! Syud it is heart rending to see the entire avenue of trees in the Chandni Chowk hewed down! It is wanton vandalism. There is no knowing where they will stop. The matter is of more than local interest – they are blotting out history … Fancy even the Hindus have permitted their sacred pipal trees to be removed by the roots.

A visit by the secretary of state for India in November 1917 found Asaf being given the responsibility of drafting a representation to the government on behalf of Delhi's leading citizens. Asaf was impatient with the 'footling local demands' it contained but found there was not much flexibility in changing the substance of the text. The preamble, though, was his to write as he wished and 'I worked into it a reference to Delhi as "the cradle and grave of mighty empires"' and also the hope of 'the termination of India's non age', meaning its servitude and political submission. Left to himself, 'I would have urged self-determination and full self-government'. That the secretary of state was not given the opportunity to attend a public reception intended in his honour occasioned more articles, editorials and letters. Much of this again was a play on words and a showing of literary excellence aimed at British officialdom.

The point perhaps was that for Asaf and those like him, no Englishman could count himself automatically as their superior: their own education and, more importantly, their English qualifications and experience of living in England ensured that. It was this sense of equality that underwrote their nationalism at the time, and from it also came a mood of defiance which others, less privileged, would have both admired and envied. At one stage, responding to a communication from the government of Delhi that did not address him correctly, failing to add 'Esquire' after his name, Asaf drew the attention of the chief commissioner to

> an omission in the said order, accidently I presume and is I am sure, the result of the clerk's scanty familiarity with polite forms of address.

Needless to say, this letter was as much for a general audience as for the addressee since it was published in full in the *Bombay Chronicle*.[7] The only Indians entitled to have 'Esquire' added after their names while being addressed in correspondence were members of the ICS and barristers, that is, those who were also members of an English Bar. Similarly, while appearing before British magistrates, Asaf was 'averse to the prevalent use of age old expressions implying self-abasement, such as *huzoor* (your majestic honour)'. He preferred 'the reciprocal attitude of respect between the Bench and the Bar which was sought to be maintained in England'. On one occasion he was appearing before a magistrate – an Irishman – who 'had the habit of describing as "silly" any questions or remarks of counsel which appeared to him irrelevant'. When a question he posed to a witness was termed as such, Asaf says 'I immediately put down my brief and told him: "I am aware of no such expression in law. A question can be relevant or irrelevant and you have a right to rule out an irrelevant question. But I will not have the word silly."' Apparently, the magistrate 'was cured of his habit'!

This sense that he was no less than any Englishman in India, and in fact was better, comes through often – especially when he is demonstrating his command of English and knowledge of English mores, and then using this to contrast local bureaucratic arbitrariness with the high standards of 'true' English behaviour. This was in many ways the hallmark of nationalism in India as it had developed till then and is best summed up by the title of a 1901 book by a pioneer of Indian nationalism, Dadabhai Naoroji

(1825–1917), titled *Poverty and Un-British Rule in India*. This view that the colonial state in its actions was not 'British enough' is certainly something Asaf consistently put forward in this early phase of his public life and it is fair to assume this was not only for tactical reasons. Recently returned from England, he saw no reason why British standards could not be upheld in India.

We get an illustration of this in July 1917 when a public meeting was planned by the Delhi Home Rule League to protest an internment order on Mrs Annie Besant by the Government of Madras. Asaf Ali was served with an order withholding permission for organizing such a meeting. His response was a long letter to the *Chronicle* that took up almost half a page of the broadsheet:

> The Chief Commissioner has shown that means are not lacking, if a bureaucrat takes it into his head to display disregard of constitutional rights of the people . . . Do they realize they are doing the greatest *disservice* to the cause of the empire in thus ruthlessly alienating the sympathies of which they stand in sore need?[8]

Possibly the intention was to underline that his critique was not just some local-level grievance but the articulation of a point of view that was wider and sought to cut through the claims of racial superiority:

> If the World struggle is for the assertion and reaffirmation of the Rights of Man, if the world war is raging to vanquish despotism . . . no deviation is possible for the government of India from the principles for which the world is fighting the Central Powers. You cannot profess one formula in the West and act contrariwise in the East. But I have infinite faith in the British democracy with which we will have to deal ultimately. A bureaucrat may strike a discordant note here, or a misguided official may sound a discordant note there, but the heart of the British democracy beats true to the noble impulses of Humanity . . .

To our contemporary understanding, upholding English mores and usage as the gold standard of acceptable conduct was itself an indication of an enslaved mind; but such debates were a necessary staging post in the much longer journey to intellectual freedom.

December 1917 saw Asaf in Calcutta on behalf of the Delhi Home Rule League for the annual Congress session. He was not satisfied attending as a casual delegate and felt there should be a Delhi branch of the Indian National Congress. He was apparently even more ambitious and suggested that the next Congress session – of 1918 – be held in Delhi. His point was that 'never in the history of the Congress had a session been held in Delhi – now the capital of an alien and autocratic government'. An annual Congress session in Delhi would be akin to the 'invasion' of the citadel' necessary to shake the 'wooden mind of the bureaucracy'. The government must be made to realize, his argument ran, that shifting of the capital from Calcutta would earn them no respite from political and nationalist awakening. The shift certainly had had as one of its principal motives the need to move the seat of government some distance away from the cockpit of political activity that Calcutta had become.

The Congress session in Calcutta was the first Asaf attended. He had stayed away from the 1915 and 1916 sessions – in Bombay and Lucknow, respectively – conscious that there was over him 'a heavy cloud of suspicion, thanks to Mohammad Ali'. The advice that Jinnah had given him to 'lie low' was something he had kept in mind.

The Lucknow session of the Congress stands out for several reasons. At it the decade-long rift between the 'moderate' and the 'extremist' factions within the Congress was set aside. Following the partition of Bengal, the extremists had wanted the expansion of the Swadeshi movement and boycotts to the whole country, and the extension of the boycott beyond that of foreign goods to any form of cooperation with the government. The moderates wanted the agitation confined to Bengal and no extension of boycotts to other fields. Apart from these tactical differences, the two had a great deal in common – more than is generally conceded. Neither demanded independence immediately and saw the path ahead as one of progressively greater involvement of Indians in the governance of the country and reforms in the nature of the colonial state. They differed principally on tactics, degree and on the pace of change, but most visibly in the intensity of the rhetoric employed against the government. Matters soon came to a head and the differences were both animated and accentuated by personalities, with the firebrand B.G. Tilak heading the extremists and the reflective and measured-in-tone G.K. Gokhale leading the moderates. At the annual Congress session in 1907 in Surat, delegates in the opposing groups had come to blows and the Congress effectively split into two separate camps. The police had to be called in to clear the meeting hall and the viceroy was later to write to the secretary of state that the 'Congress collapse' at Surat 'was a great triumph for us'. The senior leaders in both camps had much to regret but despite their best efforts their respective radicals had led the packs and rapprochement was difficult.

By 1916 all this was in the past. G.K. Gokhale had died in February 1915, leaving the moderates rudderless and dissatisfied with Congress inactivity in the intervening years. Tilak had been jailed in 1908 and returned only in 1914 from Mandalay in Burma. The stage was now set for the rift to be healed as both sides saw the costs of disunity. The Congress had seen a new entrant in the form of Mrs Annie Beasant. Her long stay in India and the reputation she had built as a Theosophist catapulted her to the highest levels of the Congress. She played a leading role in uniting the Congress. A unified Congress thus came to meet in Lucknow in 1916 and the healing of the rift itself made this a landmark Congress meeting. This session had, however, an even greater significance as it also saw a meeting of minds between the Congress and the Muslim League on the highly divisive issue of representation for Muslims in elected bodies.

The colonial government in 1909 had introduced a package of reforms providing for an expanded Indian representation in legislative councils of different provinces and in the Imperial Legislative Council. The idea of Indians having a presence and some say in the governance of their affairs goes back to the 1860s – in form or stated policy at least, if not usually in substance. Indians were first associated with governance as nominated members, and then gradually elected in small and restricted elections, as stakeholders in local bodies such as municipalities. With the 1909 reforms such representation made a start at the level of provincial legislative councils and in the central Imperial Legislative Council. These reforms were therefore generally welcomed, although there was some disappointment over the limited powers granted to the councils and the fact that the elected members would be a minority, with the majority of the seats reserved for nominated or official members. For instance, of the sixty members of the Imperial Legislative Council, only twenty-seven were elected.

What, however, was divisive in the 1909 package, or the Morley–Minto reforms (as they were known after the then viceroy and the secretary of state for India respectively), was the introduction of separate electorates for Muslims and also allotting Muslims more than proportional (in terms of their share of population) seats. Separate representation had been a demand for many Muslims on the grounds that few of them had the chance of being elected – both because they were a minority in most provinces of British India and also because relatively fewer Muslims even in the Muslim-majority provinces fulfilled the educational and property qualifications required for seeking representation. Many leading Hindu politicians opposed this and the Congress as a whole saw the provision of separate electorates as a malign initiative to divide and rule. Over the years the issue acquired a momentum of its own as a power-sharing formula between Hindus and Muslims proved elusive and was one of the great unresolved what-ifs of the first half of the twentieth century. But at the time, this was principally an elite preoccupation for both communities: 'the largest constituency under the Indian Councils Act of 1909 had only 650 voters and there were only 4818 electors for the twenty-seven elective seats on the Imperial Legislative Council.'[9]

The Muslim League, dominated so far by feudal grandees and British loyalists, also faced a dissatisfied constituency with its pro-government stance gradually evoking criticism, the early signs of which, as we saw, were evident in Aligarh even a decade earlier. If the 1909 reforms were a considerable shot in the arm for the League, as we saw the annulment of the partition of Bengal in 1911 was a setback. Jinnah's influence in the Muslim League meanwhile had increased, although he was not an original member and had only joined in 1913. He had criticized the impulse that led to its foundation, and his position was that it needed to work alongside the Congress and adopt a critical position vis-à-vis the government.

The Lucknow session was the venue in which these different views were sought to be reconciled as far as possible. The outcome was a compromise. Most significant in this was the concession by the Congress accepting separate electorates for Muslims. What this had meant in practice was that Muslim voters would be apportioned to specific constituencies designated as 'Muslim'. In these Muslim voters would elect a co-religionist. In effect there were two voter lists: one general and one Muslim. Since the voter list was made on the basis of religion, no Muslim could vote for a non-Muslim and vice versa. Constituencies, contestants and voters were all segregated on the basis of religion This also meant that in practice constituencies that were not really territorial, and in some cases a particular area or locality, could have two constituencies: one 'General' and one 'Muslim'. The system applied to all the provinces of British India barring some such as Delhi, the capital city.

Separate electorates had been generally viewed negatively in Congress circles, so their acceptance in Lucknow was a big concession to the Muslim League. This was matched to some extent by corresponding concessions by the Muslim League. The mutual concessions meant that seats reserved for Muslims were fixed in excess of their percentage share in those provinces where they were in a minority but this was reversed for those provinces where Muslims were in a majority. Thus, in Bengal where about 52 per cent of the population was Muslim, seats reserved for them comprised 40 per cent of the total; in Punjab with Muslims comprising over 54 per cent of the population, only 50 per cent of the seats were reserved for them.[10]

The Congress–League pact had many opponents, both in the Congress and in the League. Yet one of its principal protagonists was B.G. Tilak, recently released from prison, and he stood taller than anyone else in the Congress at the time. Apart from being a leading figure of its 'extremist' wing, his postures of defiance against the government led to an enormous mass following. In the 1890s in his native Poona and Bombay he had successfully married popular religion and history to current political issues by organizing the Ganapati and Shivaji festivals. He had been jailed for 'sedition' more than once. Therefore he was seen as a votary of his co-religionists and to many Muslims his was the most prominent face of the 'Hindu Congress'. A 'joint author' was M.A. Jinnah, a critic of the League's feudal grandees and their constant kowtowing to the government. Between the two they got enough support in both parties to agree to a compromise.

Sarojini was an ardent admirer of this achievement, in particular of Jinnah's role. Writing to Syud Hossain on 13 February 1917, she noted that 'though [Jinnah] did not and could not evoke any passionate enthusiasm or affection [he] has created for himself an abiding respect and confidence in the minds of both communities. He fails to arouse affection but he certainly creates trust and respect because of his level headed and sincere convictions . . .' Some months later, on 18 November, she wrote to Syed Mahmud about a short sketch she had written on Jinnah for the *Bombay Chronicle*. She referred to him in the latter as 'the man you [Syed Mahmud] respect and dislike' and said that she had titled it 'An Ambassador of Unity'. Jinnah, she had written, 'is frightfully pleased with it, though there is some severe criticism of him'. Possibly this sketch was the basis for the introduction Sarojini was to write to a collection of Jinnah's speeches which was published in 1918.[11] He was, she wrote, 'essentially a solitary man', someone with 'a large political following but few intimate friendships' and outside of law and politics 'he has few resources and few accomplishments'. Jinnah would never be able to establish that 'instinctive and inviolable kinship' that made Mohammad Ali 'a hero of the Muslims' and Mahatma Gandhi 'a living idol of the masses'. But it was 'testimony to his personal triumph' that he stands approved 'not merely as an ambassador but as an embodied symbol of the Hindu Muslim Unity'. The title has stuck perhaps because it provides to many such a contrast between the

Jinnah of the second decade of the twentieth century and that of the fourth decade. Because of this contrast the title bestowed by Sarojini itself became over the years deeply controversial in India.

~

To Asaf, Calcutta was a revelation and Delhi certainly appeared a 'squalid settlement' in comparison. Yet despite all of Calcutta's grandeur he noted the dismal character of its 'native quarters'. At the session itself he found most of the important leaders and delegates 'in fashionable European costume and hats'; only Tilak was in a dhoti. When 'Vande Mataram' was sung with a chorus and orchestra Asaf found his eyes filling with tears and, in that moment, he felt that although 'insignificant and of no account individually, I was also a note in this grand orchestration of human aspiration'. Clearly, he was now getting fully into the stream of nationalist politics.

Asaf heard the speeches of the figures then at the head of Congress: Surendranath Banerjee's rhetoric 'ebbed and flowed in a well-modulated voice'; 'B.C. Pal roared like a lion'; Sarojini 'sang her words with a lilt'; 'Tilak spoke in a voice of almost no volume or timbre. He was not heard but was uproariously cheered.' Asaf made a request that he be allowed to speak and was asked to do so on a resolution condemning the internment of the Ali brothers. He saw this as 'a good return on the unmerited calumny he had faced' and spoke in Urdu for about ten minutes and 'earned repeated cheers'. Asaf's idea – which may well not have been just his – that Delhi host the next session found support, was accepted and 'we returned to Delhi feeling triumphant and full of zeal'.

The task ahead now was to establish the Delhi unit of the Congress. This was easily done by converting the Delhi branch of the Home Rule League into the Delhi Congress. Raising funds and enrolling volunteers was a more arduous task into which he writes he 'threw myself heart and soul – as publicist through the platform and the press'.

~

Through this frenetic political activity and his work at the Bar, we get a sense of Asaf as an earnest and serious young man. Other interests, in particular Urdu poetry, remained, and he continued to compose verse and try to get it published in different outlets, but this interest was weakening. His was, with the notable exception of Sarojini, a male-oriented milieu and if he sought feminine companionship there is little record of it. Possibly many of his friends in Delhi were married and with families of their own but we have very few references to any women in Asaf's life outside the relationships within the family.

There is a single reference to a young woman, Khurshid, in a letter to Syud: 'Khurshid has gone to Bombay . . . I am rather cross with her for leaving Delhi without my consent but she says she had to obey her mother.'[12] The latter Asif described as a 'damnable hag'. He wrote also that he 'was hoping to bring her [Khurshid] to the right path when her people decided that she should be spirited away from Delhi'. We cannot say whether this was a younger relative or a romantic relationship, but the letter to Syud asked him to see Khurshid, 'encourage her [to] strike for release from her mother's slavery', and persuade her to return to Delhi 'if her old mother has not already disposed of her in some other way'. This last phrase, though, seems to indicate a complete absence of romantic interest but, whatever it was, this is a solitary reference of its kind in many letters which are full of talk about other men but no women.

But he did have time for relaxing. On one occasion, around the time of the Delhi Congress, Asaf recalled going for a break with a friend to stay for a fortnight in Mehrauli, in the environs of Qutab Minar.

> We filled our time with long walks among the ruins, exploring the successive strata of the archeological remains of at least three of the early Delhis – of Prithviraj, the Ghoris and the Aibaks or slave kings. We also read Plato together. In the evening we would go to the grassy square before Balban and Altutmish's tombs and carry on our Socratic discussion.

Friends from Delhi would frequently join. 'Spring was at its height and the dry and scented air of Kutab was itself an ecstasy.' Clearly this was a male-oriented group. Possibly the views he had about arranged marriages since Liaq had further hardened and the circle he moved in precluded his meeting women with his interests. There must have been pressures from his relatives on him to marry and start a family. His mother certainly tried. We find Asaf writing to Padmaja Naidu, Sarojini's daughter, from a dak bungalow in Rohtak on 11 September 1919: 'Most probably by the time you get this, my dear mother would have "fixed me up matrimonially". I have in sheer exhaustion given up the struggle and resigned myself . . .'[13] But it was his resistance that prevailed. If he chafed at the obstacles to a marriage of choice, he does not say so in his stray jottings about this time. Whatever the reason, this is a part of Asaf's life we know little about and the unfolding of this private part of his personality was still some time into the future.

# 9

# Pushing Back

As Asaf's activism grew, he noted that his role was increasingly drawing the attention of the police and the local intelligence authorities. Efforts to disrupt meetings he was addressing became more frequent. On one occasion 'police agents' stood at the outskirts of a meeting and 'chucked stones into the audience', inviting 'instant retribution from the public'. On another occasion some old shoes were thrown at him as he entered the compound of the court and he 'noticed a sardonic smile' on the face of the police officer on duty. The president of the Bar told him that this was the 'recognition of his public activity'. As his local profile grew incrementally, he was frequently in touch with some of the major leaders of the Congress and of the emergent national movement. But possibly doubts still remained about his connection with the intelligence agencies among Mohammad Ali's numerous supporters and admirers for, as mentioned earlier, he was to inexplicably resign as secretary of the Delhi Congress unit in early 1918.

In April 1918 the viceroy convened a war conference to be attended among others by Gandhi. Sarojini Naidu was in Delhi at the time but was not invited: 'she was only a poet', was Asaf's sarcastic assessment. A meeting was therefore arranged which both she and Gandhi would address. On learning that the latter would speak in Hindustani, Sarojini was apprehensive: 'Gandhi did not know Urdu and the Delhi audience would be critical.' Asaf recalled Sarojini's nervousness and her asking C.F. Andrews, his old teacher in St Stephen's College and now Gandhi's close associate, 'whether his old man was going to address the meeting in Hindustani'. Andrews was certain that speaking in Hindustani would work: 'My old man will win through, you may be sure.' Both Asaf and Sarojini were unconvinced: 'It would be a crowded meeting, loudspeakers were not known and they [the audience] had never heard Gandhiji before.'

In Asaf's recollection, Gandhi in homespun clothes and with a villager's turban spoke in broken Hindustani using expressions – possibly from Gujarati – which would have been understood quite differently in Delhi from their original Gujarati meaning. Used by any other person these 'would have tickled the audience to a titter'; but Gandhi had the audience spellbound. Asaf commented to a friend, 'This is the eloquence of sincerity.' Nevertheless, Asaf also noted the general assessment amongst his colleagues in the Home Rule League and in the Congress which remained largely inspired by Tilak's rhetoric: Gandhi was 'an honest, self-sacrificing crank, but not a politician of any mark'.

As 1918 progressed, the momentum of politics in Delhi accelerated which, Asaf writes, 'shattered the nerves of the Delhi administration'. With the forthcoming Congress session, efforts to mobilize support, raise funds and enrol supporters moved up several notches, with the local administration clearly not amused. He and Neki Ram Sharma, an upcoming politician and powerful orator from nearby Bhiwani, were barred from addressing public meetings under the Defence of India Rules. The order served on him referred to the 'reasonable grounds for believing that Asaf Ali, Barrister at Law, Delhi, has acted and is about to act in manner prejudicial to public safety and to the Defence of British India' and that he should 'refrain from addressing public meeting in the Delhi province'.[1] The order was served on him on 12 June and was immediately the subject of numerous column inches in the form of news reports, Asaf's commentaries and angry editorials in the *Bombay Chronicle*.

Both Asaf and Neki Ram attended meetings thereafter – but sat through them quietly – regularly evoking a huge response as 'dumb speakers'. In one meeting in which both were billed to speak but did not while occupying their designated places as speakers, Asaf became in the *Chronicle* the 'muzzled speaker' who got a 'record ovation'. The meeting itself was to highlight the conditions of Indians in South Africa but this local issue dominated the proceedings. The reading of the chief commissioner's order against Asaf Ali and Neki Ram was greeted with 'deafening cries of shame'.[2] For the *Chronicle* the gag order was an opportunity to further develop its critique of 'Haileyism' in reference to the chief commissioner of Delhi, W.M. Hailey, and the column 'Imperial Delhi' noted that this 'reactionary bureaucrat has supplied a fresh illustration of his worst tendencies'.

Asaf, however, wanted to push this particular envelope further and, lawyer that he was, soon detected a loophole in the order in that it related to 'public' and not to 'private' gatherings. He therefore felt that a meeting held indoors and limited to registered members of the Home Rule League would be outside the ambit of the ban order. Some other lawyers advised against this: 'it was not lawyer-like to court prosecution in order to test a point.' Asaf's response was that he was not acting as a lawyer but as a citizen engaged in the 'preservation of civil rights'. But, clearly, he knew he was going to cross a line. The opportunity was there, with the Home Rule League Day falling on 16 June.

A meeting was thereafter publicized for members of the Home Rule League to be addressed by Asaf Ali and Neki Ram Sharma. Naturally, this announcement, seen as an explicit act of defiance of the recently issued order, 'created a sensation'. At the entry to the Laxminarain Dharmshala – the building in Chandni Chowk where the meeting was to be held – arrangements were also made to enrol new members to the League. The Laxminarain Dharmshala was incidentally the site of many Home Rule League meetings and was regarded as its 'storm centre'.[3] In Asaf's later recollection, on the day of the meeting 'several hundred new members were enrolled at the gate', and the audience consisted of a thousand or more including several plain-clothes policemen. At the time, however, he was at pains to emphasize how strictly he was acting within the limits of the permissible and the meeting was entirely a private affair confined only to members of the League, some of whom may have joined just before the meeting. Entry to the hall where the meeting was held was also strictly controlled to keep non-members out.

Asaf was setting the administration up for a public fall and it fell into the trap.

Asaf was arrested some twenty days later on 6 July, and recalled being 'filled with a strange feeling of elation'. Possibly for him his actions were a vindication of his personal integrity after the blows his reputation had received in the past three years; he had embarked on this risky venture for precisely that reason: 'This was my baptism and I could not henceforth be denied the genuineness of my credentials.'

His mother, 'tense but seemingly calm and dignified', was the most affected: 'You are my only child. Did I bring you up for this day? May God protect you.' Brushes with authority for middle-class Muslims in Delhi were always unnerving; the elders in his family, still haunted by the events of 1857, 'used to tremble at the very mention of anti-government agitation'.[4] But this issue was now a public spectacle, and the press and the *Bombay Chronicle* in particular made it into an all-India show. Asaf's mother was interviewed and was perhaps tutored on what to say. The paper quoted her to the effect that 'This was the first happiness she has known since she became a widow at the age of 20 some 30 years ago'; and that 'her son is doing his best for the constitutional freedom of India and no sacrifice is too great for that righteous cause'.[5]

Possibly the *Chronicle* also found a public hungry for gestures of defiance, so no detail of the arrest was too small to be printed: Asaf was to provide graphic detail for its reports. Taken to the kotwali, the old city's historic police station, it was revealed to him that 'I was sitting only a few paces from the cell in which Ghalib the poet is said to have been confined once . . .'[6] News of the arrest was described as having created unrest:

> Uncommon sensation and indignation prevails in Delhi. The general belief in his innocence and the unjust action of the authorities in molesting the most popular leader of public opinion have won the overwhelming enthusiasm for Mr Asaf Ali. A public committee

for the defence has been immediately instituted with Rs 10,000 as a nucleus.[7]

Asaf was quickly bailed out, which was disappointing, 'since it took the elation of martyrdom down by many pegs'. His aim, however, really was a 'forensic duel' in a courtroom and he aimed to make as much capital out of this in the media and elsewhere as possible. The *Bombay Chronicle* connection now played a major role, and as the trial grew closer, space in the newspaper devoted to the case grew from some columns to whole pages and more. Messages of support and sympathy poured in from across the country and a senior counsel from Bombay was engaged to conduct the defence. When the trial began on 18 July, the 'Court room was packed to capacity and large crowds filled the court compound'. 'Coming out of the Court Mr Asaf Ali was greeted with copious showers of rose petals and cheers and shouts of "Vande Mataram" punctuated the intervals between the court room and the car.'[8]

Asaf did not venture into this contest without several serious concerns: being found guilty could mean conviction for at least a few months if not longer, his possible debarring and the loss of his career. The stakes were now much higher than a letter or an article in a newspaper. He was advised by many of his friends to look for a way out: 'It was alright for the Tilaks and the Mrs Besants, whom the people had supported with hundreds of thousands and showered gifts on but not for you at the start of the only career left.' Apparently even Abul Kalam advised prudence. He had received an informal advance notice and an implied warning from the public prosecutor in Delhi about the difficulties he would face and also a suggestion that he could seek a way out. Asaf stuck to his guns but went through many anxious moments.

There was also the more than occasional despondency at the weak support he thought he was getting in Delhi: 'I meet with sniggers not infrequently! They think I am being tried for treason and therefore they must not be seen talking to me or sympathizing with me.' We also find him writing to Syud on 10 July: 'I write to warn you not to put any faith in the high-sounding names.' In the first flush of enthusiasm after his arrest numerous persons had pledged financial contributions but he noted that of the defence fund of Rs 10,000 expected, 'actually only 1840/- has been promised of which only Rs 75 has been collected so far. They are all talking a lot but no work done'. What hurt more – and for this Asaf blamed a clique in Aligarh – was a spurious story being circulated to the effect that the entire prosecution was a sham and a conspiracy. He complained to Syud on 9 July: 'Just think those dammed *Bahanchouds* of the Aligarh sect who call my trial "a move by the government to restore me to public confidence".' The context was obviously the earlier controversy about his being a government informant. 'Who will expect me to have patience with such *Madharchouds*?' he asked. But in contrast to the lukewarm response in Delhi, support in the rest of the country was strong. Telegrams of encouragement from important leaders including Mrs Annie Besant poured in. Horniman's message from Bombay ended: 'Stick to your Guns.'

As the trial commenced on 18 July and continued for the next ten days, the *Bombay Chronicle* maintained its detailed coverage.[9] The criminal proceedings against a barrister were significant enough to attract attention outside nationalist circles. The *Times of India* also reported on it in some detail.[10] The magistrate hearing the case, George Spence, had to be brought from another province as the Delhi officers could not be expected to pronounce on the infringement of their own government's order. Asaf's lawyer was imported from Bombay, thanks largely to the support of the *Bombay Chronicle*.

The defence's argument was that the Delhi administration held a grudge against Asaf for his writings criticizing them in the *Bombay Chronicle*; but the case actually hinged on what constituted a public meeting as opposed to a private gathering. The judgment found the accused 'contumacious' – someone stubbornly and wilfully disobedient to authority – and 'improper' but also had to concede that there had been no infringement of the chief commissioner's order as the meeting was not 'public' but a 'private' one; there was therefore no alternative but to acquit.[11] In one account Spence was given a punishment posting thereafter.[12] But his career in the longer term does not appear to have suffered: he was the law secretary to the Government of India in the 1940s and Asaf would meet him in the Central Legislative Assembly.

The verdict was an emphatic victory for the two defendants. The technicality or the loophole Asaf had identified had worked. 'We were wildly cheered and garlanded and walked out on a carpet of rose petals in the court compound. And I suddenly became well known in the country.' The *Bombay Chronicle* later put together all its reporting and editorializing on the case and the judgment in the form of a little booklet titled *The Asaf Ali Trial* and it was advertised for sale in the paper for months afterwards. The nature of the case, the support of the *Bombay Chronicle*'s editor Horniman, and the presence of Syud, who wrote the introduction to the book, meant that Asaf's had not been a silent struggle.

He had taken a big risk, possibly thinking he needed to play a high-stakes game to fully clear his name and retrieve his reputation from the charge of being an informer. The ordeal and the final judgment in his favour undoubtedly marked a step forward but did not change everything, and reservations about him persisted in the Congress hierarchy. He wrote to Syud on 9 October 1918: 'persecution cannot be tolerated after a certain limit . . . I feel sick and disgusted.' But there was also support for him: 'I think Akka means to do her best for me, but I feel uncertain about the result.'

Notwithstanding such doubts, victory in the legal 'forensic duel' he had set up may well have strengthened the belief that his future lay in more of this: constitutional and legal battles in the full glare of publicity in which the finer points of law and fair play were contested, and victory came from knowledge, skill and finesse, not necessarily the application of force. For someone like him, equal to India's rulers in knowledge and education, nationalism was also demonstrating your personal worth, even your superiority, and the political task ahead could be to accumulate incremental gains like this. But such thoughts existed perhaps in the background and would assert themselves only gradually, for the period of four years or so that lay ahead was one of mobilization, agitation and of more demonstrative and less clinical action.

Amidst all this, another major event was looming: Delhi's first Congress session scheduled for the closing days of 1918. Compared to 1916 or the subsequent sessions in 1919 and 1920, the Delhi session was comparatively uneventful. The big draws, B.C. Pal and B.G. Tilak, did not attend; the former because of a prohibitory order denying him entry into Punjab and Delhi; while Tilak was away in London pursuing, unsuccessfully as it turned out, a defamation case he had filed against the journalist Valentine Chirol of the London *Times*. The Congress did provide Asaf the opportunity to push for a particular 'bee in his bonnet' and it remains a minor footnote in the city's modern history. This was that Delhi be expanded by carving out Ambala from Punjab to form a new province which would also have its own legislative council and high court. He was thus perhaps amongst the early protagonists of a full-fledged Delhi state.

Asaf was part of the team responsible for arrangements of the Congress session but was disappointed at not being given a bigger role or to be included in any of the Substantive Committees. 'I was not only a mere youngster but was still suspect in the eyes of some. So, the Congress came and went and left me where I was.' Asaf's proximity to his two personal mentors, Hakim Ajmal Khan and Dr Ansari, who were key figures in Delhi at the time, gave him an enlarged role and profile; he was still building up a reputation block by block.

Despite this pessimistic personal assessment and, in relative terms, the still largely placid tenor of politics in Delhi, in a wider frame the pieces were falling in place for an intense confrontation that would characterize 1919 in India. The end of the world war was accompanied by expectations that change was in the offing. The Home Rule League, the Congress and the Muslim League may have each contributed to this expectation of change but there was also a larger general sense that after such a carnage in Europe the government would now advance with speed down the path of conceding a larger quantum of self-governance to Indians. The Great War had seen the demise of three European empires – the Austro-Hungarian, the Ottoman and the Russian – and 'self-determination' was emerging as the new buzzword. The government for its part had also encouraged such expectations, conscious of the need to keep public opinion on its side, given India's huge contribution to the war effort with over a million troops in action in different theatres. In August 1917 the British government had promised 'the increasing association of Indians in every branch of the administration and the gradual development of self-governing institutions'.[13] As the war ended many felt that the time had come for these assurances to be made good.

If India on the whole seemed to be on the threshold of a new phase of its history, Delhi too had a transformed political persona. Because of the activities of the Home Rule League and the Congress and Muslim League sessions in end 1918, the city would now be much more in the eye of the storm than could have been anticipated even a few years earlier. A government official had assessed:

> I have no hesitation in saying that no other city in India enjoys the unenviable notoriety that Delhi enjoys for simmering popular discontent and even active contempt for British institutions and the British point of view. The result is that within a few years of the change of capital the people of Delhi have become adept in organizing demonstrations and using strong language from the pulpit and in the press. Once Delhi decided to assume a hostile attitude, the suggestion was taken up by other towns connected with Delhi by railway and postal communications.[14]

Early in 1919, the government had enacted the Rowlatt Act – named after the Home Member of the Viceroy's Council. This aimed at strengthening capacities in the law and order machinery to deal with revolutionary acts carried out by terrorist groups. The spectre of the Russian Revolution had loomed large in the minds of many officials. The new law was aimed at creating a mechanism to 'short circuit the processes of law in dealing with political crime'.[15] Consequently, legal safeguards available to those so charged were to be considerably eroded. Politically conscious sections of Indian public opinion, led in particular by the Indian National Congress, denounced the move; Gandhi had earlier announced a 'Satyagraha' against the move were the bill to be enacted. Despite opposition in the Imperial Legislative Council, the bill was enacted into law in March 1919.

Asaf recalled, 'The term Satyagraha and its scope were wholly new in the public life of the country.' He understood 'civil resistance': 'if a government rode roughshod over the inherent rights of the people, their obvious remedy was disobedience of such laws as were unbearable.' But Satyagraha appeared to be different; for Asaf the expectations from a Satyagrahi 'were formidable and forbidding'. Gandhi had visited Delhi in February 1919 and, in a meeting at the house of S.K. Rudra, the principal of St Stephen's College, explained the requirements: 'The Satyagrahi must forswear all worldly attachments and taking his firm stand on the truth be ready in his pursuit of truth to suffer unto death. Satyagrahis should pledge themselves publicly. The smallness of their numbers should not weigh with them.' The group in Principal Rudra's house was small – no more than twenty – with some of them being members of the Home Rule League including Asaf. Others included Swami Shraddhanand, a firebrand Hindu activist, part political animal, part religious mendicant and grassroots intellectual, who was very popular and a crowd puller for Hindus – possibly at that time in the same league as Mohammad Ali for Muslims.

Gandhi's aim was to form a Satyagraha Committee for Delhi. In Asaf's recollection 'Swamiji was the first to declare that he was fully prepared to pledge himself' and others followed, raising the number to fourteen. Asaf says he hesitated before adding his name to the list. He wanted time to consider because of the high expectation from a Satyagrahi and explained his thought process: 'I was not capable of rising to the dizzy heights of renunciation and self-imposed austerity of an almost saintly order but I decided to accept Satyagraha in the spirit of political civil resistance.' He wrote to Syud about this on 8 March 1919:

> I am not yet decided about the Satyagraha vow. The movement as explained to me by Gandhi seems to lend itself to staggering unwieldiness and does not appear to be very far from the borderland of fiasco . . . The idea in the abstract is I admit unique for testing the

> spiritual faith of a people. But tremendous must be the difficulties of realizing the idea in practice.

When he did join, despite his own earnestness he was also astute enough to decipher that none in the group who volunteered saw non-violence in the spirit that Gandhi understood it but found in it the great value of expediency in the current situation.

The Rowlatt Satyagraha demanding that the legislation be abrogated soon gathered momentum in Delhi, amongst the Muslims in particular. For them, as Asaf said, 'any stick was good enough' to beat the government, given what had happened to Turkey in World War I. Militarily defeated by October 1918, it had sued for armistice and Constantinople was occupied by Allied forces. It was now clear even to its strongest supporters that the dismemberment of the Ottoman empire was imminent and the future of its head, the caliph, in doubt. And, unlike in the past, this time the danger came directly from the British. To many who supported the Ottoman empire, its sultan was especially significant as he was the custodian and defender of the holy places – the Khalifa. The institution of the Khilafat was not less than 'the Viceroyalty of the Prophet of Islam' so ordained by divine law.[16] The more discerning would point to the relatively recent origins of this great regard for the Ottoman sultan as the 'Khalifa'. The historian Jadunath Sarkar was, for instance, to write to this friend and fellow historian G.S. Sardesai amidst growing pro-Ottoman and pro-Khilafat sentiment in India: 'The Sultan of Turkey was never recognized as the Khalif by any Muhammadan ruler of India as every such ruler, according to the strict theory of Mohammadan Law, called himself the Khalif of the Age.'[17]

Yet these were academic arguments. On the ground, veneration for the caliph often ran deep and sometimes even amongst those not particularly religious. As we saw earlier, Asaf had been moved to involuntary tears at the sight of the Ottoman sultan in Constantinople – 'the last vestige of Muslim freedom and greatness' – and this despite what he described as his 'rationalism', but because of his 'upbringing in a Muslim home'. Concerns about the Khilafat and the fate of the holy shrines merged imperceptibly with anti-Rowlatt sentiment: both issues could after all be traced back to the same source, the actions of the British government.

A hartal or general strike was called for in Delhi on 30 March 1919 to protest the Rowlatt Act and it garnered support from different quarters. There was a fracas over some sweet shops not being closed and five persons were killed in police firing. The hartal thereafter was extended, and in the following two weeks there were more fatalities due to police firings. Already, however, the main action was shifting to Punjab where the defining act of the Rowlatt Satyagraha was to be played out. This was on 13 April 1919 at the Jallianwala Bagh in Amritsar where a large gathering was fired upon, resulting in a horrendous number of fatal casualties. How many were killed remains disputed: the government accepted a figure of 379; nationalists claimed a number at least four or five times as many. The number of those wounded was even larger. The horrified reaction to this spanned the entire country, and to Asaf it appeared as if 'India was in the throes of a revolution'.

# 10

# In the Throes of Revolution, Piety and Hindu–Muslim Unity

In Delhi, in the aftermath of the police firings and deaths, a surge of Hindu–Muslim unity gripped the public imagination. At its centre was Swami Shraddhanand. Too many in Delhi caught up in the nationalist agitation – a combination of anti-Rowlatt and pro-Turkish or Khilafatist sentiment at that point – the symbolic high point was the swami being invited to the historic Jama Masjid to address the Friday congregation. After the Delhi shootings and killings on 30 March, the swami had confronted some soldiers and, baring his chest, challenged them to fire. News of the incident spread and he was catapulted to becoming one of the principal leaders of the protests in Delhi. On Friday 4 April, the swami spoke to the congregation gathered to offer prayers that day for those martyred in the police firing. 'It was an unbelievable and never to be repeated scene. A Hindu Sanyasi in his ochre robes preaching from the very pulpit of the greatest mosque in India.'[1] In one recollection 'Swamiji started his address with a sloka from the Vedas and he ended his speech with the *Gaitri mantra*' and the almost entirely Muslim audience extolled his talk.[2] All those present would have been conscious of the import of the occasion.

The swami had only two years earlier taken sanyas, discarding his given name of Munshiram, his clothes and all his other worldly possessions, donning the ochre robe, and finally performing his own funeral rites;

he had then taken the name 'Shraddhanand'. Over the past two decades he had developed a reputation as a charismatic advocate and activist for Hindus and Hindu causes, and had frequent brushes with Muslims for his sharp critiques of their proselytizing activity and perceived aggression and with the law for his incendiary rhetoric. Somehow the nationalist stirring of the time and the interface with Gandhi transformed this traditionalist and activist for Hindu causes into a satyagrahi who then became a 'living symbol of Hindu Muslim unity'.[3] Two days after the Jama Masjid speech, the swami was invited to another important site of Muslim Delhi: the Fatehpuri Masjid.

The idea of Hindu–Muslim fraternization in mosques spread. In Bombay Sarojini accompanied Gandhi to a mosque and, eloquent as ever, delivered a speech: 'united prayers from the far flung provinces would go forth to the Almighty to deliver them from life destroying black bills.'[4] But perhaps what she said was less important than the fact that a Hindu woman was addressing a gathering in a mosque. Yet beneath the veneer of a nationalist upsurge united against a draconian legislation lurked all the risks attendant on mass agitation. Gandhi was to be arrested en route to Delhi and the Punjab, and as news of this spread, violence erupted in several places followed by the massacre in Jallianwala Bagh in Amritsar. Gandhi, shocked at the violence and by the difficulties in ensuring a non-violent satyagraha, suspended the campaign on 18 April 1919.

The Rowlatt Satyagraha was a milestone in the evolution of Indian nationalism and Indian politics. In one assessment it 'was the first countrywide agitation to be launched against the British government and it not only transformed nationalism in India from a movement representing the classes to a movement representing the masses, but it also paved the way for Gandhi's emergence as a dominant figure in Indian politics'.[5]

~

In many ways the early months of 1919 saw a genie coming out of the bottle. The anti-Rowlatt agitation; the massacre at Jallianwala Bagh;

growing Muslim concerns over the fate of Turkey and the caliphate; a Congress energized by the unconventional approach of Gandhi who was steadily moving to its helm – these were all factors that came together and coalesced with the strong, if still hazy, urge for freedom from British rule.

In this moment of churn, Asaf appeared to combine different roles. First, he was a political activist, a key lower-level player. The police reports of the time name the Hakim, Dr Ansari and Shraddhanand as the major leaders of the movement in Delhi. Asaf is generally mentioned as a 'secondary leader'.[6] He was also a public advocate and journalist; apart from his stump speeches he was also writing regularly for the *Bombay Chronicle* with blow-by-blow accounts of the satyagraha in Delhi and on the city's nationalist politics in general. And finally, his political activism was also merging with his legal work as numerous cases were instituted against other political workers for rioting and other offences. His activity extended to the environs of Delhi; at one stage Asaf found that he was 'dividing his time between Delhi and Rohtak, motoring down to Rohtak in the morning and working in Delhi for the rest of the day and writing sheaves of press messages at all odd hours'.

At that point, Asaf may have been rethinking his own approach to politics, seeing the limitations of wordplay with colonial officers to establish his background as being no inferior to theirs. In Hindu-majority Delhi, Asaf identified Hindu–Muslim unity as a critical component for the future and was looking for a platform to construct a durable programme of political action. One idea that gained traction was of reducing the slaughter of cows on Bakr Id, a hugely sensitive subject for obvious reasons then as it is now.

While this idea was being tentatively explored, Asaf received an invitation to address a public meeting in Deoband and saw this as an ideal opportunity. Deoband was the location of one of India's most important Islamic institutions of learning, the Dar ul Uloom, established almost contemporaneously with Sir Syed Ahmed's Muhammadan Anglo-Oriental College in Aligarh in the aftermath of the 1857 seismic wave that battered north India. If the latter saw Western education and modernization as the way forward for Muslims in India, the Deoband seminary founders had drawn the opposite conclusion and retreated inwards to a concentration on classical Islamic education and learning.

For Asaf the visit was a 'revelation'. What appealed to him the most was that in this small town there was 'a fine body of men of profound learning, the simplicity of whose life was inspiring'. Students from Afghanistan, Central Asia and even China were attracted enough to come and study; erudite professors whose fame had drawn these students sat on primitive mats to address them; their living quarters had the same 'utter simplicity'. But Asaf also noted that the syllabi followed were six centuries old, 'comparative theology was nonexistent', and while 'knowledge of Islamic law and jurisprudence was deep and immense, they did not seem prepared to examine precedents in the light of changing circumstances'. Asaf discussed the possibility of a modernization of the syllabus with some of the teachers but drew a blank: they were 'supremely self-satisfied'.

In engaging with Islamic clerics or the ulema in Deoband Asaf had a more specific objective in mind: the issue under consideration in Delhi, that is, cow slaughter. He noted that his own views were clear: while he did not like the idea of having to 'pander to superstition', whether Hindu or Muslim, he was prepared to promote cow protection 'on purely economic grounds' as the rural economy depended on it. In addition, the issue was a major one for Hindus, and recurrent rioting and violence occurred because of it. For Asaf therefore

> it was only politic to initiate a good neighborly gesture . . . To kill men and women in the zeal for protecting an animal could not be a religious or rational act, nor would it be a religious or rational act to exercise a right in a matter obnoxious to Hindus . . . the mere maintenance of peace required a rational solution.

The answer could not lie in a 'self-denying ordinance'; after all, how long would self-denial hold? In Asaf's discussions in Deoband he therefore asked 'could not Indian Muslims win the friendship of Hindus by forgoing beef altogether?' Some responded that while this would be ideal, the poor subsisted on beef which was cheap. Others had a more fundamental point:

in deference to Hindu sentiment cow slaughter could be reduced to the minimum but a total ban was not possible because that would in effect concede the principle of cow worship or veneration. This would be against the fundamental Islamic principle that only 'God was worthy of worship'. Asif recollected that he 'pushed the debate a little further': how can you claim this freedom for yourself and also expect support for the Khilafat movement from the non-Muslims? He found that his interlocutors were prepared to go 'any far' [*sic*], short of conceding an outright ban. 'They wanted only the two and a half days of the Bakr Id, out of the whole year, to be reserved for the possible exercise of the right to slaughter cows, which they were further prepared to reduce to a symbolic assertion of the right.'

Asaf returned to Delhi gratified and elated at this opening. He shared the details and intricacies of his discussion with several people, among them Hakim Ajmal Khan.

Asaf's activism on cow protection had, however, a much wider context than his individual effort and this was the steady rise in pro-Khilafat sentiment amongst Muslims in 1919 and 1920. Mushirul Hasan, a careful historian and easily the leading authority on the subject, wrote: 'The *Ulema* were at the heart of Muslim concern over Turkey. From their Madarsahs and Mosques they suddenly emerged on the national scene to dominate the course of the Khilafat agitation.'[7] Their activism added a new edge to existing politics – whether of the Muslim League or of the Congress – because 'for them everything was to be decided according to the Sharia; to join the Khilafat committee was a religious duty; to wage Jihad against the government and to boycott foreign goods was made obligatory by the sharia'.[8] Seminaries had suddenly acquired a new importance and profile, and Deoband was at the top of the list.

Concern over a general 'threat' to Islam had been brewing amongst the ulema for at least a decade coinciding with the political turmoil in Turkey. By 1919 this overlapped with the wider nationalist ferment in India after the end of World War I. Both causes acquired even greater potency and energy with Gandhi himself moving to the forefront of the Khilafat agitation. Following the suspension of the Rowlatt Satyagraha Gandhi had watched the interest that the Khilafat issue generated in India and saw this as the platform on which a wider nationalist agitation could be constructed, advancing satyagraha as a principal technique of nationalist politics. Speaking in May 1919 he had said that the Khilafat question 'was the greatest of all, greater even than that of the repeal of the Rowlatt Act, for it affects the religious susceptibilities of millions of Muslims'.[9] Hindu–Muslim unity was central to Gandhi's vision and Hindus coming to the assistance of Muslims would tie both to each other and to the national movement.

In these circumstances activists and leaders in Delhi decided to convene a 'Khilafat Conference', possibly the first of its kind in India. Asaf was one of the secretaries of the reception committee, 'arranging the reception, boarding and lodging of delegates and guests, drafting resolutions and detailing the duties of volunteers'. He was also keen that the progress he had made on the cow slaughter issue be sealed by a resolution adopted by the Conference. The two principal leaders of the Khilafat agitation in Delhi (in the absence of the interred Ali brothers, removed from all activity since 1915), Dr Ansari and Hakim Ajmal Khan, were on board and therefore it had appeared to him a formal announcement through a resolution was likely.

But the best-laid plans of young men often do not work and there were numerous unexpected glitches. For one Gandhi was not properly received when he arrived. The team deputed to receive him with due fanfare on arrival at the railway station was late and Gandhi had to make his way to his place of stay escorted only by his host: Principal Rudra of St Stephen's College. Asaf himself was delayed in reaching the station and on meeting Gandhi later was subjected to an angry tirade over his lame excuses: 'You must have been standing on your head,' Gandhi told Asaf, 'when you received my telegram otherwise there could be no confusion.' Asaf acknowledged that he was to blame and the rebuke was, he wrote, 'amply deserved and I tried to take it with good grace'. But he also reflected later that while it may appear strange, the fact was that 'in spite of what had happened since the Satyagraha campaign and Jallianwala etc., Gandhiji was not yet regarded as a very important person; neither Hakimji who was chairman of the reception committee nor Ansari thought it necessary to receive him at the station'.

Asaf also faced what he called 'a second ordeal' that was worse. He had hoped that the Delhi Khilafat Conference would have as its high point an authoritative statement on cow protection and cow slaughter. Hakim Ajmal Khan decided, however, to defer the announcement to a few weeks later to the annual session of the Muslim League that he was going to preside over. Asaf in his letters of invitation for the Khilafat Conference had projected it as culminating in an authoritative statement on cow protection and 'felt mortified for, after what was stated in my invitation, it might look like securing the participation of the Hindu leaders on false representation'. However, he was reassured when Hakim Ajmal Khan explained the cow protection issue along with this background at the conference.

But there were larger forces at work and – perhaps unknown to him – others too had given much thought to this question. In particular, Gandhi certainly had, and was unconvinced that wading enthusiastically into the issue was the right approach: 'Mr Asaf Ali has, in the notices he sent about the meeting, mentioned the subject. My humble opinion is that the issue of cow protection may not be raised on this occasion by the Hindus.' The logic behind this position was clear: Hindus should not use their support for the Khilafat to extract concessions on the cow protection issue. 'Though I yield to none in my reverence for the cow, I do not wish to make my help in the Khilafat conditional on anything.'[10] Possibly he had an intuitive understanding that there were numerous minefields on this path.

While the cow slaughter issue figures significantly in Asaf's recollections of this time, there were other issues that dominated the Khilafat Conference. The younger participants, Asaf included, wanted a resolution calling for the boycott of British goods, a tactic employed against the colonial state since the protests against the partition of Bengal in 1905. The 'elders', including the conveners of the conference, Hakim Ajmal Khan and Dr Ansari, were opposed. This was, they argued, too drastic a step for this stage and should only be considered later when all else had failed. Gandhi too was opposed: boycott, he said, 'savoured of hate' and was therefore 'violent'. As he said this, Asaf was left wondering 'Who among the Muslims would appreciate this?' When presented, the boycott resolution created a certain amount of tension. Its supporters were worried about the opposition not so much from Gandhi – 'for Gandhiji was only [*sic*] a honoured guest', as Asaf saw it, but from the Muslim elders. In Asaf's recollection Gandhi made 'a passionate speech strenuously opposing boycott', which he pronounced 'violence in thought'. He was questioned from the floor about the alternative and he replied promptly: 'Yes, Non-cooperation.'

In November 1919, Asaf wrote, 'none of us had any idea what it meant'. In Gandhi's explanation 'this meant withdrawing all cooperation from the British and their institutions – schools, law courts, services – giving up titles and finally stopping the payment of taxes'. He urged that 'as against the big and comprehensive idea of non-cooperation, boycott was a trifle and should be dropped'. The elders, Asaf found, 'were flabbergasted' at this approach but went along because it was a 'distant and impracticable scheme and therefore more innocuous than boycott'.

This conference in Delhi merited a mention in Gandhi's autobiography as the occasion he introduced the concept of 'non-cooperation'. In Gandhi's account the idea emerged almost spontaneously. He was called upon to speak to a somewhat impatient and critical audience immediately after an enthusiastic protagonist of boycott had delivered a fiery speech. Gandhi recalled that he was 'handicapped for want of suitable Hindi or Urdu words. This was my first occasion for delivering an argumentative speech before an audience especially composed of Musalmans of the North' and also because he was 'faced with a critical if not hostile audience'. In response he

> had cast aside all shyness. I was not there to deliver an address in the faultless, polished Urdu of the Delhi Muslims, but to place before the

> gathering my views in such broken Hindi as I could command. And in that I was successful . . . I could not hit upon a suitable Hindi or Urdu word for the new idea and that put me out somewhat. At last I described it by the word 'non co-operation', an expression that I used for the first time in this meeting. I had not then a clear idea of all its manifold implications.[11]

In the end both the boycott and non-cooperation resolutions were adopted but it was the idea of non-cooperation that gripped the imagination of those present. In Asaf's description: 'The delegates represented the millions of angry, excited and impatient Muslim men and women who were spoiling for a fight. Boycott of British goods was a weapon they understood and were bent on wielding and now non-cooperation meant a bigger, more comprehensive boycott of the British government.' Asaf saw the Delhi Khilafat Conference's adoption of non-cooperation as the way forward. It was a landmark event as this 'paved the way' for its endorsement by the Indian National Congress a year later, in 1920.

A little later Asaf was gratified when the Muslim League in its Amritsar meeting in December 1919 adopted a resolution, as Hakim Ajmal Khan had anticipated and worked towards, that 'called upon Muslims to show their regard for Hindu susceptibilities by voluntarily giving preference for non-bovine species for sacrifice at Bakr Id'. The Congress, also meeting in Amritsar thereafter, however, recorded a resolution of thanks for this 'giving up' of cow slaughter. Asaf saw in this the germ of a potential conflict: 'What was intended as a gesture, and was expected to expand under voluntary effort, was seized upon to make it appear that Muslims were to abstain from cow sacrifice altogether.'

This divergence prompted Asaf to write a long letter to Gandhi in January 1920. It is interesting that it addresses him as Mr Gandhi; these were still early days of the journey by the end of which Gandhi would comprehensively dominate all aspects of Indian politics as a Mahatma.

Asaf's main point was that the Amritsar Congress did not realize 'all the difficulties besetting this question' and 'Hindus would be better advised to take nothing for granted'. In brief his point was that the language of the Muslim League resolution was a careful compromise and this should be understood so that 'high hopes should not be raised among the Hindu masses lest they should become the seeds of undesirable complications'.

Asaf had a good sense of the delicate compromise the Muslim League resolution was, as it was based on Hakim Ajmal Khan's address. On his return from Deoband Asaf had first gone to him to convey the gist of his discussions with clerics in its seminary; in fact Asaf says he translated the address into English from the hakim's Urdu text. He was very conscious that, in the enthusiasm of the times, few would realize the very narrow space on which the compromise stood.

Gandhi's response about a week later suggests that he fully grasped Asaf's concern: 'I shall certainly take every step to see that there is no misunderstanding regarding the cow slaughter resolution. I quite agree with you that no false hopes should be raised regarding the Mahomedan attitude on [the] point and that all propaganda on our [Hindus] part among Mahomedans should be avoided.'[12] In brief, the compromise, such as it was, remained a tenuous one and its fragility would be repeatedly demonstrated.

The period after the sessions of the Muslim League and the Congress in Amritsar in December 1919 was an exciting one. For one the Ali brothers, their period of internment over, returned triumphantly to Delhi from Amritsar where they had attended both sessions immediately after their release. Asaf noted that the response was 'an amazing upheaval of public feeling and demonstration of joy and enthusiasm . . . Their triumphal procession was perhaps the biggest Delhi had seen within living memory. They floated on the crest of an oceanic wave of public enthusiasm.' He was, however, silent on whether the breach with Mohammad Ali was now healed, and it appears likely that it was at least put aside. Possibly others including Sarojini Naidu had played a role in advising Mohammad Ali to let the matter rest. But there are no signs now of the older intimacy: the long and candid conversations, impromptu dinners and parties. The Ali brothers were now in fact in a different and certainly much higher orbit than Asaf, and this plus the passage of time possibly made the older relationship impossible to recreate.

To many the change in Mohammad Ali was particularly marked: 'jail had turned Mohamed Ali into a bitter critic of the Raj. As a symbol of his protest, he began to wear half-moons in his grey cap and Khuddam-i-Kaaba badge, compared with his European style of dress in previous years.'[13] The Khuddam-i Kaaba, or Servants of the Kaaba, was set up as an organization in response to widespread concerns about the safety and sanctity of Islam's holiest shrines in Arabia, in particular that the disarray in the Ottoman empire might lead to control over them passing to a non-Muslim power.

Then there was an outburst of activity to devise concrete ways to follow up on the non-cooperation resolution. In early 1920 a meeting was organized which Gandhi, Tilak, Lajpat Rai, Dr Ansari, Abul Kalam attended. At issue were the components of non-cooperation to be embarked upon – beginning with the return of honours and giving up of honorary posts, to withdrawing from educational institutions, non-payment of taxes, etc. Asaf had the opportunity to observe Tilak closely in these deliberations. Since no definite conclusion had been reached by the time Tilak left (as he had other public engagements), Gandhi was, according to Asaf, perturbed. Tilak noticing this and in response to a question said that it could be taken for granted that he would support and subscribe to all decisions taken. He then added after a pause, 'Because I am prepared to go much further.'

Asaf was asked by Swami Shraddhanand to translate Tilak's speech at a public meeting from English to Urdu. Tilak approached the theme of his address – India's freedom struggle – by detailing the contest of good against evil in Hindu mythology. For Asaf the most electrifying moment in the speech came as Tilak reached his denouement: 'Don't imagine for a moment that I want to work for you or India's freedom.' At this the audience was 'spellbound but mystified and waited in tense expectation for its elucidation'. This came accompanied by cheers from the audience in the concluding sentence: 'I would have wanted, worked for and suffered for freedom wherever I might have been, on the face of this earth. It is the demand of my nature.'

Such fiery stuff was the mood of the times and Asaf was also learning fast. He visited Mathura for a public meeting around this time and said that he laced his speech, 'typical of trump oratory of the time', with something new and along the lines of Tilak's speech. He was building on a tip received: he could win Mathura's heart and soul 'if my speeches were larded with Hindi and with Hindu mythology associated with Krishna'. He took this seriously and was, he recollected later, paid a fulsome compliment by Swami Shraddhanand who prefixed a 'Pandit' to his name.

Over the next year these sentiments would mature and strengthen. The Treaty of Sevres in August 1920 imposed by the victorious powers in World War I, in particular Britain and France, on Turkey deprived the latter of major territories. But what had the strongest impact in India was that the Arab parts of the Ottoman empire were transferred to British and French control, who in turn raised its former tribal chieftains to the status of monarchs. The net impact – and the one that mattered to public opinion – was that the Ottoman sultan was no longer the caliph of the holiest shrines of Islam. Some, even amongst Indian Muslims, recognized the invidious nature of Ottoman rule over the Arabs but veneration of the idea of the caliph ran deep. Demands that the Ottoman sultan's earlier status be restored to its original position were made by leading Muslim figures and supported by Gandhi, but there was no real chance of these being met even halfway.

There were other grievances cutting across Hindus and Muslims. Public opinion in India was outraged at the reception Brigadier Reginald Dyer, the officer who had ordered the firing at Jallianwala Bagh, received in England. He was hailed as 'the Saviour of the Punjab' in his homeland. A government report on the Punjab developments leading up to the

Jallianwala Bagh massacre was seen as a whitewash job. Demands for severe punishment were not heeded, adding another layer of grievance. 'Non-cooperation' with such a government seemed logical, even necessary.

As the strands of 'non-cooperation' and 'Khilafat' merged, Asaf would have been encountering avenues he was unfamiliar with. From verbal and legal duels and addressing Home Rule League meetings of like-minded people, nationalism was now becoming something different – infused with not just Hindu–Muslim unity, but also Islamic piety and a heavy dose of Hindu devotionalism.

At the end of 1919 came another development of significance at the initiative of Abul Kalam, the Ali brothers and others: the convening of a meeting with leading ulema from acclaimed Islamic institutions – such as at Deoband and Firangi Mahal of Lucknow. The latter rivalled Deoband in the quality of its instruction and its faculty. The meeting in turn led to the formation of the Jamiat ul Ulema-i-Hind, a countrywide association of Muslim clerics. Asaf noted, 'Many an educated person in public life who had learnt in more than half a century of British rule to think in terms of freedom of conscience, or rather freedom from religious authorities, privately deplored this come-back of the Mullahs. They saw it as a reactionary step.' Jinnah certainly felt that. Clearly these are thoughts that had occurred to Asaf himself: much as he had admired the simplicity and learning of the Deoband ulema, he saw also their fixed world view; their inability to change and their complacency with tradition.

But Asaf saw also the potential strength that the ulema carried in their wake and he posed the counterargument to his own doubts: the moment was a decisive one in a struggle that was non-violent and the ulema would play an important role. After all, the government was 'employing all means in its power, including the parading of support from certain loyal maulvis and saints or pseudo saints'. The ulema finally endorsed the non-cooperation programme and also issued a fatwa or a religious ruling that 'all cooperation with the foreign government was a sin'.

Despite his own doubts or conflicted opinion regarding the ulema and their role in politics or about mixing politics and religion, there is little doubt that Asaf was now fully engaged with all aspects of Khilafat and non-cooperation. He was later to write about a particular incident during the Delhi Khilafat Conference when he had been called to the stage where senior ulema were seated, by Hakim Ajmal Khan. Asaf had been very busy for the past few days, and had therefore not shaved off a significant stubble on his face. On the stage he was congratulated for his beard – seen as a sign of a devout Muslim – by some he knew, perhaps as a joke or in sarcasm. This was taken more seriously by others, and 'before I knew where I was', writes Asaf, he was proclaimed from the dais 'as a model of reclaimed Western educated youth', with an appeal made for others to follow his example! Thereafter, in his recollection, others including Dr Ansari had to follow suit. 'Khilafat beards' and even the title 'Maulana' were the trends of the day.

Asaf said he would re-emerge as 'Mr' only after some years and that too only 'from the wreck of the Khilafat edifice'. But at the time, he had fully embraced the spirit of Khilafat and non-cooperation: 'After growing a beard under the circumstances prescribed, I felt that Bond Street suits and fancy shoes were out of place.' Because of Gandhi 'homespun [was] the badge of the new outlook'. The problem was how to get it, there being no homespun shop in Delhi. When he mentioned his difficulty to his mother, she pointed to the fact that 'homespun and hand-woven cloth was available in our own home in the form of cloth spread over the floor'. She was distressed, however, when Asaf insisted on having his clothes made out of the floor coverings. But, as he explained, 'I had already given up everything connected with the Western mode of living – wine first of all – except books and furniture.'

He also related how the Muslims of Delhi hailed the transformation: 'it seemed a great thing to many that one who had been at the top of fashion until yesterday had renounced everything . . .' Possibly a hitherto Westernized barrister identifying with the mass of other citizens appeared to many emblematic of the changing times. But Asaf was also now sufficiently embedded in the grassroots of the national movement to understand and appreciate that theatre was also an inseparable part of all politics.

Just how infectious the entire mood was is illustrated by another episode in which Asaf and a clutch of Delhi activists and leaders were en route to Nagpur for the annual sessions of the Muslim League and the Congress in December 1920. Asaf was in the same compartment as Hakim Ajmal Khan and Dr Ansari, neither of whom had as yet made the crossover to khaddar. The latter was to preside over the League session. A couple of stops before Nagpur, Asaf says, Hakim Saheb 'suddenly turned to me and in a sweetly familiar tone' asked if Asaf could spare a set of clothes in khaddar. Asaf could and did. But Asaf also does not fail to mention that at the venue itself he made sure of securing for himself a place in the 'European camp' where non-vegetarian food would be available! Yet his mentor's move to khaddar showed how far the moral balance in public life in India was shifting in favour of the discourse being given by Gandhi. Piety, your comportment and your clothes – all were now inseparably part of nationalism.

However, not everyone agreed with this march to confrontation. The government had announced in end 1919 a package of further devolution of power to elected representatives. Known as the Montagu–Chelmsford reforms, after the secretary of state for India and the viceroy, respectively, these were conscious of the new mood sweeping India and of the need for incremental advance over the 1909 package. In essence, in this package administrative departments of provincial governments were divided into two: those that were 'transferred' and would be administered by elected representatives as ministers; and those which remained 'reserved', that is, would be headed by officials. In both cases the provincial governor remained overall in charge. This provincial-level 'devolution' was less than what many had expected but it was still something and had supporters keen to take advantage of this opportunity for authority and influence. Many in the Congress, including prominent faces, preferred to work with this, rather than go down a path of confrontation with vague and, what many felt, unrealizable demands.

The Nagpur session was Asaf's fourth and the liveliest he was to attend. Prominent leaders such as C.R. Das, Lajpat Rai, Madan Mohan Malaviya and finally Jinnah himself, who were opposed to non-cooperation, suddenly found a new situation confronting them in Nagpur with most of the delegates ranged against them: the large mass of delegates were firmly for Gandhi and non-cooperation. And it was this view that finally prevailed. Almost all fell in line but Jinnah was left standing largely alone and high and dry in opposing non-cooperation.

The Nagpur Congress was a seismic shift in nationalist politics which saw the Gandhian era of the Congress commence. The Khilafat mood swept along many in the Muslim League. By the same token it was the end of Jinnah's high position in the Congress, and in Indian politics generally, which he had come to occupy as the architect of the League–Congress pact at the Lucknow Congress. For one who had been regularly cheered earlier, he now faced in Nagpur the ignominy of being shouted down by supporters of Gandhi and Khilafat, as he opposed both non-cooperation and according such prominence politically to what was essentially a religious issue concerning distant Turkey. Gandhi for non-cooperation and the Ali brothers for Khilafat were now the new icons and the alliance between them effectively put paid to all others.

Asaf in his autobiographical notes does not refer in any detail to the Jinnah part of the story of the Nagpur Congress, although he does mention there were serious warnings against non-cooperation. The omission is intriguing since the personal element in the drama of this political clash was intense and Asaf personally knew the protagonists on either side. Supporters of the Ali brothers openly scoffed at Jinnah. In one account 'Shaukat wooed each and every' leader to win them over to the Gandhi camp within the Congress 'except Jinnah whom he had begun to regard as a personal enemy'.[14] 'Boos, hisses and catcalls' amidst cries of 'shame, shame' and 'political imposter' were the responses Jinnah received in the public sessions, and a biographer concluded that this was 'the most bitterly humiliating experience of his public life'.[15]

What made it worse was that his young wife, Ruttie Jinnah, was present. She had been in Lucknow at the site of Jinnah's great triumph

– the Congress session of 1916 – and perhaps it was in that heady atmosphere that they had decided to marry. The marriage in April 1918, as soon as Ruttie was eighteen, had caused a storm – in public and also in Ruttie's Parsi family. Ruttie was young and fashionable and, with the twenty-four-year age difference with Jinnah, it was a pairing that always attracted attention and news. She also unwittingly became a target in the moves to cut Jinnah to size. In Nagpur that day, at the Congress pandal there were some objections to how Ruttie Jinnah was dressed, and she had no real choice but to leave. She was, in fact, dressed with perfect propriety, but those opposed to Jinnah made an issue of her sleeveless blouse – 'part of the hate campaign that the Jinnahs had been facing ever since they got to Nagpur'.[16] On their journey back to Bombay too the Jinnahs were heckled and hooted; it was admittedly a considerable humiliation for Jinnah with Ruttie there to witness it.

It is possible that Asaf's silence on this when he wrote his memoirs over two decades later was because it was still difficult to recount the demolition of someone he had admired and looked up to. Or perhaps the silence was also because Asaf had seen the merit in Jinnah's stand but moved in the opposite direction as he was conscious this was a time for choices to be made.

At Nagpur Asaf was elected a member of one of the Congress committees – certainly an advancement in his status. He was also elated to find *The Asaf Ali Trial* booklet on sale at the session, although he was conscious that 'I was among the small fry'. But he was clearly happy with his new position. The Nagpur session left a great impression and two decades later he recalled the

> heartwarming sight . . . [with] thousands of khaddar clad wearing what had come to be described as a Gandhi cap (it was really a Rampuri cap). It was a trek of the dispossessed to claim their own land. The flush of hope and the glow of pride lit up every brow. Oh! For a breath of that air once again before one dies. The scenes of communal fraternization were a sight for the Gods. Hindu and Muslim went out of the way to embrace, conciliate and befriend the other. If unity were the only

condition of Indian freedom India was free then – free of fear of the foreigner and free of mutual distrust.

The change from the first Congress session that Asaf had attended in Calcutta just three years before was striking: then most of the delegates and important leaders, with Tilak among the few exceptions, had been in European dress; the small changes that Asaf was part of in Delhi were part of a much larger macrocosm.

Once back in Delhi the realities of non-cooperation had also to be dealt with and their impact was felt in different ways. Beginning from early 1921, different planks of the non-cooperation platform were being implemented: return of government honours, boycott of government educational institutions and more dramatically of foreign cloth, which was often publicly burnt in large bonfires.

Asaf gave up his legal practice in line with the programme.[17] The practice had never been spectacular; he was still regarded as a relatively junior lawyer and was too preoccupied by politics to give the time and commitment it required; but it was significant and he commanded good fees. Without it, his debts mounted, as he had a household and establishment to support, and there was no option left but to sell his ancestral lands in Nagina. It was a difficult and painful decision, and many advised him against 'heroic self-immolation'! Despite this willingness to stretch his limits of safety, the decision finally taken would long haunt him. He was to later write: 'Of all the losses I have suffered in the course of my career, and there are not a few, I have never ceased to regret the necessity of selling out.' What it also meant was that he was cutting himself off from a future in the politics of a major province and would now have only Delhi in his horizon.

There were other problems – political issues bound to come up in any political protest based on street-level activism. Police reports adversely commented on Asaf's role in the boycott of elections held under the

1919 Montagu–Chelmsford package of devolution; in particular that he 'practiced general intimidation through his volunteers at polling stations and organized a partial social boycott of candidates'.[18] Another accusation that gathered even more traction was that supporters and non-cooperation activists had attempted to prevent the burial of a supporter of the government.[19] This attained visibility as Gandhi himself called such actions 'cruel and sinful'. Asaf consistently denied any such action and the charge was in fact untrue.[20] It was nevertheless a matter of time before he was arrested in December 1921 and sentenced to eighteen months in prison.

Asaf's arrest was part of a larger government crackdown on Congress activists and leaders. The Ali brothers too were arrested – for calling on Muslims to not serve in the army. The list of those jailed was a long one comprising the bulk of the Congress leadership. Asaf's statement issued after the arrest suggests that it was prepared in advance, with knowledge of the buttons to press to touch the sentiments of its target audience:

> I am too ill to hope that I shall survive the rigors of jail life but I am proud to say that I have deliberately sought it for the sake of my conscience and my country . . . Our bones may lie bleaching in obscure dungeons built of sand and maintained out of our nation's money, but over our unknown graves shall rise the noble edifice of our country's freedom.[21]

He was to spend a year and a half in jail in Delhi and then in Mianwali in Punjab. In jail he corresponded with Gandhi who would occasionally print extracts from Asaf's letters in his newspaper *New India*. In February 1922, when Asaf was in jail in Delhi he wrote: 'it is a matter of no surprise to me that my health has appreciably improved since my incarceration . . . the discomforts of prison life will be throughout our lives the most cherished of our memories, like the scars of warriors . . .'[22] The letter incidentally also asked Gandhi to 'give my love to my Akka, I mean Mrs Sarojini Naidu'.

Asaf's upbeat and inspired letters to Gandhi indicate his spirits were high and he saw the jail term, as others did, as a necessary baptism to cement their position in the Congress hierarchy and in the country's political life. He was probably aware his letters to Gandhi would be broadcast to even wider audiences, and the jail experience would have strengthened his confidence and boosted his self-esteem: he was now indubitably part of the large, significant enterprise that Indian nationalism had become.

Yet during this time the situation outside was far from satisfactory. The two planks which supported the Khilafat and non-cooperation movements – Hindu–Muslim unity and non-violence – were facing considerable resistance and in fact were under great threat. That Gandhi was not among those arrested was a tactical decision of the government waiting for the movement to take a turn that would leave the nationalist leaders no option but to call it off.

# 11

# Anticlimax

The communal situation had started deteriorating in mid-1921 deep in the south among the Mappilas. Here, religious fervour fanned by Khilafat slogans and the general mood of protest enabled by the Non-cooperation movement converged with local factors and injustices. A random incident of police firing on a crowd of Khilafat supporters and rumours that a mosque had been destroyed had an incendiary effect. Government offices were attacked and sacked. The attacks spread to killings of Hindu landlords and forced conversions, and soon made it indistinguishable from a communal conflagration. The Mappila uprising may have had agrarian roots – the protesting Mappilas were peasants – but it also had strong communal overtones with protesters being Muslim and their landlords Hindu. The Mappilas could be put down only by the end of the year, after the army had been called in to assist the police; 2,000 people had been killed. The Mappila riots had an all-India impact – perhaps because they went so clearly against the prevalent narrative of Hindu–Muslim unity and non-violence. Rationalizations have continued over the decades, pointing to the essentially agrarian nature of the issue. But the damage was done and it was considerable; it was a dampener for all those who had been energized and inspired by the Hindu–Muslim fraternization that the Khilafat movement had originally engendered.

Non-violent non-cooperation that was so confidently anticipated soon faced other setbacks. In February 1922 in Gorakhpur in the United Provinces, a Khilafat-cum-non-cooperation procession turned into a village mob and attacked a police station killing twenty-two policemen. This violence in the police station of Chauri Chaura led Gandhi to call off the Non-cooperation movement. He was arrested soon after: the tactical moment for which the government had been waiting had come.

The Khilafat impulse was also not to fare much better but the reason for this lay in Turkey. It faced a major crisis when Turks themselves questioned the dual – spiritual-cum-temporal – status of their sultan. In contrast to the nostalgia-tinged view of the Ottomans, so strong in India, as the last surviving Islamic power and of its sultan as the spiritual head of all Muslims, a new Turkish nationalism was looking to the future, not to the past. A new political force in the form of Mustafa Kemal abolished the caliphate in March 1924. To Mustafa Kemal, the caliph was an anachronism in a modern Turkish state. That the caliph would be finally overthrown not by external imperialists but by Turks themselves meant that the entire basis for the Khilafat movement in India was now in question. What was once the platform to construct Hindu–Muslim unity was now a discredited lost cause.[1] The supporters of the caliph in India and those prominent in the Khilafat agitation were left bewildered, angry and helpless. While some led by the Ali brothers and others remained faithful to the idea, its public credibility had gone.

In the anticlimax of the collapse of the Khilafat and Non-cooperation movements, communal violence intensified and spread. One set of figures illustrates the impact of this breakdown in communal relations. In one count there were sixteen communal riots between 1900 and 1922; between 1923 to 1926 there were seventy-two.[2] Why this should have happened is difficult to answer. Each communal incident had its own peculiar local cause and conflicting grievances underwriting it. In a letter to Gandhi, Asaf referred to a situation in which press reports made 'every street brawl' into a communal fight and where 'every worthless delinquent who bears a Hindu or a Muslim name is held up as a type of civilization which each name is supposed to represent'.[3] Yet, in the aggregate, clearly there were general, and not merely local, factors at work. Political mobilization brought in its wake communal rancour, especially when religious figures on both sides had been agents of such mobilization. As the larger envelope of non-cooperation and Khilafat got tattered and eroded, the need grew to mobilize support for elections to the provincial assemblies and other bodies in which greater elected representation was now possible. This fanned more primordial instincts. Amongst Hindus, movements of shuddhi – in effect reconversion to Hinduism – received a fillip post the Mappila riots and was matched by the tabligh, which was tantamount to proselytizing, amongst Muslims. Both sides also emphasized tanzeem and sangathan, which essentially meant strengthening of religious identity. The environs of Delhi – in the Punjab and the United Provinces – were to a great extent the focus of these activities.

Asaf was released from jail in June 1923 and would have encountered a sad reality far from the euphoria of the Delhi Khilafat Conference or the Nagpur Congress. The leaders of Khilafat and the Congress appeared powerless to control the deteriorating communal situation; there was also a revival of the older debate within the Congress on the efficacy of non-cooperation. Many felt that not contesting elections for positions in bodies emerging from the devolution of power announced by the government was self-defeating.

Provincial assemblies or councils and the Central Legislative Assembly had seats that were open to election and 'Council Entry' seemed to some to be an essential political adjunct to protest and agitation. The devolution at the provincial level meant ministerial berths would also be available. Elections to seats in municipal councils and boards were also similarly sought after and were seen as useful to cementing local strength and position. Those who thought so were the 'Swarajists' and they were to band themselves into the 'Congress Swaraj Party', in effect a separate party within the umbrella of the Congress. Those committed to non-cooperation opposed any such moves. The differences between the two camps often became acrimonious even though there was much the two sides agreed on.

Asaf himself had a small part in this debate. His thinking converged with the Swarajists led by C.R. Das, Madan Mohan Malaviya and Motilal Nehru. He explained his reasoning in a letter to Gandhi in February 1924:

> bitter experience, careful thought and perhaps also a certain degree of impatience to reach a more immediate objective, have led me to the Swarajist camp – not to seek responsive cooperation but to evoke intensive noncooperation. I have patiently heard both sides and have regretfully noted much extravagance in both types of zealots.

Just three years earlier he had regretted the absence of leaders in Delhi who understood how to lead agitations. The downside of political mobilization and mass politics was that there were so many fault lines in the existing milieu, and any of them could turn incendiary. Electoral politics and pressurizing the colonial state through orderly means appeared to him to be more sensible. For Asaf now 'for a true non cooperator . . . Swarajism is a natural development' as it would enable further pressure to be put on the government.

Asaf's letter to Gandhi also expressed the anguish many felt at the breaking down of Hindu–Muslim unity:

> The virulent cancer of communal distrust has found a favourable region round about Delhi. Those who are fighting it know what it is to combat a disease, which is neither fatal nor incurable, but which is hourly sapping the vitals of the nation. Forgive my saying so, but the ill-disguised insincerity of most of our leaders, both Hindus and Muslims, is the sole cause of its continuance.

Asaf was gradually discovering first-hand the debilitating impact of communal polarization in other ways. The summer of 1924 saw a wide swathe of north India consumed by communal violence. In July that year in Delhi, there was major rioting and all the principal leaders of the non-cooperation and Khilafat movements – Mohammad Ali, Hakim Ajmal Khan, Swami Shraddhanand, Dr Ansari and others – appeared helpless to control things on the ground. A nonplussed Mohammad Ali wrote to

Gandhi on 12 July 1924: 'We the Congress have decided to admit defeat and leave the maintenance of peace to the guns of the police.'[4] This sense of incomprehension and frustration was widespread. Sometime later, on 15 July 1926, Jawaharlal Nehru wrote in frustration to Syed Mahmud in response to the latter's letter detailing efforts to restore amity in Bihar: 'I am more and more inclined to think that the only remedy is to scotch our so-called religion and secularize our intelligentsia at least. How long it will take I cannot say but religion in India will kill that country and its people if it is not subdued.'[5]

There were numerous efforts to restore some semblance of the earlier spirit of togetherness between the two communities. Gandhi undertook a twenty-one day fast in September 1924 after massive rioting and an orgy of violence engulfed Kohat in the North West Frontier Province (NWFP). The fast was undertaken in Delhi in Mohammad Ali's house. Political efforts made included the holding of a 'Unity Conference' but a historian's assessment of these events is that 'after all the ballyhoo things ran their course much as they had before'.[6] Asaf was active in all these events supporting the efforts of his seniors such as Ajmal Khan and Ansari. In all likelihood he was absorbing, consciously or otherwise at this time, the sense that Hindu–Muslim relations had a centrality that could not be underestimated. If this was a basic fact most would readily concede in principle, perhaps as a Delhi Muslim he was more acutely conscious of the need for it to be more than a principle and an actual plank of any political initiative.

Other efforts at communal unity included appointing Sarojini Naidu to the post of president of the 1925 Congress session held in Kanpur, a decision for which Gandhi was principally responsible. Possibly, given the many divisions within – including between those wanting to participate in elections and seek office and those against – she would have been a relatively non-controversial figure and one who could work with both sides. She would be the first Indian woman to hold that post and she also stood out for her unwavering commitment to Hindu–Muslim unity. Her speech in Kanpur rose to the occasion: 'I who have dedicated my life to the dream of Hindu Muslim unity cannot contemplate without tears of blood the dissensions and divisions between us that rend the very fabric of my hope.' They were, she said, in an atmosphere 'tense and dark and bitter, with unreasoning communal jealousy, suspicion, fear, distrust and hatred'.[7] Sarojini had spoken extempore and hers was a voice of transparent sincerity.

Her admirers and friends found much to inspire them in this address and many were moved to tears. But others were less impressed; eloquence had its limits, particularly in a situation everyone agreed was grim. An exasperated Motilal Nehru had asked, 'But what did she say?'[8] The *Times of India* found her remarks the perfect target for its sarcasm, noting that in a land of many famines there was never a famine of words: 'The prodigal wealth, the exuberant extravagance of Mrs Sarojini Naidu for example if spread would serve for a dozen humbler banquets.'[9]

Syed Mahmud in Bihar – in his native Chhapra and in Patna – also faced a similar conundrum as the downturn in Hindu–Muslim relations came as an anticlimax to the heady days of Khilafat and non-cooperation. He had been active in both and Syed's ascendancy through the hierarchy of both organizations was marked. Clearly his nationalist credentials, long background in the Congress, activism in Aligarh and for the Home Rule League, and European doctorate all played a role. He was also married to a niece of Mazhar ul Haq, a senior figure from Bihar in the Congress and Muslim League, which no doubt also helped. In his personal life he was conservative and a deeply devout Muslim; even in jail and in very bad health he would fast each Ramzan.

By 1921 he was general secretary of the Central Khilafat Committee. Active also in the Non-cooperation movement in response to Gandhi's call, he discontinued his legal practice in Patna and, following what became a rite of passage for many of a new generation drawn into the freedom movement, was jailed. He quickly rose up the Congress hierarchy in Bihar and his position in 1923 as joint general secretary of the Congress, along with Jawaharlal Nehru, suggested an ascendant political career.

*Syed Mahmud (left) and Jawaharlal Nehru, possibly in the early 1920s*

A close friendship with Nehru had also developed. They had been contemporaries at Cambridge in 1909 but being together in a political struggle meant a new bond and also a new quality to their relationship. From quite early on, a hierarchical pattern also seems to have crystallized, with Syed Mahmud, although slightly older, assuming a position of deference. We find him writing to Nehru on 30 November 1923: 'Sri Krishna and the Hindu's ideal of life always appealed to me but I never had the fortune of meeting a Hindu before I met you – who had appealed to me in actual life. Now I try to see and realize that idea through you.'[10]

He also displayed an almost excessive sentimentality and emotion, something that had been evident in his earlier friendship and infatuation with Sarojini. To the restrained and reserved Nehru this was frequently irritating: 'May I say a thing to you which I have wanted to say for some little time? Why are you so emotional or why do you exhibit your emotion so much? Surely emotion should not be cheapened, it is too valuable a commodity.'[11] Everything being pitched in too high a key was seen as 'soppiness' by Nehru who grew up in the bracing environment of a British public school. Nehru was to write on these lines more than once: 'I am afraid you have a bad habit of exciting yourself. Excitement and agitation of mind are not helpful in solving a difficulty.'[12] Such putdowns, gentle and otherwise, do not appear to have deterred Syed Mahmud: 'the only present that I can offer for your thirty fifth birthday is my life long devotion and fidelity to you and the Nehrus'; and 'I am painfully conscious of the worthlessness of my devotion but then, my boy, just like a dog I have nothing else or better in my possession to give my master – a thought which sometimes makes me bitter and sad.'[13]

The downturn in communal relations after the collapse of the Khilafat and Non-cooperation movements saw him drawn to the conclusion – which became in time a kind of political ideology – that his community would be secure only by maintaining a strong presence within the Congress. This belief tied him even closer to the Nehrus, both Motilal and Jawaharlal. The communal cauldron of the mid-1920s would also often see him isolated within his own community. At the naming ceremony for his newborn son, he caused, he wrote to Nehru, 'a little flutter amongst the small Muslim group present here this morning, by giving him your name'. There was shock at this: 'I could easily read from their faces what was passing in their minds . . . religion was in danger.' He went on to say, 'My children are extremely pleased to see their little brother is given your name. My wife is pleased too; but she seems to be little afraid of public opinion.'[14]

From the mid-1920s Syed was frequently in Allahabad on Congress work and here his friendship with Jawaharlal acquired an additional and most unusual feature. He had started teaching Kamala Nehru, Jawaharlal's wife, Urdu and thereafter, during her stay in Europe for medical treatment, they corresponded for some years; possibly the aim was also to improve Kamala's Urdu and English writing abilities. Some of her letters to Syed Mahmud have survived and these bring out Kamala Nehru's heartbreaking sense of inadequacy vis-à-vis the Nehru family, her feeling that she lacked education and sophistication:

> I wish I was like Sita and other great women . . . Now if you try to be like Sita people will make fun and laugh at you . . . No one told me that I am not educated but my hurt told me and it tells me nearly every day that I am not educated. I do not know the world so I am quite in darkness.[15]

On an earlier occasion: 'It really breaks my heart to think I have not sufficient education . . . I am no use in the world [and] am making it heavier every day by doing nothing only eating and sleeping.'[16]

Kamala Nehru invariably addressed Syed Mahmud as Doctor Sahib and signed off as 'Your Sister'. In the letters there is alongside a great deal more about the lot of women and in particular she consistently urges Syed Mahmud to pay more attention to his wife and make arrangements for educating his daughters. 'Where are the girls now and what they are doing? For God's sake do not waste time. You must do something for them as soon as possible.' And about his wife: 'Please teach her English because one cannot do anything in this world without knowing some foreign languages.'[17] And there is also on occasion a hint of admonition – quite likely as a response to Syed Mahmud commenting on his wife's shortcomings, possibly that she was too timid: 'Is it fair to blame us when we are frightened of every little thing. I shall always blame men for our cowardice. If you want my sister to become brave and help you in your needful hour you must try to talk to her quietly about your difficulties.'[18] On another occasion:

> I am not at all convinced that purdah has the virtues you suggest . . . I do not suggest that women should come out of purdah at once. If you accept my suggestion they should come out of their house gradually so that they become accustomed to moving about and seeing men. My sister is intelligent. She will act as I say if you allow her to.[19]

But Syed Mahmud's innate conservatism ran deep, perhaps this was especially so where his family was concerned, and we find Kamala remonstrating: 'From your inactivity in the matter I have started feeling that you do not desire to educate your daughters . . . Perhaps you think female education is hardly worth anything because they are to remain in purdah.'[20] Clearly Syed Mahmud's attitude to his wife and daughters was a subject of discussion in the Nehru household. On one occasion Kamala informed her husband of a booklet in Urdu on the appropriate training of women that Syed Mahmud had sent her. Evidently this booklet was

*A photograph of Kamala Nehru holding a garland, possibly taken in the early 1930s*

a conservative Muslim tutorial on the place of women in society and the result was an irate letter from Nehru: 'it is a little surprising that you should patronize such absolute trash . . . I was amazed that any man should be foolish enough to write such rot.'[21] Purdah was an issue that others too raised often with Mahmud but without much effect. We have the Mahatma writing a decade later, on 11 April 1938: 'tell Begum Mahmud with my love that she has no right to invite me till she has given up the purdah. Has not the Prophet said that the real purdah lies in the woman's chastity.'[22]

Syed Mahmud's growing distance from many Muslims, even as he became more proximate to the Congress and in particular to the Nehrus, was noticed by others in the Congress hierarchy. Rajendra Prasad, a major figure in the Congress in Bihar, was to comment in a letter to Motilal Nehru on 11 April 1926:

> He is entirely with us and prepared to help us. But . . . for about two years he has not been in the good books of our Musalman friends who have been trying by all means to run him down. His influence among his co-religionists has been considerably reduced . . . While I love him and regard [*sic*] his as one of the most fair-minded and straight Mussalmans I cannot conceal from you that for those very qualities he is not liked by many of them.[23]

Asaf faced the consequences of this downturn in communal relations in a more personal way. He was the official Swarajist candidate in the November 1926 elections to the Central Legislative Assembly from Delhi in a triangular contest. Election to the Central Assembly would have moved Asaf to a higher notch of politics and he was therefore deeply invested in the idea.

But underpinning this election was, even by then, a story of bitter factionalism within the Congress and within the Swarajist camp itself. The latter was a divided house with one group in favour of contesting elections to the legislatures and another going even further and accepting ministerial office in the provincial legislatures – something Congressmen had so far opposed. Amongst the Swarajists Motilal Nehru led the opposition to the idea and his old rival Madan Mohan Malaviya was in favour. The latter along with Lala Lajpat Rai founded the Independent Congress Party, putting its own candidates in opposition to the Swarajists. All of them were Congressmen but the rivalry ran deep. The Independent Congress Party was also close to the Hindu Mahasabha, founded by Malaviya in 1915.

There was a Hindu–Muslim dimension to the rivalry as well and Asaf was at the centre of this. The other two candidates were both Hindus, one from the Independent Congress Party. In many ways this was a prestige contest because Delhi was, because of being the capital, a joint or general seat – not a reserved Muslim seat. Some newspaper reports described it as especially important because it was the only joint electorate seat in the entire Central Legislature. By fielding Asaf, a Muslim candidate in a constituency with a predominantly Hindu electorate, the Congress Swarajists were also making a symbolic point; although Asaf, because of his background, was anyway possibly the strongest candidate it could have put up, barring Hakim Ajmal Khan and Dr Ansari who were unwilling to enter this fray. The result was a disappointment: Asaf was defeated by a reasonably high margin by the Independent Congress Party–Hindu Mahasabha candidate. Behind the statistics of the loss is the story of a deeply polarized electorate, a highly communalized situation in Delhi, and serious infighting within the nationalist and Congress line-up that further cemented the communal division.

One close observer had commented in the run-up to the election in a letter to Congress President Sarojini Naidu: 'The Muslim and Hindu votes are in the ratio of one to two . . . the result is a foregone conclusion: the Muslim candidate loses simply because he is a Muslim.'[24] For his friends and supporters his defeat was therefore 'a matter of very great regret, if not a positive shame, that the Hindus of Delhi do not realize the importance and significance of the Delhi elections and swayed by communal currents are determined upon putting up Hindu candidates on communal tickets'.[25] Asaf was later asked the reasons for his defeat and his response was published by the *Bombay Chronicle*: 'Since the sanguine events of 1919 . . . the pendulum of Delhi's mentality has swung back to the extreme point.' Delhi, he noted was, now 'a storm centre of *Sanghathan*, *Shuddhi*, *Tanzeem* and *Tablighi* movements' which had vocal exponents in the city. He blamed Lala Lajpat Rai and Pandit Madan Mohan Malaviya for his defeat, believing they took 'fullest advantage of the worst features of communal tension in Delhi'. Asaf assessed that almost all Muslims in the electorate voted for him but very few Hindus. He remarked, 'The Musalmans may have been actuated by communal motives as well; but not a word was said or written appealing to them on my behalf which had the faintest tinge of communalism.'[26]

Asaf's campaign had received a fair amount of support from the Congress leadership. Abul Kalam Azad and Sarojini addressed meetings in his support and the latter would have tried to make sure the Congress machinery worked effectively for her friend. Special attention was paid by the most important Swarajist leader at the time, Motilal Nehru, who had selected Asaf Ali as the party candidate. As the Delhi result was announced, Nehru was campaigning in the United Provinces and his anger and bitterness at the outcome was evident. It was clear to him that what was at play were also leadership rivalries as well as religious prejudices, and he pointed to the 'wrong that Malviyaji and Lalaji had done by opposing the [Swarajist] Congress candidate in Delhi'. The Swarajist Congress had, he said, deliberately chosen a Muslim 'as the best reply to those who were saying that under the joint electorates Mohammadans had no chance'; he had told Malaviya and Rai that they could suggest any Muslim of their choice and he would have Asaf's candidature withdrawn. But what took place instead was 'a bitter communal campaign to defeat the [Swarajist] Congress candidate', and therefore 'nationalism and patriotism was being sacrificed'. Elsewhere Nehru was to say in another public meeting: 'Lalaji opined that Swaraj was impossible unless there was joint electorate, but he destroyed that very principle by his conduct at Delhi [where he] appealed to communal passions and defeated Asaf Ali. With what face therefore can he recommend joint electorates.'[27]

Asaf's personal bitterness and disappointment were obvious but there is also the suggestion of a more fundamental rethinking. His defeat meant that 'even I, a confirmed believer in the ultimate desirability of joint electorates' could not 'close [my] eyes' on its effect on the principle of joint electorates. He would not have 'the courage to advocate joint electorates for some time to come' and 'the Musalmans of Delhi would be fully justified in demanding an equitable adjustment of their rights'.[28]

Apart from holding Lajpat Rai and Malaviya responsible for lending their names to the campaign against him, Asaf also blamed Swami

Shraddhanand. The swami's supporters denied this but Asaf's charge did have a wide currency.[29] In April 1919 Swami Shraddhanand had epitomized the spirit of Hindu–Muslim unity and his address at the Jama Masjid was frequently invoked by nationalists of different hues as epitomizing the very spirit of the Indian freedom struggle. However, by late 1926 things had moved full circle and on 23 December of that year, shortly after the elections, he was murdered by a Muslim fanatic.

The polarization of the intervening period had seen the swami critical of Muslim actions and of Islam. In one account: 'From the end of 1923 to early 1925 the swami produced a stream of articles, pamphlets and books all concentrating on different aspects of a broad Muslim conspiracy that threatened the very existence of Hinduism.'[30] Much of this was perhaps also in response to critical attacks by Muslims on Hinduism and the Arya Samaj, or personal attacks on him.

Perhaps even more than these polemical exchanges, one single incident had brought the swami into the centre of a communal cauldron that was at its boiling point. In March 1926 he had performed a shuddhi, converting a Muslim woman to Hinduism. She had, unknown to her husband and against his will, made her way to Delhi from Karachi with her three minor children, approached Shraddhanand and sought conversion. The husband found her some five months later and instituted a case against the swami and his son and son-in-law of a conspiracy to abduct his wife and children. The case was decided by December 1926 and it acquitted Shraddhanand and his family members. It did, however, succeed in further blighting the atmosphere and sharpening the Hindu–Muslim divide in the city. The court's verdict came after the election but the entire run-up to the polling occurred in the midst of this bitter controversy and the intense communal tensions it generated.

In that particular situation it is hardly surprising that Asaf lost. But even the election result was a side show to what happened some weeks later when the swami was assassinated at his home by a Muslim charged up by a ferment of indignant animosity over the shuddhi, which many Muslim newspapers had strongly condemned.

The impact of the swami's murder was felt nationwide but with particular intensity in Delhi. For those trying to stay away from both sides of the divide, as Asaf was, the going was particularly hard. A public meeting was held on the afternoon of 26 December 1926, three days after the murder, in the Queen's Gardens (now Azad Park, behind the Town Hall in Chandni Chowk). It was presided over by 'Narain Swami, President of the All-India Aryan League' and Lala Lajpat Rai was one of the main speakers. Asaf was also one of those invited to speak. Quite possibly, the effort was to calm tempers and reassert the spirit of Hindu–Muslim unity that had characterized public life and the nationalist agitation in Delhi until just a few years ago; if so, they failed. As Asaf spoke, a press report noted, he was 'frequently interrupted'.[31]

A press release issued by Asaf and published by the *Times of India* gave more details. Asaf announced in it his resignation from the Congress:

> I resign my membership of the Congress to draw attention to the gravity of the enormous progress of Hindu Muslim tension in north India, the speeches delivered yesterday at the monster meeting addressed by Lala Lajpat Rai, Mr Jayakar, Professor Ramdeo and others being symptomatic thereof. The shocking outrage perpetuated by an unhinged assassin, deplored and condemned by Muslims of all shades of opinion, was made the occasion for laying it at the door of a deep laid Muslim conspiracy, which is utterly unfounded, and for appealing to Hindu youths for laying down their lives for the communal cause, and finally Mr Ramdeo offensively asserted that the Vedic Dharma would vanquish all other religions and its flag would fly from every mosque.

But it was more than the speeches that Asaf found so reprehensible:

> Five Muslim wayfarers including an old man were brutally assaulted soon after the outrage, the old man since died and not a word of condemnation or regret over the wanton assault on unoffending wayfarers was uttered by any. Until the Congress concentrates on the effectual settlement of Hindu Muslim relations to the exclusion of all other questions it has no claim on my allegiance.[32]

Highlighting the resignation of a Muslim from the Congress and also pointing to the deep-rooted animosities between the two communities were part of the editorial approach of the *Times of India*, close as it was to the official establishment. This was nevertheless a sad end to the first phase of Asaf's interface with nationalist politics and mass agitation. The resignation, whether an emotional reaction or a calculated political ploy, had little impact. But the communal divide had taken a toll on Asaf personally. He had lost the election but was also gripped by a sense of being rudderless while navigating the morass of communalism versus nationalism. It was another dramatic development that would provide a new direction: it would cement Asaf to a course of trying to bridge the communal divide. It also meant a firmer conviction that the Congress was the best platform to achieve this. Another phase of Asaf's life was now beginning.

# 12

# A Change in Status

In February 1928 Sarojini wrote to Syud Hossain after a long gap about soon seeing him face to face again 'after all these years'.[1] Her reference to this long gap – 'these long-crowded years' – requires some explanation for much had in fact happened to this member of the original London trio. Syud had moved in January 1919 from Bombay to Allahabad. The move, coinciding with the nationalist upsurge through 1919, was to edit a new venture of Motilal Nehru's, the *Independent.* It was meant to be a nationalist platform that would articulate the particular perspectives and views of the senior Nehru. Implicit in the decision to set up the paper was to provide a rival voice to the moderate and more conservative *Leader*, founded by Madan Mohan Malaviya a decade or so earlier and also published from Allahabad. Their rivalry was obvious in the mid-1920s, but clearly it ran even deeper.

Syud's fiery writings in the *Bombay Chronicle* appeared to be what the *Independent* needed. Horniman recommended him for the post and also agreed to release him for some time. Perhaps the original intention was that the move would be temporary and would see the *Independent* through its establishment phase.[2] For Asaf, Syud's move to Allahabad and editorship of the *Independent* meant that he 'had the columns of a second daily, besides the *Bombay Chronicle*, at my disposal as their special correspondent and columnist. I also wrote now and then for other dailies and I sometimes filled as many as four to five columns by Press telegrams or by mail.'[3]

Syud's tenure in Allahabad turned out to be most eventful for entirely unexpected reasons.[4] He arrived there in January 1919 and stayed at the Nehru family home, Anand Bhavan, for want of suitable accommodation elsewhere. Quite soon, or at least within a few months, the thirty-one-year-old Syud and the nineteen-year-old Sarup Kumari, Motilal Nehru's oldest daughter and Jawaharlal's younger sister, were in love or at least they both thought so. By the last quarter of the year – certainly by December 1919 – an elopement, even a secret (sometimes described as 'informal') marriage followed.[5] A garbled version of events had possibly reached Asaf in Delhi, for he wrote anxiously to his old friend on 19 February (the letter does not mention the year, which is probably 1920), 'I am dying to have a word from you on a subject which is feeding "gossip" here, in Aligarh & in Bombay.' This was that 'Syud is engaged to marry Miss Naidu' – obviously Motilal Nehru's and Sarojini Naidu's daughters were being mixed up. Asaf exclaimed, 'Never was I more suddenly taken by surprise.'

Asaf would have soon learnt the truth for this could obviously not be kept secret. The wrath of the establishment descended squarely on the hapless young couple. Motilal and Gandhi worked together to put the clock back. Sarup was packed off to the Sabarmati Ashram near Ahmedabad where she was to spend some months undergoing what she, at least, saw as a very austere penance. Clearly both the senior Nehru and Gandhi were outraged at the idea of a Hindu–Muslim liaison and annoyed that Sarup had behaved so thoughtlessly. Some months later, in May 1921, she was married to Ranjit Pandit and in time would become better known as Vijaya Lakshmi Pandit. Syud, in turn, already scheduled to accompany a Khilafat delegation to London in February 1920 was encouraged, perhaps even helped, to prolong his stay in Europe and thereafter move to the United States to establish himself there as a kind of spokesperson for the Indian National Congress. He would spend the next quarter-century there. The matter was satisfactorily 'settled' as far as the Nehru family was concerned. The gossip and the scandal never fully died out but it was managed and contained.

Sarojini was present at the Sarup–Ranjit Pandit marriage in Allahabad, 'a very pretty and simple affair'.[6] She wrote to her daughter that the bride was 'in a coarse handspun sari presented by Gandhi man [*sic*] so all of us wore our plainest clothes to match'; Sarup looked 'a picture of happiness'. Sarojini also commented, 'Poor Syud. My heart ached for him all the time.' But she noted 'how thankful I was that it had all ended like this because Sarup did not really care and Syud never really cared either'. We can only guess at Sarojini's reasons for saying this. She possibly saw the Syud–Sarup entanglement as no more than a juvenile episode: she had grown-up children of her own after all and was accustomed to their sudden infatuations. She may have thought that this had acquired a larger-than-life character because one party was the daughter of Motilal Nehru and because of the Hindu–Muslim dimension. In any event she would have seen the impossibility of it having any future given the forces arraigned on the other side – in particular Motilal Nehru and M.K. Gandhi. Deeply committed to Hindu–Muslim unity herself, perhaps she also saw, with even greater clarity, the importance of being circumspect in forging the most personal of relationships across what was undoubtedly a divide.

Syud would therefore henceforth be located in the United States The startling elopement/marriage episode certainly interrupted the Syud–Asaf relationship. At the very least the letters exchanged frequently between Bombay and Delhi, and then Allahabad and Delhi, stopped altogether, or at least were not preserved, and there is no record of them meeting after this episode. There seems to have been a similar break between Syud and Sarojini: if their correspondence continued, no trace of it remains until she wrote in February 1928. In any case their discreet meetings in the Taj in Bombay were a thing of the past.

It is fair to assume that in both sets of cases, Asaf–Syud and Sarojini–Syud, with distance and time, the older relationships would have changed and the converging paths of youth were now more distant from each other even if they had not diverged. Asaf had been exposed to the rough and tumble of politics and the realities of Hindu–Muslim polarization while Sarojini's own profile and public responsibilities had multiplied. She was after all now a past president of the Congress. She was also being sent on an important journey: many in the Congress felt that an outreach to the United States was essential to explain the viewpoint of Indian nationalists and correct misperceptions that the British authorities created about them amongst American intellectuals and others. Sarojini was believed to be best suited to this mission. The latest letter to Syud was in fact related to her forthcoming visit to the United States in 1928 and more would follow with regard to the arrangements for that visit; while they would frequently meet during her stay in the United States, perhaps after the visit the links became fainter.

---

With his departure for the United States Syud largely passes out of this story and will reappear only towards its end. For the next quarter-century or so he lived in the United States, returning only in March 1946. Barring a brief visit in 1937 he was therefore physically distant from his older friendships, in particular with Asaf and Sarojini, as we have noted. It was inevitable that Syud would be largely divorced in any direct sense from the pace of developments in India. New York, Los Angeles and Washington were the cities he seemed to have spent the bulk of his time in. Living the life of an exile or near exile in the United States at the time was a different experience from what his counterparts in England or even in Europe may have faced. India was to most Americans a distant place, remote not just geographically but also from their everyday priorities and their politics. Seeing India through British eyes was inevitable for most Americans. A small and slowly growing diaspora would gradually make its presence felt but, in the 1920s and 1930s, Indians were very much an exotic species in the US.

In his initial years in the US, Syud devoted himself to becoming a figure in the lecture circuit as an interpreter of India, of Islam, of the Orient but most all as a critic of British rule and as a protagonist of Indian nationalism. In a recent biography Syud is described as having had some success: 'refreshingly different from the American stereotype of an Indian, Syud had obviously impressed his audience and the press.' Possibly he saw himself as 'an unofficial Ambassador of Gandhi'[7] and charged with the responsibility of educating public opinion about India and its quest for freedom from British rule. Alongside the lecture circuit there was also some journalism and efforts to establish a news magazine that would put forth the nationalist perspective for American readers.

This could not have been an easy life. The remuneration from lectures was not huge and also showed a natural tendency to plateau and then fall once the novelty wore off. So it appears that in the mid-1920s Syud was thinking of returning to India but possibly found that the way back was not easy. Why this should be so is not clear but that he was on a British government blacklist was a contributory factor. His charm and his ability as a public speaker were qualities that worried British intelligence which monitored his early success in the lecture circuit.

As the US sank into the Depression things became more difficult. Lecture invitations shrank further and that income could no longer sustain him and his somewhat extravagant lifestyle. Even during his London years Syud had frequently entreated friends to bail him out financially and letters to Syed Mahmud at the time contained passionate appeals to rescue him from humiliation and penury. A foreword written by Asaf, his oldest friend along with Sarojini, to a book on Syud after he died, referred to him as someone who 'squandered his personal life as a reckless spendthrift'.[8] Syud was often to rely on the generosity of friends in the US too. An otherwise sympathetic modern biographer has noted that at this time 'Insinuations of Syud's fondness for his drink, murmurs of financial impropriety, and whispers of flings would invite severe opprobrium, and blot what could otherwise have been a sterling reputation'.[9] A university appointment in Los Angeles helped somewhat and he spent eight years in that city. The US entry into World War II and the Japanese thrust into South East Asia revived public interest in external affairs and on Asia, and Syud's presence in the lecture circuit also witnessed an uptick before he returned to India in 1946.

But on the whole Syud's life in the US has a somewhat unfulfilled quality to it, as if fate and circumstance had joined to shrink the stage he would occupy. An émigré existence when the world was turning upside down in India and in which his closest friends were playing big and small roles, their lives and personalities matured and shaped by imprisonment and political struggle, casts a comparatively sad shadow on his life.

Sarojini's February 1928 letter to Syud had also contained news on what was happening in India, about which she painted a somewhat sombre picture: 'the "inner" workings of the nation are tragically bad. Alas! There is no cohesion, no concentration, no sustained consciousness of the gravity of the issues to be faced.' What weighed with her were the different sectional divides: 'The Hindu Muslim gulf is wider and deeper than ever, the Brahman non Brahman quarrels more acute and disastrous than before.' To a dejected Sarojini the situation looked bleak also because 'There is no single leader today big enough to coordinate all the disregulated forces in the country. Mahatmaji has, whether deliberately and cruelly, through exhaustion and loss of vision, withdrawn into a sort of nun's cloister.'

The picture she drew was not inaccurate nor exaggerated, given the deep conflicts even within the Congress (such as those reflected during Asaf's failed election bid), the overall communal division reflected in the differences between the Muslim League and the Congress, and the growing stridency of bodies such as the Hindu Mahasabha which had many sympathizers within the Congress. But for Sarojini, being Sarojini, the personal was always significant and the letter is also full of news about common friends. There is inevitably a reference to Asaf who she wrote 'has become somewhat middle aged!' She explained, 'He has lost so much of that old irrepressible charm.' But more to the point, 'he has fallen in love with a young Bengalee girl of 18 whom he met for 2 days somewhere and he is very keen to marry her. But I fear and I have told him so. It will not be a success.'

By 'young Bengalee girl' Sarojini meant a young Hindu girl. Her disapproval is clear enough. We do not know whether she had already met the young woman concerned; it is unlikely. The disapproval is likely to have sprung from her knowledge of the Syud–Sarup Kumari experience and a sense of what a Hindu–Muslim marriage would mean at the time. Perhaps she was also apprehensive about the age difference and feared things would go awry once the initial euphoria of requited love faded. She had seen from even closer quarters the whirlwind M.A. Jinnah–Ruttie Petit courtship and marriage, with its age difference of twenty-four years, and then the consequences of social isolation and basic incompatibility as the relationship faded.

Sarojini was a friend of Jinnah but was also to become a pillar of emotional support to the young Ruttie. 'So Jinnah has at last plucked the blue flower of his desire,' she had written to Syed Mahmud on 28 April 1918 as news of that marriage became public. She had tried, unsuccessfully, to dissuade Ruttie, notwithstanding her great admiration for Jinnah. 'I think though the child has made far greater sacrifices than she yet realizes,' but she went on to say, 'Jinnah is worth it all – he loves her.' Possibly Sarojini had hoped, despite all her qualms, that the marriage would work out and would soften and even humanize Jinnah. But that did not happen. By the time Sarojini was sailing for the United States, about a decade later, the marriage was in tatters, in spite of the birth of a child; Ruttie died while Sarojini was in the United States.[10] So Sarojini's doubts about Asaf at forty and a 'young Bengalee girl of 18' are understandable. Moreover 1928 was a far worse time for a Hindu–Muslim marriage than 1918 had been for a Parsi–Muslim match, given the intensified communal friction in the country.

In September 1928 in Nainital, Asaf Ali, then nearing forty, married Aruna Gangulee, then still a teenager. Apart from the obvious religious divide and the considerable difference in age, what was unusual was that this was not a union following a sudden infatuation or dramatic falling in love but was seemingly carefully thought through by both parties.

We know only the bare bones of this story. An old acquaintance, Maya Roy, whom Asaf had first met as a student in London, invited him to

Allahabad in January 1928 to meet Aruna who was visiting and staying with her sister Purnima Banerjee. Maya Roy was also a house guest at the Banerjee house. Aruna had studied in Nainital, and on completion of school, was keen to study English literature in England. Her parents were insisting on an arranged marriage and Maya Roy, taking Aruna's side, suggested Asaf as a possible groom to Aruna. After all, he was someone interested in literature and politics, and was a prominent barrister. What other factors were behind this most extraordinary and unconventional suggestion are lost now, but the significant point is that both, after meeting, seemed open to the idea. Aruna's father opposed the match, but he died in March 1928, and despite familial opposition they were married in September 1928.

Aruna's family background was unusual. Her mother, Ambalika, was the daughter of Trailokyanath Sen, described as being famous in Brahmo circles in Bengal for his devotional songs. Aruna's father, Upendranath Gangulee, had lived as a young man in the US and England and discarding the general preference for administrative, academic or other white-collar jobs, joined the hotel and restaurant business. He thereafter went on to manage in Kalka a unit of the then famous Kellner chain of railway restaurants and refreshment rooms. Kalka was an important stopping point en route to the summer capital Simla and Kellner being a well-established chain suggests that Upendranath was doing well in this chosen line of work. He was to go on to establish his own restaurant in Nainital, another favoured hill station for the English in India, and Nainital would become the Gangulee home town.

One of his brothers, Nagendranath Gangulee, had a PhD from an American university and achieved some distinction as an agronomist and agricultural scientist as a professor at Calcutta University. When a Royal Commission on Indian Agriculture was established in 1926, he was included as a member, a considerable distinction at the time. Nagendranath married into the Tagore family, to a daughter of Rabindranath Tagore in 1907, and it was Rabindranath who had financed his and his brother's study in the US. The marriage itself did not last beyond the 1920s and Nagendranath was to be the cause of much grief to Rabindranath. More relevant to Aruna's and Asaf's story is that Nagendranath was to get married again – to Maya Roy. It was this connection that led Asaf to visit Allahabad in early January 1928. Another of Upendranath's brothers was to achieve fame as a film director. In brief, notwithstanding the somewhat unconventional – for the times – choice of career by Upendranath as a restaurateur, his was a family of standing, even distinction.

Aruna was brought up in an anglicized home atmosphere. She recalls that her mother 'felt that unless we spoke, wrote and thought in English, we wouldn't get on in life'. By the latter, 'I think she meant that they would not get married in families that really wanted girls who spoke English fluently and with correct accent.' Her mother believed, 'Girls who are educated in Bengal, they may be read very well in English but they cannot speak English with a correct accent.'[11] Aruna's early schooling was, not surprisingly, in Lahore, in a Catholic missionary-run boarding school – the Sacred Heart Convent – no doubt to reinforce the 'Englishness' considered so desirable in all well-established Brahmo families. At thirteen she professed a desire to become a nun – an early sign that she had her own view of things; this independence of thought would grow and strengthen, even multiply, in the years ahead. This undoubtedly adolescent phase so alarmed Aruna's parents that she was brought back to Nainital to complete the rest of her schooling.

Thereafter her parents were keen that she get married; their preference would have been a well-placed civil servant, or perhaps an army officer or someone well established in the corporate world. She wanted to study further: she dreamt of Oxford or Cambridge. She was in Allahabad in January 1928 en route to Calcutta where she intended to work in a girls' school as the first step to making her way to London. Her younger sister Purnima Banerjee (1911–51), whom she was staying with, had been married at fourteen to the son of a well-known Allahabad lawyer Pyarelal Banarjee.[12] Purnima Banarjee would also emerge as a radical Congresswoman in the 1930s and 1940s, undergoing jail terms and taking part in different agitations against the government. She was later to be amongst the handful of women members of the Constituent Assembly. In contrast to their more conventional male siblings, both daughters of Upendranath and Ambalika would turn out to be very unusual women.

There are different accounts of the early meetings of Aruna and Asaf in Allahabad. Asaf had stopped in Allahabad while returning from Calcutta where he had gone to attend the annual Muslim League meeting in December 1927. One biography of Aruna suggests that Asaf proposed marriage soon after they met, at which she was 'at once pleased and perturbed'.[13] She wanted to get her parents' consent and 'suggested therefore that she and Asaf remain in touch through correspondence'. According to her own recollections recorded in the 1980s, in 'the beginning of our friendship . . . it was nothing more than a friendship'.[14] Their first meeting was in early January 1928 but what is intriguing is that barely a few days later both the *Times of India* and the *Bombay Chronicle* announced the impending wedding.

The *Times of India* on 18 January 1928 carried a news story: 'The engagement is announced of Mr Asaf Ali, Barrister, Delhi with Miss F Ganguli, daughter of Mr W N Ganguli of Naini Tal. The marriage will take place in about three weeks' time at Delhi under the Civil Marriages Act.' This reporting has some factual errors in the initials of Aruna and her father. But the point is what the headline made clear: why this was news and not just another marriage. 'Mohammadan to Marry a Hindu Girl' was the title, with the subheading: 'Asaf–Ganguli Engagement'. The *Bombay Chronicle* on the same day had carried a similar announcement – 'Hindu Muslim Wedding' – and it differed from the *Times of India* article only in providing the additional information that Miss Ganguli was a niece of Professor Ganguli, a member of the Royal Commission on Agriculture. It also, giving the name correctly, identified the bride-to-be as 'Miss A Ganguli'. Both news articles had mentioned that the wedding would be solemnized under the Civil Marriages Act.

There was clearly no effort at keeping it under wraps to the extent possible – if that indeed were possible. Had they decided to get married immediately after their meeting in Allahabad and Asaf on return applied for a civil marriage licence which sparked off the news reports? Could he have done so without consulting Aruna's father? What is clear is that there was no effort to keep this a secret, and it is possible that Asaf had no desire to follow in Syud's precedent of an elopement or an 'informal' secret marriage. He – or perhaps both of them – were embarking on this venture very much in the public eye. That this was so is suggested by the fact that about a week after these reports Asaf spoke to the *Bombay Chronicle* about the impending marriage. The article's title, 'Love at First Sight', suggests the chronology of the relationship.[15] Asaf is quoted as saying, 'The whole affair took place with lightning rapidity' and 'he discovered in her a kindred spirit'. There is clear understanding of the full ramifications of their decision: 'We knew we would raise a tornado but all pioneers have to put up with such things.' As in the earlier reports, this one too mentioned that the wedding would take place under the Civil Marriages Act and also that 'There will be no conversion of either party, each maintaining his or her faith'.

This article was perhaps not entirely accurate when it said: 'Scarcely any opposition is said to have been offered to the proposal by her father and other relatives.' It, however, also pointed out that Asaf had 'gallantly weathered the storm' of 'opposition from his own people'. But the report was entirely accurate in this assessment: 'In an atmosphere surcharged with communal passion and prejudice the announcement of the engagement . . . has caused a sensation in Delhi society.' The news was certainly sensational.

The next day the *Bombay Chronicle* had on its back page a large studio photograph of an attractive Aruna seated on a chair, captioned: 'Miss Ganguli, the accomplished niece of Prof Ganguli whose engagement to Mr Asaf Ali has just been announced.'[16] The photograph, now blurred with time, shows the young Aruna not as a shy demure bride but someone at her ease, confidently staring back at the camera.

However, about a month later, on 20 February, another news report ostensibly based on a press statement from Aruna's father 'W N Ganguli' (whose initials were again incorrect) stated that 'the announcement was premature and that it was without his sanction' and 'the proposed marriage is now definitely postponed till legal and other difficulties are solved. It is not true that the marriage [will] take place shortly as was announced.'[17] The wording of this second announcement is somewhat ambiguous: it does not deny the possibility of a marriage in the future, but only that one is not imminent.

It is hard to discover what exactly happened between Aruna, Asaf and Aruna's family in those initial days. We can surmise that her father disapproved and the initial negative reactions to the press announcements would have reinforced his disapproval, leading to the second announcement. In Aruna's later recollection, 'My father's main objection was that he [Asaf] was not financially very well off . . . [and] . . . the difference in age.'[18] Clearly the religious factor would have loomed so much larger than life that it need not even be mentioned. Her reaction – or at least how she remembered it decades later – was, 'I will wait till you agree. There is no hurry as far as I am concerned.'[19]

Aruna's father, however, died shortly afterward in March that year. Asaf paid a condolence visit to Nainital, and both he and Aruna reaffirmed their decision to marry. The wedding, in view of the family tragedy, was postponed and it took place in September 1928 in Nainital in an Islamic ceremony in which Aruna took the name Kulsum Zamani. There was subsequently a registered or civil law marriage in Delhi.

Her mother is said to have reconciled herself to the marriage and Aruna's sister Purnima attended the ceremony. But her uncle, the professor of agricultural economics, tried to have the marriage stopped on the grounds that she was a minor and he was the head of the family. It would be some years before he would come around. There were many others who came out in the open with their opposition. On the other side of the divide, too, the reactions were no less severe. Aruna remembered her 'mother-in-law . . . [being] flooded with letters saying what is this? He belongs to a Syed family . . . How can this happen?'[20]

~

Alongside the uniformly negative familial reaction on both sides, the political and social reactions were even stronger. Aruna said, more than half a century later, 'I did not expect the explosion of political opposition.

The Hindu Mahasabha got to know about it when the news appeared in *The Illustrated Weekly of India*, I think with my photograph with Asaf Ali.' Aruna's memory was of the Hindu Mahasabha saying 'they would kill that Brahman woman'. The conservative leader and the founder of the Banaras Hindu University, Madan Mohan Malaviya, it is said, 'would turn his face away from Aruna when the two were thrown together at Congress gatherings . . . he could not endure the thought of a Bengali Brahman girl marrying a Muslim'.[21]

The reactions were newsworthy enough to make it to the national level and the *Times of India* was to carry a more detailed analysis summarizing Hindu and Muslim press reactions to a Muslim Congress leader marrying an upper-caste Bengali girl.[22] The paper noted that 'it is very disturbing that this bold step in practical national unity has been received with snarls and sneers'.

The Hindu nationalist *Milap*, founded by Lala Lajpat Rai, openly suggested a political motive, writing:

> Mr Asaf Ali, Barrister, is a Congressi leader of Delhi. In the last elections he was unsuccessful and was thereupon taunted by the Musalmans that the Hindus whose side he had taken had not even given him their votes. But this did not shake Mr Asaf Ali's iman (faith) and he remained a champion of Hindu Muslim unity. Now 'Congressi' Hindus are highly pleased that Mr Asaf Ali is going to marry a Hindu lady, Miss Ganguli. They believe this novel method of bringing about Hindu Muslim unity will prove more successful. We for one have no faith in this new method; but our narrow mindedness may not appeal to 'Congressi' Hindus who are now turning very broad minded.

The sarcastic tone clearly suggests that many in Lala's camp saw the Congress's efforts with Muslims as an exercise not just in futility but also one involving a suspension of disbelief.

Another paper, *Sandesh*, was less sarcastic and more frontal in its view in the article 'The Vile Act of Mr Asaf Ali':

> If social relations with Musalmans increase, every Hindu must . . . feel anxious about his daughter or sister. It is just the result of Moslem culture that just as soon as a man sees a woman his attention is fixed on her. In Hindu society it is considered bad manners to ogle a strange woman, even a marriageable maiden . . . need it be told how censurable it must be to attempt to lure a woman of another faith?

It continued:

> Barrister Asaf Ali a Musalman leader whom the Hindus called their own has today proved treacherous to the Hindus . . . This is a most vile act. When they see such instances, Hindus begin to feel that every Musalman is unfit to be trusted – that you never can tell when he will cut your throat – and therefore he is regarded as an enemy.

And it harped further on Asaf Ali's 'betrayal': 'When even Nationalist Musalmans turn out such lamb slayers, it is necessary that Hindus should regard every Musalman as a red lamp, as a danger signal.'

The *Ranagarjana* by contrast focused on Aruna's role in this 'extremely painful news':

> Where did this craze for marrying Musalmans, that has entered the minds of our girls, come from? We think it is the result of English education. Idiotic ideas of individual freedom enter the heads of young men and women on account of this education, and it is these ideas that are at the bottom of this social and economic revolt.

If this was a representative sample of conservative, even nationalist Hindu reaction, it is matched by those amongst Muslims. The *Times of India* attributed to Maulana Shaukat Ali an editorial in the *Khilafat* which said, 'The Hindu is a creature that knows how to destroy others when they are sleeping.' It remains unclear whether Shaukat Ali's ire was on account of Asaf's marriage but another Khilafatist paper *Medina* waxed indignant about the match with this bit of sarcasm referring to the fact that Asaf had met Aruna in Allahabad while returning from the Muslim League session in Calcutta: 'The Calcutta League was very successful. For because of it one Musalman found a bride and firm and lasting unity was established between Hindus and Muslims. Shout Hindu Musalman marriage *ki jai*.'

There were positive reactions too, but these appear somewhat muted, almost as if startled by the audacity of it all. The *Bombay Chronicle* quoted an Urdu newspaper *Riyasat*: 'We congratulate Mr Asaf Ali on this proposed marriage and we hope that this marriage will serve as an example to others . . . [as] . . . one of the ways of achieving Hindu Muslim unity.'[23] The *Chronicle* also reported the proceedings of a Bombay Youth Conference that had passed a resolution welcoming 'The Gangulee–Asaf and other similar marriages which have been or will be celebrated', and condemning 'those newspapers and other peoples who have persecuted these married couples'. The newspaper did not fail to report that such resolutions were 'not passed unanimously' but 'the fact that they were passed at all is sufficient indication that the heart of the youth . . . is sound that they are all yearning for a political solidarity that will not countenance petty racial and communal prejudices'.[24] It would be fair to say that the outrage and condemnation was far in excess of those voices showing understanding and support.

In contrast to the many – perhaps overwhelmingly – negative reactions in public there must have been quieter responses of support from friends and associates. Some expressed support not so much in words but by treating it as a personal matter, and continued to maintain close relations with Asaf and increasingly with the couple. For the younger family members of Dr Ansari's family, Aruna was soon 'Bhabhi'. Abul Kalam Azad had often stayed in Kucha Chelan while visiting Delhi and continued to do so. There were other prominent figures who were supportive, including Sarojini Naidu who must have put her doubts aside once the marriage had taken place and, most significantly, Gandhi. In Aruna's recollection:

> When I began to meet Gandhiji after my marriage, I remember that he spoke of it as a symbol of Hindu Muslim unity. I protested that I married Asaf not because he was a Muslim but because of the affinity we felt over shared interest in English literature and the impression he made on me with his knowledge of history and philosophy, his agreeable personality and refined manners. But Gandhiji insisted that our marriage had symbolic significance.

Gandhi's 'endorsement' or support merits examination. He had opposed the relationship and brief 'marriage' of Syud Hossain and Sarup Nehru, been active in separating the couple, and delivered long lectures to Sarup on the fundamental unsuitability of the match. That was, however, eight years earlier, and the Khilafat/Non-cooperation phase with the subsequent breakdown in communal relations lay in between. Yet this intervening history could have played no real part in changing Gandhi's mind.

As recently as in 1926 he had strongly opposed his son Manilal's relationship with Fatima, a Gujarati Muslim girl in Cape Town, South Africa. Manilal was then based in Natal and involved with running the Phoenix Ashram. They were in love and Fatima had declared she would convert to Hinduism. Gandhi's views then bring out his fundamental opposition to such a marriage as 'contrary to dharma'. His letter to Manilal said: 'if you stick to Hinduism and Fatima follows Islam it will be like putting two sheaths in one sword . . . It is not dharma, only adharma, if Fatima converts just for marrying you. Faith is not a thing like a garment.' He had, however, also a larger objection. 'Your marriage will have a powerful impact on the Hindu Muslim question. Intercommunal marriages are no solution to this problem.'[25] An eminent biographer of the Mahatma has concluded that a marriage of this kind by his son, with the girl converting to Hinduism, 'would at one stroke ruin Gandhi's attempts to bring up unity . . .' and therefore Gandhi's principal reason for opposing the marriage was political'.[26]

So what explains Gandhi's liberal position and the support, or at least the acceptance, he extended to the Aruna–Asaf marriage? Possibly the knowledge that there was little he could do to dissuade Asaf or Aruna and that his opposing the idea would be counterproductive both politically and personally in terms of his relationship with the Asaf Alis. But perhaps also because Asaf was not in the actual front line of the political leadership: the marriage may have attracted attention but it would not have the implications that one involving a person whose family was very prominent and well connected may have had.

The interval between January 1928, when Aruna and Asaf first met, and the marriage in September is long enough for both to have evaluated what they were embarking on. Reflecting on the initial public outcry and reactions before the actual marriage would have focused their minds clearly on the path ahead. Years later Aruna digressed into her own personal life when detailing Jawaharlal Nehru's marriage. Writing of Motilal Nehru's efforts to arrange a match for his son into one of two prominent Kashmiri Brahmin families and dispassionately weighing the pros and cons of each of the girls, she noted:

> This clinical account of the comparative merit of the Mulla and Sapru girls reminds me of the mortification I felt when, like them, I was subjected to inspection with a view to matrimony. My parents were understandably anxious. My younger sister Purnima had married and joined the home of Pyarelal Banarjee a leading lawyer of Allahabad. This led relatives and family friends to wonder what was wrong with Aruna. I for my part abhorred the idea of being married off to a stranger. The problem was resolved when I met Asaf Ali at Allahabad.[27]

Her younger sister Purnima's marriage, unusually carried out before the older daughter was married, was clearly the outcome of parental pressure. It was not a particularly happy marriage.[28] So Aruna's desire not to stick to the beaten path and strike out on her own is understandable. Perhaps with Asaf too, the sentiments were similar. His earlier engagement to Liaq indicated his distaste for a conventional arrangement; perhaps this view had persisted, even solidified, and that explains his long bachelor status till he met Aruna. Even so, that he would marry a young Hindu girl from a reputable family is surprising. Did he see his marriage as a form of political statement? Or as a means to social and political mobility: if nothing else, he would be noticed as someone different? Or was he just swept of his feet, deeply in love and decided to take the plunge regardless? No doubt these very questions would have been discussed even by his close friends and supporters, with no finality attached to the different explanations that came up. Whatever the reason, and whatever the weightage attached to the different possibilities, their marriage does show in both Asaf and in Aruna a willingness to act on the courage of their own convictions and take difficult decisions if they thought they were doing the right thing.

# 13

# Domesticity and Confrontation

Outrage and criticism apart, the marriage faced other more personal hurdles before it found its balance. Asaf's ancestral house in Kucha Chelan may well have appeared primitive to young Aruna, brought up with more modern Western conveniences. On returning from England Asaf himself had had difficulties readjusting to living there. How would Aruna, with her convent school education and anglicized Bengali family background, cope with daily life deep in the by-lanes of the old city? She later recollected: 'When I first came to live in Delhi after my marriage in September 1928, I belonged to an entirely different hybrid Anglo Indianized background. There I found it difficult to fit into a Muslim Indian way of living, hoary with customary manners and traditions.' She is described as being 'shaken' by the 'kitchen bound domesticity and seclusion of women' and believed to have said later, only half seriously perhaps, that had she known what life in a typical Muslim home was like, she would not have married Asaf Ali![1]

The nineteen-year-old showed a lot of determination and staying power. She did not accept Asaf's offer that they move out of Kucha Chelan to a modern flat as that would have left his mother bereft. 'Special toilet arrangements were made for her, and it was accepted that the customary observance of seclusion would not apply in her case.'[2] Aruna settled down in the old haveli – amidst 'open drains running alongside the congested streets' – initially managing as well as she could and then settling down to become a member of its community. But it was also apparent to her that the twenty-year age difference with her husband and her own youth meant that the transition to being the wife of a public figure would not be an easy one. In her recollection, in the early days after the marriage, 'I was almost in purdah . . . not that my husband believed in it, but I just felt shy. I felt, oh, I would be abused, rather I seemed to have put my foot into something for which I was not prepared.'[3]

We get a sense of her diffidence and awkwardness when, a little after the wedding, the couple was invited to a dinner party by a senior civil servant, Brijlal Nehru, at his residence in New Delhi (called 'Lutyens Delhi' today). Brijlal was a nephew of Motilal Nehru; the occasion was that Motilal was in town and Jawaharlal would also be joining them for dinner. Brijlal's wife Rameshwari Nehru was active in women's issues and later would also be active in Gandhian efforts to work with Dalits. Despite her husband's career in the civil service, she was drawn to nationalism and was arrested in the 1940s during the Quit India movement. Towards the end of her life Rameshwari would be head of the Harijan Sevak Sangh, one of the important Congress organizations. All this was in the future, however; in the winter of 1928 at the time of the dinner party, Brijlal Nehru had recently been posted to the capital city and Rameshwari had thrown herself into social work and established the Delhi Women's League to this end.

Asaf was acquainted with Motilal because both were practising lawyers and their common involvement in the Congress had drawn them closer together. As we had seen, Motilal was a supporter of Asaf's failed bid to get elected to the Central Legislative Assembly and had taken his defeat as a political setback for himself. Motilal was a leading 'Swarajist' and Asaf was part of the large group that supported his view that the Congress should supplement its agitational and protest activity with participation in the legislative bodies set up by the colonial state even if they had only limited mandates. That Asaf would be invited for a private dinner for Motilal was therefore not surprising. Yet the evening in Brijlal Nehru's bungalow had, in Aruna's memory, a subtext: 'the establishment Nehru' had invited the Asaf Alis because their 'seditious clansmen from Allahabad were visiting'.[4] Motilal and Jawaharlal were obviously the 'seditious clansmen'.

The communal situation in Delhi and the rest of the country was, especially with Asaf present, an obvious conversation point. But there would have been others. Much, if not all, of this was way beyond Aruna; she recollected later: 'I felt lost in what struck me as a sombre gathering of elderly persons talking about the problems of the day of which I was utterly ignorant.' Jawaharlal arrived late, coming straight from a speaking tour in the Punjab 'all covered in dust' and Aruna was 'dazzled by the first, close look of him'. She also recalled that 'he looked me up and down with amused curiosity'; she 'was wearing a silk sari and some jewellry [*sic*] – a dolled up slip of a girl destined to decorate drawing rooms'.[5]

At the dinner party, 'Rameshwari Nehru must have realized, with womanly intuition how acutely uncomfortable I felt, among persons much

Photo Section, PMML

*Aruna Asaf Ali possibly soon after her wedding in September 1928*

senior to me in age. She came over to me and asked me about my family and my interests.' And in the following weeks, 'Rameshwari saw that I was a frightened young thing bewildered by the sharp change in environment from a missionary college and a westernized home in Naini Tal to a Muslim home in the walled city.' Aruna thereafter joined Rameshwari Nehru at the Delhi Women's League; she evidently found in her one of her early mentors who bolstered her confidence and gave her a glimpse of life outside domesticity, and she was grateful. 'Rameshwari Nehru taught me the procedure of calling meetings, preparing minutes of discussions, keeping of records and monitoring the implementation of decisions.'[6]

Her husband was also, at this very early stage of the marriage, another guide. They had exchanged letters after the first meeting in Allahabad, and Aruna remembered that his letters were 'most educative . . . they were answers to my questions'; she also noted that they had a 'professorial element'.[7] He was also something of a tutor, giving her books on politics and literature. One of Aruna's biographers noted: 'Asaf proved a more than adequate substitute for formal tutors . . . He helped her to appreciate social and political problems of the times.' We find amongst his recommendations the poetry of Alice Maynell, T.S. Eliot and Asaf's old favourite 'The Hound of Heaven' by Frances Thompson. One book that Asaf gave to her stuck particularly in her memory and this was the proscribed *India's First War of Independence* by V.D. Savarkar. In her words: 'I was thrilled by it. It politicized me.'[8] There were others too; Bernard Shaw's *The Intelligent Women's Guide to Socialism*, Virginia Woolf, Ibsen are the ones mentioned, but probably in the early years after marriage there was a great deal more. Asaf's own political profile and interests would naturally have been an equal catalyst in this evolution of her political awareness and consciousness.

Perhaps quite early she may have decided that motherhood was not in her list of chosen priorities. Asaf and Aruna were not to have children – and we can only guess the reasons. In an account of a confidant of Aruna's, but dating to half a century after the marriage, the decision was hers that there would be no children. The reason he gives, or the one Aruna supposedly gave to him, was that 'she feared that a child born to them was unlikely to be accepted by one community or the other'. She was therefore 'disconcerted by the prospect of her children being given Muslim names and being brought up, especially if there was a girl child, in the way of life she saw around her'. In this account Asaf, with 'surpassing gallantry', accepted this decision. He told his mother – the one person who would have been most inquisitive about this issue – that the absence of children was on account of his 'sterility', thus deflecting pressure away from Aruna.[9]

This is the only marker we have to illuminate this most private of domains. Perhaps this was indeed the explanation but equally there are logical arguments against accepting it. Why should children be such a problem when getting married and living for a length of time in Kucha Chelan was not? Quite simply, we do not know. But once having reached a decision and conclusion, Aruna would have steered her own course no matter what.

The supercharged political environment in the country would have had a formative influence on Aruna, now in the midst of an intensely politicized life as the wife of a rising Congress activist in Delhi. At around the time she first met Asaf in Allahabad in January 1928, educated sections of the Indian middle classes were outraged over a portrayal of India by an American writer, Katherine Mayo in her book *Mother India*. This was a notoriously biased depiction of India and Indians, concentrating on the deplorable treatment of women, untouchability, the hypocrisy of educated Indians especially those in politics and finally, in contrast, the high-minded idealism of the colonial establishment and its officers. The central problem the book identified with Indian – or rather Hindu – society was its rampant sexuality and tendency towards sexual excess with attendant consequences that Mayo identified as homosexuality, rape, prostitution, etc.

The book would be dismissed as a 'drain inspector's report' by Gandhi and there were many strident denunciations, including a fair number in print. The book was aimed primarily at an American readership but it had a huge impact in Britain and of course in India where it was translated into a number of Indian languages. Many in India suspected, quite correctly as it subsequently turned out, that the book was more than the fulminations of an American writer bent on executing a hatchet job. They suspected the hand of the colonial state's propaganda machinery, as the book in effect also amounted to a criticism of the demands for self-rule by nationalist Indians and advocated continued British rule. That the main target was Hindu society and Hindu men also suggested to many a further variant of 'divide and rule'.[10]

While *Mother India* was being widely talked about and criticized, there was another colonial initiative that similarly outraged and united even more strongly different shades of Indian opinion. In November 1927 the British government announced the appointment of a commission to examine the working of the constitutional system in place since 1919, exploring greater representation of Indians and devolving more power and authority to elected representatives in provincial assemblies and also at the Centre. This body would also make recommendations about the future course of governance reform in India.

To an extent the decision to appoint such a body followed from the 1919 Act itself: it had contained a provision for its review within ten years. That period would have, however, expired only in 1929; the appointment of a commission two years earlier had much to do with the divisions within British politics on the future of its Indian empire. In 1927 the Conservatives were in power and faced the likelihood of electoral defeat at the hands of Labour. To pre-empt the possibility of a Labour government constituting the commission that would recommend India's future course of constitutional development, the Conservatives decided to set it up in advance so that its composition and, to the extent possible, its major recommendations would be in line with their thinking. The broader context is that this was the first decade after the Bolshevik Revolution in Russia and the Conservatives in Britain were apprehensive that 'radical' politicians of the Labour Party would tinker too much with India.

The aims of the commission would have appeared unexceptionable to many in India. The problem, however, was a typical colonial blunder but one inherent in the nature of British colonialism in India: the commission was constituted without a single Indian member. Virtually the entire political spectrum in India joined together in its boycott. The older divisions between Hindu and Muslim politicians, between the Congress and the League, and within the Congress itself – such as the Swarajists, the Malaviya and Motilal Nehru groups and others – now suddenly appeared less significant and this 'insult' instead came to occupy centre stage. By end 1927 a taunt by the secretary of state for India – that Indians never came up with ideas they could all agree upon – further consolidated this convergence. It led to the formation of an all-parties conference, comprising virtually the entire Indian political spectrum, to draft a new constitution for India. This finally appeared by mid-1928 in the form of the Motilal Nehru report, as the senior Nehru was one of its principal drafters.

Meanwhile the all-white commission, named after its chair John Simon, had arrived in India in February 1928 and from the start faced hostile demonstrations in the different cities it visited. In Lahore, during one such demonstration, the veteran nationalist Lala Lajpat Rai was badly beaten up by the police, an act that further inflamed public opinion across the country. Lajpat Rai, along with Malaviya, had been blamed by Asaf for leading a communal campaign that led to his defeat in the 1926 election to the Central Legislative Assembly. But the way he was assaulted and his death soon after caused an outrage that went beyond their personal differences. We can easily assume Asaf was as affected by this incident as anyone else.

So, the period of Asaf Ali's initial meeting with Aruna and up to their marriage in September 1928 was on the whole a volatile spell for the Indian national movement, which must certainly have been a factor in the incubation of their relationship.

In April 1929, some seven months into their marriage, Aruna was present along with Asaf at a landmark event of the freedom movement. She used to accompany Asaf Ali to witness debates of the Central Legislature. Asaf, despite his loss in the 1926 election, had maintained an interest in Central Legislative issues and debates. 'So if there was any keen, good debate – he always knew the agenda of the Assembly – he would go and I used to accompany him.' Anyway, 'I had nothing else to do. I knew nobody in Delhi,'[11] Aruna would say. One suspects that alongside a fledgeing interest in politics, the young Aruna may also have found it a relief to leave the closed confines of the old haveli in Kucha Chelan to spend some time alone with her husband during the day. And so it was that on 8 April 1929 both were present in the visitors' gallery of the new Council House building adjoining Raisina Hill at the heart of the still under construction new imperial metropolis. Aruna was seated separately from Asaf, in the ladies' gallery. As it happens, Brijlal Nehru was also present at the gallery and Rameshwari was in the ladies' gallery.

That day the visitors' gallery was full: the speaker of the house Vithalbhai Patel was expected to deliver an important ruling. Under consideration were a 'Public Safety Bill' and a 'Trade Disputes Bill' introduced by the government; their enactment would empower it to deport foreigners indulging in subversive activities and also curb strike actions by trade unions. These measures were aimed at curbing the activities of British communists amongst trade unions in India. The bills had been strenuously opposed in the Assembly at different stages. At one stage the Public Safety Bill was defeated with the speaker of the Assembly, Vithalbhai Patel, casting his vote against it; the viceroy subsequently gave effect to its provisions through an ordinance. Further consideration of the Trade Disputes Bill depended on the ruling Patel was to give, which was keenly awaited and much discussed as another contest between the government and nationalists in the legislature. Vithalbhai Patel was incidentally, along with Motilal Nehru, one of the leaders of the Swaraj Party.

Asaf was standing, with Brijlal next to him. In one of those bizarre, almost comic, coincidences, as the speaker rose to deliver his ruling, Brijlal commented to Asaf: 'And now Mr Patel is going to throw his bombshell.' Asaf describes what happened next:

> suddenly a loud noise was heard. I saw a flash between the first and the second Government benches, and for a flash of a moment I wondered quite irrationally whether the Govt had arranged some kind of fireworks to divert our attention, when down went the second bomb and exploded with a terrific retort and fumes filled the chamber and then some shots were fired.

This was Bhagat Singh and B.K. Dutt throwing two bombs into the chamber along with some revolutionary literature. They also fired some shots from a revolver and shouted slogans. Aruna remembered that 'there was a lot of commotion. We could not move and get out of the building . . . I remember all the time there was talk and talk and excitement.'[12] Asaf's own recollection adds further detail. He was standing in 'the part of the gallery where Bhagat Singh happened to be seated right in front of me'. He in fact remembered seeing Bhagat Singh a day or so earlier before the bombs were thrown:

> I first saw him in the gallery of the Assembly, sitting close to the distinguished visitors' Gallery just above the government benches, a day or two before he threw bombs into the Assembly. I remembered this when I saw him under arrest soon after he had thrown the bombs and fired three or four shots into the pit of the chamber.[13]

Bhagat Singh and his associates in the 'Hindustan Socialist Republic Association' had in fact chosen this day quite deliberately to amplify both their protest against these measures and to create maximum impact. Bhagat Singh's earlier visit to the chamber was to study its layout and finalize their modus operandi.[14] In the ensuing panic the gallery emptied, although Asaf and Brijlal Nehru remained as they were both looking for their wives. Neither Bhagat Singh nor B.K. Dutt made any effort to escape, and Asaf overheard the former telling a police officer, 'Don't worry we shall tell the whole world . . . we did it.'[15]

A day or two later Asaf was approached by Bhagat Singh's father to defend his son. He observed, 'It was an incident of such grave consequence that normally lawyers were not prepared to come forward to defend him.' Asaf agreed to do so and sought a meeting with the young men as their defence counsel.[16] He found 'both of them extremely human and gentle although one would have believed that they would be rather ferocious and hard. I had numerous occasions after that to interview them and I found Bhagat Singh a most lovable person and BK Dutt one of the most affectionate.' Both were, he said, 'two of the bravest young men I had ever come across'. Asaf believed that Bhagat Singh's 'conception of the kind of revolution he wanted to bring about in India was not a mere change of rulers from the foreign to the indigenous but it was a far larger one'. Bhagat Singh was not 'smitten by communism but his approach to political, social and moral problems certainly derived from the Marxian conception of a socialist order'.[17] Asaf read out a statement on their behalf in June 1929 and mentions also appearing for them later in the High Court.[18]

The legalities of the case were less important as both were determined *not* to plead 'Not guilty'. The gravity of the Delhi offence was, however, not a match for the even more serious charge that Bhagat Singh was soon to face: that of assassinating a British police officer. In December 1928, he had shot the police officer in Lahore under the mistaken impression that this officer was the one responsible for a lathi charge in which the nationalist leader Lala Lajpat Rai was injured. Rai was greatly revered in Punjab and he died a few days later of a heart attack; that this was on account of his wounds was the general impression, although the government denied it. The assassination of John Saunders, the young British police official, happened a month later on 17 December 1928 after which Bhagat Singh evaded arrest and then went on to throw the bombs in the Central Legislature. Bhagat Singh's and Dutt's arrest for the Council House episode was soon linked to the Lahore case and consequently the defiant young men acquired an even higher profile and became cult figures across the country.

A young Aruna absorbed this from the vantage point of the wife of an established politician in Delhi. She recalled that on hearing that her husband was going to defend Bhagat Singh and B.K. Dutt she was 'very excited' and insisted on attending the proceedings.[19] The trial was closed to the public but Asaf as the defence counsel could get her permission to attend the proceedings in a small courtroom set up within the jail premises itself. At the commencement of the trial a newspaper noticed and commented that the only outsiders allowed into the courtroom were the parents of Bhagat Singh, Mrs Asaf Ali and a few pressmen.[20] As the prisoners entered the makeshift court, they started raising slogans. Asaf recalled: 'B K Dutt shouted "Down, down with imperialism" in stentorian tones and Bhagat Singh rounded up by "Long live the revolution". Their voice(s) nearly brought down the low roof, and the committing magistrate . . . suddenly grew red in the face.' Handcuffs were ordered.

Aruna, electrified, remembered 'that was the first time I had heard "Inquilab Zindabad"';[21] it struck 'untouched chords of the inner being, that were dosed with complacency fed on Anglo India's cheap dope. The originator of *Inquilab* looked the blustering magistrate straight in the eye when he ordered handcuffs on the prisoners. Once the hands were in chains, he repeated the slogans.'[22] 'Inquilab Zindabad' had been coined as a radical slogan by the poet-cum-activist Hasrat Mohani in 1921 but it was Bhagat Singh's raising it in defiance that was to hugely popularize it in times to come.

Asaf said he had tried to persuade Dutt to plead not guilty to the charge of throwing a bomb as both bombs had been in fact thrown by Bhagat Singh. Dutt did not agree and both were sentenced to life imprisonment. Bhagat Singh was sentenced to death later for the Lahore assassination and finally executed in March 1931. While still in jail he, along with a number of other young men, went on a hunger strike demanding to be treated as political prisoners – with more facilities and better diet – rather than as common criminals. One of them, the twenty-five-year-old Jatin Das, also implicated in the Lahore assassination, died on 13 September 1929, after a hunger strike spanning sixty-three days. It would be true to say that this entire chain of events and its final tragic end electrified India.

The assassination in Lahore, the bombs in Delhi, and the hunger strike in jail were shaping a different strategy of resistance and protest. It was not new in itself. From the late nineteenth and early twentieth centuries individual acts of violence targeting the colonial state had regularly, even if not frequently, punctuated the chronology of the otherwise staid public life in India. But from the 1920s such acts were embedded in a different context: they were in many ways almost consciously a counter to the Gandhian narrative of non-cooperation or any other form of resistance to the government with non-violence as its bedrock. These two separate trajectories were part of the national struggle for independence and have remained inherent in other movements too. The tension between them was never reconciled. The non-violence narrative certainly gained strength and in time became the defining discourse of Indian nationalism but it never had a discursive or narrative monopoly. Thus the debate between these two streams had never been absent but certainly Bhagat Singh and his associates gave to it a new intensity. We can imagine they left the young Aruna more influenced by their end of this polarity than she was probably even aware of at the time.

Asaf, older and more experienced politically, would have disagreed with their tactics, much as he liked and admired Bhagat Singh and Dutt. He had witnessed at reasonably close quarters the playout of the Wyllie assassination by Dhingra as a student in London and then the failed attempt in Delhi in 1912 to assassinate the viceroy. In his later recollection of his role in the Bhagat Singh trial in Delhi he noted:[23]

> It is often said that it is far more difficult to live to serve one's ideal than to die for it, and again it is said that it requires courage of the highest order to face unspeakable hardships and growing cares and anxieties from day to day and from moment to moment.

To him, then, 'the momentary courage which like a flash in the pan leads one to the battle front or to acts which end on the gallows, is only but a phase of fragmentary heroism'. This was written after 1947 and clearly Asaf was then juxtaposing his own experience of the freedom movement as politics as opposed to Aruna's involvement in the struggle as revolutionary activity. But that was still in the future.

These events form the background to the Lahore session of the Congress in December 1929. Asaf Ali attended it with Aruna accompanying him and she recollected seeing Jawaharlal Nehru as he was taken around the city on horseback: he was 'smartly dressed in black sherwani . . . on a magnificent white horse' and 'he looked every inch the knight errant of the freedom movement'.[24] Perhaps she had by now sufficient grounding of the political context she was then situated in. Or perhaps not: she was someone typically impatient with legal and constitutional moves and issues.

Asaf certainly would have been aware that notwithstanding the many stirring moments the Lahore Congress witnessed, deep differences had already emerged in the unity suddenly and unexpectedly forged across the Indian political spectrum by the Simon Commission's appointment, its arrival in India, and the initiative to draft a consensus constitution by way of the Nehru report. The latter contained recommendations the Muslim League could not stomach: in particular it suggested doing away with separate electorates, something that had been anathema to many in the Congress, notwithstanding the Lucknow Pact of 1916. The Hindu Mahasabha had even stronger objections to the principle of separate electorates. The report tried to compensate for its recommendation against separate electorates. For instance it endorsed the demand for a new Muslim-majority province of Sindh to be carved out of the Bombay Presidency, and for the Muslim minority in the United Provinces it recommended reserved seats for Muslims in joint electorates. But separate electorates had become a cherished position for many Muslims. What the Nehru report offered instead was not enough for many, perhaps most, Muslims. These compensatory positions were in turn deeply resented by many Hindus who demanded there should be no special treatment for any community. To the report's critics it appeared that keeping this section of Hindus – the Hindu Mahasabha for instance – on board had been a higher priority for the report's authors than forging a common front with Muslim opinion.

Various compromises were in fact attempted, not least by Jinnah, but none finally worked. Gandhi's breach with many of the former Khilafatists and most prominently the Ali brothers was now wider than during the communal downturn after the collapse of Khilafat. To Mohammad Ali the Nehru report was simply 'Hindu Raj'. In December 1928 Jinnah is reported to have referred to 'a parting of the ways' with Hindus. Sarojini characteristically kept trying to push things in a more positive direction and arranged a meeting in Bombay in August 1929 between Jinnah and Gandhi. The Ali brothers also attended. But this was just one more failed attempt.

Within the Congress the mood was frustration about the inaction during the second half of the 1920s and also impatience to respond to the insult that the Simon Commission represented. The younger generation of Congress leaders, such as Jawaharlal Nehru and Subhas Chandra Bose, wanted the Congress to set a clear goal for complete independence. At the annual Congress session in Calcutta in December 1928 a compromise position – full dominion status rather than full independence – was worked out. There was a condition attached: unless dominion status was conceded within a year, by 31 December 1929, a civil disobedience movement would be launched to secure complete independence. The following year, in the absence of any noise from the government regarding dominion status, the Congress in Lahore under Jawaharlal Nehru's presidency declared 'Purna Swaraj' or complete independence as its goal.

It was clear that the next round of confrontation with the Raj was now on the cards but it was left largely to the Mahatma to decide what form this would take and how it was to be implemented. By March 1930 the decision was taken: the target was the colonial salt laws. The tax on salt was, in Gandhi's explanation, a metaphor for the whole of British rule in India: 'It has impoverished the dumb millions.'[25] It may have appeared an eccentric even quixotic target at first – making salt from seawater in violation of the extant law – but it integrated the idea of struggling for freedom with opposition to an unpopular tax. On 12 March the march to Dandi began from Sabarmati Ashram in Ahmedabad. By the time the march concluded about 385 kilometres away at the coast in Dandi on 6 April, the political protest had assumed larger-than-life proportions across the country.

# 14

# Climbing the Political Ladder

As political activity intensified in Delhi, Aruna was in the beginning entirely in the background: 'I was as if watching everything from behind the scenes.' On 13 April 1930 a procession and a hartal had been organized to commemorate the 1919 massacre at Jallianwala Bagh. The launch of the Dandi March a month earlier had seen supportive agitation across the country and in Delhi there had been many arrests. There was therefore a paucity of speakers to energize protesters and it was a nephew of Dr Ansari who persuaded her: '"*Bhabhi aapko bolna hai aaj*" . . . I said, what can I say? In between I had been reading Vinayak Damodar Savarkar's book *The Indian War of Independence* and anything that came to me. All that was my political education.' She stumbled through her speech in her broken Hindi and finally 'I broke into English' but 'in those days anything served the purpose'.[1] And with this, during the salt agitation phase, she made her entry into active involvement in the freedom struggle.

This involvement owed much to another early mentor, Satyawati Devi, a granddaughter of Swami Shraddhanand. Rameshwari Nehru had provided the template of an anglicized woman from the upper classes of Indian society entering public life. Satyawati Devi was an alternative, more subaltern, model and one that would steer Aruna towards more radical postures: 'Had it not been for Satyawati, I wonder if I would have ventured out of my sheltered domestic life.' Aruna said she had doubts whether with her foreign missionary education and her 'westernized habits' she could adjust to what was expected from a Satyagrahi and feared that 'I would remain an outsider'.[2] But 'Satyawati's burning zeal was infectious. I was drawn to her and could not stay away from the great fight.'[3]

The question was: how could they infringe the salt laws by illegally making salt in landlocked Delhi? The answer was found in the Delhi suburb of Shahdara:

> Satyawati and some of us decided to break the salt law in a marshy vacant lot where the sub soil water had a high salt content. About fifty of us made illegal and muddy salt, of which we made packets for distribution rather like *prasad* (consecrated offering). This went on for ten days, after which the police swung into action, to disperse the law breakers with lathi charges and teargas shells.[4]

Aruna was arrested in October 1930 and was sentenced to a year's imprisonment for a speech that was seen as propagating and inciting violent action. Asaf had already been arrested and sentenced earlier in September 1930 for six months as part of the salt protests. At one stage both were in the Lahore jail – separately in the men's and women's sections – and allowed occasional meetings. When political prisoners were finally released, Aruna's release was delayed by some days because she could not be placed in the same category of political prisoners who did not advocate violence. Without stretching the evidence, it is possible to discern ideas that had begun to influence her other than those of her husband and the Congress. The Bhagat Singh episode and trial would still have been fresh in her memory. She recounts:

> When I met Gandhiji in Delhi after my release, he wanted to know whether I had really incited people from the path of nonviolent noncooperation. I had to confess to him that having recently read Savarkar's book on the Indian struggle for independence in 1857, I could not help being influenced by it and did refer to it quite often . . . in my speeches.[5]

She would be arrested and imprisoned again, as we shall see, in 1932. Wives of senior Congressmen being arrested and jailed was no longer a novelty, but someone in her early twenties undergoing the experience was news. Each jail term was marked also by acts of defiance, and as news of these travelled outside the prison walls, her public profile acquired greater depth. The advice she offered the magistrate before whom she was produced after her first arrest in 1930 made headlines in the nationalist press: 'If you agree with me conscientiously, I appeal to you to resign your post. Give British prestige a hard knock.'[6] At one stage a hunger strike while in jail led to solitary confinement in a men's prison. There was public outcry as news of this leaked out. In her recollection, 'The British made me a heroine.'[7] On her release and return to Delhi, she was taken in procession from the railway station to Kucha Chelan.

Scattered through Aruna's later writings are numerous references to the mentoring she received first from Rajeshwari Nehru and later from Satyawati Devi. Both were women with a deep sense of public service but otherwise very different. Each left their own individual stamp on the much younger Aruna as she thought about and crafted her own role on a wider stage. What is surprising is the absence of Sarojini Naidu who should have been a powerful presence too, given her old friendship with Asaf. She moved in the highest echelons of the Congress leadership and would have been in regular touch with the Asaf Alis, during visits to Delhi and in Congress meetings elsewhere. She does figure in Aruna's later recollections but almost entirely as someone her husband was a 'fan' of and not as an influence in her own evolution.

How was it that Aruna did not count the eminently suitable Sarojini among her mentors? In part it could be that in 1928 and 1929 Sarojini Naidu was out of the country for long stretches. Her visit to the United States in 1928, which had occasioned the restarting of correspondence with Syud Hossain, was in fact part of the Congress strategy to reach out directly to influential quarters there in the wake of the publication of

*Smt. Rameshwari Nehru*

Mayo's *Mother India* and the negative impressions it created. But Sarojini was at the centre of events in India as the salt agitation began and was present at the coast when Gandhi and his all-male band of marchers arrived in Dandi, a little village on the coast, on 5 April 1930, having completed a 385 kilometre march to the sea to make salt in violation of the law. Her letter to her daughter described the excruciating food – 'a mess worse than dog's food' and thanked God for a reasonably clean bathroom. But Sarojini characteristically found the right words as Gandhi picked up a lump of natural salt at the seashore the next day; she dramatically cried out: 'Hail Deliverer.'[8] Another account has her saying 'Hail Law Breaker.'[9] These ricocheted around the world as the press party present on the occasion flashed this symbolic defiance of Empire far and wide.

Some weeks later, on 21 May, she was at the Dharasana salt works in present-day Gujarat, leading a protest against this government factory in one of the most dramatic confrontations of the Salt Satyagraha. Column after column of disciplined Satyagrahis were beaten down without them offering resistance but determinedly trying to enter the premises guarded by the police. Sarojini was arrested there along with numerous others.

Therefore, Sarojini's absence in general from the list of those whom Aruna counted as her mentors does merit a pause. Was it that she was choosing her own circle rather than finding a place in her husband's? Or did she find Sarojini's long and easy familiarity with Asaf and Asaf's devotion to Sarojini somewhat threatening and didn't want to give Sarojini the satisfaction of becoming her protege? On Sarojini's side, she may have sensed something in Aruna that was different – something more radical and self-willed, less amenable to control – and therefore kept a certain distance. Perhaps the half-expressed doubts in the letter to Syud were further cemented? She had then written about Asaf wanting to marry Aruna: 'It will not be a success.' Could it be Aruna now sensed this disapproval?

Also likely is that now Asaf's own path was different from Sarojini's. As is often the case, friends of youth or relative youth drift apart as both sides mature and interests and profiles diverge. While they were both part of the same joint enterprise, Sarojini had always been on a different level from Asaf and gradually this made more of a difference than it had earlier.

If Aruna's involvement in the Salt Satyagraha suggests the breathless and boundless enthusiasm of a new initiate, Asaf's own experience conveys the sense of an organizational man going about his business methodically. As noted, he had been arrested and jailed in September 1930, before Aruna's first arrest. On his arrest he was described as the person in charge of the Delhi Congress or its 'Dictator'. The terminology was in the style adopted by the Congress at the time. Mahatma Gandhi on his arrest in May 1930 had designated Abbas Tyabji as 'Dictator' of the Salt Satyagraha. The term had caught on. As arrests of the top echelon continued, Dr M.A. Ansari was to become Congress 'Dictator' on the arrest of Maulana Azad. Asaf was thus designated as 'Dictator' of the Delhi Congress 'War Council'. Press reports refer to him as being the 'third dictator' suggesting that others had been arrested before him.[10]

There is a certain stoicness to the whole process of protest, arrest and imprisonment. These were the reactions of a seasoned Congressman and freedom fighter going about the required business in a systematic way. There was, however, a larger change in the air. Contrary to the expectations of many in the Congress leadership, the Salt Satyagraha and the Dandi March had comprehensively gripped the nationalist imagination and galvanized the party's rank and file. After the 'Purna Swaraj' resolution in Lahore, agitation and protest constituted for many the need of the times. The government on its part was surprised at the success of Gandhi's quixotic idea of building up civil disobedience through the conscious infringement of the ubiquitous salt laws. After floundering for some years, the national movement appeared to be back on a linear trajectory with confrontation with the colonial state at the centre of the frame. The internal communal fissures and conflicts would have seemed, at that heady time, something of the past.

But at least some in Gandhi's disciplined band saw such a conclusion as a delusion. In this view the fault lines of the past, far from going away, had deepened and were of greater concern. Most prominent of this group was Dr Ansari, Asaf's senior in Delhi, close friend and mentor in public life and easily now the most important Muslim Congressman. Ansari seemed to register with greater clarity than others a central weakness of the Congress that nationalist protest and agitation could so easily camouflage: Muslim support for the Congress had dwindled since the heady days of Khilafat and non-cooperation almost a decade earlier. Important Muslim leaders such as Jinnah, the Ali brothers and many others had stayed away from the Salt Satyagraha. Shaukat Ali had in fact described it as aimed at establishing 'a Hindu Raj' in India. As we saw, the Motilal Nehru report too had failed to reassure Muslim opinion. Its most significant recommendation was doing away with separate electorates and the Congress's moving away from this key concession was enough to condemn the report in the eyes of many Muslims. Ansari was a key supporter of the report's recommendations – including doing away with separate electorates – and his support was invaluable particularly because he was a Muslim. But he had a larger concern that was also very specific. In his view the earlier agitations in 1919 and 1920 had been based on the premise of exemplary Hindu–Muslim unity. In 1930 there was a changed situation as the preceding years had seen a calamitous decline in the communal situation.

Ansari put forward these views in a letter to the Mahatma in February 1930 after the Lahore Congress but before the announcement of the Salt Satyagraha.[11] His basic premise was put forth as: 'Hindu Muslim unity is not only one of the basic items in our programme, but according to my belief, and conviction, *the one and only* basic thing' [emphasis in original]. The letter pointed out that in the run-up to the Lahore declaration he had pointed to 'our internal dissensions, unpreparedness and weaknesses' because of which it was not advisable to proceed on a confrontational path with the government. The current situation was 'the lowest watermark reached in Hindu Muslim disunity' and therefore: 'You are taking a great responsibility on yourself by declaring war against the government. The situation today is quite the reverse of what it was in 1920.' In brief this view was tethered around the perception of the shallowness of Congress support among Muslims and therefore a fear that this would not just impart a fragility to any enterprise taking on the Raj head-on but was fraught with other dangerous consequences.

The Mahatma gave a detailed reply: 'I agree that the Hindu Muslim problem is the problem of problems. But I feel it has to be approached in a different manner from the one we have hitherto adopted.' The new approach was spelt out: 'the third party, the British, has got to be sterilized. There can be no charter of independence before the Hindus and Muslims have met, but there can be virtual independence before the charter is received.' In effect the Mahatma was saying that Hindu–Muslim unity would follow India's independence rather than be a precondition for it. It is a debate that would periodically recur but for the time being the die was cast. The letter also acknowledged Ansari's value to the Congress and to him personally. 'If all this be hallucination I must perish in the flames of my own lighting . . . It does not matter at all if we do not see eye to eye. It is well with us if our hearts are pure as I know they are.'

Much the same point was made by Syed Mahmud: Muslims were indifferent to the Congress and in this situation civil disobedience would degenerate into Hindu–Muslim riots with official encouragement. Gandhi is believed to have said in response that he was conscious of this danger but there was no way out but to keep moving forward.[12] Syed Mahmud was later jailed during the Salt Satyagraha and shared a jail cell with Motilal Nehru and Jawaharlal. Before the launch of the salt agitation, he had sounded the same note of caution with Jawaharlal Nehru too: that greater priority should be accorded to building communal harmony; that Muslims were on the whole distant from the Congress; and that non-cooperation or civil disobedience would disintegrate into Hindu–Muslim riots. If, in the rest of Syed Mahmud's relationship with Jawaharlal he was sentimental, often lacking in confidence, and usually ready to defer, on this one point a consistent difference remained; it was similar to the position Nehru later encountered with Asaf Ali and Maulana Azad. For Syed Mahmud, the central political issue to be addressed first and foremost was Hindu–Muslim unity and how this could be cemented. For Nehru, on the other hand, the communal problem would be resolved relatively easily in an independent India without the British.

Why should a protest and an agitation against the British end up with Hindus and Muslims inflicting violence on each other? Possibly the fear was that once mobilized and charged up, sentiments and passions are difficult to control and older grievances and fault lines such as communal divides flare up. This was after all the experience of the 1920s; in Ansari's words: 'Immediately after the setback of the NCO [non-cooperation] movement, there was a reaction which, instead of keeping the Hindus and Muslims together, made them fight each other as they had never done before. Unity patched up to fight a common foe always breaks down as soon as the fight ceases.'[13] Put simply, the apprehension may have been that an agitation by Hindus in which Muslims were absent or thinly present could well end up in them turning on the latter.

Possibly this general point discussed between Ansari and Gandhi was also being discussed in wider circles within the Congress. Should agitation against a colonial state await a consolidation of Hindu–Muslim unity, which was evidently absent, given the negative Muslim response to the Nehru report? 'Does this not mean,' S. Satyamurti, a senior Congressman from Madras, wrote to Gandhi, 'a charter for extreme communalists to go on obstructing? Even when Swaraj is obtained, there will be extreme communalists. Other free countries have their communal problems but have not allowed minorities to dictate to the nation.'[14] To an extent this was a generic problem: should even a small minority hold up progress to build up a consensus for national freedom? Possibly the answer Ansari would have given is that Muslim disillusionment and alienation was deeper than was being acknowledged – this was not a question of a small disgruntled minority – and embarking on a path of confrontation with the government would only make the situation worse.

We do not know where Asaf stood on this divide but, given his proximity to Ansari and Sarojini Naidu – Ansari's letter had pointed out that she agreed with his approach – it is almost certain he would have shared this position. He was not yet in the upper echelons of the party hierarchy and his views may not have been listened to. What we can be certain about is that for Asaf the communal downturn after the heady phase of Khilafat and non-cooperation had been a searing experience and he had witnessed it first-hand in Delhi. At a personal level the reactions to his marriage had revealed the depths of communal antagonism that existed. Finally, it is likely that he shared Ansari's dismay at the growing gulf between the Muslim League, whose meetings he had attended recently, and the Congress; and between Jinnah on the one hand and the Nehrus – both father and son – and Gandhi on the other.

We know that Asaf was fully involved in Ansari's efforts to consolidate Muslim support for the Congress and here the strongest critics of this initiative were the Ali brothers. In July 1929 a 'Nationalist Muslim Party' was formed with this aim: of strengthening Muslim support for the Congress and trying to ensure that important figures such as

Jinnah, even if not the more radical Ali brothers, were supportive of the Congress. These efforts failed quite spectacularly – in part because of opposition from the more conservative sections within the Congress such as Madan Mohan Malaviya; they were convinced that the Congress leadership, unless pressured otherwise, would make too many concessions on Muslim seats in the provincial assemblies and the Central Legislature. The Ansari group also faced damaging criticism from many Muslims – in particular the Ali brothers – who accused them of being renegades and traitors. Sarojini Naidu in particular tried hard, but also without success, to bridge the growing breach between the Ali brothers and Gandhi, once the strongest of allies during the Khilafat phase just a few years earlier.

Within a few months of such efforts, by early 1930 it became evident that the attempts to forge a broad Muslim phalanx of support for the Congress had not made headway. This was mainly why Ansari and his supporters objected to embarking on a fresh confrontation with the government. Dr Ansari was, however, also a staunch Congressman. Once he found that his objections were not being heeded, he had adopted a lower profile. But as the agitation began and one after the other leaders were arrested, he responded positively to appeals made to him to take part. He was himself arrested and sentenced to jail in August 1930. Not to be in the Congress was, in brief, unthinkable – regardless of even fundamental differences – for 'to leave the Congress would be to commit political suicide'.[15]

The round of confrontations following the Dandi March, during which Gandhi and many other senior Congress leaders were jailed, ended in a series of negotiations and an agreement between Gandhi and the viceroy in March 1931. Under the terms of the Gandhi–Irwin agreement, political prisoners were released, Asaf Ali among them; Aruna's release followed a few days later. But the scene had shifted to a much larger stage. In terms of the understanding reached with the viceroy, Gandhi would be attending a Round Table Conference convened in September–December 1931 by the British government in London to which different shades of Indian political opinion and different parties were invited.

An earlier round of the conference had concluded in January 1931 and had been largely inconsequential, with the Congress not attending. The forthcoming round would have Gandhi attending as the sole representative of the Congress. The government had thought of the Round Table Conference as a way forward to break the deadlock arising with the boycott of the Simon Commission. By inviting all the principal Indian players to discuss the commission's report and its recommendations about further constitutional change in India, the government was also seeking to correct the blunder of the all-white Simon Commission. Gandhi's agreement with Viceroy Irwin appeared to paper over the Congress's demands of complete independence or at least immediate dominion status. Many were bewildered at Gandhi's willingness to compromise and agree to what in effect was a truce, particularly when the Civil Disobedience movement had drawn a strong response across the country and put the government on the defensive. But perhaps Gandhi understood better than others that an agitation could not continue indefinitely.

However, the Round Table Conference could not break fresh ground. For one, the Congress-led agitation and protests had led to a perceptible hardening of attitudes amongst both British officialdom in India and many in the political class in Britain. Many were appalled at the viceroy directly negotiating with Gandhi and thereby elevating not just his prestige but the status of the Congress-led freedom movement as a whole. Winston Churchill spoke of the 'nauseating' spectacle of Gandhi 'posing as a fakir' and 'striding half naked' to 'parley in equal terms with the representative of the King Emperor'.[16] This was not just the fulminations of an arch imperialist but a more general sentiment. Then, in the second round of the conference itself, differences on the question of Muslim representation and separate electorates became more pronounced. Other complexities also emerged, with separate electorates now being demanded also by 'Depressed Castes', Christians, Sikhs, Anglo-Indians and others. Most prominent in this was the question of representation for Depressed

Castes or the 'untouchables' – a demand forcefully spearheaded by Dr B.R. Ambedkar in the deliberations of the conference, and this pushed to the back burner, for some time at least, even the Hindu–Muslim question.

With no general agreement with the government in sight, Gandhi himself was arrested again in January 1932 soon after his return from London, and civil disobedience resumed. Both Asaf and Aruna were again arrested – this would be her second jail term – as were many others. The government this time was prepared and launched a counter-offensive of strong repression. By end 1932 the movement was flagging and government circles were beginning to feel triumphant. Many activists wondered what the agitational phase since 1930 had achieved. Others felt that Gandhi's step-by-step approach was eroding the foundations of imperialism – slowly but surely.

In August 1932 the government announced that the 'Depressed Castes' would also be treated as a 'minority community' and become entitled to separate electorates. To Gandhi the Hindu–Muslim issue appeared to be deadlocked with no easy way out. Carving out the Depressed Castes from the Hindus as a separate political entity had become a more immediate and significant political threat. Still in prison, he began a 'fast unto death' in protest. Begun on 20 September the fast ended on the 24th with an agreement between the Congress and Ambedkar: there would be no separate electorates but seats would be reserved for the Depressed Castes. The government too signalled its agreement to this.

Such issues preoccupied the Congress and its leadership even as it became clear that civil disobedience was petering out. Within the Congress, internal questioning began on how to sustain a nationalist momentum in these circumstances. An older impulse reasserted itself, similar to that of the 'Swarajists' or the Congress Swaraj Party at the time of the Non-cooperation movement, with many in the Congress of the view that elections to legislatures should not be boycotted but contested and won to demonstrate the strength of nationalism. This group felt that using constitutional means and platforms available to push a nationalist agenda from within the legislative bodies should be an option, apart from agitational tactics such as non-cooperation and civil disobedience. Asaf Ali belonged to this group, writing to Mahatma Gandhi in June 1933: 'Our forces which are intact want a change in strategy and a new enthusiasm for a new objective . . . It is merely a question of change of strategy and of tactics.'[17]

This approach was anathema to other Congress leaders committed to the idea of non-cooperation and civil disobedience and wedded to the idea of agitation till Purna Swaraj or complete independence was attained. In Asaf's case we note, however, a consistency in his approach from the 1920s when he had stood from Delhi as a Congress Swarajist and lost in a communally supercharged election. Some important figures such as Jawaharlal were critical of this approach entailing a softening of the agitational posture. Asaf had also written to Nehru at about the same time he had written to Gandhi:[18]

> If the Congress keeps out of the show and prefers to remain in opposition outside the legislatures, the opportunities for tinkering in the provinces will be utilized to delay the precipitation of a real political crisis and the great day, which we all hope for, may recede further away. But with the Congress in office or in opposition in different provinces . . . much may be achieved.

Nehru's response in October 1933 showed how differently this issue could be viewed:

> Personally I think a withdrawal of civil obedience would be a blunder of the first magnitude . . . I do not see how the issue of Council entry arises now. According to the most optimistic estimates any new Council will not begin functioning for three or four years. Practical politicians do not lay down their immediate programme for a contingency which may occur three years later or may not occur at all.[19]

Nehru's reference to a 'new Council', or a new Central Legislature, was to a new Constitution that was expected following the Simon Commission report and the Round Table Conference.

Asaf was only one of many pushing the approach that the next round of elections, in 1934, to the existing Central Legislature should be contested in any case. In May that year a number of Congress leaders met Gandhi to urge him to suspend civil disobedience and encourage 'Council entry' of Congressmen after contesting elections. Heavyweights like C. Rajagoplachari, Rajendra Prasad, Sarojini Naidu and M.A. Ansari led this group. A compromise was thereafter worked out. 'Mass civil disobedience' was called off but 'individual civil disobedience', by which Gandhi meant himself, would continue. The Mahatma was also persuaded into endorsing a dual policy of struggle both within and outside the legislatures. The road was now clear for those Congress leaders who wished to participate in the elections to the Central Legislature due later in the year.

The Delhi seat in this election had a special significance: as mentioned earlier, Delhi had a joint electorate, and the political constituency's location in India's capital loaded it with optical value. Dr Ansari was the acknowledged Congress leader in Delhi and had been so for many years. He was, however, not interested in contesting. This was on account of his ill health but it is possible he felt that, having played a major role in the national affairs of the Congress, he was now above the cut and thrust of a single constituency's politics. In any event his decision not to contest meant a potential vacuum and Asaf Ali was the choice to fill it as the Congress candidate.

But there were problems – and Asaf had faced these in the 1926 election. While he was an established Congress leader of Delhi, he lacked Ansari's national stature. Delhi was a Hindu-majority constituency and it had a joint electorate. Asaf explained these complexities in a letter in July 1934 to Khaliquzzaman, an important Muslim leader who was associated, as were many others at the time, with both the Congress and the Muslim League.[20] 'In Delhi,' Asaf wrote, 'it is practically certain that the Hindu Mahasabha will contest the seat if I am put up.' He had after all contested and lost the election in 1926 to the Hindu Mahasabha-backed candidate when communal polarization had ensured he would not get many Hindu votes. He wrote, 'it [is] also equally certain that the Muslim reactionaries will contribute their quota to the same'. By this he meant that he was now on the wrong side of the Muslim League and therefore the Muslim vote could not be counted on fully. There was now the added complication of his marriage and it meant loss of support from both ends of the spectrum: 'the great objection of the Muslims to me is that I am a Congressman and a pro Hindu and have married a Hindu lady and the greatest objection of the Hindu Mahasabha is that I have married a Hindu lady; so the two sections seem to share this objection in common, failing to find any other . . .'

There was certainly substance in these fears. For instance, in October 1934 that year, as electioneering for seats to the Central Legislature was peaking, a body describing itself as the 'Delhi Muslim Association' passed a resolution to the effect that since the Congress had 'failed to nominate a true Muslim representative', the Muslims of Delhi were 'urged not to vote for Mr Asaf Ali'.[21] There was also the possibility that the more conservative sections within the Congress led by M.M. Malaviya would put up a rival candidate on behalf of a breakaway Nationalist Congress Party or support the Hindu Mahasabha's candidate. Asaf's opponent was Rai Sahib Nanak Chand of the Hindu Mahasabha, someone believed to be favoured by official circles.

But the debits and doubts on Asaf's side were compensated greatly by the Congress realizing the significance of the Delhi contest: a Hindu-majority constituency where it had put up a Muslim candidate. The election therefore saw some heavy lifting by the principal Congress leaders. Jawaharlal Nehru, otherwise strongly opposed to the whole effort of the Congress in contesting elections to win legislative seats, noted in his diary in November 1934: 'I am specially interested in the defeat of . . . Nanak Chand of Delhi.'[22] Ansari played a key role. He contributed substantially in financial terms to Asaf's campaign as he did for many other Congress candidates across the country. And he also put his personal political weight behind Asaf; clearly, this was for him the election of a close personal friend and equally the making of a political statement. Other Congress leaders – Vallabhbhai Patel, Sarojini Naidu, Rajendra Prasad and

C. Rajagopalachari – pitched in. On the day before the polling Gandhi sent a telegram to Asaf Ali, the text of which was published in newspapers on election day: 'I hope every Delhi vote will be cast in your favour.'

Asaf's victory was by a considerable margin, and to him and others in the party it was a symbolic vindication of the Congress position that joint elections were workable and the only way forward.[23] Asaf Ali had 3,424 votes compared to Nanak Chand's 949. The headline describing his victory was 'Delhi Vindicates Joint Electorate'.[24]

~

The end of civil disobedience and these elections to the Central Legislature set the stage for a wider political process. Following the Simon Commission and the tortuous and inconclusive discussions at the Round Table Conference, the Government of India Act of 1935 was enacted by the British parliament and it provided for provincial governments accountable to elected assemblies. The old system of transferred and reserved subjects was ended; all government departments would have elected representatives as their heads as ministers. The party with a majority in the provincial legislature would form the government which would be headed by 'premiers'. The electorate was also substantially widened from about 6.5 million to 30 million across the different provinces of British India. While the governor retained substantial powers, this was nevertheless a significant change and power shift at the provincial level. Elections to these provincial assemblies were held in different parts of British India in February 1937. The Congress did well in these and thereafter went through an intense internal debate on whether to form governments in those provinces where it had gained a majority. Gandhi was to finally tilt the balance in favour of the Congress accepting office. Many who had led agitations, and been non-cooperators and habitual prison-goers, were now ministers and even premiers in different provinces. This was a greater devolution of power than had earlier been the case, and many believed these governments offered the Congress the pedestal it needed for the last phase of the freedom struggle.

The Act of 1935 also had federal provisions, that is, on the structure of a central government. Essentially it introduced to the Centre the system that had existed in the provinces, with transferred and reserved subjects. These federal provisions did not, however, come into effect; in the Central Legislature the older system continued unchanged.

Asaf was now an opposition member from the Congress at the Centre; on the other side were government officials in charge of different departments. He clearly gave importance to this new role and more importantly saw his position as one which he had trained himself for and had worked towards. It revealed a grassroots politician growing in significance and acquiring a new profile. Asaf was to now focus on defence and foreign affairs, and gradually, he noted, 'I established a reputation as the Congress expert and spokesperson on these subjects. Even the Government benches began to pay attention to what I said.'[25] But this transition from agitational politician and lower court lawyer to being a Congress voice on defence and foreign affairs also required major adjustments and changes.

For non-officials to speak authoritatively on foreign affairs was difficult, given the monopoly over information and views exercised by the Foreign Office. Moreover there were only a very small number of knowledgeable persons in the field outside the government. He reflected: 'When you are on an opposition bench, the biggest handicap is the paucity of "matter".'[26] By this he meant not having sufficient evidence to easily make a meaningful contribution to the debate on any particular issue. This could be made up by being 'insensitive to irrelevance' and not mind 'the claptrap and usual vitriolic vituperation'. Rhetorical speeches and good demagogy could be a substitute, in other words, for lack of substance. As a younger man making his reputation in the Delhi branch of the Home Rule League and in the Khilafat protest he had used this technique and as an approach it had worked well. 'I indulged in this species of tub thumping in the early phase of my public life.' But now, even when 'I held audiences spell bound, or drew tears or cheers from them, I felt ashamed of stump oratory'.

He had therefore started discarding these tricks of 'the speaker's trade'. This meant becoming the kind of speaker who 'even at the risk of leaving audiences cold . . . tried to encourage on the part of my hearers an unimpassioned consideration of solid facts'. This shift – from agitation and mobilization at a local level in which being a good orator meant intuitively understanding what the audience wanted to hear to using the knowledge and logic of a sober political figure – was neither a quick nor an easy one:

> I must confess my failure, after twenty years' experience, with large audiences. They expect and appreciate fireworks. Even if you give them information of the weightiest character, they remain dissatisfied. They expect you to hold their attention with resounding phrases: a blow at the idea or person or institution they hate, or hyperbolical praise of what they hold dear or in high estimation.

Asaf was possibly, and even perhaps unconsciously, sketching out the dilemmas of transition which other public figures were also undergoing from the mid-1930s. The Congress had emerged as a major victor in the 1937 elections, winning clear majorities in six of the eleven provinces and becoming the single largest party in three others. What should the balance be between dissent and opposition on the one hand and governance on the other? It was a great dilemma the Congress faced. There was thus an almost natural rush and desire to form provincial governments – to use such power as was available – to implement policies and programmes of their choice. No doubt there would have been the equally inevitable desire to dispense patronage. The difficulty was of reconciling this with opposition to the colonial government: the journey to freedom was after all far from over. If significant achievements were to be expected from an elected government compared to a bureaucratic Raj, the attendant risk was of factionalism over the spoils of office and patronage.

The Congress did move finally to form governments in the provinces in which it had won an electoral majority: Madras, Bombay, the Central Provinces, Orissa, Bihar and the United Provinces; and then also went on to form the government in Assam and the North West Frontier. Within a year Nehru felt that the Congress had lost momentum by such office acceptance and the difficulty of reconciling being in power in provinces with being in opposition mode at the Centre had taken a toll.[27] Many had anticipated this and Gandhi had for instance written about office acceptance in August 1937: 'These offices have to be held lightly not tightly' and 'they are or should be crowns of thorns, never of renown'.[28]

There were other transitions for Asaf. M.A. Ansari died in May 1936. Asaf's association with him had begun soon after his return from England a quarter of a century earlier. 'My back is broken and I feel myself a helpless orphan after Dr Ansari's death,' he said in a public condolence meeting.[29] This certainly summarized their relationship in many ways. Ansari was a close friend, a mentor and a guide and most of all the closest link to Gandhi someone like Asaf could possibly have had. Hakim Ajmal Khan had died in 1927 and Ansari's death now also meant that Asaf had become in effect the senior Congress leader in Delhi. The mantle of leading the Muslims in the Congress or the 'nationalist Muslims' would similarly now devolve on another old friend, Abul Kalam Azad.

Another transition involved the Ali brothers – once friends of Asaf but with whom his relationship had taken a bitter turn almost two decades earlier and never recovered thereafter. Mohammad Ali died in 1931 and Shaukat Ali in 1938. Following the collapse of the Khilafat movement the brothers had in many ways personified the gulf that many Muslims felt separated them from the Congress. For the Ali brothers, in the last phase of their lives the Congress appeared more and more to be an exclusivist Hindu party and those Muslims who were associated with it – such as Ansari, A.K. Azad and Asaf Ali – were traitors. With the death of the Ali brothers, Jinnah would become the tallest leader in the Muslim League at the national level.

The League's performance in the 1937 elections was not creditable given the profile it had adopted at an all-India level: even with the separate electorates it won only 109 of the 482 Muslim seats. It did not do well even in the Muslim-majority provinces of Punjab and Bengal. For those in the Congress who felt triumphant at the League's poor showing, its own roots were revealed to be shallow: the Congress won only twenty-six Muslim seats and in fact it had put up only fifty-eight candidates for the Muslim seats. Moreover the Congress forming governments in a number of provinces provided the League a potent platform to mobilize on the grounds that Muslims were being oppressed and discriminated against. Ironically, Jinnah the constitutionalist and the moderate would now successfully make the Muslim League into a significant platform for channelling real and imagined Muslim grievances against the Congress and putting it on the defensive, especially in those provinces where it formed the government.

For Asaf, membership of the Central Legislature meant an even wider canvas than intervention in debates on defence and foreign policy. There was also a broader acquaintance with Congressmen from across the country and other legislators, and this meant frequent consultations with them and a wider field of activity than his earlier focus on Delhi and its hinterland. In the Central Legislature he was the Congress chief whip and later the secretary of the Congress Legislative party. Perhaps now, out of the shadow of Dr Ansari and Hakim Ajmal Khan, he was dealing from a position of greater equality with others in the same position as himself: the large mid-level of the party.

One close acquaintance, perhaps even friend, was the Madras politician T.V. Sathyamurthy (1887–1943), who was also a member of the Central Legislature and with whom Asaf was to interact closely on the range of issues the Congress party dealt with from the mid-1930s onwards. Sathyamurthy was his senior – not so much in age but in the Congress pecking order – and his legislative career had begun in the Madras Legislative Council in 1923. In 1935 he was the president of the Provincial Congress Committee of Madras and was a serious contender to head the provincial government in Madras after the 1937 elections; but intra-Congress factionalism meant that C. Rajagopalachari got the post.[30]

Sathyamurthy and Asaf appear to have got along well, as is suggested by such of their correspondence as has survived. We find in them a free communication of views and also frustrations. On 24 April 1937 Asaf wrote: 'Have you heard my latest epigram – "Most of the world suffers from handicaps but India suffers from Gandhicaps" and that the "Gandhicap" is "almost the superlative of handicap".' The epigram, Asaf wrote also, was irresistible although 'I love and respect the dear old man too much to make fun of him'.[31] Both Asaf and Sathyamurthy were part of the group concerned that more agitational voices would tilt the balance against the Congress contesting elections and forming the government in the provinces it had won elections in. Nehru was sympathetic to the agitational approach, and we find Asaf writing on 13 August 1936: 'I fear Jawaharlal may suddenly take the bit and gallop away, if he happens to "shy" at acceptance.' Such views also reflect the private sentiments of those close to real decision-making levels but not part of them. We have for instance Asaf writing on 24 April 1937 with some rancour: 'Have you noticed every Tom, Dick and Harry has been summoned for consultation to Allahabad? But, I believe our Leader has the collective wisdom of all of us put together. And, after all, what are we – just legislators – mere sentries guarding the gates of the mighty one's Palace.' To this Sathyamurthy had replied that he entirely agreed 'that the working committee is perhaps more unapproachable than the government of India. People of ideas are kept at arm's length.'[32]

Yet despite such occasional griping, in the mid- and late 1930s Asaf was active in the Congress, secure in the upper ranks of its hierarchy as a member of the Central Legislature and as the most prominent Congressman of Delhi at the time. Perhaps he may have felt a sense of contentment at the trajectory of his personal and political life, built up in many ways block by block. Certainly, he valued his membership of the Central Legislature and may have also felt the overall direction of the Congress was positive, with just the right balance of agitation and constructive governance, although the growing strength of the Muslim League under Jinnah was a cause of worry. He was to move further up the Congress hierarchy, becoming a member of the All-India Congress Committee (AICC) and then its apex body, the Working Committee, in 1940. That his old friend and someone he admired greatly, Abul Kalam Azad was now the Congress president was no doubt related to this advancement. There were others in it he knew well, particularly Sarojini who was a member as a former president of the Congress. Syed Mahmud was also a member and had been for some years, reflecting his strength in the Bihar Congress, his position in the national hierarchy and his proximity to the Nehrus.

We know far less about Aruna's preoccupations and interests at this time. As a couple both were recognizable figures even in those Congress circles that were more exclusive. A fellow Congressman of Asaf in the Central Legislature recalled Aruna in the mid-1930s playing 'the hostess for our Party's evening get-together'.[33] Both were present at another controversial wedding – although it was much more high profile than theirs – when Jawaharlal Nehru's daughter Indira married a Parsi, Feroze Gandhi, in March 1942.[34] Perhaps the Asaf Alis were largely seen as a couple who lived the Congress creed of Hindu–Muslim unity, the defining motifs of their lives being nationalism and the freedom struggle, rather than the established upper-middle-class pursuits of a successful career as a lawyer or something similar, accompanied by social success in the elite circles.

But their social circle did appear to be wide, extending beyond the Congress circle. The civil servant B.K. Nehru – son of Brijlal and Rameshwari Nehru, early friends and mentors of Asaf and Aruna – noted that in 1940 when he had returned to Delhi after a posting in London, 'The Asaf Alis belonged to the same social set as ourselves'. About Aruna he recalled 'she was no negligible player in our fun and frolic'.[35]

For Aruna, after the hectic activity and two jail terms that characterize the first four or five years of her marriage, the subsequent decade or so seemed a more placid phase. However, there was not a complete severance of public activity. There was activity in the All-India Women's Conference with occasional meetings in different parts of India and Aruna's presence in these would invariably figure in news reports. But certainly, there is less about her in the newspapers and she appears to have almost consciously lowered her profile.

For a time, she was quite taken up with radio broadcasting – still something of a novelty in India then. Over 1936 and 1937 she regularly gave radio talks on subjects that sound distinctly quaint today but were perhaps then the staple and had resonance in a different age. Very likely the subjects or title of each talk was suggested by the Delhi radio station itself. These were both in Hindi and in English, so clearly her skills in the former were improving. Some of the titles have survived thanks to the details of radio programmes being published daily in newspapers. The Hindi broadcasts included: *Girls and Social Work; Domestic Quarrels; Domestic Etiquette; Mid-summer Showers;* English ones for example were: *My Favourite Records; The Work of the Municipality*, etc. A series of radio talks on *Wedding Customs across the World* was much appreciated. An article otherwise critical of the Delhi radio station's programming and content noted appreciatively: 'The series by Mrs Aruna Asaf Ali on the marriage customs of various countries were much enjoyed. She has a special gift to speak on the mike and the listeners are fascinated by her charming voice.'[36]

It is possible that Aruna was trying out a number of roles through this period after being thrown into the politics of the Salt Satyagraha and civil disobedience soon after her marriage: reading voraciously, active in the All-India Women's Conference, trying out radio broadcasting, and perhaps also engaging with her redoubtable mentor Satyawati Devi on other fronts. But she seems to have consciously adopted a low profile in Asaf's election campaign; perhaps her being out in the front would have been politically too sensitive given the communal considerations involved. None of these roles was all-consuming. Asaf later suggested in his writings, with a degree of conjugal disapproval, that her interests were sequential and often jostled with each other for primacy:[37]

> Once an idea has caught her imagination, she rides it to gallop until the tired steed has to be discarded or put to rest. First the social pony, Saraswati Bhawan, trained to perfection, fell from favour. And Irwin College took its place. Then Irwin College faded out and the Women's Conference succeeded. One day the Women's Conference was abandoned and journalism followed as the next quarry, and serious

> study filled the hours. But the political bias swelled all the time to the point of flood . . . The governing passion of the time claims all her energy and time.

'Saraswati Bhawan' referred to Mrs Rameshwari Nehru's Delhi Women's League. Possibly Asaf saw it largely as a social circle and hence the reference to 'social pony'.

So Asaf, who knew her best – if anyone could claim to know her at all – perhaps saw her as restless and possibly seeking something new that would become her chosen track. A larger change in Indian politics, amidst a wider geopolitical turmoil in the form of a world war, would catalyze this restless energy into the channel she sought.

# 15

# Ahmednagar

The outbreak of war in Europe in September 1939 had as its immediate impact the resignation of the Congress-led provincial governments in late October. This was on the grounds that India was not consulted before Great Britain made it a party to war against Germany in Europe. The real point of contention soon became the Congress wanting a clear commitment from the British on sovereignty and freedom after the war. Such assurance was not forthcoming, and so despite the private sympathy many in India felt – and possibly most of the Congress Working Committee (CWC) shared – for Britain's situation with its back against the wall by Hitler's Germany, the confrontation between the Congress and the colonial government had already germinated.

The British had in fact made an arrogant and fatal miscalculation as far as India's position in the war was concerned. By dispensing with even a formulaic consultation process with the elected bodies in India and then not backing down from this position, it narrowed options for the Congress and pushed it, much against the will of many Congressmen, into more confrontational positions. On their part British officialdom – both in London and in New Delhi – saw the Congress attitude as a stab in the back. Some prominent Congress leaders, in particular C. Rajagopalachari in Madras, tried hard to resist this turn to confrontation but without success. Asaf Ali himself had much sympathy with this approach of avoiding confrontation. The Congress decision that its legislators stop attending sessions of the Central Assembly had left Asaf and many like him disappointed. But it was difficult to argue against the predominant view and the government's arrogance made positions such as his weak.

There was alongside a more significant political shift under way. For the government the familiar way to deal with the Congress was to build up the Muslim League so that the contest was no longer between the Congress and the British Raj: there was a third party. The viceroy's statement in October 1939 summed up this approach with classic governmental obliqueness: 'It was unthinkable' to move forward 'without again taking counsel with those who have been in the recent past so closely associated in a like task'.[1]

The period of the Congress provincial governments had been the window the Muslim League needed to recover from their less-than-optimal performance in the 1937 elections. League propaganda against the Congress ministries had many planks. Optically most powerful were the alleged enforced singing of 'Vande Mataram', bans on cow slaughter, encouragement of Hindi and Devanagari at the expense of Urdu and the promotion of an anti-Islamic education scheme. It is debatable how much of this was truth and how much exaggeration but much of it fell on fertile ground.

Syed Mahmud had been made minister of education in Bihar when the Congress formed the provincial government. His case was singled out for the Muslim League's propaganda machine that a Hindu Raj had been foisted on Bihar. In some accounts, his long years of nationalist politics and in the Congress had made him a natural to be the premier of Bihar heading the Congress government. His progress up the Congress ladder had been steady: he had been a general secretary of the Congress till 1936 and a member of the CWC from 1934. Azad certainly thought so and was later to write: 'Syed Mahmud was the top leader of the province when the elections were held.' There were of course opposing arguments to his candidature as premier but the point was of perceptions. And when he was edged out from the top job in the province, it buttressed the Muslim League's claims of anti-Muslim discrimination.

Syed Mahmud's basic approach was that the minority community's concerns needed to be addressed frontally since 'reconciliation was only possible with concessions on both sides, and that the Hindus in particular being the stronger party should be generous'.[2] Both during the period of their government and after the resignation of the Congress ministries, as the Muslim League's profile grew, Syed Mahmud would frequently find himself its principal focus in Bihar, even as his pleas to the Congress for greater accommodation were viewed with growing suspicion or at least impatience by colleagues in the Bihar Congress convinced that Muslims were making unreasonable demands.

In March 1940 his mother-in-law's funeral in Chhapra was boycotted, at the instance of the Muslim League. Mahmud wrote to Nehru on 23 March 1940: 'The limit has been reached indeed. This is your country. My poor wife is feeling this very much. Amongst the Musalmans this is the greatest form of insult conceivable.'[3] How much of an issue this was then is brought out by letters that colleagues and fellow Congressmen wrote to him – in solidarity and shock but also in frustration. Rajendra Prasad was to write: 'This is a most outrageous thing and no words are strong enough to condemn the act. But we are living in a strange age and unthinkable things are happening all around.' Similarly, Jawaharlal Nehru: 'this is scandalous . . . the Muslim League is deliberately not only trying to sabotage the whole conception of Indian freedom but also poisoning personal life and lowering the standards of public life.'[4]

The Muslim League had, upon the resignation of the Congress ministries, called upon Muslims to observe 22 December 1939 as a 'Day of Deliverance' from the Congress. A little later, in March 1940 in Lahore, the League adopted the 'Pakistan Resolution': that only the creation of autonomous and sovereign Muslim-majority states in the north-west and the east of the subcontinent would be acceptable to the Muslims of India. The term 'Pakistan' here is strictly speaking a misnomer: the word did not figure in the text in much the same way as 'Quit India' did not figure in the August 1942 Congress resolution that launched this agitation against the British.

But that is what the headline was and it has remained that. The 'Pakistan Resolution' was by no means a point of no return but it did underline that Hindu–Muslim differences had solidified further and the accumulated polarization of the earlier years was taking a toll.

It also underwrote how the terrain of the Hindu–Muslim debate had been shifting in India from the 1930s as demands for dominion status or full independence made these realistic possibilities. The question was increasingly not one just of Muslim representation: whether separate electorates were the best means of ensuring adequate representation to a minority. With two large Muslim-majority regions in the east and west, the question also was: what should be the relationship between a Muslim province and the central government? In a sense this brought together the two fundamental aspects of the Hindu–Muslim interface in political and constitutional terms in pre-1947 India: a communal and representational issue given the fact that the Muslims were overall a minority in India and in most of the provinces; and also a federal question in that Muslims were a significant majority in Punjab, Bengal and the NWFP, and sought recognition of this in the relative distribution of future power between the Centre and the states.

B.R. Ambedkar, the backward-caste leader, wrote in detail about this in his book *Thoughts on Pakistan* which appeared within months of the March 1940 Muslim League Resolution. There was, he noted, in the Muslim-majority provinces, an anxiety 'to see that the independence of the Muslim governments was preserved'. This was because it was possible to envisage situations in which these provinces were 'made subject to a central government predominantly Hindu and endowed with powers of supervision and even interference in [their] administration'.[5] In brief the issue had shifted from one of representation alone to one which considered the balance of power and legal authority between the provinces and the Centre. The Muslim League increasingly now demanded a constitutional structure with a weak Centre and strong provinces. The Congress view was the opposite: such a weak Centre would lead to a fragmentation of the whole country.

To correct the drift towards a confrontation with the government following the resignation of the Congress ministries, the Congress did make overtures to the government in mid-1940 – largely at the initiative of C. Rajagopalachari and perhaps much against the Mahatma's own inclination – but these were spurned. While doing so, Viceroy Lord Linlithgow had also raised questions about the Congress's capacity to speak for all of India. Its authority, he said, was 'directly denied by large and powerful elements in India's national life'.[6] The subtext obviously was that the Congress was not representative of Muslim opinion. Early in 1940, Azad as Congress president had written to Jinnah suggesting that the Congress could consider a multiparty government at the Centre for the duration of the war. Jinnah had refused to even engage or explore the idea with someone he termed 'a Muslim showboy' Congress president. These contestations continued over 1941 in the midst of a 'no war' 'no peace' situation in the Congress–British Raj interface.

Many prominent Congress leaders including Nehru, Azad, Patel and Rajagopalachari were arrested for speaking against cooperation with the war effort. Asaf and Aruna too were arrested, the former in December 1940 and the latter in February 1941.[7] For both now going to jail was not a new tribulation; both appear matter-of-fact about it and would have regarded themselves as seasoned at it although it had been a decade or so since they last served prison terms. The existing government records reflect their new status and public profile. The sentencing magistrate referred to Asaf as 'one of the old leaders of Delhi' who had been in jail 'a number of times for taking part in antigovernment activity'.[8] Some months later he surprised the Delhi authorities by seeking a 'western diet' if it was possible. After a search for precedents – which did not seem to exist – the request was agreed to.[9] During Aruna's sentencing in February 1941 to twelve months of simple imprisonment, the magistrate noted that he had 'convicted her twice before in 1930 and 1932' and recommended that she be given higher-category status as a prisoner, noting also that she was the wife of a member of the Legislative Assembly.[10]

Japan's attack on Pearl Harbor in December 1941 and its astonishing advance across South East Asia radically altered this choreography. The attack on Pearl Harbor meant the entry of the United States into the war: a European war and a Sino-Japan war was now transformed into a world war. Singapore fell to the Japanese in February 1942 and Rangoon in March. With the Japanese in Burma there was a real danger to the Indian empire and the war was no longer an abstract issue for Indians. The internal political situation in the country therefore assumed a new significance for the British.

The British government dispatched Sir Stafford Cripps to India in March 1942 to offer new proposals that could, it believed, be the basis for a cooperative front between the government and the Congress. Congress leaders arrested had also been released piecemeal and the period saw protracted negotiations. The 'Cripps proposal' in essence was dominion status after the war and, immediately, a 'national government' with participation of all political parties. There was some ambiguity about the national government and its powers but there were other sticking points. Contained in these proposals was the idea that those parties which did not want to stay within the future dominion would be free to opt out – clearly a major concession to Jinnah and the Muslim League and, or so it appeared to many, an implicit acknowledgement that the Muslim League demand for separate sovereign states in the Muslim-majority parts of the country had registered and received some extent of official recognition.

The idea generated much debate and concern within the Congress and suspicions about the government's malign intentions but was not the principal reason why the Cripps Mission failed. The sticking point concerned the viceroy's powers and that the national government would have nothing to do with all defence-related matters. The failure to reach an agreement during Cripps's visit also had much to do with the viceroy who disliked the whole approach of parlaying with the Congress when it had adopted a posture of defiance at a time when Britain was fighting for survival.

Alongside, divisions within the Congress were also taking their toll. By July 1942 C. Rajagopalachari, then certainly amongst the four or five tallest figures in the Congress, had resigned from the party over disagreement with the dominant party view on two central issues. First, with regard to the Muslim League he proposed agreeing to the demand for separation of the Muslim-majority areas if they so wished. Second, he opposed the hard line the Congress was embarking on and the agitational approach it was veering towards, following the failure of the Cripps Mission. Both stances isolated him within the party but it is also clear that he was by no means alone in holding such views. To someone like Asaf it would have appeared that calculated and clinical reasoning was taking a back seat to sentiment and inflammatory rhetoric.

The stage was now set for the CWC deliberations of August 1942 that led to the adoption of the 'Quit India' resolution and the crackdown on the Congress that followed. The wave of arrests that followed the CWC meeting in Bombay on 8 August 1942 had been meticulously planned by the Government of India and instructions about the procedures to be followed sent to all the provinces well in advance. The resolution adopted by the CWC was not, however, intended as a point of no return, but only an additional point of pressure on the government in the hope that it could catalyze an invitation to negotiate. The term 'Quit India' was not used in the resolution. But the speeches in the session were belligerent and there was enough in the resolution to give the government formal cause to act. In any case Prime Minister Churchill in London and Viceroy Linlithgow in Delhi had been looking for the appropriate moment to strike and they felt they had enough cause. The attitude of the Congress since the outbreak of World War II and the recent string of British military defeats in South East Asia had brewed a cocktail of frustrations in both Delhi and in London that needed release. Banning the Congress, incarcerating its leadership and putting down any protests with a heavy hand seemed to be just that release.

Asaf was in Bombay from 4 August for the CWC meeting and staying with a friend, K.F. Nariman, a prominent lawyer and Bombay Congressman. While in Delhi he had received a tip-off about the impending arrests and that they were timed for immediately after the CWC meeting. Aruna joined him from Delhi on the 6th with further confirmation that orders had been issued 'for our arrest and detention in a special concentration camp – in a fort'. The Government of India leaked, then as now, like a sieve. The same source had also updated Asaf that 'the confidential correspondence between the Viceroy and the Secretary of State contained suggestions about deporting Gandhi to Uganda but finally the proposal was dropped'. Asaf, however, noted that 'none of us gave full credence to this information'.[11]

When Aruna came with further confirmation, others in the CWC remained disbelieving of 'these Delhiwallas' that there would be a government crackdown on the Congress. In Aruna's recollection, Sarojini Naidu and Maulana Azad were somewhat scornful, saying, '*Yeh afimchi ki kahani hain. Aisa nahin hoga, arre* these are all rumours' (These are tales of opium eaters. Nothing like this will happen).[12] The CWC, Asaf recalled, 'could not dream of any precipitate action on the part of the government' because it did not think it had thrown down a gauntlet. But for the British, beleaguered and defensive, the Congress attitude represented a stab in the back: to the official mind, the Congress leadership needed to be taught a lesson.

On the early morning of 9 August his host woke Asaf up: 'Are you awake? They have come to fetch you and me.' Aruna accompanied them to the railway station, Victoria Terminus. They found Sarojini Naidu, Maulana Azad, Nehru and other Congress leaders similarly arrested. As the train pulled away Asaf looked at Aruna on the platform: 'Her face was livid with suppressed anger and heaven knows with what rapid trains of thought or gusts of emotion – not personal only, although she had as much reason as I had to wonder [if] this would not be a goodbye for good.'[13]

On the train Asaf found himself soon in the restaurant car 'to regale ourselves with the dainties provided by the Bombay government whose involuntary guests we were'. Gandhi was on the same train, along with the Working Committee and the prominent leaders of Congress. Accompanying him were his faithful secretary Mahadev Desai, Mirabai or Madeleine Slade, and Manibehn, Patel's daughter. Also on the train were a number of prominent Bombay Congress leaders including the mayor of Bombay Yusuf Meherally, Nariman – Asaf's host – and others. 'As we passed station after station, we found the platforms guarded by the police, with not even railway staff or porters on the platforms.' Despite what appeared to be a tension-filled and eerie atmosphere outside, the mood inside was upbeat: the Maulana in particular was full of mirth. 'I thought,' writes Asaf, 'it was due to the sudden cessation of prolonged tension. We felt for the moment a load of cares was off our minds.' But there had been some anxious moments earlier. The senior police officer on duty in Bombay at the railway station, a tall English deputy inspector general of police, 'dressed in serge and wearing a felt hat', was 'promenading the station platform with an air of satisfaction – obviously at a preconcerted programme being almost fully carried out'. He asked Yusuf Meherally to move to a compartment where other Bombay Congress leaders were, addressing him as 'my boy'. Meherally had stretched himself to his full but still very short height and rejoined: 'You call me a boy! I am the Mayor of Bombay!' Asaf recalled that it was with difficulty that a scuffle was prevented and a truce affected by the 'silver tongued Pattabhi Sitaramayya', a former president of the Congress and its fiftieth-anniversary historian.[14]

As the train neared Poona, the word spread that Gandhi and his party would be detraining there. Their prison was to be the Aga Khan palace in Poona which the government had secretly rented for this very purpose. Sarojini, the only woman in the CWC, was to be jailed along with the Gandhi party. The Bombay Congress leaders would also alight, to be taken to the Yerwada prison. Those remaining – the CWC – had been in different train compartments from Gandhi and his party and from the Bombay Congress members. In Poona as 'Gandhiji, Mrs Naidu, Mahadev Desai, and Manibehn walked past our compartment, some of them waved to us'. Asaf noted, 'A few of us had an uncomfortable feeling that we might not see Gandhiji again . . . I at any rate felt that this might be the last time I was seeing the great man.' He elaborates:

> The scene before me was unspectacular: a puny, sparsely clad old man accompanied among others by three women (one of them a widely known poet and another an Englishwoman wearing coarse Indian homespun). Yet it stirred in my mind memories of Herod, Pilate, the grand priest of the Jews, Christ and the Cross, mixed up with pictures which future historians might draw in a sequence of parallelism.[15]

Some actual scuffles also took place in the Poona railway station. Nehru jumped out of his compartment's unbarred window when he saw some stray Congress workers being beaten up by the police on the platform and had to be restrained by force.

The CWC members soon reached their destination: their prison was the Ahmednagar fort. The original sixteenth-century Nizamshahi structure was now a British military garrison. It had been used intermittently as a prisoner-of-war camp – during the Boer war; for German internees during World War I and for Italians in World War II – but clearly this group was more distinguished than any other incarcerated previously. The inputs Aruna and Asaf had received from their source within the government – that they would be locked up in a fort – had been entirely accurate. The government had felt that it was sufficiently secure and cut off for the detainees to be held in secret. Other options had been considered both for Gandhi and for the CWC leaders. The possibilities had included Aden, Sudan and Uganda, for the object also was to teach the Congress a lesson. Practicalities and wiser counsel prevailed and the fort in Ahmednagar was decided upon; it would be where Asaf Ali and eleven other members of the CWC would spend nearly three years with just each other for company.

They alighted from the train and were put on a bus 'having a low roof which made the Maulana and the rest of us bend their heads little too low, and almost to the point of doubling our bodies'.[16] En route, as it became crystal clear what their destination was, some felt their historical imagination kindle. To Azad, the fort brought to mind 'several forgotten footprints of time'. As they neared the fort and its ramparts became visible, he looked to see if he could identify its moat that had been described by the medieval historian and Akbar's favourite courtier Abul Fazl (1551–1602), and later by General Arthur Wellesley (1769–1852), in time more famous as the Duke of Wellington. Azad could not spot the moat and wondered if it had been filled in the past century and a half.[17] Asaf Ali's thoughts also turned to history:

> Aurangzeb's grave is scarcely fifty miles from here. And I often say to myself: 'And the Mughal empire was buried with him.' It is a strange coincidence that, sitting in this fortress prison of Ahmednagar we are witnessing the guttering of the British power's candle . . . The Union Jack is daily hoisted on the bastion which faces us. I say to myself 'This is the last of it. It cannot float in India after this war.'[18]

We have an unusually detailed picture of this group of detainees and the cloistered lives they led in Ahmednagar fort because a number of them kept diaries, including, as we know, Asaf himself. The more diligent of such diarists included Pattabhi Sitaramayya. He combined in his daily writings a detailed catalogue of different activities, discussions and pastimes along with a vast amount of trivia he picked up either from his co-prisoners or from his reading. In addition, Jawaharlal Nehru and Maulana Azad also wrote a great deal about their lives in the three years spent in Ahmednagar Fort.

The prisoners numbered twelve in all, with ages ranging from the early forties to the late sixties. The three obvious leaders were Maulana Azad, who was president of the Congress, Vallabhbhai Patel and Jawaharlal Nehru. G.B. Pant came next in the hierarchy, possibly because he had been the premier of the United Provinces, British India's largest province, following the 1937 elections. He had not travelled on the special train with the rest of the party. The police party sent to arrest him early on the 9th morning was nonplussed when he refused to get up from bed and sent word that they should return at a more appropriate time. His sheer bulk made them adopt a more prudent course of action and he was separately motored down from Bombay a day later. The others included Asaf Ali, Syed Mahmud from Bihar, Shankarrao Deo from Maharashtra, Prafulla Ghosh from Bengal, J.B. Kripalani from Sindh, Harekrushna Mahatab from Orissa, Narendra Deva from the United Provinces, and Pattabhi Sitaramayya from Madras. While each of them knew the others because of political activity, nevertheless three years together in a confined space meant an unusual intimacy and camaraderie but also its own set of frictions and tensions. Sitaramayya wrote:

> Little did we, a small compact body . . . who had been meeting month to month for years, expect to spend time together in a building eating at a common table, chatting, playing, joking . . . Acquainted we had been for years, we have known little of each other, less of one other's families . . . We were representing different provinces and therefore temperaments having different systems of cooking, eating and regaling ourselves.[19]

Certainly, at the beginning none expected a long incarceration: the impression was that after being locked up for some months the path to negotiation would open up. That had been the pattern in the past.

This was not the first prison experience for any of them but it was possibly the longest for most, although Azad noted that he was earlier continuously in prison from 1916 to 1920. It was also perhaps the most rigorous in terms of how tightly contact with the outside world was controlled. Perimeter security and insulating the prisoners from any external contact was entrusted to the custodians of the fort: the army. The internal administration of the makeshift prison was the responsibility of the Bombay government. Azad wrote soon after arrival at the fort:

> Defense Department has taken us under its charge. The entrants are checked according to the list provided by the police. All possible arrangements for security and for snapping our contact with the outside world are in place. Beyond this they are not concerned. Internal

arrangement is entirely in the hands of the Home Department of the Bombay government. Real substantial action is the concern solely of Central government.[20]

Initially no letters, newspapers or books were allowed. Shankarrao Deo recalled:

> For the first one month we had no connection with the outside world. Nobody was allowed to come inside or go outside. No interviews, no letters, no papers, nothing that could help us have some glimpse of the happenings outside were allowed. The jailor himself had become a prisoner like us. He had to live with us for 24 hours. The warders and sepoys were also given accommodation in the jail, in the fort. And if some outside help was necessary generally the British soldiers were asked to come and help.[21]

The jailer and the warders were also closely searched on entry and exit from the jail on the rare occasions they ventured out.

In the initial weeks the prisoners focused on settling down. All being prison veterans, none of them were greatly impressed by this medieval fort now a makeshift jail:

> We drove to the Fort, passed an English sentry, alighted from the bus inside it at an inner gate to which a few yards of a high gradient road led and the doors opened before us and shut behind us. But none of those huge grating doors which guard a central jail, none of those liveried sentry sepoys with arms on their shoulders! It was rather an unprepossessing gate through which we came to a large quadrangle, enclosing an ill kept lawn in the middle with a broad verandah all round on three sides covered by a Mangalore tin roof, and with terraced halls looking old and dilapidated.[22]

These halls, some 20 by 25 feet, separated by partitions of asbestos sheets, were their accommodation. There was electricity – two 'punkhas' in each hall – and coir mats but 'the odour was musty and semi cadaverous later on developing to faecal intensity'. The windows opening outside had been recently bricked in; clearly the authorities were taking no chances. In each hall 'there was a huge cushion chair . . . a small frail dinner chair, a chest of drawers and a small almyra, a wardrobe – some big some small; a wash basin and a water carrier'. The mosquito curtains were 'of various ages, some of which may have been heirlooms from Shivaji's days'.[23] Clearly the accommodation had been made ready in a hurry and the furniture was taken from government guest houses and offices in the vicinity. Over time British Tommies would be called in to break down the bricked-in walls and the windows could be opened.

But each step forward required brushes with the authorities. This was not so much with their jailer – 'a poor creature', 'half timid and half awe struck' – but with the deputy commissioner of the district and the inspector general of prisons, both of whom would in turn only act on instructions from New Delhi relayed by their superiors in the Bombay government. Each of the Congress leaders, and even more so collectively, were at their best in brushes with authority, no matter what it was. On arrival the jailer had 'served them a heapful of bread and butter in a "Thali"'. The mistake was to have taken the 'the tea paraphernalia' to the Maulana 'which sent him 'into a towering rage'. The tea was 'promptly refused unless served in trays and accompanied by cups and saucers, spoons and forks, kettles and cutlery'.[24] The Maulana was fastidious about tea and the concoction being served was an abomination to him – a 'whole lot of lives are not enough to cover the distance' of milk and tea, he wrote in his prison letters which have many pages and verses devoted to tea and how it is to be correctly made and consumed.[25] The group therefore did without tea the first day but the demand was conceded and the process of settling down began.

Gradually the regimen of no newspapers was eased although letters would be censored and were invariably delayed. There were strict limits on the number of letters that could be sent or received and were only allowed to relatives. 'Large portions of the incoming letters were blacked out with a brush! The fate of the outgoing letters, we assumed, must have been the same.'[26] With the newspapers trickling in after about three weeks came information from the outside of the violence that had taken place countrywide as news spread of the arrests of the nationalist leadership. Asaf wrote on 2 September:

> I was moved to the very depths of my being when I learnt last night that Delhi was in the grip of an upheaval of anger for several days. Hell, it seems, was let loose almost at the start, when the police shot dead 12 demonstrators and injured God knows how many . . . Is it a wonder that the result was counterviolence by the people?

The fact is that at the CWC meeting before the arrests and crackdown Asaf was in the minority arguing against any precipitate action such as giving an ultimatum, and adopting a resolution that would be seen as the Congress's Quit India call to the British was just that. But he also saw clearly the responsibility of the government in mishandling the whole situation. 'Did they not know that by putting a match to the powder magazine of public resentment and by shutting up precisely those persons who constitute a veritable fire brigade, they would sabotage the very war effort they were so concerned about?'

A number of convicts from the Ahmednagar jail had been provided by the administration to act as helpers and also as cooks but their turnover was rapid and they needed supervision by the detainees. Looking after a group of important politicians was not their core competence. In the early weeks of imprisonment an internal order was established by the detainees. First the food and the menu had to be improved. The entire party understood the importance of cooperative endeavour:

> We are busy allotting duties to the members and rotating them every week. The voluntary system is encouraging but everyone should make themselves familiar with every set of duties. Breakfast implies

> knowledge of preparing omelets and toasting bread, besides making tea and coffee and egg flip [*sic*]. Night meal includes frying potatoes.

Conversation at mealtimes would often go into the minutiae of food. But this was an India-wide congregation of well-informed and highly inquisitive individuals. Regional variations in food and cooking and of the varieties of ingredients were therefore dissected in considerable detail. For instance:

> Dalia, how is it to be prepared, a comparison of brown bread with white, whether the brown bread is really whole meal or merely coloured, why we are not given hand pounded rice, what par boiled rice is – which many amongst us had never heard of, how it has in Bengal and Tamil Nadu, obviated the need for hand pounded rice . . . whether fish or mutton should be fried or cooked, and if the latter, how much of ghee or in their own fat, whether masala should be added or not . . .[27]

One can imagine these details of cooking would have been a novelty to them, this not being a subject any of them would have given much time or thought to.

Then a badminton court was set up. This too was taken seriously and tournaments were organized to relieve 'the tediousness of life': 'Although there are only six or seven players some of whom have to be forced into the court like sheep into the slaughter house. But the tournament itself is conducted with all due ceremony, the bell, the book, the tossing, the score the umpire and linesmen.'[28] None of the players were athletes and 'ere long, by the beginning of October, four friends (players) had a bad elbow and they changed hands i.e. two right handed began laying with the left and one left handed with the right. The fourth discretely gave up for a long interval.'[29] Possibly most of the prisoners had carried with them the personal belongings they had in Bombay. In Ahmednagar fort they were informed after the initial settling in that they could ask for clothes from their respective homes.

And finally, among these pastimes was gardening, initially a passion for Asaf and Nehru, but others joined in too. This required overcoming the objections of the jailer; this was wartime and news of escapes from prisoner-of-war camps in Europe made headlines across the world.

> Even the small pits dug for the garden have upset the people here. Nor is their fear groundless. We learn that the Military is eternally obsessed by the one thought that we may escape. It is not possible to change their minds – even if we may convince them that we are of a different sort . . . they continue to think that if you dig up the ground for a garden . . . you are excavating an underground tunnel.[30]

Evidently persuasion worked, and by end October, about ten weeks or so into their detention, Asaf wrote, 'gardening has become an absorbing pastime for Jawahar and myself now . . . We started sowing three or four days ago.' Soon thereafter: 'We had the privilege of witnessing the first appearance of the seedlings yesterday. Patel noticed it first and then Jawaharlal shouted the glad tidings to me and I felt like a child securing his first toy.'[31]

Gardening provided also the basis for much philosophical musing. To Asaf, 'Gardening is a cooperative endeavour . . . No garden can spring up without collective labour, care and constant tending. In life, too, it is the same. Some prepare the ground and others raise seeds. And often, yet others, reap the harvest.'

A few weeks later, 'morning glory began to flower a week ago, beginning almost from the bottom of the creepers . . . I spend quite a bit of my time, and so do the others, particularly Patel, Jawaharlal and even Maulana in visiting and examining each seedling and appraising them.' Another shared pastime was birdwatching. After a year and a half in Ahmednagar, Nehru learnt of Asaf's interest in birds and was to write that his 'knowledge of birdlore is considerable'.[32]

This enforced seclusion was for some an extraordinarily creative period. This was after all a diverse and highly talented group of individuals. Nehru noted at one stage in a letter in 1943: 'You may be surprised to learn how many languages are represented in our group, nearly all of them in a scholarly way. Of classical languages: Sanskrit, Pali, Arabic and Persian. Of modern Indian languages Hindi and Urdu, Gujrati and Marathi, Bengali and Oriya, Tamil and Telugu and Sindhi . . .'[33] Through his incarceration, Nehru penned his famous *Discovery of India*. Azad, Asaf Ali and Narendra Deva corrected his drafts on some points. Maulana Azad wrote a collection of letters, none of which were posted; they were later published as *Ghubar e Khatir*, which also remains a classic. Narendra Deva delved deep into the intricacies of Buddhist philosophy and Pattabhi Sitaramayya sought to update his *History of the Indian National Congress* into a new edition. As noted earlier, he also kept a voluminous diary: a witty and amused glance at their life together in prison that was to be published later as *Feathers and Stones*. Asaf Ali also wrote many pages on his prison experience, reflected on his times, and put together a part autobiography.

# 16

# The Journey to Jail and the Divides Within

This long incarceration meant that this circle of twelve people unexpectedly found the time and the space to actually think about, discuss and debate the issues they had been grappling with for most of their adult lives. And many of those conversations – as they gardened, cooked and walked – were inevitably about how to attain a free India and what it should be like once they attained it.

What had brought the group together to Ahmednagar were the tactical swings in the national struggle for independence and this remained the main issue throughout the long period of imprisonment. The passage of the 'Quit India' resolution may have seen the CWC present a united face in public but there were deep and major differences within on a whole range of issues: approaches to the war; attitudes towards the Muslim League; differences between the left and right wings on the economic programme of the Congress; and clashes between those predisposed towards confrontational postures vis-à-vis the colonial state and those who favoured more measured approaches; and, finally, on the question of Centre–state relations and their relative powers. This was not surprising; the Congress had always been a broad church and within it there were different perspectives, ideologies and personalities constantly battling for precedence.

But since the outbreak of the war and the resignation of the Congress ministries the central dividing line was on the question of confrontation with the government and the intensity of the agitation if one was embarked on. The divisions amongst the Ahmednagar fort detainees were also clear. Maulana Azad, Asaf and Syed Mahmud formed one group and their clear preference was to avoid positions of confrontation in the midst of the war. The opposing group led by Vallabhbhai Patel included Shankarrao Deo, J.B. Kripalani and Prafulla Ghosh. The balance of those in custody, such as G.B. Pant, P. Sitaramayya and others, would generally follow Nehru, and it was to him that the Maulana and Asaf looked for getting the CWC to moderate its position about head-on confrontation with the government.

Asaf himself was fully convinced about the downsides of agitation, as we have seen. 'I have remained a Swarajist all the time, that is, a believer in the parliamentary procedure.' This was a diary entry in August 1943 after a year of imprisonment. A year later, in August 1944, after two years of imprisonment, his views were no different; the confrontationist path adopted by the Congress at Gandhi's instance was a mistake:

> In my opinion 1942 was a wrong occasion. The entire war period should have been devoted to parliamentary activity . . . In the end would have come the award – or otherwise a struggle. But Gandhiji and his group precipitated a crisis prematurely and Jawaharlal simply abdicated his reason. And now we are in [this] 'quandary'.

The frustration of being locked up during what he saw as a critical period weighed heavily on Asaf, as indeed it did with the others. But for him the need for a Congress initiative to make peace with the government was a more urgent priority than it was for the others. This feeling had been with him for some time and he was to write in July 1943, as the completion of a year's imprisonment neared:

> I have been utterly out of tune with the Working Committee since the Allahabad meeting of April May last year. I was with C R [C. Rajagopalachari] and but for Maulana, I would have resigned right then and been out of it all. And again in July last year at Wardha, I was on the point of resigning. But because it would look as if it was to avoid imprisonment, I refrained from resigning. I could not endorse

> Gandhiji's programme of mass struggle, although at the time it seemed as if it might not come to that. The approach of struggle in the middle of the war, seemed to be wholly wrong. Maulana felt the same way and so did Mahmud. Even in Bombay, last August, I made it clear that it was only as a matter of discipline that I was yielding.

We can perhaps decipher two impulses rolled into one: first, that agitations in the absence of substantial Muslim support to the Congress should be avoided, and second, that embarking on an agitation in the midst of a war was a wrong tactic. In prison, as the months rolled by, the sentiment that something should be done to conciliate with the government grew.

> For weeks, nay months, I have been discussing with Maulana and some others the sorry plight to which Gandhiji's blunder has reduced all of us and the country. Maulana had, on his own, come to the same conclusion. So had Mahmud. All three of us had opposed the July and August resolution as suicidal. Some others also, it seems, felt the same way but they do not admit it. Jawaharlal is fully aware of it: but he is not one of those who can retrace a wrong step without feeling humiliated and is therefore obstinately reluctant to admit Gandhiji's Himalayan blunder . . . Others too, of the Gandhian party await some face-saving occurrences.

In Asaf's telling, Maulana Azad came to the conclusion in November 1943 that something needed to be done. A change had taken place in New Delhi with Wavell, earlier the commander-in-chief of the army in India, now the new viceroy. The Maulana felt that the time was ripe for a rapprochement and for the Working Committee to write to the government to begin the process. In Asaf's account the terms of the communication would be that in view of the terrible famine conditions in Bengal and the government's resolve to carry the war to the Japanese-occupied territories, the CWC was prepared to forget the past and cooperate with the government and all parties. The idea was first broached to Nehru and Patel who were not opposed to it per se but wanted the new viceroy to take the first step. Therefore they, according to Asaf, 'hummed and hawed'. Azad and Asaf wanted to take the initiative.

Azad thereafter convened, or rather gathered together in the largest room, the CWC members for a discussion that began on 15 November and went on for about a week. The outcome was predictable: Vallabhbhai opposed and Nehru was lukewarm to the idea. There was no real chance of securing the outcome Azad wanted. The long consultation was often acrimonious and heated. Asaf's sentiment at the end was: 'The future is full of gloom if these people do not make up their minds about the problems. They seem to expect too much from their masterly inactivity.'

For some in the CWC, to embark on a new line without Gandhi's explicit approval verged on a kind of heresy. This group included Patel, P.C. Ghosh, Shankarrao Deo and perhaps others too. In Nehru's words: 'To criticize any step taken by Bapu is *lese majeste*. That is the hiatus between the so-called Gandhi members of the WC and the others.'[1] Similarly, Asaf was to write: 'Patel and the others rely on Gandhi to do everything for them.' Nehru, he felt, was in the same category: notwithstanding the power of his analysis that made him disagree with Gandhi, in the end he would fall in line.

After this prolonged deliberation, when it became clear that the majority would not go along with him, Maulana Azad spoke again in conclusion. He threw out, in Nehru's description, 'a very remarkable and significant hint about the communal problem. This was that we should tone down a little towards Govt (not giving up our position in any way but still) and then with its help we should be able to solve the problem easily.' Essentially what Azad was putting forth was a pragmatic proposal: taking on both the Muslim League and the government together was not easy or advisable, and conciliating the latter would help in dealing with the former. Nehru wrote further in his diary: 'This took my breath away for it opened up new vistas, entirely new approaches. If this was the objective then obviously the old arguments built on different premises, hardly applied.'[2]

Nehru's response and surprise suggests a novel point had been raised for the first time. This in fact was not so and since the formation of the

Congress ministries in 1937 there had been much discussion about the growing distance between the Congress and Muslim public opinion. The Muslim League certainly made much of this; but in the eyes of many Congress leaders this could be disregarded: after all it was a party that had been worsted in the 1937 elections and therefore lacked credibility. Yet there were others who were concerned at the rapid growth of the Muslim League and how this was exposing the shallow base the Congress had amongst Muslims. Certainly, the Muslim League under Jinnah had been effective in an intense propaganda campaign that anti-Muslim governments were in power in those provinces with Congress governments. The gains the Congress had registered in the 1937 elections and the confidence this generated that the Muslim League was becoming a spent force were misleading.

These concerns grew following the resignation of the Congress ministries. Rajagopalachari for one was convinced that the Congress now faced a real problem both of the Muslim League consolidating itself and of its own growing distance from Muslim opinion. To a great extent this both flowed into and from his larger concern that the Congress should not, post resignation, move into an agitational phase against the government when the British had their backs to the wall in the war against Germany and Japan. Others had been sounding warnings on these lines – not least the Muslim CWC members. Syed Mahmud had written to Nehru frequently on these lines. At one stage soon after the resignation of the Congress provincial governments, Nehru wrote to Syed Mahmud on 12 December 1939: 'The communal problem as such is there of course but it is a very minor problem. The real problem is a political problem – the conflict between an advanced organization like the Congress and a politically reactionary organization like the League.'[3]

Someone like Syed Mahmud could be easily silenced by Nehru's arguments but the problem did not go away. In the period up to their arrests in August 1942 Syed Mahmud continued to write to Nehru on these lines and their correspondence reveals their differences but also the relationship of deference which overrode them. On 2 February 1942 Nehru wrote that in his view Jinnah's and the Muslim League's attitude was 'governed by the desire to prevent radical changes or the democratization of India *not* because of a Hindu majority but because the radical elements will put an end to semi feudal privileges'. By insisting that 'no political progress is possible till his conditions are accepted', Jinnah was 'putting the cart before the horse'. In fact, Nehru wrote, there was no solution possible 'however hard we may try, as long as the third party (the British) is not eliminated'.[4]

Mahmud's point was, however, different, as he made clear in his reply to Nehru on 5 February:

> You say '... Jinnah puts the cart before the horse', but they (the Muslim League) say exactly the same thing about you ... Your argument is not a new one. We have been telling them this for the past twenty years – let us win freedom and then we will decide about the spoil. But their reply is – this is the argument of the stronger party. The stronger party thinks it can defeat the weaker party if a conflict comes about before the departure of the third party ... This is a very reactionary argument indeed. But I realize also that this is their conviction. This reactionary argument used to be put forward by the upper-class Muslims only a few years back, but this is now fast becoming the conviction of the Muslim masses hence the danger.

There was no real way out of this conundrum that was visible to these actors and possibly Mahmud, deferential and admiring of Nehru, realized this: 'I look to you for guidance as I did all my life, for my politics is governed by my personal relations while your personal relations depend on your politics. This is the tragedy.'[5]

After the failure in the November 1943 consultations to bring the other CWC members around to his point of view, Azad – in discussions with Asaf and Syed Mahmud – had reviewed in detail Congress–Muslim relations. Asaf recorded his own frustrations about this old friend:

> He [Azad] has been an apologist of Congress policy rather than an incisive critic. Personally, I think it is time that merciless self-criticism was undertaken by nationalist Muslims and Hindu Congressmen. Results are the soundest test in politics. A compromise that secures desirable results is infinitely better than sticking for sound but barren principles. Indian Muslims as a bulk are dissatisfied with the policies of the Congress, howsoever well intentioned they may have been.[6]

Since the Cripps Mission, one concept that had generated much discussion was that of self-determination for the Muslim-majority provinces or in general of the future constitutional relations between the Centre and states. As noted earlier, the communal issue had been merging with a larger federal issue and what should be the relationship between a Muslim-majority province and the Centre in a Hindu-majority India. In Asaf's view this was a reality that had to be faced. He wrote in his diary in March 1944:

> Nothing is easier for me than to say 'that Pakistan is the most undesirable for India as a whole and for the Indian Muslims'. But if we refuse to have anything but the best the situation may get worse. In the evolving world we have often to be content with the second or next best.

To him therefore if this indeed was inevitable, recognition of the principle of self-determination was preferable to a union that was forced. 'If there is to be a Pakistan, a treaty will have to be negotiated by it with Hindustan.' But discussions with Nehru also showed a different way of looking at this issue.

> Jawaharlal made it clear in the end that the big economic plan by which he intended to tackle the problem of India's poverty would not be realizable if the communal tangle continued to come in the way. And therefore he would rather agree, of course unwillingly, to let the Muslims separate where they could. He would then have a

strong central government in the rest of India and proceed with his economic programme.

For Nehru, in brief, a strong Centre was an inescapable requirement since the object of securing independence was to bring about an economic and social transformation of the country. How much had Asaf thought through the confederation idea? Did he see its contradiction with the reality that had emerged over the past century of a strong central authority in the shape of British colonial authority? Could a weak Centre have a unified and effective foreign policy and be an instrument for economic change? We do not know since he mentions Nehru's views without any great comment. But perhaps to Asaf Ali if the price to be paid for a more harmonious Hindu–Muslim interface was a weak Centre in an Indian commonwealth in which different regions and provinces had considerable power, it was a necessary cost and could be paid.

Some were suspicious about Asaf talking about an Indian confederation or a commonwealth. One of his diary entries is: 'My talk with Vallabhbhai on my idea of a Commonwealth of India has travelled in some form to the different "clubs" here. Jawaharlal brought the news to the Maulana that I was described as going one better than Jinnah.' Because he was a Muslim, the impression among some was that he was a fifth columnist for the League. Asaf commented, 'There is no limit to narrowness, suspicion and a fanatical adherence to the idea that only that political structure which some of these gentlemen have in view is the best.'[7] But reactions on this issue had the potential of becoming truly acrimonious. Asaf's discussions with other CWC members brought out just how deep the waters were on the Hindu–Muslim issue:

> Some six months ago when I spoke in similar terms to Narendra Dev[a], he held that the principle of self determination could not be permitted to be exercised by anybody except by the population of India as a whole. He further said that those who thought along these lines – we were talking of Muslims – would have to be 'driven out' of India.

> I stopped the talk with the rejoinder 'Try it'. Since then I have not discussed politics with him. On earlier occasions I decided to eschew discussions with Kripalani for similar reasons.

He described also a discussion with Shankarrao who flew into a rage and said, 'Every inch of ground is mine – the land of five rivers and Peshawar are sacred to me.' Asaf comments, 'He could not see that if the Muslim majority in certain parts of India wanted self government and this was denied it would mean the imposition of Hindu rule on them. It is a pity that even tried and tested patriots cannot talk of these things in a rational way.' These divisions, arguments and counterarguments reflected on the whole the uncertain state of relations in political terms between Hindus and Muslims in many parts of the country. Within the Congress these could be minimized on the surface and party discipline would project overall unity; but the differences remained seething beneath the surface.

In addition to these and other political differences over principles and tactics, there was of course the inevitable play of personalities and individual likes and dislikes. Asaf wrote about Patel: 'He seems to consider everyone who does not agree with his point of view as a sort of delinquent.'[8] Nehru, similarly, despite his enormous respect for Maulana Azad, was to write: 'I always feel at a slight disadvantage in discussing anything with him. I cannot adopt my usual free and easy manner as this might rub him up the wrong way . . . He has an astonishing mental grasp and a prodigious memory – but the 18th and 19th centuries cling to him.'[9] Nehru was also to describe Prafulla Chandra Ghosh's irritating manner: 'he smiles at the wrong moment and appears to look around for applause'.[10]

Enforced inactivity in close proximity obviously fostered its own tensions and frictions. The strain of being locked up for a prolonged period with no break from the monotony of prison life compounded existing political differences despite the individuals, mature and well rounded as they were, being conscious of the strain each was under and being extra careful to not upset others. Asaf had written: 'When human beings are imprisoned together for a long time they cannot help jarring on one another, particularly if they are ill assorted temperamentally and by cultural background.' But on occasion frictions would surface unexpectedly. In August 1943, almost to the day of their arrival in the fort a year earlier, Jawaharlal Nehru wrote:

> This morning at breakfast quite unexpectedly, there was a heated interchange of aggressive language between the Maulana and me. It was not much and it lasted barely a minute. Nothing really offensive was said by either of us; we kept more or less within the bounds of propriety. But the tone and manner exhibited irritation against each other – not only present irritation but a little fund of stored up irritation.[11]

The specific cause was trivial, almost juvenile. 'A new kind of dalia was prepared, or rather it was prepared in a new way.' The Maulana had commented that it was now more difficult to digest to which Nehru had responded to the effect that his digestion was fine.

> This remark of mine somehow upset Maulana. It is clear that my references to my own good health, which had not been infrequent in the past, had somehow got on his nerves . . . Maulana said something about my arrogance in regard to my health. I retorted that I was proud of my health and physical condition and it was distressing enough for me to have to hear so much talk of disease and illness. There were a few more remarks and counterremarks.

Later both were remorseful and apologized. Nehru wrote privately of his own excessive conceit and 'veiled contempt for the physical weakness and ailments of others' and said he decided to express his regrets, but the Maulana 'forestalled me and at the next meal together he expressed regret before all the others . . . he is the perfect gentleman'.

# 17

# The Pain of It All

During this long incarceration every aspect of the daily lives of the prisoners was under the microscope of the prison and provincial authorities. The reports they sent were closely scrutinized by the Government of India officials, and frequently shown to the viceroy. There was a weekly medical examination of each prisoner the report of which – apart from listing basic health parameters – would also contain a brief description of the individual's state of mind and body. Instructions to the prison authorities about the entitlements of the prisoners had been precisely laid down including 'special privileges' in view of their status. Thus, the numbers of bars of soap, toothbrushes, daily diet allowances, towels and so on were documented.

In terms of material well-being, the detainees were not physically deprived. As conditions in their prison in the fort stabilized so did their entitlements. The latter, when compared with conditions in a 'normal' prison, were clearly based on the recognition that each of the prisoners was a person of standing and high political status. A sum of Rs 100 per month – not a small sum in those days – was allocated as expenditure for each prisoner towards the costs of their diet, toiletries, etc.[1] Some newspapers and periodicals were supplied at government cost; others could be ordered from within the Rs 100 limit. Personal parcels were allowed after scrutiny as were books sent by the members of their family or ordered by each individual.

But this material minimum was hardly the point. This was a politically supercharged period and each of those imprisoned was there after great personal sacrifice. Most were constantly plagued by doubts about the confrontation they had embarked on. Almost all the prisoners were not in good health and the prolonged incarceration meant a further deterioration. Over the first year – between August 1942 and end 1943 – some of the Ahmednagar inmates seem to have gone through a particularly bad time. A comparative chart of their weight in this period reveals that Abul Kalam lost over 40 pounds (18 kilograms), Mahmud 32 pounds (14.5 kilograms), Pant 19 pounds (8.5 kilograms), Nehru 16 pounds (7 kilograms) and Asaf 9 pounds (4 kilograms). One pencilled note by an anonymous officer on this report reads unsympathetically: 'probably some of them had been too fat when they were bought in'.[2] Medical attention was minimal, with their jailer-cum-doctor the only recourse in most cases. Anything needing more specialized attention required clearance from the Government of India after the Bombay government had given its recommendations. Proposals for examination by a specialist were scrutinized minutely on file, some of which fortunately survive if only to establish how little government functioning has changed. Often the highest levels of government were consulted; attitudes there were generally against leniency and this would have influenced the judgement of those down the bureaucratic chain.

On occasion whether a specialist should be permitted depended also on the political personality of the individual in question. On a proposal that Vallabhbhai Patel be allowed a visit by the physician who treated him regularly, the viceroy himself was to comment, 'I am prepared to resist this strongly.' This was because 'Patel is the worst offender of the lot and very largely responsible for the violence that took place in August 1942'. The viceroy also noted that 'the last time he was "in" he escaped by a faked condition of high blood pressure arranged by his doctor'.[3] On a representation by a senior politician Shri Prakash that Narendra Deva – one of the 'few scholars of his eminence in ancient Pali' – be released on account of his poor health, the Home Member of the viceroy's Executive Council minuted: 'If he puts politics above Pali the choice is his and he cannot have it both ways.'[4]

In Ahmednagar fort, Syed Mahmud shared a room for about fifteen months with Nehru, who often nursed him for long periods and frequently noted in his diary how very ill Mahmud was. At one stage he listed the more serious ailments: 'Filaria, heart trouble, gall bladder, serious eye trouble, persistent spitting out of blood, pyorrhea.'[5] He wrote for instance in May 1943:[6]

> Obviously Mahmud is a case for a hospital. But both in his case and Vallabhbhai's there is an initial difficulty. We are supposed to be living in an unknown place although everybody knows exactly where we are kept. Anyway, they are not supposed to know. So, if anyone is sent to hospital or elsewhere this very transparent veil of mystery is torn up.

In Ahmednagar Asaf had noted about Mahmud that he was 'the only person here to whom the ritual side of religion has as much meaning as its spiritual realm'.[7] Mahmud's insistence on fasting through Ramzan did not, in Nehru's view, help. His health, along with that of some others, was a matter of great concern to the entire group and there would be frequent run-ins with the jailer on the inadequate medical treatment they were receiving.

At one point, in the summer of 1943, the entire group was inoculated against cholera amidst reports of mounting cases of the disease. Mahmud had an extreme adverse reaction to the vaccine and Nehru was to note:

> The last three days have been unusual for me. I have done little except nursing Mahmud. His condition suddenly became rather serious. His temperature went on mounting . . . It was obvious that all of this was not just a reaction to the vaccination. Perhaps the vaccination had roused up latent disease; indeed, much of this is not latent, it is obvious enough . . . Yesterday morning I spoke to the Supt [superintendent] with some vigour, and I fear harshness. My anger was of course directed against the Govt . . . I told him that it was scandalous that serious hospital cases like Mahmud and Vallabhbhai's should be treated casually here.[8]

Amidst all this, the relationship with Mahmud's family also continued and we find Nehru as concerned as his wife had been over a decade and a half ago. He wrote to Indira Gandhi on 20 November 1943:

> I wrote to you long ago about Dr Mahmud's daughters. You wrote to either Sarvar or Hamida and apparently had no answer. I should like you to try again . . . It is difficult to move these people. They fall into certain ruts and remain there . . . I do wish you could manage to get the girls to come to Anand Bhavan. If Mrs Mahmud could come also, it would be good for her.[9]

Correspondence into and out of the prison was obviously closely monitored and censored. On one occasion soon after their arrival in Ahmednagar, Asaf complained about letters from Aruna not being given to him. The Government of Bombay acknowledged that four of her letters received in as many weeks 'have been forwarded to the Chief Commissioner of Delhi as she is evading arrest'. On Asaf's protests and saying 'hard things about the officials who were behaving like panic stricken fools' and whether 'correspondence between husband and wife would blow the British empire to pieces', the matter was further referred to the Government of India. Richard Tottenham, then additional secretary in the home ministry in Delhi, was to send what Asaf termed a 'laconic' reply: 'Such instructions are being issued as seem to be necessary.' We do not know whether the letters were ever delivered but the episode is revealing of the government's paranoia.

There were, alongside, numerous comments made on specific remarks contained in personal letters on file, and an evaluation of whether they indicated a change in political perspectives. Often there were detailed considerations of what precisely constituted a letter of a purely domestic or private nature, and so on.

Books requested by the prisoners would be procured, as mentioned earlier, or their relatives permitted to send them, but such lists of requests or the books received would be carefully vetted and scrutinized. On one occasion P.C. Ghosh complained of difficulties in getting the kinds of books he was looking for, being 'interested in ancient Sanskrit literature'. After prolonged consideration by both the Government of India and the

Bombay government, a solution was found: a government official became a member of the Bhandarkar Oriental Research Institute Library in Poona and borrowed the books Ghosh wanted. But such consideration was rare and there was an obvious element of arbitrariness in the entire set-up. The well-known journal *Modern Review*, to which Nehru had a regular subscription, was not permitted, along with a number of other publications.[10]

In time these restrictions would be relaxed but the Intelligence Bureau kept under very close scrutiny what was actually delivered, occasionally complaining about the sheer volumes (literally) involved, which had to be gone through before being passed! Within the government there were frequent debates on whether restrictions should be imposed on the prisoners' access to printed material, with vast amounts being mailed to them from across the country and abroad. One irate official wrote in May 1943: 'there is no need for us to be unduly assiduous in protecting the detenus from rubbish.'[11] Others actually, and somewhat incredibly, saw the control they had over what the prisoners read as an opportunity: 'Several pamphlets have recently come to our notice, issued by various political parties or groups in India, which we think it would be good for persons like Mr Gandhi and Pandit Nehru to read. We can easily arrange for such pamphlets to be addressed from various places in India ...'

Occasionally the question would arise of a prisoner being required for appearance in some legal matter. On one such occasion in late 1943, a legal notice was to be served on Asaf requiring him to give evidence on an issue he had been involved with, concerning the Delhi government. The chief commissioner of Delhi formally sought the advice of the Government of India on this. After consultation the following approach was deemed most appropriate:

> It would seem to be inept for *us* to have the notice delivered to Mr Asaf Ali calling upon him to appear if at the same time we are to tell him that he can't appear. The Deputy Commissioner should I think send the notice to Mr Asaf Ali c/o the Bombay Govt and we might

at the same time tell Mr Iengar that Mr Asaf Ali cannot of course be allowed to comply.[12]

'Iengar' or H.V.R. Iyengar was additional secretary in the home department in the Bombay government and the point person in the province for all matters concerning the political prisoners in Ahmednagar fort and in the Aga Khan's palace in Poona.

Soon after their arrival in Ahmednagar had come the news that Mahadev Desai, Gandhi's devoted secretary, had died on 15 August at the Aga Khan palace and was cremated there. Maulana Azad's wife died in April 1943 and, while he knew she was grievously ill, the news of her death was conveyed to him after some delay. Kasturba Gandhi, who was sent by the government to be with Gandhi in the Aga Khan palace in Poona, died there in February 1944. The inmates of Ahmednagar fort would receive other such tidings regularly and each such piece of news would accentuate their sense of helplessness and their doubts about what exactly they were doing locked up while such tragedies were taking place. Asaf Ali learnt of the death of his mother-in-law by reading a brief obituary notice in a newspaper in April 1944. The previous year, in March 1943, the death of Satyamurthy – his friend and colleague in the 1930s in the Central Legislature – had similarly depressed him. 'Death is the most certain fact of life. Who can escape it. And yet life resists it even in the midst of pain. What makes us want to live?'[13]

In Poona, Sarojini Naidu's health was also a matter of concern. In January 1943 it was found that she had lost about 16 pounds (7 kilograms) since being jailed in August 1942: 'She herself does not complain – she is a difficult patient,' one report noted.[14] In February 1943 Gandhi had begun a twenty-one-day fast in protest against the government's allegations that the Congress was responsible for the widespread disturbances and violence after the party's leadership was jailed in August 1942. The fast ended on 3 March. There had been real concern, not only amongst the public, but also in the government that he might not survive. It is possible that Sarojini knew that there was a move to release her, but she had insisted that no action be taken till Gandhi's fast was over. In the last week of February an official noted: 'it might look somewhat odd to release her immediately on medical grounds while we still continue to keep Mr Gandhi himself as our prisoner.' By March, however, there was even greater worry: 'Mrs Sarojini Naidu's health has considerably deteriorated. She is seriously ill.' She may have had an inkling that she could be released on medical grounds, and wrote to the government:

> all my life I have been in poor health and there is therefore no special need for special anxiety on that score . . . It is clearly my duty as well as earnest desire to be with Mahatma Gandhi and render him every assistance in my power. I could not on moral grounds justify to myself the unseemliness of taking advantage of purely technical reasons however valid.[15]

The government, however, no longer wanted to take a chance and she was released in March 1943.

Although Asaf was, even by the standards of the national movement and the Congress, no novice at undergoing imprisonment, the incarceration in Ahmednagar took an enormous physical and mental toll. His frustrations over Congress policy and the inability to counter the growing strength of the Muslim League amidst communal polarization are obvious enough. Perhaps he missed being in the Central Legislature – something which he valued and enjoyed. But alongside these political frustrations there was a more traumatic personal crisis – principally on account of Aruna. His mother had died in 1941, and while he did have other relatives on his mother's side, Aruna was, as far as he was concerned, now his major and only responsibility.

Her story had, however, taken on a separate trajectory almost as soon as the train with the imprisoned Congress leaders steamed out of Victoria Terminus station to different prisons. She had exchanged a few pleasantries with Maulana Azad at the railway platform and gathered that he was, in his capacity as Congress president, supposed to have been at a public meeting at the Gowalia Tank Maidan that morning to unfurl the tricolour to mark the conclusion of the CWC meeting. Aruna said later that she had made up her mind on an impulse – 'I am going there' – and she did go. Arriving at the Maidan she found that the police had given orders to the assembled crowd to disperse.

> I quickly scrambled up the dais, announced to the people the arrest of the leaders and pulled the cord to hoist the national flag. Hardly had the flag been unfurled when the police started lobbing tear gas shells into the crowd. The men and women ran helter skelter with tears streaming from their eyes. The experience of that morning made me decide that I would not again tamely enter jail by offering Satyagraha.[16]

Aruna secretly returned to Delhi and remained in hiding. Police reports revealed that she was involved in creating disturbances in Delhi and also carrying out acts of sabotage in the widespread agitation that had accompanied the news of the Congress leaders being jailed. There was soon a hunt for her with an award of prize money for information leading to her arrest. Evading arrest and thus 'underground' but travelling to different places, she soon gained the reputation of being a fearless freedom fighter.

Asaf in jail was plagued by worry but also largely in the dark about what was happening. The absence of information and the feeling of helplessness consumed him, and he remained in this state through virtually the entire period of imprisonment. He shared his worries with some of the others and also recorded them in his diary. We get from this a tantalizing glimpse of his relationship with Aruna as one based on immense personal love and caring, but also one which, from her side at least, was intensely political.

He learnt quite early of Aruna's hoisting the national flag and of the dispersal of the meeting with tear gas. 'This made me most anxious about Rene [Aruna]. The anguish of suspense lasted nearly three weeks till I received a brief note from her which she wrote on the 21st [August] and which was delivered to me on the 27th after it had been duly scrutinized by the Home Department . . .'[17] Aruna was called Rene at home ever since she was a child and that is how Asaf referred to her in his private diary. In letters to relatives – his and hers – he referred to her or asked about her using the name Kulsum, the Islamic name she had used for their marriage. This was to evade censorship: the hope was that the censors would assume Kulsum was one of Asaf's relatives. As a regular trickle of newspapers began for the inmates of Ahmednagar fort prison, his worries multiplied on seeing stray reports about Aruna evading arrest and public notices calling on her to surrender. A few days after their wedding anniversary Asaf wrote:

> For the first time in 14 years I nearly forgot the 5th September, our wedding anniversary . . . Every time we have not been together on the anniversary we have reminded each other by telegram of what to us was a day of destiny. Although it is not one of the major calamities of this universe, this oversight marks a breakdown of a hallowed tradition of our personal life – of which little is left to us in the stormy political weather we have been living [through].

Aruna was soon to be formally declared an 'absconder' from justice. Asaf's reaction was: 'I was terribly annoyed by the description of her as an "absconder". But perhaps it cannot be helped. She knows the conditions best. To me it appears that it would hurt her dignity to give herself up.' His own view about the politics of underground or undercover activity was clear:

> I think all underground activities are, in the very nature of things, demoralizing . . . Rene I am sure has gone underground only to be spared from being rendered inoperative. From a selfish point of view I don't like it . . . However, from a larger point of view, when I remind myself that she is doing what she thinks is best for the country and the people, I cannot but feel proud of her.

That he was conflicted is obvious; while he disapproved of covert activities and being underground, perhaps more upsetting was that she had decided to embark on this course of action on her own and certainly without any prior discussion or agreement with him. We do not know if they had ever discussed in the past their future courses of action in the event of a government crackdown. It is fair to say that Asaf would have assumed a replay of what had happened during civil disobedience a decade earlier. Certainly, there had been no sign (of which we are aware) that Aruna would so resolutely make up her mind against jail and the well-trodden path of Satyagraha.

Letters to and from Aruna were frequently delayed and sometimes not received at all. As we saw, within a few weeks of being jailed, Asaf had realized that some of Aruna's letters to him were being impounded. Nevertheless, the occasional letter from Aruna would supplement the news about her conveyed in a guarded fashion to other inmates by their relatives. From his prison diary we get a sense of the evolution of their marriage.

> Our correspondence during the days of courtship fills a sizable box. How we probed each other's mind, and how I filled her with such choice delicacies of the spirit as I hoped she would appreciate. For fifteen years we have lived together, until lately I her mentor and she my apt but not uncritical follower.

But in fact the relationship had started changing quite early in the marriage and here Aruna's own political journey was the driving factor. Political work and prison in tandem constituted an education with obvious results. 'After her second term of imprisonment she began to take in much individually, and her mind began to expand and blossom in its personal climate.' But he still felt a strong sense of responsibility towards her:

> I was her creator – a pardonable pride – and her tactful preceptor . . . I still flatter myself to think, without meaning any slightest reflection on

> her individuality and originality, that I am her leader in every matter, and therefore whatever she does in life, whether after consulting me or otherwise, I am primarily and finally responsible. [18]

But this pattern had changed and it would be realistic to add an element of resentment in the mix of emotions Asaf was having at the time.

A sense of responsibility towards his wife, whether or not it was justified, meant enhanced worry on two counts. The first was personal and the other political. There was an obvious concern about her physical well-being and safety. Equally pronounced was the anxiety because Aruna had embarked on a course of action he profoundly disagreed with: going underground. 'I would regard it as more appropriate for Rene to come right out into the open and challenge the validity and immorality of their infamous orders and go behind prison bars after exposing the inequity of the rulers.'

But the political and the personal were obviously mixed up.

> I wish Rene had gone to prison. It would have meant much more rest than she can enjoy outside; and it would have set me at rest too. Isn't it curious that I, who want with all my heart to see her free and happy, now wish to see her in gaol? I am all the time afraid that they will implicate Rene in some serious charge, if only to prove their contention that responsible Congressmen and women are encouraging violence.

This was written in November 1942, and by February 1943 Asaf felt that these worst fears were coming true. He read in the newspapers reports of the viceroy writing to Gandhi that the Congress was behind the mob violence that followed August 1942 and that 'even now there is an underground organization, in which the wife of a member of the Working Committee plays an important part'. The organization, the viceroy went on to state, 'is actively engaged in planning bomb attacks and other acts of terrorism'.[19]

Such news reports added to Asaf's gloom and appears to have pushed him into a deep depression. We get a glimpse of Asaf as he appeared to others through Nehru's jail diaries. The viceroy's letter meant that Asaf had, Nehru wrote, 'made himself quite ill'.[20] Some weeks later the situation was no better: 'Asaf continues to be in a limp condition, lacking all interest in any activity and generally unwell.' While others also had their own set of problems, either because of health issues or personal worries, Nehru wrote sometime later, 'Poor Asaf is the worst hit of all. Partly because of Aruna.' Things did not improve as the year progressed. In mid-April 1943, in Nehru's assessment, 'he has completely gone to pieces'; and some weeks later, 'he is unhappy, troubled, incapable of doing anything, cannot even read consecutively, lies in bed most of the time'. For Nehru the deterioration was surprising: 'He looks terribly aged and quite down and out. I cannot understand how any person can go to pieces like this. The worst of it is that he realizes it and admits it.'[21] If this appears judgemental, even unfeeling, perhaps it was. Nehru had himself noted at one stage with regard to Asaf's condition and worries about Aruna: 'How would I have felt if Kamala or Indu had functioned in this way and I in prison? I wonder.'[22] The Congress leaders were in prison together and for the same cause, and prone to similar anxieties; but each different personality was unhappy in its own way.

Asaf's own diary entries also record his descent into depression. In early January 1943 we find him writing, 'I have not felt so terribly down in the dumps in the past five months as today. Quite suddenly about mid day, I collapsed into the deepest mental depression – and imagined all sorts of horrible things happening to Rene.' And a few days later: 'I have tried hard to relax my mental tension about Rene. Why should human beings be so consumed by their emotional attachment?' His own self-examination was often remorseless: 'I have become so hyper sensitive about Rene. This has made me a phenomenon at once pitiable and disgusting. Maulana and Jawahar have hinted that I should exercise my will and pull myself together. It was humiliating. And yet, despite every effort, I fail to get over it.' Perhaps he may even have felt resentful of those who were widowers such as Jawaharlal and Patel and the Maulana; or those, like Syed Mahmud, whose adult children looked after their mothers and managed the family's affairs. In the mood he was in he felt what was possibly an exaggerated burden of responsibility for the very young woman he had married and who had thereafter plunged into politics in his wake, but now carved out a path very different from his.

This depressive mood eased slightly after the first year in prison but never fully lifted. There is occasionally an element of reproach directed at Aruna for being the cause of this anguish:

> Alas! Rene will never realize, in the present flood of her innocent and emotional elation, how I have suffered on the score of her risks . . . Rene must have worked herself up, as she always does, to the highest pitch of Satyagrahi zeal for her plan to deliver India from bondage even as Joan of Arc did in the case of her motherland. But the mental faggots are for me . . .

In this mood he was inclined to always imagine the worst, and it was almost as if he could anticipate Aruna's frame of mind better than she could herself. In January 1943, he received a letter from her written in Urdu and signed Kulsum Zamani (Aruna's 'Islamic' name) to mislead the censors into thinking it was from one of his female relatives. She wrote of having cut her hair to a shorter length: 'She has either bobbed or Eton cropped her hair.' To Asaf this was a sign that she was 'Active, legitimately proud of her achievements but emotionally tense and almost morbid and tragic'. To him the only conclusion was 'this is indication enough that underground life is robbing her of peace and rest'.

We know also that at least some of this worry and concern made its way back to Aruna. Perhaps Asaf's own letters, coded and through third parties to escape the censor, contained a hint of these sentiments, even reproach; or perhaps others in Ahmednagar also wrote to family and friends outside about Asaf's condition. Asaf's letters to other relatives were certainly full of gloom and doom and made no attempt to disguise his depressed frame of mind. We get a sense of Aruna's reaction from his dairy entry after receiving a letter from her. 'She is shocked at my despondency and bitter pessimism. She says I thought you were one of the few persons alive, evolved and integrated. Further she conveys to me the conclusion of an "academic" debate, that tyranny whether dictated by love or hate is bad, and it is the personal right of an individual to be free to travel to the furthest limit of one's responsibility'. This was an obvious reference to some earlier discussion between them because Asaf's wry comment in the diary was: 'How my chickens have come to roost.' That he was losing control of her was undoubtedly a source of anguish even if he resisted a bald statement of this fact.

A little later Asaf wrote that Aruna had written to him again and this had made 'me think and think hard. She has taken me to task and has asked me to be my "brave and courageous self" and "the beacon that you have been"'. What had made Asaf think was a reference in the letter 'to two generations mine and hers, and the difference in outlook'. Asaf noted, 'If so, instead of a beacon I must be a stumbling block.' The contrast between Aruna's activity and underground profile while Asaf was in a depression in jail underlines how much the relationship had changed. The twenty-year age difference was now playing a role – and Asaf was conscious of it.

Asaf Ali's depressed state of mind drew much unsympathetic comment, on his personality, in the internal consideration of the government. He was conscious, even in the despondent state he was in, that he should be careful what he wrote in his letters. 'Often I pour out my heart in long letters intended for Rene, and then consign them to the flames since I do not wish to subject my sacred thoughts and feelings to a public exhibition to the censor.' But enough would get through. In the files dealing with the state of mind and health of the prisoners there is occasionally an element of glee that a good lesson is finally being taught to agitational leaders. There is a marginal note by a home ministry official on a letter from Asaf to his sister-in-law Purnima: 'Self pity is not an admirable trait.'[23] On his general condition such comments are also frequent:

> Mr Asaf Ali is a highly strung, nervous individual with a [tendency] towards hypochondriasis. This latter has become more marked [page torn] months and the absence of direct communication from the prisoner [page torn] together with the anxiety called by the nature of her activities [page torn] lack of information as to her exact whereabouts

> have been [page torn] factors. He also appears to be considerably depressed at her fail [page torn] to surrender herself to government as apparently desired by him.[24]

The prisoner's health being a barometer of his political conviction is the sense that underwrote such official assessments: that is, those who were ill were actually so because they regretted the steps that had landed them in jail. That they had all blundered their way into prison and were now looking for a way out was also the general assessment of senior officialdom, especially the Englishmen amongst them. In Poona in September 1943, a year into the incarceration, Madeleine Slade, the Englishwoman who had accompanied Gandhi to imprisonment in Poona, had a minor medical issue of shoulder pain, leading to this dispatch from the governor of Bombay to the viceroy:

> I feel it worth reporting that Miss Slade has been showing signs of wanting release on medical grounds … but physically she seems quite well and is putting on weight … The Inspector General of Prisons tells me he has the impression that she is very tired of it all and wants to get out. I have been wondering whether this is so simple as it seems or whether Noah wants to send out the dove to see what the weather is like outside.[25]

The viceroy had responded, 'I agree about Noah.'

If nothing else such detailed consideration of minor issues reveals more about the anxieties of the colonial authorities than about those imprisoned.

One particular CWC member attracted more than his share of attention, as much for his political stance as for his medical condition. His ill health weighed greatly on Syed Mahmud and by mid-1944 he was deeply concerned in particular about permanently losing his eyesight. In August 1944 he secretly wrote a long, rambling letter to the viceroy, the thrust of which was that he had opposed the passage of the Quit India resolution in the August 1942 meeting of the CWC; and in earlier meetings too he had opposed the launch of an agitation against the government. 'I went to the Bombay meeting to oppose the proposal which I did with all my might . . .' In brief Mahmud now sought his release on the grounds that he would not take part in a movement against the government or impede the war effort in any way. The letter is long and discursive and at places unmistakably ingratiating, detailing the many English friends he had; that he was 'enthusiastic about the war efforts'; and that he had been 'a persistent and ardent advocate in the Congress Executive of giving unconditional help to the war efforts'.

The long letter was greeted in the Government of India with glee. Reading the file today we can almost hear the shrieks of joy in North Block in New Delhi, the location of the ministry of home affairs, that at least one, and hopefully only the first, of the Congress leaders had cracked and seen reason. Tottenham, additional secretary in the home ministry, noted: 'We have known for some time that he has been anxious to secure his release on medical grounds . . .'[26] The Home Member in the viceroy's Executive Council was more forthcoming, terming the letter 'an amazing production':

> A man who writes like this cannot be a public danger. In fact, I doubt he was ever dangerous. He is merely one of the Muslim dummies with which the Congress dress their shop window . . . It is possible that he was opposed to the August resolution but bullied into acquiescence . . . his attempts were merely brushed aside which shows how ineffective a person he is . . .[27]

Syed Mahmud was released on 6 October 1944. He had spent well over two years – 788 days to be precise – in prison, virtually all the time in very poor health. The others in jail assumed almost automatically that his release was on account of his medical condition. Gradually, however, the full facts emerged when the government issued a clarificatory statement that he was *not* released on health grounds.

His release gave to the outside world a first-hand account of life inside the fortress and the initial garbled accounts appeared to the inmates to be a form of black humour. Some press reports noted that 'older people played chess or cards and in the evening some girl inmates take to badminton'. A printing error had changed 'agile inmates' into 'girl inmates'. Nehru noted wryly, 'Girls! Considering that we have not seen anything resembling a girl or a woman ever since we left Bombay 26½ months ago.'[28] Yet this amusement or bemusement apart, Syed Mahmud's step was demoralizing for all. Asaf wrote in his diary:

> It is the matter of the greatest surprise to me, Maulana and to Jawaharlal – with whom Mahmud was sharing a room – that all this time he did not allow any of us to get the slightest inkling of it. I am genuinely sorry that his indiscretion has exposed him to disagreeable criticism and affected the whole of his future. I fear he has committed a serious mistake. Had he taken Jawahar or Maulana, preferably Jawahar, into his confidence, he could have secured his object without attracting any blame. After all he has suffered two years or more and had behind him the work and service of a lifetime.

He also noted: 'At least one of our colleagues said: Who can you believe, now?'

# 18

# Preparing for the World Outside

The Mahatma was released from custody on 5 May 1944. After his last fast he was in poor health and the government was taking no chances. In any case the internal situation was now calmer; the war situation had turned in favour of the Allies and no great threat was expected from his release. As news of his release reached Ahmednagar fort there was some discussion amongst the inmates on what his next steps would be. Asaf's own thoughts were focused on the possible implications of this for Aruna. Clearly his hope was that Gandhi would be able to convince her to give herself up and be arrested: 'I am praying hard that Rene may be guided to seek his advice and terminate the long agony of my anxiety about her. He alone can talk her out of the tangle of self-imposed banishment and its trials.' About a month later he again wrote in his diary, 'It is surprising that Gandhiji has not advised Rene to surrender yet. Why, I ask myself in anguish.'[1]

Clearly Asaf was overestimating Gandhi's powers of persuasion and even influence over Aruna, and also underestimating her determination and conviction. In actual fact, not long after his release, on 9 June 1944 Gandhi had written to Aruna: 'I have been filled with admiration for your courage and heroism. I have sent you messages that you must not die underground. You are reduced to a skeleton. Do come out and surrender yourself and win the prize offered for your arrest. Reserve the prize money for the Harijan cause.'[2] The prize referred to the substantial police reward offered for her arrest after she had been declared an absconder.

Asaf obviously did not know of this letter or even that soon afterwards Aruna and a small group of those underground with her had travelled secretly to Poona to meet the Mahatma and explain what they were doing. In her later recollection close followers had opposed the meeting: 'Was it not improper for the apostle of non-violence to receive one who was known to have promoted violent acts of sabotage?' In her account Gandhi's response to the advice that he should refuse the meeting was that 'he could not refuse to receive anyone who wanted to see him. As for the police who were enforcing the alien rulers' law, it was for them to stop Aruna if they could, and if she came to the Ashram it would be at her [own] risk.'[3]

The viceroy's letter to Gandhi in early 1943 referring to the wife of a Working Committee member being implicated in organizing acts of sabotage – which had driven Asaf into a frenzy of depression and anxiety – was not disinformation or exaggeration. Aruna admitted that many who had originally gone underground later dropped off from clandestine activity on the grounds that actions being taken to sabotage the British war effort were against Gandhian principles of non-violence. She did not agree: 'We were careful to draw a distinction between planned dislocation of Britain's imperialist war effort, on the one hand, and senseless destruction of life and property on the other.' A pamphlet titled 'A B C of Dislocation', possibly authored by her or brought out by her group, had said:

> Dislocation is a common and effective method used by enslaved and oppressed peoples against their rulers . . . Thus, if telegraph lines are cut, fish plates on railway lines are removed, bridges are dynamited, industrial plants put out of order, petrol tanks set on fire, police stations burnt down, official records destroyed – these are all acts of dislocation. But a bomb thrown at a market place or a school or a *dharmshala* is not dislocation. It is either the work of agents provocateur or misdirected energy.[4]

In brief, the aim was not sabotage as an end in itself; rather, 'our object was to bring about a mass uprising'.[5] The fact that she made no secret of her views was perhaps another reason why she remained so high in the government's target lists. The *New York Times* in a report in September 1942 described her as a prominent Congress leader. The report said that she had written to foreign correspondents in India and described their activities as 'short of taking life, everything is permissible'.[6]

We have an unusually detailed account of the meeting that Aruna and some of her 'underground' colleagues had with Gandhi after he was released. Possibly the meeting took place in June or July of that year. Reading this account, drafted by one of Gandhi's followers, certainly gives the impression of neither side conceding their own points of principle.[7] A woman worker, almost certainly Aruna, is described as cross-questioning Gandhi: 'You told us we should be our own master after your arrest . . . We acted according to our light. Your recent utterances make us feel that we have been let down.' Gandhi's response was apparently that he accorded no blame but 'when a thing is wrong, I must say so'. The woman worker admitted that the force of public opinion was behind Gandhi 'but you cannot expect everyone to become a perfect being which your method implies'.

In Aruna's recollection, however, through most of the meeting Gandhi had just listened to her and her colleagues and confined himself to saying, '*Tum sab moorkh ho* [You are all foolish]. Can this country be saved by a handful of people?' The meeting was 'etched on my memory as a vivid illustration of the Mahatma's sympathetic understanding of viewpoints other than his own'. A day or so after this meeting Gandhi released a statement to the press giving his answer to a 'question most discussed with me by visitors is whether I approve of underground activities'. Clearly the meeting with Aruna and her colleagues was on his mind. His answer was categorical that underground activities 'should have no place in the technique of nonviolence'. He also said that while such activities 'may be shown to have imagination and enthusiasm, I have no doubt that they have harmed the movement as a whole'.[8]

After this Aruna wrote to him and the letter underlined both the depth of her own conviction and brought out the respect and adulation Gandhi now commanded even from those who fundamentally disagreed with him:

> If only I could honestly feel that our mode of resistance was wrong, life would be so simple. To be permitted to act under what is known as the willing suspension of disbelief or better still blind discipline would take an enormous load of my shoulders. But you are bent on testing our mettle. We will now go into voluntary inaction for a while.[9]

It seemed nothing was settled and Gandhi's response on 2 August acknowledges this:

> You must not discover yourself unless you feel the wrong of secrecy. You must not be displeased if I hold an opinion which does not coincide with yours . . . I have not judged anyone. I have given my opinion about certain acts. You will harm the cause by acting against your judgement. See me when you like. Don't be in a hurry. Don't be sad.[10]

Aruna's secret and underground existence therefore continued and this would not be the only time she would be in disagreement with Gandhi A confessional statement from an arrested underground activist contains this vivid description of her at that time:

> Mrs Asaf Ali was a liberal, enthusiastic, warm hearted and inspiring type of woman. Though her judgement of persons was not so correct and she often overestimated any worker's ability, she was a great organizer. More and more I used to come in her contact, I felt that she was a very able woman possessing great capacities for initiative and leadership.[11]

An intelligence report of April 1943 noted that 'Mrs Asaf Ali was the chief leader of the movement in Delhi'.[12] Another report ranked her with other leaders of the underground such as Jayaprakash Narayan in Bihar, Achyut Patwardhan in Bombay, Ram Manohar Lohia in the United Provinces, and others.[13] Each was to acquire iconic status and this was now her peer group. The bulk of her underground existence was in Delhi, although she also spent time in Calcutta and Bombay and travelled widely, it was the city she knew best and where she and Asaf had many friends. New associates here included the strongly leftist journalist Edatata Narayan, with whom she remained closely associated in the 1950s – which let to some amount of talk, as we will see.[14]

Many stood by her, offering help and secret hospitality. But not everyone did and some were candid about the dangers. Thus B.K. Nehru, the son of Asaf Ali's old friend Brij Kishore Nehru, with whom Asaf and Aruna had been friendly in the late 1930s, recalled: 'Sometime in 1942 she telephoned me one evening if she and her companions could take shelter in our house.'[15] He refused and the reasons were obvious. He lived in No. 2 Tughlak Lane in the heart of government Delhi; 'Given my relationship and my antecedents, it was probably already under surveillance.' If he had agreed he would have lost his job and her arrest would have been certain. 'She understood the reasons and I heard nothing more from her till everybody was released in 1945.'

She seemed to have captured the imagination of the country at the time with a public profile that would endure. To a public deeply impacted by nationalism she embodied a spirit of sacrifice and resistance that could only be admired: she was after all still a young woman (she was then thirty-five) with a husband in jail and who was struggling for her ideals virtually alone. We do not know how fully Asaf during his incarceration grasped that his wife had acquired an independent, iconic status of her own. But there is no doubt he did have some inkling of the popular adulation for Aruna. He recounts that one day in October 1944, 'Narendra Deva showed me a paragraph in the *Leader* . . . It refers to Aruna as one of the rising stars, whose name is becoming popular for new babies.'[16]

Asaf reflected on this and the entry says much about his melancholia and depression. 'Even this does not assuage my pain. I may feel proud but it does not hurt me the less to think what it has cost her and I dare not think of what it may cost her.' It had also become clearer to him that she was not going to be bound by Gandhi's or anyone else's advice. Were there other concerns that were present but remained unvoiced? It is natural to posit that he may have had doubts about her fidelity and jealously wondered about relationships forged in the heat of the struggle as underground, outlawed political activists. These fears may also have been further compounded by the realization that she had outgrown him and the life he had created for them in the past decade and a half.

News to this effect also came from other sources. Syed Mahmud released from prison after his apology appeared to have continued being in touch with his friends inside jail. Correspondence of a purely personal nature was permitted and a coded post card summed up the position as follows: 'Your niece's condition is not satisfactory. She is very obstinate and has refused to listen to the family doctors.'[17] And there were other disguised hints, in letters to him or to one of his co-prisoners, that preyed on his mind. One from Calcutta referred to 'Sabina having left her husband's house and not wanting ever to return'. Asaf was to write after receiving this: 'This has left me utterly shocked and miserable.'[18] Perhaps it was now becoming clearer that more had changed since his incarceration than just the wider world and India itself.

At about this time a letter from a neighbour in Kucha Chelan drew a depressing picture of the 'unpleasant state of disrepair' which the house was in. With his mother dead and as neither he nor Aruna were staying there, it was falling to pieces. 'Natural', wrote Asaf, for 'the shadows of the evening are gathering fast round me too . . . I know that the visible structure which houses the eternal – I and also Rene – are destined to dissolution. I am dissolving rapidly.' Clearly there was a mix of emotions: real worry and fear about what could happen to Aruna, dread that she no longer loved him and the distinct possibility of losing her, all this with admiration for her courage and determination.

There is alongside the belief that, somehow, he was responsible for his wife's predicament and she was being targeted because she was his wife. A censured portion from one of Asaf's letters contained the following sentences: 'Here is a lonely woman driven from her home for the heinous sin of self-respect and patriotism, to suffer in innumerable ways in exile and who has been hunted and hounded for 32 months and more like a culprit.' This was, the letter went on, 'vindictive persecution. What English woman placed similarly would have been treated thus. I don't mind what happens to me but to treat my wife like this is the limit.'[19] If his view was indeed that Aruna was being targeted on account of his political position, he was deluded. His wife had now an independent political personality. The time and distance from her earlier life in Kucha Chelan had possibly given her a different perspective and an alternative context in which to view her husband. His inclination towards constitutionalism and incrementalism, as opposed to agitation, must have almost certainly smelled to her of political conservatism, the beliefs of someone who did not really want to change the status quo. The age difference and their now different political views had taken them down radically different paths.

One of Asaf's last diary entries in prison – of December 1944 – sums up his mood, and possibly that of others confined along with him: 'The grey monotony of this place – fancy twenty-eight months of incarceration at one place – is enough to wear out one's freshness and the capacity to work.' Perhaps morale was at its lowest ebb then. But he found a survival strategy and solace in 'metaphysical excursions and poetry', which were like 'refreshing gusts of wind'. He writes, 'Once a poem grips you, it will not be denied entry even if you are dying; like truth it will out.' Nehru was to note in January 1945 that Asaf had 'been writing rather good Urdu verse'.[20]

Survival strategies differed and, for each of the prisoners, had evolved and changed over time in the fortress. One of them shows just how slowly time could pass or how bored they often were: Azad would talk, Asaf noted, 'at random for the sake of amusement'. Asaf would occasionally join in and it became then 'a game of playing with words or ideas, parodying well known poets and so on. It is an interesting past time [*sic*].'

Years later Shankarrao Deo would reminisce on the long sojourn in Ahmednagar: 'We have the happiest memory of this period of our lives'![21] But after nearly thirty months, even the most die-hard optimist amongst them would have been bored and exhausted by the daily monotony of life in jail. Nehru had written in his diary in early December, 'Release seems as distant as ever,' but also noted that 'it is likely that we might be discharged next spring'.[22] As 1944 drew to a close and the new year began, the sense that major changes were in the offing grew. News of the poor health of many of the leaders spread and was frequently raised in the press and questions regularly posed to the government in the Central Legislative Assembly.[23] Possibly this mood infected the prison inmates too. Certainly, there was some change in Asaf's state of mind or perhaps he was just tired of his own melancholia. Nehru writing in end January 1945 noted, 'Two years ago and even a year ago Asaf Ali was in a bad way – physically rather broken up with various ailments and mentally even more so. He has pulled himself up . . . He keeps better health. He is a pleasant companion with wider interests than many of us.'[24]

There was enough coverage in the press now to indicate that the government was thinking of separating the CWC and dispersing them to jails in their respective provinces. This was an obvious bureaucratic first step to their release, but clearly the government now seems to have decided that continued incarceration in Ahmednagar was no longer necessary and cases of plague in Ahmednagar city made it risky. Although nothing was known for certain, for the prisoners themselves, 'our impending transfer has filled our minds and interfered with the normal routine of our lives here'.[25]

The likely dispersal had led to a resumption of deliberations – after a long gap following the acrimonious ending of the discussions in November 1943 on the need to conciliate with the government. Now, the main line of division and the point of discussion was the chain of events that had landed them in Ahmednagar and the Congress in seeming wilderness. A subtext of this was the communal question and the position that the Congress should take with regard to the Muslim League and with the issue of Muslim representation in general.

By early March these meetings were taking place regularly. Nehru wrote in his diary, 'we have been meeting every afternoon for two hours'. And on 8 March, 'we have had five such meetings'. Their aim was to get to know each other's mind so that a common position could be maintained even if they were dispersed to different jails and communications between them became difficult to arrange. There were many specific issues: should the refusal to have meetings with outsiders, even relatives, continue as long as the custody continued? What was the committee's position on the communists and the socialists, the communal issue, the impact of global changes on India, etc.? It was agreed they would continue to refuse meetings with outsiders unless there was some very important contingency. On the communists it was generally agreed that there was a continued need to keep them at arm's length since they were unquestionably 'against Congress policy and attacked Congress during a period of action'. The socialists by contrast were acceptable: 'the general opinion was that we must not push out any group. We had to widen and strengthen the Congress and not to make it into a narrower body.'[26]

These broad policy issues would have possibly seen a consensus of opinions. By the third week of March, however, more sensitive areas were being touched, and on 19 March Nehru wrote: 'There has been a burst up at our afternoon talks.'[27] This happened when Azad embarked on a reflective and introspective discourse on the events of 1942 and the fateful decision that had led them to Ahmednagar: 'he felt now that he should have resisted Bapu's argument still more.' There was possibly more than an implied criticism of Nehru for changing his mind on the final decision to launch a movement against the government and also of Gandhi and those who had fully supported such a move. The discussions continued the next day; Nehru tried to 'explain as calmly and objectively as possible the effects on my mind of various incidents, so that I could understand myself and show to others the changes I underwent in the course of those months preceding August 1942'. In his telling:

> When, however, I saw that this [the 'Quit India' resolution] was inevitable, that Bapu's mind was fixed and determined, then further argument was not useful. I had to make my choice. There was no difficulty about the choice. It was inconceivable for me to remain aloof from such a movement . . . Looking back, I said, I am not very sorry for what I did or for what happened. I do think it could have been

> better if the approach could have been different if, in fact our approach of August could have been consistently followed in previous months. But facts are seldom in our control and things took their own course.

Next to speak was Patel; his view of the past decisions was different and his 'tone was full of suppressed anger, pain and bitterness'. The obstacles Azad and others had presented to the path of confrontation were clearly still uppermost in his mind. Patel said

> he had long suspected that Maulana and others had long felt the way they had spoken about events prior to August 1942 . . . he wished to say with all emphasis that he did not agree with Maulana's analysis and he was firmly convinced that the attitude and steps taken by Bapu had been correct and inevitable . . . He resented this attempt to show that he and his colleagues had not only been wrong but also what they proposed then was dangerous to the Country.

The discussion that followed was acrimonious, and when it concluded the next day, Nehru noted, 'I am presently hardly on speaking terms with Vallabhbhai and Kripalani . . .'

It is not known whether Asaf spoke and participated in this discussion. He might have kept quiet as perhaps most others did: the differences were hardly new and had been gone over several times in the past. Many of them may have felt that continued recrimination over the past was pointless, and with the divisions in the CWC being clear enough, there was no need to wade into them again. In any event, when they were finally released, it would be a changed reality each would have to confront.

The actual move out of Ahmednagar began from end March 1945. Barring Kripalani and Asaf, the others were sent to jails in their home provinces. Asaf was dispatched to Gurdaspur in Punjab, because the Government of Delhi did not want him to be jailed in a city under its jurisdiction.

Kripalani was sent to Karachi in Sindh – perhaps technically his home province but with which he had had little to do for at least two decades. He was, Nehru wrote, 'amazed and it struck him as a huge joke'. Asaf's health through this time was not good; in mid-May the secretary to the viceroy wrote that he was ill in the Gurdaspur sub-jail: 'he is a sick man [and] we should probably release him soon . . . he is not thought to be likely to give trouble in present circumstances.'[28] A letter from the viceroy subsequently revealed that while the central government had been prepared to release him even earlier because of his ill health, 'the Delhi Administration were against it'.[29]

The nervousness of the Delhi authorities is suggested by its actions when Asaf's train arrived from Ahmednagar and the accompanying police escort realized that a halt of some hours or a whole day in Delhi – before he could be put on the train to Gurdaspur – was now unavoidable. News of his arrival in Delhi had reached earlier and waiting at the railway station were a large number of Congress workers and friends. Asaf is described as looking 'pale and weak' and unrecognizable. He was taken to a nearby police station and then, possibly to pre-empt a large gathering and possible demonstration, driven to Ghaziabad to catch the train from there rather than Delhi. This news spread and his almost two-month-long stay in a Gurdaspur jail was regularly punctuated by newspaper reports about his precarious health, the shabby treatment accorded to him while being transferred to Gurdaspur; there were many petitions submitted to the government that he be released.[30]

This finally happened in end May and he arrived in Delhi on 28 May 1945 to what newspapers described as a rousing welcome at the railway station. Described as too weak to stand he was brought out of the compartment in a chair.[31] The next few weeks were spent in a Delhi hospital and then in recuperation in Gulmarg in Kashmir along with some other members of the CWC now also released. While in hospital Asaf read of a statement given by Nehru a day after he had been released: 'It is a matter for shame and sorrow that so many of our comrades are still behind bars. Their sufferings, unlike mine, have not hit the headlines. The world tends to forget them.'[32]

Nehru went on to say:

> Among them, it is only in the fitness of things that I must take the name of one of India's brave women, Aruna Asaf Ali. If my voice can reach her, I want to send her my love and esteem. I want to tell her that whatever she has done shall not be wasted and will bear fruit. It will leave its impression on her countrymen.

Asaf was deeply touched as he read this and telegraphed Nehru of his 'undying gratitude for nobly owning disowned, hunted, hounded, persecuted for sin of patriotism'.[33] But Nehru had perhaps erred in writing that Aruna was in the forgotten, anonymous category of activists. Her story was never far from the newspapers, and her capacity to evade arrest and travel around the country virtually at will was a subject of almost continuous interest to many.

Aruna managed to meet Asaf in Delhi in hospital. They were meeting after almost three years: Asaf had been arrested in August 1942 and they had last seen each other on the railway platform before the special train bore the arrested Congress leaders to Ahmednagar. We can reasonably surmise she told him she had no intention of ending her underground existence, possibly gave as full an account as was possible of her activities and her associates, and reiterated her commitment to what she stood for and had done. Their politics had clearly diverged, and while Asaf had certainly been conscious of this for some time, his worst fears must have been confirmed at that moment.

We can also surmise, in part speculatively, that more than their politics had diverged and there was now, if not a breach, certainly a gulf that separated them. She was a person and a public personality now in her own right, with a profile that was far higher than his. He had built his career block by block on a trajectory entirely different from the young woman's who now commanded a larger-than-life image in the country and not just in its nationalist circles.

It was not an opportune time for these realities to dawn. Asaf was, if not a mental and physical wreck, certainly a much reduced person in his own eyes and in the eyes of those who had been incarcerated with him. The past three years had taken a toll, and while the damage was not irreversible, at that moment his position was the weaker one. Aruna on the other hand was now a person tempered by struggle, fearless in many ways, and with widely expanded mental horizons. If these attributes were characteristic of her personality from the beginning – what else would explain her unconventional marriage and life thereafter – the past three years had in a sense crystallized her character. The age difference was possibly now

Photo Section, PMML

*Aruna Asaf Ali wearing khadi*

more evident than ever before – not just in physical terms but also in an emotional sense. The balance in their marriage had not just shifted; the relationship itself had fundamentally changed.

We can put all this together from certain fragments of evidence. In July, Maulana Azad, in his capacity as Congress president, made a representation to the viceroy that detained Congress workers should be released and the ban on the Congress rescinded. He also wrote a separate letter regarding Aruna and her ill health, seeking a withdrawal of the arrest warrant against her and an amnesty. The viceroy's reply reiterated that Aruna had 'done her best to promote activities of an extremely violent kind and that the orders of her arrest could not be withdrawn'. These were lengthy exchanges and found their way to the press.

On learning of this, Aruna wrote to Gandhi in August 1945 objecting to being singled out by the Congress president in this way. Her letter also suggests the tenor of the conversation with Asaf when she met him in the hospital and her misgivings about their shared future:

> It just humiliates me although I knew it is well meant. Is it because I am a woman that I have been particularized? Or is it that Asaf's health and mental anguish moved Maulana to make me a special case . . . What surprises me is that Asaf should have permitted Maulana to entreat on my behalf . . . I had made it categorically clear that whatever the consequences I would not disown my responsibility for any of the policies, programmes or directions that I have been associated with either as an individual or as a member of a group. I had also explained in reply to his questions the nature of the planned and unplanned incidents of 1942. Either he did not attach any importance to my statements or he did not realize their implications. Anyway it shows how utterly estranged we have become. I knew this might happen.[34]

This frank acknowledgement of her feelings of estrangement from Asaf was possibly also a kind of intimation to Gandhi that her marriage was over. Gandhi's letter was equally direct and uncharacteristically blunt but also an illustration of his multiple roles in the Congress leadership:

> The distress is of your own imagination. I fear that the Maulana's letter was of my doing. There was no question of isolating you from the rest or expecting you to suppress anything. You were represented as being very ill and so there is a mention of your illness . . . Asaf had no hand in it. So far as I know he came to know of the letter after it was dispatched. Will you not give him and to everyone else the liberty of free thought that you claim for yourself?[35]

The orders for the withdrawal of the arrest warrant against Aruna would be issued only several months later, in January 1946 when politics in India was poised to enter a wholly new phase.

# 19

# The World Outside

The formal announcement of the release of the Congress leadership had come in mid-June 1945. After almost three years of enforced inactivity and intense argument, each had now to step back and take stock of the fast-paced turn of actual events in the outside world. The war in Europe was over with Germany's surrender on 8 May 1945. That in East and South East Asia continued but its trajectory and outcome were now clear; Japan's surrender came on 15 August 1945 after the deployment of nuclear weapons in Hiroshima and Nagasaki. Subhas Chandra Bose had been killed in an air crash on 18 August.

The Congress leadership realized it faced a radically altered post-war reality. There was no clearer sign than the results of the British general election in end July 1945 in which the Conservatives led by Churchill, the war hero, were voted out. The Labour Party would form the new government and its view on India was unequivocal: British rule should end quickly. This was not simply by any means a linear progression of Labour's traditional stand. It reflected a new reality of a war-torn Britain in which domestic priorities of rebuilding bombed-out cities and reorienting a war-directed economy to peacetime challenges overshadowed everything else. The demands of an empire in India were a distraction and, to an increasing number of people in Britain, a responsibility they could easily live without. There was little or no appetite left for further rounds of confrontation with nationalist forces in India. If some in British officialdom would try – and often try hard – to retain a core of British influence, and even presence, in the new architecture to emerge, it was, compared to the overwhelming urge to attend to Britain's domestic challenges, not a major factor.

On 21 August the viceroy announced the elections for the Central and provincial legislatures. Immediately thereafter came the lifting of the ban on the Congress. The next step would be the construction of a new framework for the governance of a new and independent India by drafting a constitution for the country. With these fast-paced developments, the time had now come for all the contradictions between the Congress and the League to erupt.

The election for the Central Legislature was announced for end November–December 1945 and that for the provincial assemblies in January of the new year. This would be the first major electoral test for the Congress after its resignation from the provincial ministries and the launch of the Quit India movement. If this was to be a demonstration of the Congress hold on the popular imagination, it would also be a test of its popularity amongst Muslim voters vis-à-vis the League. It would ascertain whether the warnings of Azad, Asaf and Syed Mahmud in jail – that a gulf existed between the Congress and Muslims – and the prolonged internal dissensions about the wisdom of launching a mass struggle in August 1942 had any merit.

Asaf was the natural choice for the Delhi seat to the Central Legislature. Not only had he held the seat earlier, he was now the most prominent face of the party and perhaps of the national movement as a whole in Delhi. The outcome of the election itself was perhaps largely a foregone conclusion and one report described it as a 'tame affair'.[1] Since Delhi was not a reserved Muslim seat but a general constituency, the Muslim League did not put up an official candidate, but it did informally back a Muslim contender against Asaf. The Hindu Mahasabha put up a candidate who lost his deposit. The electorate was small and Asaf secured over 6,000 votes compared to his Muslim rival who got about 1,500. The Congress had, however, taken no chances in Delhi. This was a prestige seat and Asaf was now one of its prominent faces; the election campaign was launched by Nehru.[2] It had nevertheless its intense moments, including personal attacks on Asaf by the League: 'One League journal reminds Congress

Muslims that Mrs Aruna Asaf Ali is still out of purdah and nobody knows whether she has accepted Islam or not.'[3]

Such carping notwithstanding, the clarity of the verdict made the whole process appear a formality. One paper summed up the result as: Asaf 'represents the fastly [*sic*] vanishing Delhi culture.' If there was little doubt about his popularity, it continued, 'His wife, the gallant, charming and never surrender Aruna Asaf Ali has further added to his popularity.' Asaf had been 'a popular figure in Delhi' and Aruna was a 'torch bearer of liberty . . . a Bengalee by birth, a UP lady by domicile of her parents and a Delhiwalee by adoption or marriage'. The conclusion for this journalist at least was inescapable: 'Yes, people voted for Asaf because he was a Congress candidate, because he was Asaf and because of Aruna Asaf Ali.'[4]

Through the election campaign there had been another, and perhaps more significant, factor that had gripped the popular imagination, and Asaf fortuitously found himself at the centre of it. Indian National Army personnel who had supported the Japanese war effort by deserting the British Indian army and joining Subhas Chandra Bose's Indian National Army (INA) in 1942, and had been active in Singapore, Malaya and Burma, were back in India in their thousands following Japan's surrender. Bose's approach had been to forge an alliance with the Japanese and raise an army from Indian prisoners of war (POWs) taken by the Japanese to join the war against the British. There was general agreement in army headquarters and in the government that the vast bulk of them were followers and no real guilt was associated with them. The key figures were, however, the initiators who had provided the leadership and used coercive methods to compel more of their colleagues to join the INA ranks. They must be, it was strongly felt, tried both for disloyalty to the British Indian army and for crimes committed against their fellow POWs.

At about the time as the new Labour government in London was changing tack from its predecessor on the question of Indian independence came the decision to court-martial these soldiers. The government's errors of judgement were of fixing the trial by court martial in Delhi's historic Red Fort and then of selecting, so as not to appear discriminatory, a Hindu, a Sikh and a Muslim officer for the first trial. Shah Nawaz Khan, Prem Kumar Sahgal and Gurbaksh Singh Dhillon were the officers chosen and almost overnight they became household names across India. Underwriting these decisions was the greater error of misreading how intense an emotional and nationalist issue the INA trial would become.

For most of British officialdom in India – in the main army officers and civil servants – and opinion in Britain itself, this was a black-and-white issue: these officers had broken a solemn oath of loyalty that underwrites all military discipline and notions of honour. In brief, they were traitors. The British establishment felt that having themselves emerged at enormous cost from the struggle against Japan and Germany, it was unacceptable that anything but the severest punishment could suffice for those who were seen as ringleaders and the main instruments in the setting up of the INA which had collaborated with the Japanese. The men on trial had been selected and identified as the main leaders from within the large mass of captured INA personnel. They were principally officers of the Indian Army who first agreed to join the INA and then either inspired and induced or coerced their fellow officers and subordinates to do so.

Views in India were, almost unanimously, the opposite. These men were not traitors but nationalists and freedom fighters who were inspired by Subhas Bose's call to liberate the motherland. As news spread about the government's intention to court-martial them, a wave of sympathy swept the country. This also largely coincided with the lifting of wartime censorship and restrictions on reporting. As more details about the INA became public it became the recipient of progressively stronger waves of public adulation.

The Hindu–Sikh–Muslim composition of the trio identified for the first set of court martials meant also that the issue overrode the communal polarization under way in the country. They were charged with murder, abetment to murder and waging war against the king. The intention of not singling out only one religious background had the opposite effect and even the by now intense League–Congress acrimony could not ward off the criticism of the government from across the political spectrum.

The choice of the Red Fort as a venue, as far as the authorities were concerned, was in part for pragmatic reasons of easy access for the judges and legal teams; the army headquarters was close by; and the defendants were being held in the fort. But the aim was also to have a public trial rather than one in a restricted cantonment or in secrecy, to better drive home the point about loyalty and military discipline and the gravity of the offence the officers were charged with. Therefore, that the fort was seen as a symbol of India's greatness made it an appropriate venue. Viceroy Wavell agreed. To him the INA men were 'softlings' and 'cowards'.[5] Supporting them meant supporting 'the worst . . . elements in the Indian army'.[6] A public trial would reveal to all their true nature including the techniques they used to bring other POWs into the INA.

Almost from the start public comments drew comparisons with an equally symbolic and one-sided trial – that of the deposed Mughal emperor Bahadur Shah Zafar charged with mutiny, found guilty and exiled to Rangoon for the rest of his life. Subhas Bose had visited his tomb after Burma fell to Japanese forces and an INA contingent arrived in Burma to join in the Japanese offensive into north-east India. Bose's call 'Dilli Chalo' evoked images of the INA marching to the gates of the Red Fort. The trial of its officers in that very fort thus had all the ingredients to symbolically link the INA to India's First War of Independence in 1857 when Bahadur Shah, howsoever nominally, was at the head of the first national effort to rid the country of foreign rule.

The trial and the tidal wave of public indignation coincided with the election campaign for the Central Legislature. The Congress and its candidates thus found a readymade issue to funnel nationalist sentiment to strengthen its campaign. In any case, election or not, it was the sheer pace and unfolding of events that decided politics, rather than calculated, thought-out strategy.

The Congress had its own set of grievances with Bose; in particular Bose had blamed Gandhi, Patel and Nehru for having forced him to leave the Congress and strike out on his own from 1939 onwards. But all this was in the past. Bose had, with his death, become a towering figure in public perception, and the INA was his legacy and as much a force in the fight for freedom as the Congress had been when it launched the Quit India movement. The Congress leadership could hardly ignore these public perceptions even had they wanted to.

All these issues came together in the meeting of the AICC in Bombay on 21 and 22 September 1945. The venue was the Gowalia Tank Maidan where, in August 1942, the AICC had taken the fateful decision to ask the British to 'Quit India'. The September 1945 meeting of the AICC took place after a long gap with a packed agenda including discussions on the Congress's position vis-à-vis the Muslim League. But one point was especially topical. It was decided that the Congress as an organization would undertake the responsibility to defend the INA personnel being court-martialled.

Many in the Congress had doubts about Bose's approach. But its own Quit India agitation against the British in the midst of the war had enough parallels with Bose's effort, howsoever weak. The British in fact had argued that the 1942 agitation and the violent turn it took in effect aided its adversaries in the war. For the Congress any posture but of support to the INA personnel – being tried with the distinct possibility that they could face death sentences – was unrealistic. But there were reservations. The relevant part of the resolution adopted read that the Congress was 'strongly of the opinion that for additional reasons of far-reaching consequences and in view of the termination of the war, it would be a great tragedy if these officers, men and women, were punished for the offence of having laboured, howsoever mistakenly, for the freedom of India'.[7] Clearly there was an implied disapproval of the tactics Subhas

Chandra Bose had adopted but understated to the extent possible. The meeting also announced the formation of a Defence Committee to see that these 'patriotic men were properly defended'.

The Defence Committee consisted of a number of legal and political luminaries including Jawaharlal Nehru, Tej Bahadur Sapru and Bhulabhai Desai. Asaf Ali was designated the 'convener' of this group. He seems to have been an automatic choice: he was in the CWC, and was a Delhi-based lawyer and therefore in a position to follow up on a daily basis. The Defence Committee was soon active in its own separate office in Delhi and Asaf was there almost constantly. This was before his election to the Central Legislative Assembly but he must have realized that time devoted to this cause was not a diversion from his own election campaign but actually supplemented it.

The high-powered defence team and the high profile the Congress attached to the issue helped in other ways. A common defence team mounted by the Congress to defend a Hindu, a Sikh and a Muslim buttressed its claim to speak on behalf of all Indians regardless of religion. If the Muslim League contested this claim, there was little it could do on the INA issue in the face of the enormous public support for the campaign. Over the coming weeks the forthcoming INA trials became as significant as the August 1942 Congress resolution and the repressive measures adopted by the colonial state against the Quit India movement. Against the backdrop of the forthcoming elections these issues merged and crystallized into a single nationalist platform. The slight qualification contained in the AICC resolution of '"howsoever mistakenly"' provides, however, an insight into the personal thinking of principal Congress leaders. For them the correct path was political struggle – not the individual acts of extremists or joining the ranks of your adversary's enemy in combat. But this view would progressively be submerged by the wider narrative of nationalist resistance to the British.

On 15 October 1945, Bhulabhai Desai and Asaf jointly wrote to the viceroy about the forthcoming trial of the three officers selected for the first round of court martials. The trial was scheduled to begin at the Red Fort on 5 November. The letter conveyed that these officers had entrusted their defence to the INA Defence Committee – something that was already well known, with donations and letters of support coming to the Defence Committee office. It also recommended abandonment of the trial or at least its postponement till completion of the elections and the formation of new provincial governments and the constitution of a new Executive Council to the viceroy. This would put the government in a better position 'to gauge public opinion' and then it 'will be able to arrive at a proper decision whether the intended trial of the INA should take place at all and if so when and how'.[8]

The army's and the viceroy's minds were, however, made up. They were bemused at the enormous criticism they were receiving in India on this issue, angry with the Congress's tactics and frustrated that their perception of the trial – as critical for maintaining the integrity of the army of an independent India – had so few takers. The trial was to proceed as scheduled amid growing adulation of the INA and the officers on trial, bitterness over the long incarceration of Congress leadership and the accompanying crackdown: in brief, accelerating anti-government sentiment. This was in the midst of all the theatrics of an upcoming election.

For Asaf, 'constitutional' methods were preferable as a way of putting pressure on the colonial state. While he had been jailed many times and participated in all the principal Congress campaigns and agitations, his natural inclination and preference was the 'Swarajist' route rather than mass civil disobedience. Despite differences with the party line, as for instance in 1941–42, he saw also the importance of organizational discipline and keeping his differences to himself or at most confined to internal discussions. What was therefore his view about the INA and the Congress position on it? His jail diary notings appear to have no reference to Bose. He would have known little about Bose's activities as part of the Japanese consolidation and advance across South East Asia, as he was in jail the entire time, with access to only heavily censored newspapers. The letter he and Bhulabhai Desai wrote to the viceroy mentioned the point that the AICC resolution had raised regarding 'mistaken actions' carried out with the best of motives:

> It is no exaggeration to say that while some may doubt the propriety of the policies which led to the establishment of such an Army as an independent military organization under the command of its own officers, Indians of all communities, all persuasions and of all schools of political thought recognize the selfless patriotism which actuated those who took part in this moment.[9]

It is possible to infer Asaf's personal feelings from a report of his meeting with an Indian army officer, Hari Badhwar, who was a POW under the Japanese but who refused to join the INA and had possibly seen the coercive methods used to make some change their minds. He reported his three-and-a-half-hour-long conversation with Asaf Ali on 18 October 1945 to the Military Intelligence, which is how it has survived in the historical record. Captain Badhwar reported that he gave Asaf a full account of the brutal treatment of Indian POWs who remained loyal to the British Indian army and asked him 'what the Congress expected of the services when a National Government assumes power, i.e. did they intend to promote faction and communal feeling'. Asaf's reply, as is to be expected, was that the armed services would be kept free of politics. Thereafter Badhwar had provided details of the INA 'from the point of view of one of those who had suffered'. Asaf's reply had apparently included the line: 'Congress leaders had realized that those who joined the INA were far from innocent.' Asaf also told Badhwar:

> Before committing themselves to public statements Congress leaders had however asked him [Asaf Ali] to tour the country to find out public feelings. He had done so, from South to North, and found, as he moved North, opinion stronger and stronger that the INA must not be punished for their actions but should be released. This inflamed feeling forced Congress to take the line it did.

Asaf is also said to have offered the opinion that 'if Congress was in power, it would have no hesitation in removing all INA personnel from the services and even in putting them on trial . . .'[10]

The credibility of this account need not be doubted although it is unlikely that Congress leaders would have required Asaf's tour, if indeed there was a specific one of this kind, to gauge public opinion on the issue. There is little doubt that the Congress was led by public opinion on this issue but it was equally convinced that the government was tactically wrong in going ahead with the trial quite regardless of the merits of the matter. But the Congress would certainly have been aware that the views of many serving Indian officers in the army were divergent from the prevailing public consensus in the country.

Badhwar's report of his conversation was of course just what his British superiors suspected, even knew, and equally just what they wanted to hear. Having to defend and carry out a vastly unpopular decision, they sought to rationalize their actions as the right thing to do and project that it was the Congress that was being unprincipled and was opportunistically playing politics. The reality was more complex and there were two separate, each equally valid, principles in collision here. Nobody was in a better position to appreciate this than the Congress leadership itself, freshly released from a long incarceration following what the colonial state saw as a revolt during wartime or a 'stab in the back'. Asaf himself had wrestled throughout his imprisonment with the question of revolt against a foreign government when the country faced a foreign invasion. While he disagreed with Aruna's approach, he could possibly also understand it better than most. No doubt he also understood the deeper issues involved in the INA trial much more acutely than the young Captain Badhwar could. His responses to Badhwar are therefore those of an experienced politician commiserating with those who suffered at the hands of the INA, but equally that public opinion charged with nationalist fervour could not be put aside.

In the actual legal proceedings at the Red Fort, the defence was led by Bhulabhai Desai who presented virtually all arguments himself. The entire team, including Nehru and Tej Bahadur Sapru, were present on the opening day and an iconic photograph marks the occasion. But thereafter it was really Desai who was the main player. Asaf was present through the entire trial but was silent except for one cross-examination where he had a testy exchange with the prosecution lawyer. The proceedings were as much optical and political as legal, and the press reports portray Asaf throughout as a vital member of the defence. Its principal argument was one that had already been outlined in the Bhulabhai–Asaf letter to the viceroy: that the INA was the army of a provisional government of Free India which had an independent status and international recognition, and was not therefore a puppet of the Japanese. It was therefore 'entitled to make war and it did make war for the purpose of liberating this country'.

The final verdict was as expected but the outcome was not: the three officers were found guilty of waging war against the king but not of murder or abetment to commit murder. The sentences awarded were dismissal from service with forfeiture of pay and allowances, and transportation to the Andamans for life. The real fear of a massive public outcry, and of a popular upsurge that might infect the entire machinery of government, led to the sentence of transportation being remitted. In effect the three officers were free to walk out and that is what they did. For the public and nationalists of all hues it was a great victory.

On being released, amongst the first places the three officers visited was Asaf's house in Kucha Chelan. As they passed through the narrow streets of the old city, word spread and by the time they reached his house a large crowd was present: 'Joyously they marched in, followed by a crowd of friends and admirers loaded with sweets and garlands.'[11] Another report described the scene:

> News of the release was still not generally known as the three men drove to Mr Asaf Ali's house to convey their thanks to him personally. Soon afterwords however crowds gathered in the narrow valley of Kucha Chelan in which the house stood and for the next hour or two the INA men were caught in a wave of public enthusiasm. As they came out of the house the crowd cheered them with cries of 'Jai Hind' and 'Inquilab Zindabad'.[12]

It is quite probable that the residents of the locality would have juxtaposed the scenes before them with the inherited memories and the lore of the massacre carried out in Kucha Chelan by vengeful British troops on the city being retaken in 1857. But while memories of the reassertion of the might of Empire might have surfaced, the current scenes would have convinced even the most sceptical that the 'anticipation of freedom' was not now unfounded.[13]

The next day the Delhi Provincial Congress Committee organized a public meeting that Asaf presided over. The gathering was described as 'unprecedented in Delhi's history'. Asaf was reported as saying that 'He had toured from one end of the country to the other and found that there was such spirit and enthusiasm among the people as he had not heard of during the last 150 years'.[14]

There is another story within this story concerning a notable absentee in these celebrations: Bhulabhai Desai, the lead lawyer for the defence. He had left for Bombay after the oral submissions were complete and before the verdict was delivered and the decision to remit the sentences announced. He was, before his departure from Delhi, the guest of honour at a smaller gathering at (or perhaps near) the Qutab Minar. This function was both to felicitate him for the INA defence and to bid him farewell, for Desai's term in the Central Legislature had ended with the new members elected. This was in fact a somewhat sad time for Bhulabhai and many of his friends knew he had been ill used. The leader of the Congress in the Central Legislature from 1934 onwards, he had been denied the Congress ticket for the 1945 elections. He had, despite poor health, agreed to lead the INA defence team at the request of the party and undoubtedly saw his performance as a vindication of his reputation and of his integrity.

The ticket denial was a very public reprimand for an initiative he had taken with the Muslim League, to some extent with Gandhi's encouragement. It was what would be termed today a secret back channel to see if common ground was possible away from the glare of publicity and pressures of public opinion. As often happens with back channels, it all went – for Bhulabhai at least – horribly wrong.

The immediate background to this was a three-week-long but ultimately failed discussion between Jinnah and Gandhi in September 1944 some months after the latter's release from Poona on a possible Congress–League agreement to jointly form a government at the Centre, something the British too wanted. The basis for this discussion was what C. Rajagopalachari had originally recommended in April 1942: negotiate with the League on the basis of its Pakistan demand. Gandhi's proposal to Jinnah in these meetings was that he would agree to a plebiscite of all inhabitants in the Muslim-majority provinces in the north-west and north-east on whether they preferred a separate Pakistan; if that was the majority view, there would be a separation along with a mutual agreement on common defence and communications. The negotiation failed in part because Jinnah did not agree with the premise that all residents – both Muslims and non-Muslims of the Muslim-majority provinces – should take part in the plebiscite, since Muslims had the right to decide their own future.

These talks were important and their failure a setback – at least for those who believed an end to the Quit India agitation was necessary. In Ahmednagar the prisoners had come to know about the breakdown through the jailer who heard the news on the radio. In Asaf's words: 'I felt as if the heavens had come toppling about the ears . . . All was lost, I told myself.' He recalled walking with G.B. Pant and Vallabhbhai Patel discussing the breakdown and that they were 'almost like people returning from a funeral'.[15]

After this failure, Bhulabhai began a conversation with Liaquat Ali Khan who was then the deputy leader of the Muslim League in the Central Legislative Assembly. They discussed a joint proposal to be made to the viceroy for setting up a government at the Centre for the duration of the war with equal representation for the League and the Congress. Gandhi was possibly fully in the loop on these meetings and the proposals being exchanged, although he had doubts whether Jinnah would agree.

Later, both sides disowned the initiative. Jinnah said he had no knowledge of it and Liaquat washed his hands of it, saying it was no more than a private conversation. Bhulabhai was left holding a hot potato alone as news of this leaked. Misnamed the 'Liaquat–Desai pact', it was summarized by one historian as 'a non-event staged by improbable actors with an impossible script'.[16] With the passage of time, we may take a more measured view: the initiative carried all the risks of secret discussions which try to reconcile widely divergent positions and success is only possible when the respective interlocutors are fully backed by their principals.

In this case, it was not feasible that the Congress, with its leadership still in jail, would have approved – regardless of Gandhi's position and the long conversation with Jinnah. Their immediate suspicion would have been of Bhulabhai acting on his own as a means of progressing his own political career. The Congress leadership on release from jail were collectively enraged and the impression gained ground that Bhulabhai had attempted to cobble a deal with Liaquat Ali Khan and the Muslim League bypassing the CWC, that is, behind their backs while they were incarcerated. A statement by Asaf summed up at that time the CWC view: 'Nobody wants to [have a] hole and corner agreement between even responsible leaders in their individual capacity. Matters of vital interest to masses must be clearly stated . . .'[17] Whether this was actually his personal view, however, appears doubtful since he would have certainly agreed with the effort to reach some kind of an understanding with the League and was dismayed at the failure of the Gandhi–Jinnah talks.

The point is that any idea of discussing the demand for Pakistan with the League was anathema to many – perhaps even a majority – in the Congress; this was also brought out in the reactions to Asaf when he spoke about a confederation in Ahmednagar. Meeting the League halfway or discussing optimal, even if not perfect, outcomes was not a popular strategy within the Congress at the time. Jinnah's and the League's intransigence – bolstered by what the Congress saw was their rising strength and popularity – further compounded the problem and made the knot even tighter.

Bhulabhai paid the price. The INA trial did redeem his reputation but the damage was done and it was considerable. His admirers believed that the shock of being publicly dusted down, by being denied a ticket in the elections to the Central Legislature, was too much for his fragile health: he died in May 1946.[18] The story is itself a minor footnote to the crowded chronology of this time but it did perhaps reinforce one point: how very difficult the Congress–League interface was becoming and how lethal it could be to try and find common ground.

C. Rajagopalachari had been in a similar position in the run-up to August 1942 and the Quit India resolution. In April 1942 the Madras Congress, at his instance, had passed a resolution recommending that the Congress negotiate with the Muslim League its demand in the 1940 resolution that geographically contiguous Muslim-majority areas be constituted into independent sovereign states. In this line of thinking, a realistic negotiation with the League was better, given the fact that the Congress's own roots amongst Muslims were less strong than assumed. This, plus his opposition to the idea of a mass civil disobedience movement against the government at this stage, led to a situation where Rajagopalachari was given no real choice except to resign from the Congress and its Working Committee. The taking down and public humiliation were similar to what was to happen with Bhulabhai. In brief, within the Congress the search for a midway path with the Muslim League was a minefield. Rajagopalachari's position did have other takers even within the CWC, although they may well have been in a minority. As we saw, Asaf in fact wholeheartedly endorsed it. But he kept silent as others also did, but perhaps with greater cause.

# 20

# The New Radicals

The second half of 1945 was an eventful time for Asaf Ali, with his release from Ahmednagar fort and then finally from Gurdaspur jail; his election to the Central Legislature; the INA trial; his anxiety about Aruna; and – perhaps the most significant – adjusting to a changed political reality. There was also the consciousness that fundamental change was in the offing not just in India but on a global scale. And alongside all this there was one more main event: the elections for new provincial governments. Asaf himself had scored an almost one-sided victory to the Central Legislature in Delhi – and it was a valuable one for the Congress to demonstrate that it could put up a prominent Muslim candidate in a Hindu-majority constituency in the country's capital. But this could not hide the new reality revealed by the provincial election results.

By February 1946 election results from all the provinces had come in and the overall picture was clear. In the aggregate the Congress had done well, especially considering that its leadership had been locked up for a long time and that the organization as a whole had been the target of a sustained and highly repressive crackdown. It won over 90 per cent of non-Muslim votes and was the majority party in all provinces except Punjab, Bengal and Sindh. But it performed badly in all the Muslim seats, with the Muslim League possibly exceeding even its own expectations. The League won 75 out of the 86 Muslim seats in Punjab, 114 out of a total 119 in Bengal, 28 out of 34 in Sindh, and all the reserved seats in Bombay and Madras. Overall, the League won 442 out of the total 504 Muslim seats in the provinces. In the 1945 Central Legislature elections too, it had won all the 30 Muslim seats. Amongst the Muslim-majority areas, only in NWFP did the Congress perform creditably in terms of the Muslim vote.

Various rationalizations were aired: in particular, that the total electorate was minuscule and hardly representative; that the narrow upper-class electorate in the Muslim constituencies was weighted against the Congress which was a mass-based party; that the Congress organization and leadership had not recovered from the repression unleashed by the colonial state after August 1942. The 1937 electoral performance of the Muslim League had raised questions about its claim to represent Muslims and Muslim opinion in India. Those questions were, however, now answered – and pretty emphatically at that. The overall political takeaway was inescapable: the Congress's claim to represent Muslims was considerably eroded and the Muslim League's insistence that it alone spoke for the Muslims of British India enormously strengthened. In brief, the fears that Azad, Rajagopalachari, Asaf and Syed Mahmud had emphasized to the others for some time had become a reality.

Also eroded was the claim that the Muslim League was an unrepresentative party of feudal grandees. The idea of Pakistan had made deep inroads into the psyche of many Muslims in India. Jinnah would now refuse to countenance even more strongly any discussion not premised on the proposition that the Muslim League alone (and he by implication) represented Muslims in India. But while there was charged rhetoric about Pakistan as a Muslim homeland, what Jinnah or the Muslim League specifically demanded was somewhat vague and not clarified. Did he have two separate sovereignties in mind – Pakistan and India – as separate countries? Or did he have in mind a confederation of Hindu- and Muslim-majority provinces in which each would have virtually sovereign status but with a weaker central government to coordinate joint defence? What would happen to the Hindu and other minority populations in the Muslim-majority areas and vice versa? On all of these questions there was little detail from Jinnah.

As a prominent Muslim leader in the Congress, Asaf Ali was frequently asked to comment on 'Pakistan' during the course of the elections. His public pronouncements were measured and obviously clearly and deeply thought through. But that he used rational and considered arguments suggests also how seriously he viewed the potential and potency of the demand, even while dismissing it as 'nothing more than an airy bubble' or a 'will o' the wisp'. 'Advocates of Pakistan', he argued, must spell out the details of the League's 1940 resolution

> which foreshadowed the vague grouping of areas, definitely authorized the Working Committee of the League to produce a Draft Constitution which had not been forthcoming to this day. Had it been done the controversy would have proceeded along realistic lines and voters would have been able to judge whether provinces remaining outside the Federated India could ever improve the lot of those who had been allowed to nurse this illusion.[1]

Essentially, he was asking the League to spell out what Pakistan meant and how the north-west and north-east Muslim-majority areas would interface with the rest of the country. These arguments were in turn based on more fundamental beliefs and sentiments.

> [A] Nation is always a political entity and not a religious one. Hindus and Muslims are definitely two communities, but certainly not two nations . . . The Pushto speaking Pathans, Malayalam speaking Muslims and the Gujarati and Bengali Muslims do belong to the Muslim community but to lump them together and call them a nation is entirely wrong . . . I cannot see any justification for dividing a common country between Hindus, Muslims and others along the line of religious cleavages.[2]

But the ground beneath his feet was shifting faster than he and others could have anticipated when the Muslim League had adopted the 'Pakistan Resolution' in 1940. The time for rational discussions was drawing to a close, with the 1945–46 election results. The problem for someone who had emphasized the importance of legislative and constitutional struggles and means was that the new reality pointed to a federation as the only way out. But here views within the Congress were deeply divided and firmly against too loose a structure with too weak a Centre. Asaf and many others in the Congress struggled to come to terms with the implications of a federation. Opinion was also divided as to whether a federation would satisfy the Muslim League.

Possibly Asaf, as someone who had opposed the constant recourse to agitation, felt the issues more acutely on account of Aruna's political positions. For her the way forward lay not in the deliberations of a chamber that a small unrepresentative electorate had elected, but in politics led by the masses and agitation to achieve all objectives including driving out the British. So, while Asaf was one of those steering a Congress agenda through the Legislative Assembly – which consisted largely of criticizing the government for its acts of omission and commission and showing it up as directionless and weak – Aruna's trajectory was an altogether different one.

She was quoted in a public meeting in Bombay on 14 February 1946 as saying that the parliamentary programme accepted by the Congress leaders would never lead to the goal of independence. In brief, the struggle launched in August 1942 must be continued:

> Our differences with Mahatma Gandhi, Pandit Jawaharlal Nehru and others are only those of outlook. They seek to approach the goal through a parliamentary programme. They are ripe in age and experience but our experience has also taught us something. Britain will not yield to our demand unless she is confronted by us with the determination of translating the 'Quit India' slogan into its real meaning.[3]

Had she failed to recognize that British imperialism was in retreat in South Asia and that the very last stage of its endgame was under way? The mainstream politician, whether of the Congress or of the League, seemed to have a better understanding of the political realities, realizing that power was now shifting and was available to be grasped.

The public meeting where Aruna made these remarks was a facilitation function organized by the Bombay Congress to welcome her on her first visit to the city after the withdrawal of the arrest orders against her and she emerged from her underground status. Her reputation for not holding back on her convictions and her now high profile meant these remarks were reported as front-page headlines in the *Bombay Chronicle*. The same page carried the speculative and incorrect news based on a British newspaper's report that Asaf Ali was likely to be appointed India's first defence minister in a national government to be formed shortly. Talk of a 'national government' made up of the Congress and the Muslim League was clearly inspired perhaps motivated and also spurred on by various conciliation attempts between the League and the Congress at different stages. But the larger point was that of Asaf clearly playing an active role in the Central Legislature while his wife was arguing against giving it importance: the political and the domestic were obviously and very publicly at cross purposes.

Aruna's radical and fiery image was to acquire a further cutting edge in Bombay only a few days later and possibly also gave the strongest confirmation yet to the British government, if one was still needed, that the old India no longer existed. Her visit to Bombay had coincided with large numbers of Indian naval ratings – in some estimates as many as 3,000 – beginning a series of protests against bad food, racism and racial taunts, and poor working conditions. One of them was arrested for writing 'Quit India' 'on the training vessel *Talwar* which led to others joining the protests and going around Bombay city, sometimes with Congress or Muslim League flags, threatening policemen and the occasional European. There was some amount of public support and soon riot-like conditions prevailed, with shops, post offices and government property the targets. Pitched battles with the police followed and there were numerous casualties in police firings. Some trade unions came out in support. Similar scenes were soon being reported from other port cities, in particular Karachi and Calcutta, and there was unrest in military or quasi military establishments in other parts of the country. The protesting ratings included Hindus, Muslims and Sikhs, and frequently invoked communal unity.

To many it appeared that the principal bulwark of British rule in India – the military – had now been shaken. The optics and the symbolism of naval ratings going on protest strikes against the colonial authorities far outweighed the actual impact on the ground – which was not inconsiderable either. The protests, largely spontaneous to start with, also saw some leadership and activists coming from communist and socialist ranks. The Congress leadership, while agreeing that working conditions for the naval ratings should be improved, was on the whole disapproving of this largely spontaneous but increasingly violent outbreak. What was also clear to the Congress leadership was that the uprising would be put down with full force: the protesters were headed for a massacre if they did not desist.

The Congress was wary about this largely unplanned development over which they had no real control for other reasons as well. Coinciding with the outbreak of the naval ratings' protests and strikes was an important announcement from the British government in London A team of Cabinet members would be visiting India to discuss with Indian leaders the framing of a new constitution for the country and the establishment of an 'interim government' to oversee the transition to a post-British India. To the Congress this visit would be the key negotiation before full independence but the path ahead was by no means clear. This was hardly the time for a mutiny in the military and their disapproval therefore of the Bombay events and those elsewhere was evident.

In Delhi, Asaf, as the deputy leader of the Congress in the Central Legislature, introduced a motion to urgently discuss the ratings' mutiny but, possibly in agreement with the government, the matter came up for discussion only after the peak of the protests had passed. In his speech on the motion, Asaf's tone was measured and careful. The entire ratings issue, he said, had been mishandled by the authorities and matters precipitated because genuine grievances had been ignored and overlooked. The reactions to poor food, racist comments and bad conditions were natural. He went on to say, 'I am as conscious of the gravity of the situation as anybody else that the army is to be kept out of party politics. I do not want a single man in the Army who is not a patriot but I also want them to be impartially patriotic.' His speech repeatedly called for restraint and also pointed out, 'This self-imposed restraint was due to the fact – as Sardar Patel has said in another place – India's ship was nearing the shore and had to be piloted as carefully and cautiously as possible out of the shoals that lay ahead.' One report of the discussion in the Assembly noted that when a member raised the point that disciplinary action being taken against the ratings also be dropped, 'Mr Asaf Ali turned to him and said emphatically "leave that point".'[4] It is clear that Asaf found this latest insurrection avoidable and therefore not something to be supported. That was also the emphatic view of the Congress leadership.

Aruna on the ground in Bombay clearly had a different view, informed by her general perspective that only continued agitation would drive the British out. Her precise role is not altogether clear, but that she was supportive of the actions being undertaken by the naval ratings is evident. Almost from the start the protesting ratings, possibly having come to know that she was in Bombay, sought her assistance. She issued statements of solidarity and support and addressed some meetings – all of which received wide coverage in the daily newspapers.

> At last young Indians in the services are no longer prepared to submit sheepishly to the hectoring and smearing of their British rulers . . . I earnestly hope that the strikers will not permit uncoordinated and spontaneous action to mar the otherwise disciplined move they have made for the removal of their grievances.[5]

In her early statements what comes through is her expectation that mainstream political leaders from the Congress and the League would provide leadership to these protests. She had accordingly advised the strikers to approach Vallabhbhai Patel, who was also in Bombay, and seek his help. Patel had, however, advised the striking sailors to return to their barracks and call off their protests; but this advice of 'unconditional surrender' was unacceptable. Jinnah's advice to the sailors when they approached him was much the same. On learning of Patel's position, Aruna shot off a telegram to Nehru imploring him to come to Bombay. Possibly the receipt of this coincided with news from other sources and Nehru, dropping his ongoing election campaigning in north India, rushed to Bombay; but his advice thereafter was in effect no different from Patel's. The latter had in fact advised Nehru not to come to Bombay at all and when he did reach advised him to return and not meet the striking ratings.

That the Congress was not going to involve itself in the sailors' protests was now evident. To Aruna this appeared to be a betrayal of a revolutionary moment or at least a callous refusal to not side with revolutionary fervour. The absence of leadership, she told the press, is what explained the violence and the 'goonda element' – the antisocials who took advantage of the situation.

One statement from Gandhi infuriated her in particular. He had, on 23 February 1946 when the protests and the accompanying violence was at its peak, said: 'A combination between Hindus and Muslims and others for the purposes of violent action is unholy and will lead to and probably is a preparation for mutual violence – bad for India and the world.'[6] This drew a pointed and widely reported response from Aruna. It would be far easier, she declared, 'to unite Hindus and Muslims at the barricade than at the constitutional front . . . This unity is more politically sound than the one based on political or other concessions.'[7]

This was not an impulsive reaction but a thought-through position from someone who had seen at first hand all the frustrations of the Congress in forging a joint Hindu–Muslim front and was by now impatient with reasoned critiques of the idea of Pakistan, such as those Asaf was employing. It was a reaction also from someone tired of all the complexities of seeking to promote a sense of confidence amongst minorities by constitutional guarantees. Aruna's solution to the Hindu–Muslim conundrum was simple: communal unity would be forged at the barricades through mass struggle against the state rather than through political give-and-take or deals and constitutional guarantees.

Aruna also referred to Gandhi's stand that the British now in any case intended to 'quit' and therefore 'let the action not be delayed by a moment because of the exhibition of distressful unrest which has been lying hidden in the breast'.[8] This point essentially summed up the Congress attitude: that this was not the time to rock the boat through uncoordinated, unplanned protests. To Aruna this was an incomprehensible position and one 'not borne out by the facts'. 'I do not think,' she said, 'Gandhiji is justified in his belief.' In any case her larger point was:

> The people are no more interested in ethics of violence and non-violence. They just want to resist oppression. They are no more cowards. They face bullets as they never have faced lathi charges before. They have adopted a certain amount of recklessness in their resistance. They are dying but do not mind. 1942 has given the people a new life.[9]

What provoked even greater interest in this exchange was that Gandhi continued with it and gave another statement just three days later commenting on Aruna's response. It began, 'I congratulate Shrimati Aruna Asaf Ali on her courageous refutation of my statement on the happenings in Bombay.' The statement summed up Gandhi's view of Aruna's political activism: 'I admired her bravery, resourcefulness and burning love for the country.' But he went on to say 'my admiration stopped there' because he did not approve of underground activities since acts by 'a select few' would not bring Swaraj. He also disagreed with her assessment of 1942: 'I do not read the 1942 events as does the brave lady. It was good that the people rose spontaneously. It was bad that some or so many resorted to violence.'[10]

But it was Aruna's assertion of uniting Hindus and Muslims at the barricades that engaged Gandhi's attention: 'If the union at the barricade is honest, there must be union also at the constitutional front.' This was because 'Fighters do not always live at the barricade. They are too wise to commit suicide. The barricade life has always to be followed by the constitutional.' Aruna's assessment of British intentions showed 'lack of foresight' and to 'precipitate a quarrel in anticipation' was not a solution. In brief, the forthcoming Cabinet Mission needed to be engaged with seriously and 'the nation has to play the game'. To do so 'the barricade must be left aside, at least for the time being'.[11]

There was more on these lines and also on other aspects of Aruna's statement that betrayed what Gandhi termed 'confusion of thought'. In brief, 'grit becomes foolhardiness when it is untimely as this was'. Aruna was to send another reply but it was in the form of a letter rather than a press statement. Gandhi did think of publishing her letter but then ended up writing to her: 'What is the use of getting into a controversy with you in public.' His overall sentiment is summed up by one sentence in his letter: 'Will you be a rebel in all matters?'[12]

This sentiment was no doubt widely shared in the senior echelons of the Congress after Aruna's role in the ratings protests. On his release from jail in June 1945 Nehru had spoken of his admiration for Aruna's great courage and fortitude. He now referred to her and the telegram she sent imploring him to come to Bombay in February 1946 as 'hysterical'. Aruna never forgot Nehru's comment and nearly half a century later she was to write: 'I recall how I resented, at the time, Jawaharlal's use of this term "hysterical" to describe my pressing request for his personal intervention on behalf of the Royal Indian Navy ratings, whose uprising early in 1946 I regarded as a natural development of the Quit India Struggle.'[13]

How did Asaf in Delhi, an active member of the Central Legislature, take all this? He was possibly now more conscious that his wife was an independent woman with her own opinions and was her own person more than he ever could have anticipated before he went to jail and she went underground. Her angry outburst against Maulana Azad for petitioning the viceroy on her behalf, and now this very public divergence from Gandhi and the Congress, were all markers of her new self and the ideological and emotional distance between herself and Asaf, which now looked unbridgeable.

Perhaps he would have also seen some irony in this. In the run-up to August 1942 he had been amongst the voices of moderation in the Working

Committee, counselling that this was not the time for an agitation. This view was overruled in favour of the more radical option. Now when the Congress leadership was finally on course, as he saw it, to discuss future constitutional arrangements, Aruna was pushing for continued agitation. Aruna too was later to reflect on the very different paths they had taken. She saw her position not simply in terms of the political gulf that separated her from her husband but also in more personal terms and through the lens of what other women married to those in public life faced. Reflecting on Kamala Nehru and Kasturba Gandhi she wrote:

> I am reminded of the problems of adjustment my husband and I had to face, despite the shared modernity of outlook and fondness for English literature which drew us to each other. Asaf with his interest in philosophy and in Greek, Persian and Urdu literature helped to enlarge my mental horizons. But my subsequent radical tendencies – especially after 1942 – and my enthusiasm for Marxist socialism, derived mainly from my reading of Jawaharlal Nehru's and some of Bernard Shaw's works, disconcerted my husband. A liberal and constitutionalist by temperament he could not countenance revolutionary violence and was deeply distressed by my involvement in the Quit India struggle. I could only conclude that these Pygmalion-like individuals wanted to mould their wives exactly in their image.[14]

But apart from these considerations, Asaf's strongest objections were probably to the idea that 'barricades' alone were the site where communal unity could be forged. He had seen the consequences at first hand of how quickly the Hindu–Muslim unity forged at the Khilafat barricades had evaporated. He possibly now felt, much as Gandhi did, that solidarity forged against an external force in the heat of battle was too brittle a unity to be depended on.

Underwriting these differences of approach and philosophy meant a rift, which those close to Asaf and Aruna saw clearly. Among those closely associated with Aruna during the heady days of the naval ratings crisis were Kusum and P.N. Nair – both activists and in close touch with many of the ratings – and it was in their house that Aruna's meetings with the mutinying ratings had possibly taken place. Another firebrand in this circle was R.D. Puri, who was also in a close relationship with Kusum's sister Shaila. Inevitably each of them would be under close scrutiny of the authorities and their mail was subject to constant interception and snooping.[15]

We have thus a revealing letter from Shaila to Puri that provides animated detail about how things stood between Asaf and Aruna in the immediate aftermath of the Bombay developments, which came to an end by the end of February 1946 with the ratings ending their agitation. It is based on what her sister (Kusum Nair) told her after a visit to Delhi in April 1946.[16] 'Poor Asaf Ali is quite distracted' for, according to Kusum, 'Renee [Aruna] is treating him very cruelly, won't even speak to him decently'. The letter continues:

> when she came to Bombay she did not even give her address nor tell him where she was going. This of course places him in a very embarrassing position, as both being public figures, people ask him where Aruna is and he of course does not know. Really Aruna has become quite unbalanced. They are as good as separated. I feel so very sorry for Asaf Bhai and he is so attached to Renee.

Asaf had moved to 2 Windsor Place in New Delhi: government accommodation allotted to him because of his membership of the Central Legislature. The Kucha Chelan haveli was no longer in a fit state to live in, although he possibly still occasionally used it as a political office. Perhaps with his mother dead there was no real reason to stay there any more. In any case the Windsor Place residence was not a house Aruna used much, given her constant travelling at this stage. She was now, as a confidant and a biographer wrote later, only on 'visiting terms' with her husband.[17]

Yellow journalism made its contribution to the erosion in the relationship. A Bombay tabloid carried a report that Aruna was leaving Asaf Ali to marry Achyut Patwardhan. Asaf is believed to have asked

Aruna about the report and she is said to have replied, 'No, but if so you will be the first to know about it – from me.'[18]

Amidst the stirring events of the times, this domestic crisis perhaps does not amount to much. But that it was played out, to some extent, if not fully in public at least in full gaze of their friends, merits a pause. At the very least it would show how much Aruna's circle had changed, with inevitable consequences for her marriage. The age difference was now obviously compounded with an ideological and political rift.

# 21

# The Necessity and Futility of High Politics

The British Cabinet team arrived in Delhi on 24 March 1946. In the following three months the focus was on the formation of an interim government within the existing structure of the British viceroy-led administration, alongside establishing a Constituent Assembly to decide on the future political architecture of the country. It was clear that the British Indian phase of Indian history was ending, but there was a major challenge to address: the relationship between the Congress and the Muslim League, and how the British government would weigh in on this interface.

To a great extent this latest high-level British government initiative would pick up the threads from the earlier Cripps Mission of 1942. At that time – with the Japanese having overrun Singapore, Rangoon in Burma and the Andaman Islands – for the British to get Indian public opinion and the political class behind it in the war effort had been a matter of priority. Sir Stafford Cripps was a member of the Cabinet team too – perhaps its most important and knowledgeable member as far as the British understanding of the situation in India was concerned.

For Asaf the failure of the Cripps Mission had represented a missed opportunity, however deficient and imperfect. The Congress should have grasped this opportunity, rather than have meandered on and eventually stumbled on to the agitation path. But that was the past; 1946 was not 1942 and much had changed in the intervening years. The most significant difference was in the attitude of the British government. Clement Attlee, now the British prime minister after Churchill's defeat, was convinced that a transfer of power to Indians had to take place sooner rather than later. This was, after the war, the writing on the wall and evident to most in a devastated Britain whose domestic preoccupations now outweighed the demands or the attractions of an Indian empire. If there were some who did not recognize this new reality – especially among British officialdom in India – they were now in a minority, and Wavell the viceroy, one of this tribe, soon found himself more summarily overruled time and again. Britain was less interested in India now than ever before and its own difficulties overruled and dwarfed all other prior commitments. Certainly, the Congress leadership and especially Gandhi realized this and knew that the endgame was in play.

If this was a change the Congress welcomed, there was another less to their liking and one in dealing with which they were historically and otherwise at their weakest. The Muslim League was now a formidable player and the 1946 elections, both to the provincial assemblies and to the Central Legislature, had indisputably established that. Did the mantle of speaking for the Muslims fall on it alone because of this changed status? This would be one of the major sticking points in the triangular discussions between the League, the Cabinet Mission and the Congress. But there were other issues. The question was no longer simply one of adequate political representation of Muslims in those provinces where they were in a minority or of Hindu representation in Muslim-majority provinces. The question was rather also one of federation: how would the Muslim-majority provinces relate to the rest of the country and in particular what would be the balance of power and authority between the Centre and these provinces? These two questions now boiled down to a third one: would a united India remain, and if so what form would that united India take? Here there was the thorny issue of parity, with the League insistent that the issue was not of minority rights but rather that the Muslims of India formed a separate nation and there was not one country but two: one Hindu and the other Muslim. This appeared to be to many an ideological principle, almost an article of faith. But it was also a negotiating stance of strength since it began from the position that in any future governance architecture – beginning with an interim government to oversee the transition before the full transfer of power – the Muslim League must have parity or near parity with the Congress and its contention that it alone represented Indian Muslims must be accepted.

Each of these points was difficult enough but the situation was further complicated by two other factors. The first was the poor state of personal relations between Muslim League and Congress leaders. At one stage the viceroy and the Cabinet Mission team convened a conference in Simla early in May 1946 with both the League and the Congress. This began unpropitiously with Jinnah very obviously refusing to shake hands with Azad.[1] He made it amply evident that he saw a Muslim in the Congress delegation as a personal insult and as window dressing at best. The second factor was less evident, more insidious. For many British officials in India, including the viceroy and some of the governors and other senior officers, it was galling that the Congress would soon be at the helm. They were yesterday's saboteurs and the 1942 agitation weighed on them in particular. That it had jumped on to the INA trial bandwagon sharpened such prejudices, and this further cemented the logjam that dogged the Cabinet Mission throughout its stay in India.

The discussions and negotiations that accompanied the Cabinet team's stay in India were tortuous. Its focus was on two broad fronts. The immediate and pressing one was to establish as soon as possible an interim government. The seemingly longer-term one entailed developing a consensus over the process by which a new Constitution for India was to be framed and a new blueprint envisaged for a post-British India. For the British, bringing the principal political parties into a government appeared the only viable way to deal with the complexities and problems of a post-war India, of which the naval ratings mutiny was one symptom. The whole of 1946 had in fact seen numerous agitations: strikes and industrial actions, agitations by policemen, peasant militancy amidst the growing influence of communists. It was clear that, at the very least, it was better to have the principal political actors inside the tent rather than outside.

Progress on both issues was stalled because of League–Congress differences. The Cabinet Mission finally came out with a compromise which stopped short of conceding the League's principal demand of Pakistan. This envisaged a complicated confederal structure in three groups or layers. Provinces in the north-west – Punjab, Sindh and NWFP – and in the east – Bengal and Assam – formed two different groups, the common point being a Muslim majority; the remaining parts of British India with Hindu majorities constituted the third group. Each of these groupings would draw up a separate constitution for the constituent provinces or for the group as a whole if they so desired. This was not 'Pakistan' and 'Hindustan', as the League demanded, but a loose federal structure with a weak Centre with powers limited to defence, communications and foreign affairs. The groupings would have the option to secede if they so desired, an obvious concession to Jinnah and the League but clearly against the Congress's thinking. Decisions on communal or religious issues in the Central Legislature would require the majority approval of each community as well as an overall majority.

Photo Division, Government of India

*Maulana Azad and Asaf Ali (second and third from left) with the British Cabinet Mission in New Delhi*

This grouping idea had sufficient ambiguities for both the Congress and the League to initially accept it, but with radically different interpretations of what it entailed. But the contradictions between the two were too many to be papered over for too long and the agreement soon dissolved amidst mutual recrimination over who was to blame for its demise. The Cabinet Mission therefore came and went without imparting any real convergence on the League–Congress differences on the foundational issues that divided them.

If no progress was made on the longer-term issue, dealing with immediate priorities was no easier. Here the issue was of parity between the Congress and the League in the future interim government's cabinet. In the face of the impasse, Viceroy Wavell invited the Congress to form the interim government on its own. Basically, Wavell's fear was that the Congress outside the tent and in opposition would make the situation even more ungovernable in India than it already was. On the other hand, as far as the Muslim League was concerned, this was a nightmarish scenario – the worst of all possible options. Its response was to call for 'Direct Action' to achieve an independent and sovereign Pakistan.

The date of 16 August was observed by the Muslim League as 'Direct Action Day'. The communal holocaust that followed from mid-August 1946, especially in Calcutta, marked a new dimension to communal polarization. Progressively larger numbers of people began converging to the view that a partition on religious lines, even if not on the lines envisaged by the Muslim League, was the only viable option left.

Where did Asaf stand on all this? He was not by any means a principal player in the Congress negotiations with the Cabinet; that role was confined to the big three: Nehru and Patel of course, and Azad because he was the Congress president. But he would often be present when Azad met the Cabinet Mission members. It is probable that Asaf would have been in favour of the loose confederation the Cabinet Mission proposed. This had been his position for some time and also what many of the disagreements in Ahmednagar had been about. The question of allowing provinces to secede – something Asaf saw as accepting the inevitable – had often imparted to the disagreements then an added bitter intensity. For Asaf this was only pragmatism; not at all desirable in itself, but better than leaving the situation to drift while polarization continued unchecked. For him the complete absence of a settlement meant that disasters such as the Direct Action Day perpetuated by the Muslim League were inevitable.

Asaf would have therefore been in agreement with Azad describing the Congress's and the League's initial acceptance of the three-tier federal structure as a major achievement. In Azad's words: 'The acceptance of the Cabinet Mission Plan by both Congress and Muslim League was a glorious event in the history of the freedom movement in India. It meant that the difficult question of Indian freedom had been settled by negotiation and agreement and not by methods of violence and conflict.'[2] Azad's disappointment with the agreement breaking down was immense and lingered for years. What the acceptance suggested was that negotiations, agreements and constitutional guarantees had prevailed.

But possibly Asaf was conscious, as many were at the time, that the agreement was based on extremely fragile foundations and on fundamentally different readings of it by the Congress and the League. For the League the agreement on a three-tier federal arrangement was the first step towards Pakistan. For the Congress, the arrangement was temporary; it would be in place for an interim phase and would be superseded by a Constitution drawn up by a Constituent Assembly. Asaf had discussed these issues in the past and was conscious that an unwieldy, even unworkable, federal structure went against Nehru's core thinking that a strong centre was essential if India was to achieve expedited planned development and economic transformation. But to him some agreement was better than none.

Beneath the constitutional provisions were therefore more fundamental divergences almost impossible to bridge. Asaf and J.B. Kripalani had violently disagreed sometime in early 1942 during the visit of the Cripps Mission with regard to 'self-determination'. In Kripalani's account:

> In Gandhiji's presence, on one occasion, there was some talk about self-determination and, in this connection, of the communal question. During the discussions, Asaf Ali said: 'You cannot coerce the Muslim community to join the Indian Union.' This irritated me and I said: 'Why not? Did not America coerce the South to see that it did not break away from the American Union? We may not go to war about it, but we shall use all the nonviolent methods to prevent the division of India ... The discussion became heated and the matter was left at that.[3]

These differences anticipated the various disagreements in Ahmednagar and in fact were endemic to the Indian scenario in the 1940s.

So possibly Asaf was left in a small minority within the Congress holding on to a position that events had made untenable: how to maintain and achieve moderation and constitutionalism. The more significant casualty was the belief that the priority for India was communal harmony and Hindu–Muslim unity and everything must be organized around this as a central guiding principle. This position had never had many takers, but support for such a view was even weaker now for many in the Congress felt it meant allowing the Muslim League to further leverage its obduracy.

There had been a debate of long standing on this issue within the Congress dating back to the Lucknow Pact and separate electorates for Muslims. In recent years it had acquired a new potency. Syed Mahmud for instance often found himself at odds with all sections of the Congress on this matter. K.M. Munshi had thus written to him in mid-1941 as the Congress wrestled with the dilemma of whether to launch civil disobedience or tone down its opposition in a war situation: 'No one dreams of reducing the Muslims to a fifth caste. But is there not a distinct move of reducing Hindus to a secondary slavery by making Muslims a statutory majority?'[4]

Nehru, at the other end of the Congress political spectrum and one who would have disagreed with Munshi on numerous issues, then and later, was to write to Syed Mahmud in a similar vein:

> I do not understand what is meant by a majority sharing power with a minority or minorities ... when we talk about political majorities it

> means that the majority represents a political viewpoint. It is absurd for a politically advanced majority to give up its advanced views to please a politically reactionary minority.[5]

By a 'politically reactionary minority' Nehru of course meant the Muslim League. Quite possibly Asaf would not have disagreed. But perhaps he saw with greater clarity what Syed Mahmud had meant. What he sought was something more intangible, may be akin to a reassurance rather than a legally binding contract that the Congress would prioritize communal harmony as a method to deal with the League.

For Aruna all this complex reasoning and convoluted debates were meaningless since the entire Congress approach was wrong and based on faulty premises. Fired by the naval ratings mutiny experience, she saw the Congress investment in negotiations with the Cabinet Mission as a major error of judgement: 'The socialist Britisher is a half-brother of Churchill on Indian issues.'[6] To her, the way forward was mobilization and mass action alone.

Her peer group included those who had led the underground activism and sabotage during the Quit India phase, comprising a new generation of Congress radicals. This group argued against acceptance of a Constituent Assembly hemmed in by various conditionalities or of the formula of a complex federal structure with groupings of provinces based basically on religion. The core of Aruna's view was that the Congress's faulty politics explained the appeal of the Muslim League: 'Unless the Congress can take to the masses its programme of a social revolution they will be puppets in nefarious hands.'[7]

The answer to communalism lay in socialism alone. In this approach the immediate political issues are necessarily forced into the background; the central issue becomes the planning for a socialist state as without it 'the misled Mussalman peasant and worker will go on taking one suicidal step after another'. Any other approach meant compromising with first principles and betrayal: 'Our ancestors made many compromises. We are paying the wages of their sin.' An absolutist view such as this rejected the idea that negotiations, concessions and political agreement was the path to build community agreement and consensus. This, she believed, was no solution to the problem that 'small minded men had mesmerized a type of Indian Muslim for too long'.[8] Much of the assertions of Aruna and her colleagues would have sounded like high-minded sermonizing devoid of any practical suggestion to address the pressing communal, constitutional and political questions the Congress confronted as it negotiated both with the League and the departing British.

Hers was a radically different vision that rejected all the premises of the Congress approach, beginning from the representative nature of the assemblies to which its members had been elected and from which the Constituent Assembly would be formed. Thus, to set up a constitution-making body 'not representative of more than one man in a million' was an obvious 'infringement of the people's rights'. To her and her radical colleagues, the Congress's lead was 'healthy but its leaders less so'. What was needed was a new approach beyond elections based on limited suffrage (to which the Congress leadership attached so much importance).

It was true that the Central Legislature or the provincial assemblies were not elected on the basis of universal adult franchise. But since this had been the very basis of all politics in India for the past few decades, to most Congressmen her approach would have appeared anarchic, nullifying most if not all of Congress history and politics. To them, she and her group were beginning almost from first principles, from a blank slate, almost as if the past decades had not existed – and this at a time when communal polarization was at a peak and the British on the threshold of their final departure from the subcontinent. Aruna's radical critique was equally a generational one. It certainly included in its sweep Asaf Ali as representative of a 'pedantic' Congress leadership and also generational – part of an 'old group in the Congress'.[9]

These two entirely separate ideas about the Indian nation were contradictions without any possible resolution. We could also say that the debate has continued ever since on much the same lines.

What was Asaf's reaction to his wife's divergent views and her criticisms of the Congress leadership? There was little public comment on this; any such comment would have been generally regarded as an intrusion into the most private of spaces. It was, however, well known enough to come to the notice of the colonial government, which even in its dying gasps had an insatiable appetite for collecting all manner of personal information about its opponents. In describing Asaf Ali to his king emperor, Viceroy Wavell had thus noted that 'his wife is one of the firebrands of the Congress Left Wing, but I gather they do not often meet'.[10] It seems likely that Asaf was by now reconciled to the new Aruna, as were his colleagues and peers.

For Aruna, August 1942 had been that pure moment when 'The Indian came nearest to perfection'. The 9th of August was 'a solemn day – a day on which our passion for freedom burnt at its whitest, when instead of barren tears an ardent light streamed from dying eyes, and honour found brave defenders, fighting her battle'.[11] To those on the left, the upsurge represented by the 1942 protests represented the Indian masses attempting to take charge of their future. To Asaf the agitation had been a mistake and a rash and colossal error of judgement providing to the government and to the Muslim League the opening they were waiting for.

The relative strengths of these opposing points of view became evident in the AICC meeting of July 1946 in Bombay, as these tensions and contradictions played out before a larger stage. The meeting was to formally take a decision on the Cabinet Mission proposals. These had just a few days earlier been formally endorsed by the Working Committee and therefore the AICC session would have been no more than a formal endorsement of a decision already taken.

The dissenters – principally J.P. Narayan, Ram Manohar Lohia, Achyut Patwardhan and Aruna Asaf Ali – put up a dogged and determined rearguard resistance. This was decidedly a minority view, perhaps even regarded as eccentric, which relied more on its visibility and powers of articulation by a group seen as comprising younger hotheads. The vast majority present were for it, seeing the Cabinet Plan as a pragmatic step forward and the only viable option as the Muslim League had also grudgingly given its assent to it. The majority view was strong and perhaps the AICC session was an almost 'tame affair', as one newspaper columnist put it.[12]

What, however, livened up the proceedings and consequently received a great deal of attention was Aruna Asaf Ali's fiery speech denouncing the Congress leadership and criticizing Gandhi. Echoing J.P. Narayan and Patwardhan, her point simply was that all negotiations and compromises be rejected and non-cooperation launched again. Her speech drew many column inches in the newspapers but the general impact it had is best summed up by the laughter that echoed in the meeting when she addressed Gandhi and said, 'So long we have followed your advice, now you follow ours, because you say you can see nothing but darkness but we can say that we see light.' To the senior party members present, she remarked, 'If you become members of the Executive Council and walk into the Viceroy's house, there will be no room in the Congress for persons like me.'[13]

The scene that was enacted then reinforced the general response to Aruna's passion and fury. After noting that her speech 'raised the only laughter of the session', a *Bombay Chronicle* reporter described what followed next: 'The Mahatma himself joined heartily in the laughter and at the end of the speech as Mrs Asaf Ali was going down the dais beckoned to her and as she bent down gave her a whack on the cheek much to the merriment of the onlookers.'[14]

Perhaps Asaf felt a certain pride in Aruna as she confronted Gandhi at the AICC meeting in July 1946 in Bombay. Perhaps there was also a certain exasperation and even embarrassment at the laughter amongst the assembled delegates when she denounced the Congress move to accept a British blueprint for the future governance of India.

Did Aruna detect an affection behind the laughter and was touched, or did she find the response patronizing and patriarchal? We do not know, although the latter seems the better fit. She wrote about this AICC session: 'The assumption of superior wisdom strikes one forcibly in the exhibition of anger and irritation on the AICC platform.'[15] To her the issue was the absence of meaningful discussion, the ritual observance of the 'formalities of democracy' and the reinforcing of the existing system: 'A moribund Congress is what the pure power politician aims for.'[16]

# 22

# A Kashmir Trial

If Asaf Ali appears largely silent at this time, it is not only because he was dwarfed by his wife in terms of publicity and political controversy; he was also engrossed in an important sideshow to the main event of the ongoing Congress negotiations with the Cabinet Mission in India. There was a different kind of drama unfolding in the princely state of Kashmir with its Dogra Hindu maharaja and Muslim-majority population. The principal actor in this was Sheikh Muhammad Abdullah, leader of the National Conference, which he had established in 1939 by changing the name of his existing party, the Muslim Conference. The renaming was of significance: at the very least it implied a non-denominational approach to politics.

Abdullah and his party were temperamentally and ideologically closer to the Congress than to the Muslim League, which perhaps expected them to align almost naturally along the lines of the polarization in the rest of India. For Jinnah this was particularly irritating: why should Abdullah as a Muslim align himself with a Hindu Congress? Sheikh Abdullah, however, not only had a close friendship with Nehru but also shared with him socialist ideas and a radical egalitarianism. But Abdullah's opponents were not convinced and many supported the Muslim League. In brief, the communal division in British India was inevitably to have its effect on Jammu and Kashmir too. By 1941 another Muslim Conference was to emerge, declaring that Hindus and Muslims were separate nations and power in the state should reside with the Muslim majority.

In April and May 1946 as the Cabinet Mission continued its tortuous negotiations in Delhi and Simla, Sheikh Abdullah in the Kashmir Valley was questioning the legitimacy of the maharaja's continued rule in the state, and pronounced its demise simultaneously with British rule in India. His was a heady and fiery polemic of 'Quit Kashmir' which based itself on and drew parallels with the Congress's past playbook of 'Quit India'. But his rhetoric hinged essentially on an event of a century earlier: the Treaty of Amritsar of March 1846 through which the Dogra raja of Jammu had 'purchased' the Kashmir Valley. Following the defeat of the Sikhs in the Anglo-Sikh war in 1846, the British East India Company sought to reward the Jammu ruler Gulab Singh, one of the late Maharaja Ranjit Singh's principal generals. Gulab Singh had been invaluable to the British for his 'official' neutrality but much unofficial assistance in the Sikh war. By the Treaty of Amritsar he was recognized as the ruler of Kashmir in consideration for which the British were paid a sum of 75 lakh rupees. A century later, at the head of a popular agitation against the maharaja's autocratic rule, the Treaty of Amritsar became a convenient point for Sheikh Abdullah to critique Dogra rule.

The 1846 treaty, the Sheikh proclaimed, was not an agreement but a 'sale deed'. In a telegram to the Cabinet Mission team, he argued that 'the treaty by which the Dogra Maharajas came to possess Kashmir does not have the status of a treaty. The people of Kashmir wish to draw the Cabinet Mission's attention to the fact that after the British rule ends, they have a right to become independent.'[1] He followed this up with speeches denouncing the maharaja as a quisling whose time would end with the end of British rule in India. But perhaps conscious that the Congress leadership including Nehru was not in favour of this agitational mould in the midst of the ongoing discussions with the Cabinet Mission the 'Quit Kashmir' movement was suspended. The state authorities, however wary of this rhetoric and of the National Conference and Abdullah's growing influence, decided that enough was enough and he was arrested on 20 May 1946 for spreading disaffection, contempt against the maharaja, and sedition. He was then en route to Delhi to meet Nehru.

The Congress leadership was in fact unconvinced by Abdullah's logic and agitation against the maharaja. To many in the Congress Hari Singh as the Hindu maharaja of a Muslim-majority state was a bulwark against the Muslim League. Patel and some others were sympathetic to this view; Abdullah noted, 'Acharya Kripalani had an animus against our movement.'[2] Interestingly, Jinnah and the Muslim League leadership had a similar viewpoint: they both distrusted Abdullah's fiery socialism and radical egalitarianism, and were also wooing the maharaja. 'K' in the Pakistan that they imagined, after all, stood for 'Kashmir'.

More importantly, for the Congress leaders, matters were delicately poised with the Cabinet Mission and this was not, in their view, the time for random protests which could muddy the waters. It was much like the position they took at the outbreak of the naval ratings mutiny and the subsequent disturbances in Bombay and elsewhere. Moreover, the ruling princes would be playing a crucial role in deciding the direction their states would take when the British left, so it was hardly opportune to alienate the maharaja of Kashmir at this stage. The Kashmir ruler was well connected, with his clan intermarried into many of the principal princely families in India. He had, as noted, important supporters in the Congress.

Nevertheless, Abdullah's arrest when he was going to consult with the Congress leadership cast the matter in a different light. When he heard that the trial was to commence soon Nehru rushed to Srinagar with Asaf accompanying him and was arrested en route at the Kashmir border and stopped from proceeding further. A full-scale crisis appeared to be in the making. He was told in no uncertain terms by the rest of the Congress leadership to return – in part to diffuse the situation but also because of the ongoing negotiations with the Cabinet team. Nehru returned but went again to Srinagar on 24 July as Abdullah's trial for sedition and inciting disaffection commenced and Asaf Ali accompanied him again to lead the defence.

Asaf was in all likelihood well acquainted with the intricacies of the Kashmir situation. After their release from jail a number of CWC members had stayed in Srinagar and Pahalgam as part of their recuperation. Apart from Asaf the group had included Azad and Nehru, and they arrived in Srinagar early in August 1945, spending some amount of time with

Sheikh Abdullah. He therefore already had a sense of all the internal tensions in Kashmir: of Sheikh Abdullah's opposition to the ruler, those between Sheikh Abdullah and the Muslim League, and also the different views in the Congress itself on the emerging Abdullah–maharaja tussle.

This trial ranks among the milestones of Asaf's legal career, frequently interrupted as it was by his politics. It ranks with his defence of Bhagat Singh and B.K. Dutt for the Assembly bomb case and his presence on the INA defence team. The Abdullah case, however, had complexities which the earlier cases did not. He was now defending a prominent figure who was nevertheless divisive in all-India terms, given the support the maharaja had in sections of the Congress. This was also a supercharged time in terms of communal discord: the temporary agreement between the League and the Congress on the Cabinet Plan had broken down by end July 1946 in mutual acrimony and bad blood. Unlike the defence during the Bhagat Singh and B.K. Dutt trial or the INA trials where a groundswell of supportive nationalist sentiment was assured, here the position was much more delicate. This was particularly so given the maharaja's support, both within and outside the Congress.

The Sheikh Abdullah trial is largely a forgotten chapter in Kashmir's history because subsequent developments have comprehensively overshadowed it. A.G. Noorani, a noted legal expert, included it in his listing of the landmark political trials of modern India, commenting on Asaf's role: 'Asaf Ali's performance on [Abdullah's] speeches, as on the right to revolt was admirable. He lost because he was arguing before a Kangaroo court and the speeches left little to imagination. Only a sympathetic Court could have stretched this in his favour.' But it was 'an inspired performance he put up, probably the last of its kind in the history of political trials in India before independence'.[3]

Asaf spent about seven weeks in a houseboat in Srinagar. He clearly put enormous effort into this case although its outcome would have been evident from the start. In Sheikh Abdullah's recollection: 'it was Asaf Ali who took over the entire responsibility. He got the evidence recorded, cross examined the witnesses and finally presented strong arguments in my favour.'[4]

The case against Abdullah hinged on the speeches delivered by him in the first half of May in which he railed against the Amritsar treaty:

> For a paltry amount this land was sold to a *bania* . . . You must therefore say 'Quit Kashmir'. Scrap the sale deed . . . It is our right to secure our freedom from rule by the Dogra dynasty; What do the State's Hindus, Muslims and Sikhs want? They want to be freed from a life of slavery. They do not want to be victims any longer of the pleasures of the rajas and Maharajas . . . we shall end the Dogra rule after a thousand years . . . Bugle for the battle has not been sounded. When it is, avenge this shameful treachery.[5]

The charge against him was of 'exciting disaffection' and making seditious speeches. In the defence he mounted, Asaf tried to give as benign an interpretation of Abdullah's fiery polemic as was possible but also maintained the right of his client to protest. In Noorani's summary the task before Asaf was: 'He had to be bold enough to challenge Hari Singh's rule and adroit enough to put an inoffensive construction on speeches that were not inoffensive.'[6] The defence statement was in fact one that Nehru and Asaf had drafted jointly. Both perhaps were very conscious that turbulence could lie ahead for the Muslim-majority state with an autocratic Hindu ruler at the helm. Both saw the importance of cementing Abdullah's loyalty to Nehru and to the Congress. The legal defence had no real chance of success – the judgement was three years' imprisonment – but perhaps this larger objective was achieved, with all its manifold consequences for India and South Asia.

As the case reached its climax Asaf Ali had received an urgent summons to return to Delhi. He was to be sworn in as a member of the interim government. His role in the defence had in any case been completed and he rushed back to be sworn in on 2 September 1946 along with Nehru, Patel and others in what was expected to be the last administration under a British viceroy. Despite strenuous efforts of Viceroy Wavell, the Muslim League stayed away. The principal bone of contention was not unexpected: the League demanded that Muslims in the new government be its nominees alone. For the Congress this was unacceptable: Asaf in the interim government, along with two other Muslim Congressmen, was symbolic of the Congress claim that it represented India as a whole rather than just Hindus. This was a fault line that now permitted no bridging reflected in the orgy of violence on 16 August with its epicentre in Calcutta during 'Direct Action Day'.

The circumstances of the swearing-in were thus sombre. The mass killings of mid-August had continued and spread from Bengal to Bihar; communal tensions extended even further. If the prospect of governance and policymaking was attractive, the external context in terms of the political and communal polarization made this hardly viable. That an order was ending was clear but what precisely would take its place was less so. What was evident was that any real League–Congress understanding was now an extremely remote possibility.

Amidst this political churn, Syud Hossain was, after twenty-four years in the United States, back in India from April 1946. He would occasionally publish a column in the newspaper where he had first made a name for himself three decades earlier: the *Bombay Chronicle*. Sarojini Naidu was also frequently in Delhi and had been living there probably from mid-1946. She had been given the responsibility of chairing the organizing committee of an 'Asian Relations Conference' to be held in Delhi in March 1947. What did Sarojini and Syud make of the status of Asaf's marriage and of Aruna? We have few markers. Sarojini's views on Aruna would have perhaps converged with those of other senior Congress leaders: exasperation tinged with admiration at this young radical in a rush to change the world and scornful of the older generation as pedantic and conservative. Sarojini, from a different generation, was someone who had consciously tried to bridge different roles and expectations all her life and similarly find a middle path between conflicting political positions. This fiery commitment to a single and chosen course and the exclusion of other points of view – as appeared to be Aruna's general approach – is likely to have appeared as the simple-minded dogmatism of a younger generation that had not traversed the long journey to the threshold of freedom. Perhaps all her two-decade-old doubts about the wisdom of Asaf's marriage would have appeared vindicated.

Syud himself – a stranger to a new India in more ways than possibly even he deciphered – would have hardly known Aruna except by reputation. She was, as we have seen, rarely with Asaf and constantly travelling. If they met, as they must have, she would have probably regarded Syud as no more than an oddity of her husband's ancient past. What he thought we do not know but there is one cryptic comment in one of the columns penned for the *Bombay Chronicle*.

> This, of course, is a tete-a-tete – a sort of twitters – in the appropriate hour of twilight. If anywhere, where do we go from here? Is it to be 'ab initio', 'de novo', 'in camera', ex cathedra', 'pari passu', 'che sara sara, or, generally, nil desperandum? My own preference is for 'che sara sara'. It has a certain euphonious quality, besides being true to the universal mood of the moment.
>
> Or, of course, we could revert to the idea, without the sonorous Latin of destroying Carthage! But can we? How is that to be equated with the concept of 'ahimsa'? It can't. Unless, of course Aruna Asaf Ali can think of some subterranean device for liquidating Ahimsa by satyagraha![7]

We struggle to make sense of what is intended here! Is it a light, even facetious, comment on the mayhem that had engulfed Calcutta in the aftermath of the Muslim League's Direct Action Day on 16 August? This column appeared on 18 August. Perhaps Syud was making an oblique comment – even taking a dig – at Aruna's certainties when the rest of the nationalist leadership was at a loss about what was to be done in the circumstances.

How had other older relationships – at one time carefree but also close and deeply supportive – changed? One anecdotal account would suggest that the threads were picked up relatively quickly and the circle included M.A. Jinnah, much as it had done in London three decades earlier. Hosain Ali Khan, who after meeting Asaf in England in 1913 had remained a lifelong friend, says that the four – Asaf, Sarojini Naidu, Syud Hossain and Jinnah – were a quartet again in Delhi in mid-1946 much as they had been in London in 1913–14: 'These four, among whom there was perfect camaraderie, remained lifelong friends. The last time I saw them all together was in Delhi in the winter of 1946–47 in the house of Asaf Ali.'[8]

There are, however, less rosy accounts than this picture of old threads being picked up without great effort in Asaf's bungalow in Windsor Place in New Delhi, which cast doubts on Hosain Ali Khan's account. The relationship with Jinnah had to weather the polarization of the past decade or decade and a half. It is possible that Hosain Ali Khan's memory does not fully convey how strongly personal relationships would have been impacted by political positions and differences. This was after all a time when not just sides but countries were being chosen. An account of just how much things had changed comes from P.S. Gill, a mutual acquaintance of Sarojini and Syud. Gill, later to be one of India's eminent scientists, had come to know Syud Hossain while a student in the United States and through him had met Sarojini Naidu. He relates how, soon after Syud's return to India, Sarojini insisted that he (Syud) call Jinnah on the telephone. He did so, and Gill recounts: 'shortly we heard the receiver bang on the hook. Mrs Naidu asked "Syud what happened?" Dr Hossain was visibly upset and said this friend [Jinnah] has lost all sense of decency. "He has the cheek to tell me that I am in the enemy camp".'[9]

A similar picture emerges from a different source: Sri Prakasa, a long-time Congressman and, after 15 August 1947, India's first high commissioner to Pakistan. Sri Prakasa knew Jinnah from the 1920s and got to know him well from the mid-1930s during the period both were members of the Central Legislature after the election in 1934 when Asaf was also elected to it. He recalled: 'Mr Jinnah so abhorred Mr Asaf Ali who was a member of the Congress party of the Legislature, that he deliberately kept him out when he invited all the other legislators to a tea party at his residence.'[10]

This interpersonal breakdown was in both directions and extended to denying the other side any positive attribute at all. The Rajagopalachari and the Bhulabhai initiatives of 1942 and 1945 respectively showed how space had progressively contracted in the Congress where a halfway meeting point with the League could be found. The middle ground had more or less gradually vanished. While still in Ahmednagar, the jailed Congress leaders read a speech by Sarojini Naidu which 'upset' them. 'An excessively foolish speech,' wrote Nehru in his diary on 22 January 1945.[11] Sarojini had described Jinnah as the one incorruptible person in India: 'I may not agree with him, but if there is one man who cannot be bought by title, honour or position, it is Mr Mohammad Ali Jinnah.'[12] Sarojini was no doubt conscious that she was wading into very troubled waters but seeing herself as the perpetual bridge and peacemaker would have opted for a conciliatory tone in the hope of keeping alive at least some channels of communication. Perhaps she also intuitively realized that amidst the contestations and polemics surrounding the issue of minority representation, federation and Centre–state relations there were also entirely subjective issues of personality and egos. And perhaps she felt that one way to address all the contestations was to focus on the more subjective ones and pat some egos. It was, of course, in the circumstances, an entirely futile endeavour.

# 23

# Minister and then Ambassador

In the interim government the portfolio assigned to Asaf was Transport, Communications and Railways. We know of his activities through this time largely because of his administrative responsibilities. In this bleak situation, these details convey little sense of his own political or personal situation. Perhaps like most people he saw all reasonable options as exhausted and was paralyzed by the futility of it all. Or perhaps being in the corridors of power insulated him, as they sometimes can, from the chaos reigning in the country.

What we know for certain is that Wavell the viceroy, whom he now had occasion to meet, disliked him. This comes across clearly in the brief comments and character sketches he made of the new Cabinet members. Soon after the new Cabinet had been sworn in, Wavell in a letter to the secretary of state for India noted, 'Asaf is a man of no weight, looks scared and has always been rather a worm.'[1] A little later in October he had described him as 'a little rat faced man, not very attractive' but also went on to note: 'I think he has some capacity.'[2] The latter judgement is an improvement over the assessment of a few weeks earlier at the formation of the interim government. Wavell had then remarked on the Muslim inclusions – Asaf being one of three – as 'very poor specimens indeed' who had 'neither capacity nor character'.[3] The other Muslim nominees of the Congress were Syed Ali Zaheer, a Shia lawyer from Lucknow, and Shafat Ali Khan, one of India's most distinguished historians.

The harshness of Wavell's judgement gives one pause since each of the

Photo Section, PMML

*Asaf Ali (right) and Jawaharlal Nehru: no date but possibly late 1946*

three were well regarded at the time. Possibly the explanation lies with the viceroy himself. On the whole, he seldom had a favourable view of any of the Congress politicians he was in contact with, or any Indian in fact – with some notable exceptions. Given his position, such a jaundiced view would have emerged almost naturally. Also, perhaps it applied with even greater force to the Muslims in the Congress for holding up what Wavell was convinced was the best way out: an equal power-sharing arrangement between the Congress and the League. Asaf Ali's inclusion in the interim government was for the Congress as much a point of principle as it was recognition of his contribution as a Congressman. But, from Wavell's point of view he represented the impediment to the League joining the interim government. The League claimed that it alone could represent Muslims in India and the Congress stand of representing 'all' Indians was a sham. So Asaf as a 'Muslim Dummie' of the Congress – to use a term favoured by British officialdom – may well have appeared to Wavell in a particularly unsavoury light.

Possibly Asaf rubbed Wavell the wrong way for multiple reasons: the Muslim 'dummy' prominent in the Quit India movement; as someone who was at the forefront of the INA defence team that so wrong-footed the colonial authorities; and then for muddying the waters in Kashmir in the Sheikh Abdulllah trial. Additionally perhaps, Asaf, who saw himself as the equal of any Englishman, was insufficiently deferential during interactions. Being a lawyer, sharp observation or comment came naturally to him, and to occasionally poke an overbearing official in the eye would have been a temptation too delicious to resist. Wavell, privy to intelligence reports (based on intercepted personal correspondence) and no doubt to Delhi gossip, could not resist this dig at Asaf while writing to the secretary of state for India in London: 'I am told he spends a lot of his time thinking about his wife Aruna, who very seldom thinks about him.'[4] If Wavell's dislike and contempt for Asaf was for a multitude of reasons, that he was unable to control a wife with a mind of her own was possibly one more factor in his portfolio of shortcomings.

One decision of some value that can be attributed to Asaf Ali's tenure in the interim government was the ending of the practice of having religiously separated refreshment rooms and separate drinking water points in railway stations for Hindus and Muslims. Soon after Asaf's appointment, Gandhi had publicly urged him to end this practice: 'a well known Indian in the person of Asaf Ali saheb is in charge of Transport and Railways. It is to be hoped that we shall soon have the last of the shame that is peculiarly Indian . . . We have the right to assume that this unholy practice of having separate everything for every community at railway stations will go . . .'[5]

The step certainly struck a blow at a new social climate but it was only a small one, especially compared to the situation in the country as riots spread and the communal divide acquired a frightening intensity. By mid-October 1946 the interim government would acquire a new character: the League, dropping its earlier objections, now decided to join, and portfolios were reshuffled and reallocated. But this novel situation – the League and the Congress 'working together' in the same administration – neither succeeded in inspiring any real confidence nor built any trust between them. Communal violence continued in Bengal and Bihar with all the signs that it was going to spread across north India. In East Bengal a bloodbath was reported in Noakhali where large numbers of Hindus were killed, which in turn led to revenge massacres elsewhere and especially in Bihar. By mid-November Gandhi, deciding that he could not just remain in Delhi, went to Noakhali which he believed was the eye of the storm.

The semblance of unity represented by the League joining the interim government thus failed to have an impact on the ground.

Asaf's own tenure in the interim government would, however, be affected by the League's entry into it. Maulana Azad had not been included in the first set of Congress ministers as a way to placate Jinnah and the League. Now that the League itself was joining, there was no need for Azad to be kept out but a slot would have to be found or created. At this time there was a new role emerging for public figures – as ambassadors to represent a free and independent country. India was not free yet by any standards but was close enough to pass muster. Asaf was the name considered for the United States – essentially because his vacancy in the Cabinet could then be filled by Azad. There were contrary opinions – as we shall see, not least of Nehru himself – and there were rival candidates including Nehru's sister Vijaya Lakshmi Pandit who recalled later:

> Bhai as Prime Minister of the interim government also held the portfolio of external affairs and he had spoken to me several times about an Ambassadorship. He had wanted to send me to Washington but Maulana Azad was keen on the appointment of Asaf Ali and Asaf was anxious to go.[6]

Azad had also told her, 'I want you to know that I am pressing Jawaharlal to appoint Asaf to Washington.'

If this suggested deep and somewhat murky waters, there were other obstacles, not least the viceroy who wrote with evident disapproval to his sovereign some two months after Asaf's appointment as ambassador to the US:

> Nehru, by the way, succeeded in putting a fast one across me over Asaf Ali's appointment. He mentioned it to me as a possibility, and I made no comment, as I supposed he would put it up to me with other, and perhaps more suitable, names. But he apparently told the External Affairs Department that I had agreed, and had the name wired home for Your Majesty's approval without further reference. He did not even consult his colleagues, some of whom were furious.[7]

The appointment had been announced on 6 December 1946. Just a day earlier Nehru had written to Vijaya Lakshmi Pandit, who had possibly complained about the appointment, that decisions sometimes made 'were not exactly as I would like them to be, but in the circumstances prevailing in India' they were the best possible. The letter thereafter continued:

> This applies also about Asaf Ali's appointment in Washington. He is a somewhat ineffective person and I had at first not agreed to his going there. I entirely agree with you on this point. But on full consideration and in view of other opinion and factors I decided to take this step.[8]

A few weeks later we see this scornful remark from Wavell about Asaf:

> Asaf Ali, who is now in Washington is a little cock sparrow who would like to be a peacock. I am told he spent some time after his appointment designing himself a diplomatic uniform with much gold lace and finery, and was very crestfallen when Nehru said that uniforms were unfitting to disciples of Gandhian simplicity.[9]

Again, Wavell's sarcasm need not be taken too seriously: for all his bluff, soldierly exterior, he loved the pomp of the Raj as did all viceroys, and the prospect of former Gandhians now scrambling for office was the cause for much gleeful scorn in internal conversations among the many remaining British officials in India. But what of Nehru's even more withering judgement of Asaf being a 'somewhat ineffective person'? It is unlikely this was the judgement reached after observing Asaf at the ministry of railways and transport. But, by all accounts, Asaf had been an active and driven minister. Perhaps this judgement was derived from impressions gathered from their long relationship, in particular from having observed him in a depressed state for a while in Ahmednagar. The latter impression in particular may have meant that Asaf Ali would never be a figure to inspire much confidence in Nehru. So, it is entirely possible Nehru saw Asaf as ill-equipped to deal with new roles and responsibilities. After all, a lifetime in opposition and agitation is not necessarily the best qualification to be ambassador of a yet-to-become sovereign nation to what was already the most important country in the world. But there is also the possibility that Nehru, excessively possessive about India's foreign policy, would not have found anyone really up to the mark. Or finally, but also perhaps most likely, he was just placating a younger sister whom he was very fond of, who felt thwarted in her own ambitions and these remarks had that very limited purpose.

There was a larger context. The first batch of outgoing Indian ambassadors – and Asaf was the earliest of them – had few, if any, markers to guide them. There were a host of administrative issues of which Asaf did not have the faintest clue. He was, for instance, warned that he 'would find no cutlery and possibly a limited quantity of crockery in the Ambassador's residence because my predecessor, the Agent General, had been using his own cutlery etc.'. This was, Asaf noted, a 'trifling detail' but 'what I was anxious to find out whether there was a manual of Business or any annual administration reports which might give me a background'.[10] There were none: India's foreign policy had largely been in the charge of the British government and moreover the external affairs department of the Government of India was the least 'Indianized' in terms of Indian officers manning it. There were in addition strong cautionary notes on relying on the British embassy in Washington, either for precedent or for guidance. Nehru wrote to Asaf in December 1946 that relations with the British embassy 'will have to be friendly but somewhat distant, politically speaking, in order to avoid any appearance of our functioning as an outpost of that Embassy'.[11]

Soon after his appointment was formally announced, Asaf had gone to Noakhali to seek Gandhi's advice. He wrote later: 'I sought him out in Srirampur, in the interior of Noakhali, after travelling by air, jeep and on foot for many hours. He was camping in a small hut, but in the midst of many others which had suffered during the communal riots.' The advice he received on his forthcoming assignment was straightforward: 'You will represent simple living and high thinking for which the National Congress stands and of which you are a distinguished member.'

Nehru too provided general instructions on these lines: 'As the Washington Embassy is our first venture of this kind we have to step out rather cautiously so that we may not create precedents which may prove embarrassing to us later and which may lead to criticism in India and elsewhere.'[12] He also said, 'We have not been brought up to function in terms of pomp and circumstance and anything which is not considered absolutely necessary will be liable to criticism . . . A competition in pomp and display is the last thing we want to enter into.'[13] The sentiment behind this advice was commonsensical and unexceptionable but it was an onerous set of instructions to comply with to the satisfaction of all concerned.

Asaf had written of the public response in Delhi to his appointment. 'Delhi my home town was almost convulsed with elation at the news of my appointment . . . I felt chastened by the thought that there were several persons who could have filled this office with conspicuous ability.' Asaf listed Vijaya Lakshmi Pandit, Sarojini Naidu and others but went on to note an important reason why he was chosen: 'at the time the Congress wanted to prove to the world that its profession of large heartedness in politics, observing no distinction between Hindus, Muslims or others was not mere lip service to high principles.' But there was considerable dismay at the appointment in other quarters, as we have seen.

Throughout Asaf's relatively short stay in Washington – beginning from February 1947 – he was plagued by hints of his unsuitability for the job being conveyed to Nehru and others in the interim government in Delhi. He was perhaps not the only one so criticized and most political figures appointed as heads of mission faced similar issues, but possibly because he was the first, and was in Washington, the intensity was greater in his case. An early and admiring biographer of Asaf noted that criticism of him derived from the fact that 'he made no secret of his taste for wine and good food, for music and social life'. This led to 'some persons to entertain reservations about his character and private life'.[14]

As mentioned, questions about Asaf's suitability to be India's first ambassador to the United States pre-dated his arrival in Washington; they never really went away through his year-long stay there. To start with, he had a rough ride on the issue of how an ambassador ought to conduct himself or herself. Nehru had not exaggerated when he had said that the conduct of newly appointed ambassadors would be most closely scrutinized from this angle. A diversity of views on how diplomats should be maintained abroad were by no means unusual and not confined to India. But in India the interfaces between public opinion, the government and missions abroad were at their most initial phase. For a public schooled by decades of Congress critiques of excessive and disproportionate administrative expenditure by the government on itself, the winds of change also meant reining in the lifestyles of those now in the government and the few diplomats abroad were therefore often at the receiving end of critical scrutiny. But there was also a significant and articulate number of those who believed that demonstrating sovereignty meant also being able to function as the colonial masters did in terms of lifestyle and official business, and this applied especially to India's first diplomatic missions. The contradiction between these two sets of expectations is evident.

For Asaf, with his long years as a Congressman, all of this weighed heavier and possibly Aruna's austerity and approach was itself a point of critique. Gandhi himself is believed to have said to Aruna that Asaf 'spends too much money' and 'foreigners will not have any regard for us if even our Ambassadors behave in this way'.[15]

There is a revealing letter from Nehru to Asaf: 'Your demand for silver salt cellars etc., was passed on by me to Aruna. I hope she will deal with the matter.'[16] On the face of it this seems a straightforward response between friends of long standing. Possibly it was even a mild putdown and reminder that personal relationships aside, the prime minister, even if he was the external affairs minister, was not the person to be bothered with such trifles. But there was perhaps another subtle hint and reminder to Asaf of where he came from and all that he represented. Aruna was hardly likely to hunt for silver salt cellars and Asaf would have known what she would have thought of such requests. Or perhaps Nehru, irritated with Asaf's request, was taking an unkind dig at him since the state of his marriage was hardly a secret any more.

Asaf's position as India's first ambassador was an unenviable one. It was an age of transition. A new government itself born out of a nationalist agitation was stepping into the shoes of a Raj whose status it had eroded and dislodged, and yet that status was one that it also coveted. Its diplomats were expected to be at ease and on terms of equality with the new world they were stepping into while also questioning and discarding the trappings associated with the old order. It therefore fell to Asaf as India's first ambassador to reconcile these different positions. In retrospect we can see that the demands on him were irreconcilable. Perhaps he did know this but, being an old hand now at addressing contrary sets of expectations, he also knew that the way was to soldier on.

If there were occasional complaints or comments in the press about Asaf he was hardly being singled out; others too faced similar criticism and comment to a lesser or a greater degree. In the latter category was Vijaya Lakshmi Pandit herself, ambassador in Moscow from July 1947, even more visibly because she was the prime minister's sister. Her critical gaze on Asaf, however, also continued. On one occasion, possibly after she wrote telling her brother that the ambassador in Washington had distributed his own photographs at a reception, Nehru replied: 'I have been considerably put out by the Asaf Ali picture business . . . There is far too much Hollywood about the Embassy and its work.'[17] Nehru had also written to Asaf that this appeared to be a 'little outre'.

The background was that the organizers of the reception had published a brochure with photographs and brief profiles of their principal invitees. Asaf replied to Nehru that he did not 'care one jot for what others may say about me. It hurt me that the Prime Minister could credit even for a moment a report which attributed such outrageous behaviour.'[18] Nehru had sent a placatory reply: 'No one wrote to us about the story of your photograph being distributed at a party. We read about this in some American papers. Betti [Vijaya Lakshmi Pandit] came a little later and explained the facts. Your telegram also came about this at the time.'[19]

Asaf was – as he was probably well aware – an outsider to the whole business. He had not left India since his return from Britain in 1915. The general impression has remained that he had a lacklustre tenure and was ineffective, as Nehru had anticipated when the appointment was announced. That certainly was the opinion of his contemporary critics led by civil servants, both British and Indian, as well as his competitors who may well have felt that his minority status denied their stronger cases on merit. Obviously, his appointment was seen in terms of the Congress making a point with regard to Muslim support for it. 'Moslem is Named Indian Envoy to US' was the title given to the news story by the *New York Times* in reporting the appointment of India's first ambassador to the United States. The article did not fail to point out the Muslim League considered Asaf Ali a 'renegade'.[20] The British ambassador in Washington was no doubt reflecting more than just the feedback he received when he wrote that Asaf's appointment had led to misgivings in the State

Department and 'Invidious comparisons have been made . . . with the new ambassador's urbane, intelligent and hardworking predecessor as India's representative here'.[21] The reference was to G.S. Bajpai who had served as agent general of India as a part of the British embassy in Washington and thereafter as chargé d'affaires until Asaf's appointment. But the point also was that, very clearly, then as now, the British expectation was that Americans would see India and Indians through their eyes, and to them G.S. Bajpai should have been the obvious choice.

The judgement of contemporaries became in many senses that of posterity too. A history of the early years of Indian foreign policy notes that appointments such as the 'inefficient' Asaf Ali with no 'clout either in the Cabinet or with Nehru' was a 'bad omen' and 'Appointing second raters to the capitals of world powers' was both a representative feature and a weakness of Nehruvian diplomacy.[22] Such a judgement seems too harsh and even defective as it relies excessively on the assessment of civil servants of the time; it would be hard to define the expectations from the ambassador of a nation not yet sovereign and which was poised on the brink of massive internal strife.

Subsequent appointments of civil servants and others more attuned to the environment in which they would be working have also added to the general view that the early appointments drawn from the ranks of Congress activists were unsuitable. In neighbouring Pakistan, India's first two high commissioners were senior Congress figures; the anticipation was that they would be in a better position to deal with the new government there as the senior ministers staffing it were old friends and even colleagues. Mohan Singh Mehta, a civil servant who had served in different princely states in Rajputana, was sent to Pakistan as ambassador after the two Congress leaders. His judgement on his predecessor merits recall:

> Sitaram was, I think, a complete misfit in the diplomatic life. He did not know what a diplomat should do. I am told he used to entertain people in thalis, and katoris which, to my mind, is ridiculous . . . When I went to Pakistan the house was like an empty shell. Sir Sitaram functioned without any crockery, without any curtains, without any carpets . . .[23]

Thalis and katoris have in fact made their way back into Indian diplomatic and representational entertainment – a reflection on how far even the recent past is from us and how much things have changed since the time Asaf Ali was in Washington.

Aruna had posed another set of challenges to Asaf's appointment to Washington. He was keen that she accompany him there but any such expectations were soon confronted with a clear refusal; for her the question did not arise. The role of ambassador's spouse or official hostess had no appeal, nor was it compatible with her politics. In any case their personal relationship had altered irreversibly. Following the withdrawal of the detention orders against her, she was rarely in Delhi and they were seldom together.

Nevertheless Gandhi, and perhaps others, tried hard to persuade her to accompany her husband. He had written to her from Noakhali, 'You will be able to give him much help there and it would also be a service to the country.' His closing line was intended as a clincher: 'I think it is your duty to accompany Asaf.'[24] Aruna remained unconvinced; for her the issues and their answers lay in India not in diplomacy or the external world. In response to this and numerous similar suggestions, she accompanied Asaf up to Karachi, his last point in India before flying further westwards. They remained tied to each other even if not together as a couple.

For Aruna, niceties and formalities – including those imposed by marriage – were a distraction and an evasion of existing realities. Now nearing forty, her personality was fully formed. She received huge amounts of public adulation, but her response conveyed – especially to a voraciously hungry print media – that 'there was no justification for any glamorization of her'.[25] One columnist was to describe her as 'essentially anarchic' with her 'wild untamed hair and dishevelled sari' and one who would have been 'completely at home in the tumult and shouting of the French revolution'.[26]

A few days after Asaf's departure a new viceroy was in place in

New Delhi. The Mountbattens were determined to succeed where the Wavells had not and one front lay in repairing personal relationships. Edwina Mountbatten reached out to Aruna sometime in April 1947 and was rebuffed. Mountbatten wrote: 'Mrs Aruna Asaf Ali . . . reported as violently Anti British, was reluctant to accept my wife's invitation to come and meet her.'[27] Somehow this came to Gandhi's notice, and he 'persuaded her to come along with him one day as he did not approve of her attitude'. The result appeared to the viceroy 'to have been very happy, and they made real friends'. We do not know what Aruna felt but with her well-set political convictions, she was unlikely to have been impressed by viceregal attentions.

For Asaf, leaving the country without Aruna had been a wrench:[28]

> I was waiting for the time when she would relax and let me share the workings of her troubled soul. And now I had to leave her behind in India. The thread of happy domestic life which was snapped by the gravest of national crisis nearly five years ago could not be picked up again.

Time, distance and their very divergent responses to the seismic political events of the era they were living through had changed them both irrevocably. Asaf, now nearing sixty, looked back with nostalgia to a relationship which no longer existed while Aruna saw herself in a new phase of life and the country's history. For Asaf, these personal worries and larger political worries coalesced as he took off from Karachi: 'I boarded the plane with a heavy heart, not knowing what the future held in its womb for India and for individuals like me and my wife.'

A question that Asaf often encountered in the United States was of the future of India after the British left. He appears to have answered it well – not in the language of a trained diplomat but as a public figure and a politician. Thus, at a New York reception (the same, incidentally, which led to the picture business controversy) he encountered the sentiment 'uppermost in the minds of friends of India was whether the country would remain one'. Asaf recalls that he had a carefully prepared draft but realized that 'only a fragment of my prepared speech could survive; for the rest I must speak extempore and respond to the points made'. He says that in his remarks 'I referred to a question that I heard over and over again: what will happen to India if the British withdrew? And after a pause I turned round and said: "Pray, what happened to you when the British withdrew from your country?"' This he said, 'brought the roof down with cheers'.[29]

In 1947 Asaf represented the voice of Indian nationalism and an emergent nationhood that no civil servant or trained diplomat could have been a substitute for. This sounds somewhat obvious today but there was more changing in India than one bureaucratic structure being replaced by another. The new reality that homespun politicians who had been in British jails but were now in charge in India was a message that needed to be sent to the United States. Someone more trained in diplomatic niceties but who had been till recently speaking on behalf of the British government against Indian nationalism, such as G.S. Bajpai, would not have fitted the bill.

Asaf's political background showed up in other ways too. One civil servant in Washington remembered his love for rhetorical flourishes. B.K. Nehru, who served in the World Bank and was later also Indian ambassador to the United States, referred to Asaf as 'flamboyant and theatrical'. A lunch had been organized in honour of Asaf Ali by a leading American bank keen to return to India, which it had left following the Japanese advance across South East Asia in 1942. It was attended by some leading industrialists and financiers 'controlling billions of dollars'. In B.K. Nehru's account, 'we had refused them entry accusing them of cowardice and with no regard for the interests of the country but only for their profits'. He continued:

> The story of that luncheon, as I got it second hand, was that Asaf Ali, addressing the gathering, tapped his right hand *achkan* pocket and said:

'In this pocket I have twenty million dollars. But I shall spend it only on my own terms and conditions. Take it or leave it.'[30]

This was the kind of blunt talk that was perhaps possible only from a politician who had been in the trenches against imperialism.

There were also, inevitably perhaps, issues in reconciling diplomatic life in the most important Western capital with prevalent notions of Gandhian simplicity and high thinking of the kind we noted with regard to the high commissioner in Pakistan. We have Nehru writing to Asaf in June 1947 with regard to providing senior officers with air coolers:

> I do not know what the weather in Washington is like though I am told it is hot and oppressive for two or three weeks or more. It can hardly be worse than Delhi. I have not found it necessary to have an air cooler in my house and I do not see why our officers abroad cannot do without one and possibly suffer a little discomfort for a few weeks ... Everything that we can spare will go towards meeting vital demands in India for food, relief and development.[31]

~

The situation in India with all its simmering fluidity underwrote much of Asaf's tenure in Washington and added to the difficulties of being Nehru's first ambassador. We get an instance of this from what appeared to be an unrelated event. At the request of Britain, a Special Session of the UN General Assembly on Palestine was convened in April–May 1947. The background was that the British had failed to reconcile contradictory promises they had made to Jews and Arabs. The British had promised the Jews a national home in Palestine and the Arabs independence for Palestine. When the time came to deliver, the British essentially threw in the towel. War-devastated and weary, they now needed a face-saving formula to cut their losses. The Special Session was to establish a UN Special Committee to decide 'the future government of Palestine'.[32]

The session was held in New York soon after Asaf's arrival in

Photo Division, Government of India

*Asaf Ali leading the Indian delegation to the UN at its special session on Palestine in 1947*

Washington. At that time there was no permanent mission of India (a resident embassy dealing only with the UN), and he was asked to participate on behalf of India. Asaf was given instructions that, in brief, amounted to securing Indian's membership of the proposed Special Committee; he was therefore told to be 'generally supportive' of the Arab position and, finally, to 'avoid raising issues which might affect relations between India and any other country'.[33]

At the end of the session Nehru wrote to Asaf, 'you have evidently played an important part in this session' but the compliment was immediately qualified.

> It pays often enough not to give too frequent expression of views. Though you balanced your observations, when there are many observations, they are apt to irritate one party or the other needlessly

... There have been a few adverse comments here on what you said and a general feeling that it would have been better not to say so much.[34]

Nehru's general point was: 'Criticism has been made here that there was too much showmanship and not enough diplomacy.' Clearly, the additional subtext was that Asaf had not grasped the intricacies of the new role he had been thrust into. An internal noting in the ministry of external affairs recorded: 'It is clear from the telegrams and from press reports that from the very beginning Mr Asaf Ali has taken a very active part in the discussions ... His part in the proceedings appears, however, to have gone beyond his instructions.'[35]

Asaf's role was seen by many Jewish representatives as entirely pro-Arab. One influential Jewish view was:

The Indian Ambassador here Mr Asaf Ali was the worst opponent we had at the special session of the United Nations General Assembly ... Besides that while the Arabs fight us openly, he has been engaged in intrigues and double crosses and has confused many of our people by his hypocrisy and machinations ...[36]

The British too were offended but for another reason. At the same time as the Special Session was being held, the British government announced in the UK's House of Lords that it could not bind itself to any recommendation emerging from the UN. Asaf pointedly raised this matter in his intervention. Nehru wrote to Asaf about a Reuters report which described him 'as pausing and turning to the British representative and asking "Is this true? If so, what is the use of considering any item on the agenda now?"'[37] Nehru evidently saw Asaf Ali as being unable to resist the temptation of grandstanding despite the clear instructions to avoid controversies with other countries.

His critics saw Asaf as further compounding the situation by offending many Arabs when he supported the move that the Jewish Agency for Palestine may be called and its views heard along with the Arabs. At one stage he said, 'We are playing Hamlet without the Prince of Denmark

. . . where are the great representatives of the Jewish people who are also interested in this problem?' This opened the door in India for the Muslim League to castigate the 'Hindu Congress' for taking stands contrary to the sentiments of the Muslims of India. The newspaper *Dawn*, then entirely a mouthpiece of the League, commented that the Arabs could draw comfort from the fact that Asaf Ali did not 'represent Muslim India and is acting contrary to Muslim India's wishes'.[38]

At the conclusion of the session, while India did find itself a member of the Special Committee set up on Palestine, the assessment in Delhi in sum was that Asaf had ended up giving gratuitous offence to different parties. There is clearly some substance to this assessment and evidence that Asaf Ali could not resist the temptation to score debating points when the opportunity presented itself. New to the game and insufficiently briefed, he mistook an intergovernmental forum for a debating society or political gathering. As a good 'stump orator' in his early days as politician, the inclination to indulge in such oratory had probably never left him. Later, as a member of the Central Legislature, he was conscious of the shortcomings of stump speeches but the propensity to indulge in rhetorical flourishes perhaps proved irresistible.

He might have wanted to replicate Vijaya Lakshmi Pandit's performance in the UN just a few months earlier when she had deployed charm, rhetoric and sentiment in a contest with South Africa on the question of treatment of Indians in that country. But Palestine was a more complex issue, and targeting Jews or the UK was not going to get the same dividends in terms of public response that Pandit had received for standing up for equitable treatment of Indians overseas; it was this that secured her reputation as a successful diplomat.

It is, however, not difficult to sympathize with him. He was dealing with rapid changes in his life: he had come out of a long sojourn in jail less than two years ago; he had had to adjust to new roles and new environments while the ground under his feet was shifting with a partition looming ahead in India. The restraint and sympathy in Nehru's gently worded admonitions emerged from the understanding that only a colleague and a fellow traveller could have had. Nehru perhaps empathized with the difficulties of adjustment; he was, after all, in a similar place himself, although in not such completely unfamiliar territory.

But perhaps Asaf's stand at the UN session on Palestine also owed something to his awareness of the other subtexts to the issue – and we can see this with greater clarity now than contemporaries could. To him the obvious context was the looming partition of India on religious grounds and the erosion of his deeply held principle that 'religion cannot convert people into a nation'. He would therefore have been very conscious of the irony that the Muslim League, at the cusp of succeeding in its aim of creating Pakistan, opposed the creation of a separate religiously denominated Jewish state in Palestine. And he probably knew better than most others present at the UN meeting that the only way forward was an internal convergence between Jews and Arabs, rather than an externally determined partition of Palestine.

# 24

# Meanings of Freedom

When Asaf Ali left India in February 1947 to take up his assignment in Washington, the interim government was the intersection point of all the accumulated tensions between the League and the Congress. The one thing that was clear was that the British were leaving. Early in February 1947 came an official announcement from London that the final withdrawal would be completed no later than June 1948. But what was not so evident to everyone, including the British, was what, precisely, would take their place. The possibility of power being handed over piecemeal – even to provincial governments and individual princely states if so required – if there was no consensus about the new architecture was not ruled out. The freedom struggle against the British had in effect ended, and future conversations and disputations would now be about the kind of successor regime or regimes that would follow. By the last week of March 1947, a new viceroy was in place.

Mountbatten, acting from multiple motives, but most of all wanting to extricate Britain from a situation that had no good endings, announced in early June that Britain's final withdrawal would be completed by 15 August 1947. In effect, a year-long transition was now to be compressed into ten or so weeks. It was decided that the new Pakistan would be carved out by the partition of Bengal and Punjab. Communal violence, already widespread, now acquired an intensity that staggered all. The announcement of the partition and the separation of the Muslim-majority parts to constitute a new country, aimed at imparting stability and restoring order, had the opposite effect. Communal violence acquired another form, with ethnic cleansing accompanying mass killings. The worst-case scenario was now unfolding.

Asaf's reactions to these developments are not known. Did he, like Khaliquzzaman, his old friend and a Muslim League leader, blame the British for recklessly compressing the withdrawal period into an impossibly short window? Equally recklessly, they then allowed the division of assets, administration, police and, most of all, the army to coincide with the process of withdrawal. This created conditions for a catastrophic breakdown of the state machinery and chaos in north and east India. In taking this position, Khaliquzzaman antagonized Jinnah and others in the Muslim League, as it differed from their standard narrative that the Congress governments in different provinces were responsible for the violence Muslims faced and for their forcible eviction from their lands and homes. The Congress likewise blamed the League. It is not clear whether Asaf saw the futility of these old blame games when the very furies of hell seemed unleashed over large parts of India. It is most likely that he rued how the past failure to negotiate optimum outcomes, as opposed to seeking perfect solutions, had led to the situation slipping out of everybody's control.

Letters to Asaf from Nehru at this time bring out how adjusting to this new emergent reality was under way:

> the proposed so-called division of India is in fact a secession of some parts of India. That is to say, India and the Government of India continue as international persons and all our treaties and engagements with other countries also continue. Our membership of the UNO continues. In fact, there is no change in our external relations whatever because we are a continuing entity. On the other hand, the seceding provinces form a new state which has to begin from scratch.[1]

For Nehru it was critical that alongside the idea of India, its status as an international entity remain constant, even if India itself would not emerge intact from its decolonization. Whether Asaf was as clinical in his approach is not as clear. Possibly he was, because he had been after all an advocate of an amicable and negotiated parting if there was no other way out. But even if he was by now reconciled, as many were, to an acrimonious partition of British India, he was most likely mentally unprepared for the sheer scale of the violence and wholesale displacement of millions of Hindus and Muslims. Even if the signs had been discernible for some time, recognizing them for what they were was perhaps beyond the mental landscape of most.

In late August 1947 he was on his way back to India, called back for consultations, but he was probably desperate to come and see for himself what was happening in Delhi and to get a firmer sense of the India-wide situation. As ambassador, putting a brave face on distressing developments in your country comes with the territory. Certainly, he endeavoured to do so.

At a meeting with the press during the stopover in London en route to Delhi, he was quoted as saying that the violence in Punjab was the work of 'insane reactionaries' and that 'he was sure the violence would end after transfer of power had become an accepted fact'. His defensiveness was, however, evident and perhaps, as an ambassador, inevitable; it is likely he was unable to grasp the magnitude of what was under way. 'There is no difference in the disturbances that are happening in Europe.' This was of course true. Post-war Europe had not seen any reduction in conflict, but civic strife had replaced military conflict, and the ethnic cleansing and killing of ethnic Germans from what had become the new borders of Poland, Hungary and Czechoslovakia was comparable to what was now unfolding in South Asia. Asaf was possibly also trying to convince himself that things could not be as dire as was being made out when he described 'newspaper reports as exaggerated'. Confronted with the grim reality in his home country on which he has to put as much gloss as is possible, whataboutery is often an ambassador's weapon of last resort. We find Asaf to resorting to it: 'More attention has been paid to atrocities in India than had been paid to war between the Dutch and the Indonesians' and 'What difference is there between civil war in Greece and clashes in India?'[2]

He spent about three weeks in Delhi but we know little about his thoughts on the mayhem that was continuing in the city as he appears to have left no record of it. Perhaps it was too close and the cost paid too great. He would certainly have been informed about every aspect of the situation in Delhi and elsewhere as he was staying with Azad. Reports would have been constantly pouring in of the communal violence under way, of Muslims seeking shelter from vengeful Hindus, and tens of thousands of Hindus and Sikhs pouring into the city after having been violently driven out of west Punjab. No intelligence or government reports were required to grasp the situation. The Maulana's ministerial bungalow had become a mini refugee camp for terrified Muslims who had moved into its large grounds – either temporarily for shelter and refuge till the situation improved, or to stay in safety in transit before they finally exited for Pakistan.

Police firings, curfews, rioting, looting and stabbings; trains and buses set on fire and groups of refugees being attacked, made up a good part of the newspaper reports of August and September 1947. It was a time of suspicion and distrust, and in both India and Pakistan religion had become the sole criterion for evaluating loyalty and patriotism. As a prominent Muslim, the first person to be appointed as ambassador and otherwise high up in the Congress leadership, Asaf was nevertheless not immune from the rumours – the sly hints and allegations that at the time surrounded the loyalty of Muslims in India. His presence in Delhi fuelled speculation that he had been dismissed and called back for good on the grounds that his loyalties were with Pakistan. The allegation acquired enough traction for the Mahatma to debunk it in his prayer meeting in Delhi on the evening of 13 September.

Gandhi had returned to Delhi from Calcutta on 9 September, planning to go to the Punjab after hearing of the horrors taking place there. The continuing violence in the capital made him decide to stay on and he halted at the industrialist G.D. Birla's residence in the heart of New Delhi, on whose spacious lawns his daily prayer meetings were held and where he would later be assassinated. During the day he often visited victims of both axes of violence: the traumatized Hindu and Sikh refugees who had made their way to Delhi after being driven out of the western districts of Punjab and from the NWFP; and the Muslims of Delhi who became the targets for this massive swell of refugees and were being told to go to Pakistan. The prayer meetings would be gatherings of both sets of desperate and angry victims of violence, and often witnessed confrontations as raw, accumulated passions were ventilated. On some occasions there were objections to recitations from the Quran, a standard ritual at these prayer meetings, leading to the meetings being cancelled. It was as good a sign as any of just how polarized matters were, and how high passions were.[3]

At the meeting on 9 September Gandhi referred to his association with Delhi from 1915 onwards, remarking that then 'Delhi was ruled not by the British but by Hakim Saheb', referring to Hakim Ajmal Khan. He referred also to his association with Dr Ansari and staying in his house for long periods. Talking about Ansari's daughter and son-in-law, he said, 'what pains me is that they are now scared that some Hindu might kill them. They are not staying in their own house.' Speaking on these lines Gandhi then raised the subject of Asaf Ali: 'a friend of late Hakim Saheb and Dr Ansari as he is of Maulana Saheb' and who 'has been a Congressman ever since he [Gandhi] knew him' and 'was a staunch nationalist'. Gandhi referred to 'a vague insinuation' against Asaf Ali but said 'he had not been recalled but had come to consult the Prime Minister'. He added, 'It was a matter of shame that Muslims should not feel at ease with every Hindu and Sikh.'[4]

Clearly the rumour that India was recalling a Muslim ambassador had acquired wings since just a day earlier an official press statement had also announced that Mr Asaf Ali was in Delhi for consultations with the prime minister, other ministers and officials, and would be resuming duties in Washington.

We do not know who brought the allegations and insinuations against Asaf to Gandhi's attention but he must have grasped the burden this web of suspicion placed on Asaf. For Asaf himself, Gandhi's remarks must have come as a great relief, but how much difference this made to dispersing the rumours is debatable. Some weeks later Nehru was to write to Patel about scurrilous press reporting that represented 'the worst type of journalism . . . poisoning the atmosphere of Delhi and lowering our standards'. He referred in particular to 'repeated references in these papers to Asaf Ali and the most atrocious charges were made about his being an agent of Pakistan and sending munitions to Pakistan'.[5] Similarly, intervening in a debate on foreign policy in the Central Legislature in December 1947, Nehru referred again to 'some new types of papers and journals' that Delhi had been inflicted with and of 'the most malicious and unfounded and false statements in these papers about Mr Asaf Ali'.[6]

For Asaf himself perhaps, in the midst of the tragedy of August 1947 and its aftermath, one event in September may have hurt the most and also left the greatest amount of scar tissue. Asaf's old house in Kucha Chelan had also become the site of a scene that was recurring repeatedly across the city and in many parts of north India. About a hundred Muslims were reported to have taken shelter in it. The haveli itself was now rundown and post 1942 it had been largely unoccupied, except for some months after Asaf's release from Ahmednagar fort when he lived there; he then moved to New Delhi to a government bungalow in Windsor Place, after his election to the Central Legislature. But it was still 'Barrister Asaf Ali's haveli' and those who took shelter in it possibly felt they would be safer there because of the stature and high position of its owner. Gandhi himself went to meet and reassure them.[7] The press report does not mention whether Asaf Ali was present at the time – he may have already left for the United States – or whether it was at his entreaty that Gandhi went to meet one small forlorn group in particular when there were thousands like them scattered across the country.

In any case Asaf would have come to know of this occurrence and the poignancy of the occasion would not have been lost on him. How quickly and frequently history was reversing direction. The massacre in Kucha Chelan in 1857 would have seemed to have been washed clean when, just a few months earlier, the INA officers released after their trial had walked down from the Red Fort to Darya Ganj and were cheered by local residents as they went to Asaf's house. And now huddled together in the midst of another great ferment reminiscent, at least in part, of the 1857 upheaval, they would have pondered over the different meanings of freedom.

# 25

# Closing the Circle

With freedom and Partition, the different uneven strands in this history come to a close. First, the poet turned politician Sarojini Naidu: at the threshold of independence, she was the president of the Asian Relations Conference held in New Delhi in March 1947. If Nehru and Gandhi were the principal draws for the many foreign delegates who assembled in Delhi, Sarojini would have easily been the second. Her eloquence rose to the heights the occasion demanded – modern India at the threshold of its sovereignty reaching out to the rest of Asia – and those assembled had little doubt this was only the first foray into international politics of a new country. 'Comrades and Kindred of Asia'[1] is how she began. By all accounts the assembled delegates were impressed – both by the scale of the achievement of India's freedom fighters as also the intellectual quality of its leadership.

They would have also noted the unusual quality of the decolonization under way. Many Congress leaders present had been in jail less than two years earlier. There was then a Congress-led interim government in place and it was formally presided over by Lord Mountbatten – the newly arrived but last British viceroy who hosted a reception for the delegates at his regal residence at which the British flag still flew and 'God Save the King' played at the end. Yet power was visibly shifting and the shift was irreversible. To the assembled Asian delegates it was evident that the British would leave in a few months, India would be free, marking the end of a long process in which nationalists of different ideological hues had worked together and separately towards ending foreign rule. They would also have been aware that the transition under way in India would deeply touch their lives and their countries as it marked the beginnings of an unmistakable European retreat and eviction from Asia.

Yet if India in March 1947 was on the threshold of a new history, the portfolio of problems on its plate would also have been obvious to the foreigners assembled at the Asian Conference. Gandhi in his remarks had briefly referred to the underlying realities of the country and the vast spaces that separated these realities from the trappings of office or even the power shift under way:

> If some of you see the Indian villages you will not be fascinated by the sight. You will have to scratch below the dung heap. I do not pretend that they were palaces of paradise. Today, they are really dung heaps. What I say is not from history, but from what I have seen myself. I have travelled from one end of India to the other and I have seen the miserable specimens of humanity with the lusterless eyes. They are India.[2]

The immensity of India's deprivation and grinding poverty amidst its soaring aspirations would be something other Asian delegates would have recognized and understood. They came from societies that faced similar, even more onerous problems and burdens. There was, however, in Delhi at the time an even more pressing issue in the form of the looming partition of the country: the domestic and internal communal divide was poised to become an international and geopolitical fault line with fateful consequences for Asia as a whole. In the deliberations of the Asian Conference there was little discussion of this aspect. Most of the visitors were no doubt conscious of it but chose, for reasons of diplomacy and good manners, not to dwell on it.

The breach did, however, impact the conference, and despite the transparent sincerity and eloquence of the hosts, it would have been evident to the visitors. Just a week before the formal inauguration of the conference the Muslim League had announced its boycott. The Asian

Relations Conference, the League said in a statement, 'was a thinly disguised attempt on the part of the Hindu Congress to boost itself politically . . . It is absurd and ridiculous for a Hindu political party to pose as the sole cultural representative of this vast sub-continent . . .'[3] There was more on these lines including, inevitably, appeals to Muslims in other Asian countries not to associate themselves with this venture.

Sarojini Naidu, president of the conference, had lived with and struggled against this polarization for most of her life. Her principal platform which she had championed for three decades and more with eloquence, Hindu–Muslim unity, stood eroded and weakened. Her great abilities as a speaker enabled her to glide over these and other divides, the poet in her using such a broad brush on fundamental themes that contemporary divides faded in significance – for a time at least.

Privately she was deeply troubled, but given the supercharged times and her own high stature she largely refrained from public comment. Her personal views about the emerging situation in her native Hyderabad reveal, however, both her frame of mind and also the realization that a terrible time lay ahead. A rare letter to Syud from the first half of 1947 survives. She wrote on 29 June 1947: 'Hyderabad is in a strange condition of conflicting excitements, very clamorous and confusing. I wonder how many understand or care for the true and lasting interests of the state. I have a deep affection for the people and the ruler.'[4]

These sentences were written about a week before the nizam of Hyderabad had formally announced that with the British departure, Hyderabad was entitled to the status of an independent country. It was fanciful and wishful thinking to believe that he could leverage the future Pakistan to negotiate from a position of strength with the new Government of India. By mid-1947 the battle lines were drawn in Hyderabad, much as elsewhere in India, but with the difference that the nizam was now increasingly influenced by a radical group of Hyderabad Islamists who felt they could will their way to a future quite oblivious to the views of the state's vast Hindu majority. Left to himself the nizam too would have preferred an independent future using Pakistan to balance India, and this meant at least some minimum convergence with the Islamists with whom he may otherwise have had little sympathy.

As Hyderabad agonized over the way ahead, Sarojini herself was installed in a new role as governor of the United Provinces. After August 1947 this was a much more ceremonial position but it was optically important. After Partition, the United Provinces was the largest province of India and she was to be India's first woman governor. Her own views about this appointment, and whether she found it commensurate with the position she had held during the freedom struggle, are not known. Perhaps she had been long enough in public life to recognize that while she had an all-India constituency and support base, that did not translate into the kind of power local and regional politicians represented. But it does appear she was successful in the limited role that governors now discharged.

The partition on religious lines, the communal massacres and migrations – all of this had transformed what had previously been to her a mystical landscape of an ancient yet timeless land. Her own reactions to all this remain hidden. What we do know is that she used her flights of eloquence and sentiment to paper over these divides to the extent possible, as in her speech on being sworn in as governor on 15 August:

> We are reborn today out of the crucible of our sufferings, Nations of the world, I greet you in the name of India, my mother, my mother whose home has a roof of snow, whose walls are of living seas, whose doors are always open to you. Do you seek shelter or succor, do you seek love or understanding, come to us. Come to us in faith, come to us in hope, come to us believing that all gifts are ours to give. I give for the whole world the freedom of this India, that has never died in the past, that shall be indestructible in the future, and shall lead the world to ultimate peace.[5]

Possibly she saw such general evocations as the best salve in the circumstances; as someone who had tried hard and failed to prevent the nightmare of communal violence and polarization, she saw also that no more precise or relevant language could be appropriate.

She did not react publicly to events in her native Hyderabad over the course of 1948 and in particular on 13 September 1948 – just two days after her once close friend M.A. Jinnah died in Karachi – when an Indian military intervention brought the old order to an end. The nizam's prevarication had allowed a virtual coup by Islamists determined to prevent a loss of power and safeguard entitlements that would inevitably reduce with a transition to a more democratic system that integration with India represented. This view identified itself with the idea of Pakistan, or at the very least not acceding to India, and maintaining the Islamic character of the state at all costs. Alongside this a communist revolt in the rural areas spread. The state was disintegrating into an orgy of communal violence and social conflict. The military intervention effectively terminated the nizam's rule and Hyderabad was formally incorporated into India but not without a considerable amount of communal violence, much of it directed against its Muslim elite.

Photo Section, PMML

*Sarojini Naidu: no date but around the time she was the governor of UP (1947–49)*

As governor of distant United Provinces, Sarojini was removed from these dramatic developments. She had consciously identified herself with the feudal order surrounding the nizam, and it is possible that her views would have been taken as no more than the nostalgia of a woman yearning for a world that had changed irrevocably. One such cynical view of her's was conveyed to an English journalist: 'It was only in British India that Mrs Naidu was in politics; there was no nonsense under the princes; the Naidus did not agitate for freedom from feudal oppression, only for freedom from British exploitation. To hell with Hyderabad.'[6]

This was less than charitable but with a small element of truth. Sarojini was easily amongst the most visible persons in the top echelons of the Congress but as far as the stormy politics of Hyderabad was concerned, she had not been in any sense a player. So, when her voice could have made a difference – within Hyderabad and outside it – it turned out to be absent.

Sarojini Naidu died a year later in March 1949.

Syud Hossain had died a week earlier in Cairo. He had been ambassador to Egypt since February 1948, a recognition of the long years he had spent flying the Congress flag in the United States as an outpost of the Indian national movement. Much as in Sarojini's case, there is no real record available of his sentiments and views about the events of 1947.

When he had returned to India from the US in March 1946 it was to a country that he must have found unrecognizable. In part this would have been because he was staying in the new political centre of the country – New Delhi – rather than the more familiar Calcutta or Bombay. If he had some expectation that with a Congress-led interim government in place some role would come his way too, it did not happen quickly. We know that he wrote the occasional newspaper column but how he fitted into the new environment of 1946 and 1947 we do not know much about. Perhaps a fair guess would be that he would have felt a little out of place as he was returning to India after a quarter of a century.

Photo division, Government of India

*Syud Hossain (centre) as ambassador in Cairo, with office bearers of the Indian Union, May 1948*

We do know that he was in regular touch with his old friends – Asaf Ali and Sarojini Naidu. But it is also the case that they were now in different orbits. We also can be reasonably sure that Sarup Nehru – now Vijaya Lakshmi Pandit – pleaded his case to her brother for some role and position for him but there were by now many claimants for the spoils of office. As partition approached alongside a visceral communal divide his isolation would have mounted, as most of his Calcutta-based family had moved to Pakistan.[7] In the end possibly being an ambassador was the only role Nehru could have envisaged for him or Syud saw for himself. His had been also, like those of his friends, a life spent in dissent but it had been an émigré existence which had obvious limitations; during the quarter-century he was absent from India, his contemporaries had progressively graduated to larger stages in a mass movement while he was to become a kind of an outsider, a close friend no doubt but someone whom fate had taken on a different path and a different set of life experiences. He was buried in Cairo and this grave of a forgotten Indian Ambassador remains a puzzle and an enigma for the curious visitor from India.

Syed Mahmud was isolated in multiple other ways. His letter of capitulation and subsequent release from Ahmednagar certainly damaged his reputation. But he also had staying power, and when the Congress formed the provincial government in Bihar after the 1946 election, he was a minister again. To someone like J.B. Kripalani, who had also been at Ahmednagar, this was unacceptable and he had opposed the step but was overruled. He was to bitterly quote a line from the *Ramcharitmanas* hinting at Maulana Azad's and Nehru's role in the appointment: '*Samant ko nahin dosh Gosain*' (The powerful can do no wrong).[8]

If the substance of Kripalani's frustration was that this was Muslim appeasement, the experience of being a minister in Bihar as communal violence took its toll was hardly a pleasant one for Mahmud. Muslims faced public odium and were identified universally as sympathetic to Pakistan and with having suspect loyalties. Being a minister did not insulate Mahmud from the atmosphere that the violence accompanying Partition generated. He was to write to his chief minister sometime in 1948, after the worst of the violence had subsided but left in its wake an atmosphere of palpable bitterness: 'The manner in which the searches of the Muslim houses and their persons is being carried out have caused great consternation and anxiety . . . Even Muslim ladies of high families have not escaped insult. In [a] few cases burkaposh [purdah] ladies in rickshaws were stopped in the streets and searched by public.' His own house, he wrote, was subject to police enquiries on whether there were concealed arms in it and his own car 'was searched inspite of the protest of my driver'. This particular letter had ended somewhat poignantly: 'As long as I am a member of your government I ought to enjoy certain privileges.' It was perhaps also inevitable that Mahmud would personalize the tragedy he was in the midst of: 'Half my life I had to suffer such humiliation as a Congressman at the hands of British Government in India. Now it seems for the remaining period of my life I have to suffer all these indignities and insults at the hands of the Congress Government.'[9]

Apart from such issues, two larger themes comprised Mahmud's political thought at this point. First, 'that partition was a tragedy from which his community was unlikely to recover'; second, that the only way to address this situation was to strive for better relations between the two countries.[10] An early effort in this regard was directed at convincing the new Government of Pakistan to try and dissuade Sikhs and Hindus from leaving en masse and persuade those who had left to return. A telegram to the premier of the NWFP, now in Pakistan, referred to the 'noble Pathans of the Frontier' and requested him 'to take up the work in true Islamic spirit and prove to the world that even today in the midst of dark clouds of suspicion and misunderstanding a non Muslim is not only safe but feels he can live with all honour and respect'.[11]

Such appeals were being made in a situation that was irretrievably adversarial and again it was Nehru who had to remind him of the realities that existed in February 1948 about three weeks after Gandhi's assassination: 'About six months ago or more Gandhiji himself came to the conclusion that it was quite impossible for any Hindu to remain in the Frontier Province without danger . . . We have had piteous appeals from these people in the Frontier; their position has become infinitely

Photo Division, Government of India

*Syed Mahmud in 1954*

worse since the Kashmir raids.' Similarly, 'the fact is that no Hindu has any security in Sind'.[12]

In these circumstances, the question was how Muslims in India were to be reassured and this was the situation Mahmud and others like him confronted. With the assassination of the Mahatma, much of their hopes now devolved on Nehru and supporting him appeared the only logical and political choice. Seeking high office and serving under Nehru would have appeared to be one way to provide the reassurance needed, and certainly many educated, professional Muslims would have sought to make this point by seeking high office.

In 1954 Mahmud was appointed the minister of state in the ministry of external affairs, directly under Nehru. He held the post till 1957 when ill health and failing eyesight made him resign. Till his death in 1968, he, however, remained engaged in politics, and especially Muslim politics, both inside and outside the Congress as he struggled – with questionable success – to decipher how a minority should situate itself in a fractious and competitive democracy without the protections it had claimed and got from the colonial state.

Aruna continued on her predetermined and often lonely furrow, her marriage largely behind her; but the relationship with Asaf did survive – or at least some fragments of it. She was seldom out of the news, enshrined as the young woman who had unfurled the flag in Bombay that many felt heralded the launch of the Quit India movement. Interest in her as a person, and occasionally in her personal life, remained high. She continued to be scornful of all such speculations.

Her radical politics had made her a prominent member of the small but very visible and articulate socialist group within the Congress. They soon separated from it to form a new socialist party. Aruna was to leave it for the more radical Communist Party of India as her politics had diverged from older comrades such as Jayaprakash Narayan, whom she found to be moderate and 'reformist'. A parting with the communists was also

Photo Section, PMML

*Aruna Asaf Ali: no date but possibly early 1950s*

inevitable for she still admired and respected Gandhi and Nehru despite her disagreements with them. Later in the 1950s she would gravitate back to journalism, establishing the left-leaning weekly *Link*, and then a daily newspaper, *The Patriot*.

Through these changes, a constant that became stronger was loyalty to Gandhi's memory and to Jawaharlal Nehru, which also transferred in time to his daughter and grandson, both also destined to be prime ministers of India. This unwavering commitment to Nehru's successors had its downsides. These became evident when Indira Gandhi's politics in the 1970s took an increasingly authoritarian turn and later when, during the tenure of Rajiv Gandhi as prime minister, a personality cult became even more entrenched in the Congress party. Yet her image as a young firebrand at the head of the 1942 mass upsurge endured. Her austerity, integrity and a core adherence to secular and socialist ideals ensured that her aura did not diminish. This public image has endured since her death in 1996.

And finally, Asaf himself. It appears certain that he felt ill used when Nehru wrote to him about a year after his arrival in Washington that his ambassadorship would soon be ending: 'When you went there we told you that you would be expected to remain there for about a year . . . I have come to the conclusion that we would better stick to the period fixed.'[13]

Perhaps it was natural and inevitable that Asaf would blame others for this. He felt that subordinates in the embassy had worked with journalists to tarnish his record. About one of them he was to complain to Nehru that the 'latest about me is that I held dance classes at the Embassy . . . He will not stop unless he goes there as Ambassador himself.'[14] He also complained about former subordinates who he was convinced had worked against him. All this was not unusual for the time: other public figures appointed as ambassadors had the grouse that civil servants worked with their superiors in the ministry of external affairs to stymie their efforts.[15]

Photo Section, PMML

*Asaf Ali: no date but possibly 1951–52*

Underwriting this was concern about his own future in the new India – something that clearly worried Nehru too. What was to be done with this old and valued colleague in the changed circumstances? Possibly Asaf had conveyed his views to Nehru, who revealed to his sister Vijaya Lakshmi that Asaf 'had an idea that he should go to London and that Krishna Menon should go to Moscow and you to Washington'. Nehru was, however, clear: 'I do not think Asaf would fit in London or Moscow.' And this meant a re-posing of the original question: 'What Asaf will do is another problem, an almost insoluble one.'[16]

Clearly Asaf too had some inkling of this 'problem' and it added to his own doubts and insecurities about his future. He revealed to Aruna that he was considering permanently moving to England – although how he would do so is not very clear. This led to another missive from Nehru:

> Aruna tells me that you have some idea of going to England and settling down there because you seem to imagine that there would not be much doing for you in India. You are very wrong there and I think you should return to India. I am quite sure that the idea of settling down in England is wrong.[17]

Perhaps the England idea was just an idle thought, never a scheme but a tactic to engage Nehru's attention. Beneath it was a real uncertainty about what he was to do in India, especially if there was no immediate opening in the Union Cabinet. No doubt he would have received suggestions and advice, perhaps from Aruna too. Legal practice or even the Constituent Assembly were obvious suggestions. There was also his old love of poetry and literature. But these ideas were perhaps not in consonance with Asaf's own thinking. After a lifetime in politics, government office and administrative power were natural end states to aspire towards.

There was also the issue of being supportive of Nehru and not simply because of their personal relationship or because he was the prime minister. Post Partition and even more so after the assassination of Gandhi in January 1948, not having a political position alongside Nehru would be against the interests of Muslims in India. In June 1948, not long after his return to India, he accepted the post of governor of Orissa: ceremonially significant and a mark of the esteem in which the prime minister and his party held him, yet it was one more step towards the end of his political career.

He would stay in Orissa for the next four years. He corresponded regularly with Aruna, and despite their moving apart Asaf pined for her company and worried ceaselessly about her brand of politics. She now had another companion who was an ideological fellow traveller: the journalist Edatata Narayanan with whom she had worked in Delhi to bring out an underground newsletter during the Quit India phase. He would become the editor for the major venture of the weekly *Link* and thereafter the daily newspaper, *The Patriot*, which she started and was throughout associated with. The relationship with Narayanan was an enduring one and would have inevitably led to talk in the early years. An obituary when she died in 1996 had noted 'even before her husband's death in the mid-fifties, Aruna had been drawn to Narayanan personally as well as politically. Thereafter, they practically lived together, though there was no formal marriage.'[18] What Asaf thought and felt about this we do not know. But their paths had diverged for some years now, and perhaps he was reconciled to it and content that they remained husband and wife, even if only formally, that she visited him occasionally, and that some vestiges of the older companionship remained.

His sense of responsibility towards the young girl he had married never waned. He was conscious of her complete disregard for the everyday and of material necessities, and had worried about this incessantly through the entire jail term in Ahmednagar. The haveli in Kucha Chelan, which had ceased to be their home since 1942, was acquired by the Delhi Municipality for use as a primary school in 1950,[19] perhaps with Asaf's encouragement. The compensation received was settled amongst his various relatives; he made sure the balance that remained was placed in a bank deposit which would give Aruna an assured minimum income. He was no doubt thinking about her future after him. He also remained protective, almost gallantly so, of her political reputation. We have for instance Asaf writing privately to K.N. Katju, then the governor of West Bengal, in August 1950:

> My wife has now proceeded to Moscow after waiting long for her visa. I have seen some press comments in Indian newspapers which I fear are far off the mark and entirely groundless. Imagine that she has gone there as a full-fledged red to take the oath of allegiance. A more libellous statement I cannot imagine.[20]

It was a different matter that Aruna did not see the need for this protective sentiment or acknowledge it. But as in his politics Asaf soldiered on bravely in his private life.

His health was failing in these years and those who knew him well commented that it had never really recovered from the Ahmednagar years. Nevertheless, we find him expending some effort at collecting and publishing his writings. He was urged to publish his Ahmednagar detention verses which Nehru had appreciated so much. He wrote to Aruna, 'No publisher can be found. And if I decide to publish them it will mean a dead loss of perhaps Rs 2000 . . . for an old man with hardly enough to retire on, Rs 2000 must be reserved.' He did, however, publish some essays and short stories privately although he also noted: 'In another 15 years, even the few of us who can value this language will have disappeared.' Clearly, he was lonely and letters to Aruna do not disguise how much he longed for her company. 'I have got so used to being alone that even when I lie up in bed, I don't feel that I need company. And yet sometimes nostalgia for the vanished paradise overwhelms me.'[21] Later in life Aruna would confess to a sense of guilt about how things had turned out in her marriage but she had a different life to lead and it was perhaps too late.[22]

Asaf was appointed ambassador to Switzerland in May 1952 possibly also because he wanted a change and Nehru felt his health required it. There had also been differences with the chief minister of Orissa, Harekrushna Mahtab, an Ahmednagar inmate with Asaf. He died in Berne in April 1953 a few months after his arrival. Aruna was at his side when he died. She had arrived from India that very day and it was one of the few occasions they had been together in the past decade. A young first secretary recorded later his recollection of what would have been a sad time for the small Indian diplomatic mission in Berne. He noted that Aruna was 'more grieved by the calamity because she had not come earlier' and that despite their political differences 'husband and wife had remained devoted to each other'.[23]

His body was brought back to Delhi and he was buried in Nizamuddin next to his mother. The shock and grief in Delhi amongst his friends and supporters were palpable. It was left to Nehru to sum up Asaf Ali's life; he described him as 'one of the old band which was associated with the struggle for India's freedom ever since the end of the First World War'. Asaf was, Nehru wrote, 'deeply pained at the occurrences in Delhi and elsewhere of August–September 1947' for 'all that he and Delhi had stood for seemed to be denied'. He carried therefore 'many a wound hidden in the recesses of his heart'. Partition meant in effect a changed reality in which Asaf 'though fitting in had a somewhat lost look as if he was missing something he was used to'.[24]

We can reasonably conclude that the choices that each of these five protagonists – Sarojini Naidu, Asaf Ali, Syud Hossain, Syed Mahmud and Aruna Asaf Ali – exercised had much to do with the circle they found themselves embedded in however accidentally. It certainly seems so to a considerable extent. The influence of Sarojini Naidu in channelling the lives of a young Asaf Ali, Syud Hossain and Syed Mahmud into the trajectory they took is evident. Equally, for Sarojini herself we can see that the many courts that surrounded her constantly strengthened her self-image as a bridge between Hindus and Muslims within the broader umbrella of the national movement. Aruna Asaf Ali's particular path of radical positions is inseparable from her unconventional marriage to a Muslim Congressman who was himself in the thick of the freedom struggle. Some contemporaries may have speculated that her radical politics was also to be understood in terms of her husband's more moderate and constitutional postures. The strain their marriage underwent from 1942 onwards was probably inevitable and also the consequence of the circumstances they found themselves in. Yet at a time when Hindu–Muslim polarization defined so much of what was happening in India that their marriage floundered for reasons other than the religious divide is itself, in an odd kind of way, a vindication of their lives and fundamental beliefs.

We can quite effortlessly imagine plausibly different trajectories for each of these individuals. Sarojini can easily be envisaged as an accomplished woman of letters and a leader of society in her native Hyderabad or an even wider field; Syud Hossain a successful editor and journalist; Asaf Ali and Syed Mahmud as barristers with flourishing practices; and, finally, Aruna steeped in different good causes, her unusual marriage itself a statement for an India yet to be. Yet such a secure conventional trajectory was evidently insufficient for all of them when the opposing choice was to be part of 'The Great Fight' of their times, as Aruna Asaf Ali termed it. So in each of these cases it was the freedom movement that defined and finally stamped their life choices as being a curious amalgam of both success and failure. Depending on our circumstances and our inclinations we attribute different weightages to success or failure. For these five protagonists what gave meaning to their lives was the great enterprise they chose to become part of and their contributions – and those of others like them – have affected the course of our lives so many years later.

# A Note on Sources

The principal sources for Asaf Ali are his autobiographical notes and the prison diary he maintained while in custody in the Ahmednagar fort jail during the 1942–45 Quit India movement. This handwritten collection of papers/notebooks travelled with him to Washington and thereafter to Bhubaneswar. At some stage it was converted into a typescript and the collection supplemented with letters that Asaf Ali had deemed important and retained. We know that Asaf Ali did consider publishing the jail manuscript from time to time, but this project never really came to anything.

In the mid-and late 1980s as the centenary of his birth approached, Aruna Asaf Ali handed over this collection to the journalist and author G.N.S. Raghavan who had worked with her earlier on some of her books. Raghavan refers to these papers – the autobiographical notes, the jail diary and the miscellaneous letters – as the Asaf Ali Family collection, and noted that they had been carefully kept by a nephew of Asaf Ali.

The collection was thus made into a book by G.N.S. Raghavan titled *M. Asaf Ali's Memoirs – The Emergence of Modern India* (Ajanta Publications, New Delhi, 1994). It is invaluable as the principal primary source on Asaf Ali's early life, his time in England, his friends and associates, his turn to nationalist politics, his reactions to the different moods in the nationalist movement, his imprisonment, etc.

Nevertheless, the value of these memoirs as published is somewhat eroded because of the heavy editing they were subjected to. The autobiography and jail diary were not published in their entirety in the order in which they were written but excerpts were used in conformity with the chronology and thematic structure Raghavan imposed on the book to show *The Emergence of Modern India* as a parallel process to Asaf Ali's life story. We are also not sure whether some parts were consciously excluded from the publication. In addition, deciphering Asaf's own reactions can sometimes be a challenge since a fair amount of Raghavan's own comments and commentary are interspersed throughout.

These shortcomings become more pronounced because the original manuscript of *The Asaf Ali Family Collection* was unfortunately not traceable, or at least my efforts to locate it were not successful. What pass as Asaf Ali's private papers in the collections at the Jamia Millia Islamia or the Nehru Memorial Museum and Library (now the Prime Minister's Museum and Library) are small collections of correspondence and not the long autobiographical notes and jail diary which were used in his memoirs and termed *The Asaf Ali Family Collection*.

It is possible that the original is not irretrievably lost and may well be available somewhere but till such time as that happens, Asaf Ali's memoirs as published have to be relied upon as a principal source as I have done.

In addition, for reconstructing the circle of relationship contained in this book the private papers and published and unpublished writings and correspondence of Sarojini Naidu, Syed Mahmud and Syud Hossain were invaluable. These are fortunately well preserved in the Private Paper Collections of the Prime Minister's Museum and Library. In addition, Padmaja Naidu's correspondence in these collections provides a useful supplement.

Aruna Asaf Ali herself appears to have left no personal papers and correspondence behind – perhaps deliberately so. Her correspondence with her husband from the time of their marriage does not appear to have survived the vicissitudes the couple went through in 1942–45. But from the early 1930s onwards, and till the end of her life public, press and official interest in Aruna's life and politics was intense and this has enabled the reconstruction contained in this book.

# Notes

## Introduction

1. Aruna Asaf Ali, *Private Face of a Public Person: A Study of Jawaharlal Nehru* (Radiant Publishers, New Delhi, 1989), 20.

## 1. London, 1913–1914

1. Unless otherwise specified references within quotation marks relating to Asaf Ali's thoughts, reactions and emotions are from G.N.S. Raghavan (ed.), *M. Asaf Ali's Memoirs – The Emergence of Modern India* (Ajanta Publications, New Delhi, 1994) and henceforth referred to as Asaf Ali, *Memoirs*. To reduce the number of endnotes I have dispensed with references to this source unless deemed necessary.
2. Makarand Paranjape (ed.), *Sarojini Naidu: Selected Poetry and Prose* (Rupa & Co., New Delhi, 2010), 25.
3. For details see N.S. Vinodh, *A Forgotten Ambassador in Cairo: The Life and Times of Syud Hossain* (Simon & Schuster, New Delhi, 2021), 18–25.
4. Sarojini Naidu to Ranadheera, 8 February 1914, *Sarojini Naidu: Selected Letters, 1890s to 1940s*, Makarand Paranjape (ed.) (Kali for Women, Delhi, 1996), 90–91.
5. Asaf Ali's memoirs note that the visit was after the award of the Nobel Prize, which appears incorrect. Tagore had visited England in 1912 and in 1913 but the Nobel Prize was announced in November 1913, by which time he was already back in India. The publication of *Geetanjali* in English to much acclaim in England was the reason for the fanfare associated with Tagore's visit in 1913 and not the award of the Nobel Prize.
6. For Tagore's visits to England and the United States in 2012–13 see Krishna Kripalani, *Rabindranath Tagore: A Biography* (Grove Press, New York, 1962), 214–25.
7. *Times of India*, 20 August 1912.

8. *Bombay Chronicle,* 8 July 1914, 10.
9. Ibid.
10. Sarojini Naidu, *Jinnah* (Khuda Baksh Oriental Library, Patna, 1994). This little booklet is the introduction Sarojini Naidu provided in 1918 to a collection of Jinnah's speeches and writings between 1912 and 1917, titled *An Ambassador of Unity*. Sarojini Naidu famously and, in retrospect ironically, referred to Jinnah in this as an 'acknowledged Ambassador of Hindu Muslim Unity'.
11. These memories were recorded by Hosain Ali Khan in an article for the *Statesman*, 'Asaf Ali: A Reminiscence', which appeared on 17 January 1954. The full text of the article is in Asaf Ali, *Memoirs*, op. cit., 439–43.
12. Ibid., 440.

## 2. Delhi at the Turn of the Century and London, 1908–1912

1. For details of the Kucha Chelan massacre see William Dalrymple, *The Last Mughal: The Fall of a Dynasty, Delhi, 1857* (Penguin Viking, Delhi, 2006), 386–87; Kim Wagner, *The Skull of Alam Beg: The Life and Death of a Rebel of 1857* (Penguin India, Delhi, 2017), 219.
2. V.N. Datta, *Madan Lal Dhingra and the Revolutionary Movement* (Vikas Publishing House, New Delhi, 1978), 9.
3. Tim Harper, *Underground Asia: Global Revolutionaries and the Assault on Empire* (Harvard University Press, Cambridge, 2021), 119; but see in particular Datta, *Madan Lal Dhingra and the Revolutionary Movement*, op. cit., which provides a full picture of the entire episode and its background.
4. British authorities also suspected Savarkar's involvement in the assassination of a district officer in Poona and in other cases in India, and were keen to arrest and extradite him to India. Savarkar relocated to Paris in January 1910 but soon returned to London, where, acting on a tip-off, the British arrested him on arrival. He and his associates make references to a certain 'A.A.' who betrayed Savarkar in what would have been an escape attempt while in custody in England. This cannot possibly refer to Asaf Ali: there is no evidence he was associated with Savarkar or his immediate circle beyond being an appreciative member of the audience at Savarkar's speeches, or when immediately after his arrival in London, he was either staying or frequently at India House. For the detailing regarding 'A.A.' see Vaibhav Purandare, *Savarkar: The True Story of the Father of Hindutva* (Juggernaut, New Delhi, 2019), 104–06.

5. For the contrast between the early and the later Savarkar see T.C.A. Raghavan, 'Origin and Development of Hindu Mahasabha Ideology: The Call of V.D. Savarkar and Bhai Parmanand', *Economic and Political Weekly*, vol. 18, no. 15, 9 April 1983, 595–600.
6. Hosain Ali Khan, 'Asaf Ali: A Reminiscence', *The Statesman*, 17 January 1954. The article is reproduced in Asaf Ali, *Memoirs*, op. cit., 441.

## 3. Syud and Asaf in India and in England: Muslims and Modernity

1. Shaistha Ikramullah, *From Purdah to Parliament* (OUP, Karachi, 1963), 11–12. Cited in Vinodh, *A Forgotten Ambassador in Cairo*, op. cit., 8–9.
2. Vinodh, *A Forgotten Ambassador in Cairo*, op. cit., 12.
3. Christopher Shackle and Javed Majid, *Hali's Musaddas: The Ebb and Flow of Islam* (OUP, Delhi, 1997), 41.
4. Francis Robinson, *Separatism Among Indian Muslims* (Cambridge University Press, London, 1974), 124.
5. The text of the memorial submitted to the viceroy is cited in Ram Gopal, *The Indian Muslims: A Political History* (Asia Publishing House, Bombay, 1959), 98–99.
6. Ibid.
7. Ibid.
8. Syud Hossain, *Echoes from Old Dacca* (Edinburgh Press, Calcutta, 1909), 1.
9. Transcript of oral history interview Dr Syed Mahmud, Nehru Memorial Museum and Library (NMML), no. 231, 8. (The NMML stands renamed as Prime Minister's Museum and Library [PMML]). Henceforth Oral History Transcript, Dr Syed Mahmud.

## 4. Delhi: 1912–1913

1. F.A. Eustis and Z.H. Zaidi, 'King, Viceroy and Cabinet: The Modification of the Partition of Bengal, 1911', *History*, vol. 49, no. 166, 1964, 171–84, http://www.jstor.org/stable/24405055.
2. An Orient Club had first come up in Bombay in 1900 catering to the need of Indians wanting to join European-style clubs but being excluded. The Bombay Orient Club was open, however, to both Indians and Europeans. Possibly its Delhi variant, of which little is known now, was an effort to replicate something on those lines but reserved for Indians.

3. Dr Ansari's life and career in nationalist politics has been recorded and analyzed by Mushirul Hasan, *M.A. Ansari: Gandhi's Infallible Guide* (Manohar, New Delhi, 2010).
4. Ibid., 25.
5. Mohammad Ali's life and politics have been captured in Mushirul Hasan, *Mohamed Ali: Ideology and Politics* (Manohar, New Delhi, 1981).
6. Ibid., 14.
7. Ibid., 15, 16.
8. There is considerable literature on Azad and his political and intellectual world view. See for instance V.N. Datta, *Maulana Azad* (Manohar, New Delhi, 1990); S. Irfan Habib, *Maulana Azad: A Life* (Aleph, New Delhi, 2023).
9. Mushirul Hasan, *Nationalism and Communal Politics in India, 1885–1930* (Manohar, New Delhi, 1991), 70–71.
10. Ibid., 75.
11. Ibid., 14.
12. For more details on the hakim see Barbara D. Metcalf, 'Nationalist Muslims in British India: The Case of Hakim Ajmal Khan', *Modern Asian Studies*, vol. 19, no. 1, 1985, 1–28, http://www.jstor.org/stable/312319.
13. Forster to Alice Clara Forster, dated November 1912, in *Selected Letters of E.M. Forster*, Vol. I (1879–1920), Mary Lago and P.N. Furbank (eds.) (Belknap Press of Harvard University, Massachusetts, 1983), 149–50. See also Hasan, *M.A. Ansari*, op. cit., 45–46.
14. Mushirul Hasan (ed.), *My Life: A Fragment (An Autobiographical Sketch of Maulana Mohamed Ali)* (Manohar, New Delhi, 1999), 77.
15. Ibid.
16. Ibid., 77–78. Mohammad Ali does not refer to Asaf Ali by name but says that the nautch was in 'the house of a barrister who was my next-door neighbour'. During the 1912 Balkans war, Bulgaria, Serbia, Greece and Montenegro attacked Turkey and secured a swift victory, in consequence of which Turkey surrendered its European territories.
17. Hasan, *M.A. Ansari*, op. cit., 75.
18. See for instance Burak Akcapar, *People's Mission to the Ottoman Empire: M.A. Ansari and the Indian Medical Mission, 1912–13* (OUP, Delhi, 2014).
19. This is detailed in Vikram Sampath, *Savarkar: Echoes from a Forgotten Past, 1883–1924* (Penguin Random House India, Delhi, 2019), 142–49; Harper, *Underground Asia*, op. cit., 122–23.

## 5. Sarojini and Hyderabad

1. Sarojini Naidu to G.K. Gokhale, 16 November 1914, in Paranjape, *Sarojini Naidu: Selected Letters*, op. cit., 97. My treatment of Sarojini Naidu depends greatly on Makarand Paranjape's introduction to this volume, his subsequent *Sarojini Naidu, Selected Poetry and Prose*, op. cit., and the standard biography by Padmini Sengupta, *Sarojini Naidu* (Asia Publishing House, Bombay, 1966). She awaits a modern biography, and given the volume of her correspondence that is extant and the extent to which she figures in her contemporaries' accounts, that none has so far been published is surprising.
2. Margaret E. Cousins, *The Awakening of Asian Womanhood* (Ganesh & Co., Madras, 1922) 116–17, 119–20.
3. Sengupta, *Sarojini Naidu*, op. cit., 14.
4. Piara Singh Gill, *Up Against Odds: Autobiography of an Indian Scientist* (Allied Publishers, New Delhi, 1992).
5. Paranjape, *Sarojini Naidu: Selected Poetry*, op. cit., 7.
6. Harindranath Chattopadhyaya, *My Life and Myself* (Nalanda Publications, Bombay, 1948), 15.
7. Paranjape, *Sarojini Naidu: Selected Letters*, op. cit., viii.
8. Ibid., 9.
9. Ibid., 38; see also Sengupta, *Sarojini Naidu*, op. cit., 53–55.
10. Khwaja Ahmad Abbas, *Sarojini Naidu* (Bharatiya Vidya Bhavan, Bombay, 1980), 24.
11. Letters to Ranadheera Naidu dated 1 February 1914 and 8 February 1914, and to Jaisoorya Naidu dated 8 February 1914, in Paranjape, *Sarojini Naidu: Selected Letters*, op. cit., 88–93.
12. Paranjape, *Sarojini Naidu: Selected Letters*, op. cit., xxi.

## 6. Sarojini, Syed Mahmud and Syud Hossain

1. V.N. Datta and B.E. Cleghorn (eds), *A Nationalist Muslim and Indian Politics: Being the Selected Correspondence of the late Dr Syed Mahmud* (Macmillan, Delhi, 1974), xii.
2. The original letters are in the Syed Mahmud Private Papers at the PMML. They are reproduced in Paranjape, *Sarojini Naidu: Selected Letters*, op. cit., and dated from January 1916 to early 1919. Typed copies of seven of these, all dating to 1916, are also in the Sarojini Naidu Papers in the same depository. Who had them

typed and how they found their way there is not clear but possibly this was done at Padmaja Naidu's behest at the time she was arranging her mother's papers at the then NMML.

3. Sarojini Naidu to Syed Mahmud, 25 January 1916.
4. Sarojini Naidu to Syud Hossain, 8 August 1917. The letters from Sarojini Naidu to Syud Hossain are in the Syud Hossain Private Papers at the PMML.
5. Padmaja Naidu to Syed Mahmud, 6 November 1917.
6. Paranjape, *Sarojini Naidu: Selected Letters*, op. cit., xxiii.
7. Sarojini Naidu to Syud Hossain, 8 August 1917.
8. K.M. Munshi, *The End of an Era* (Bharatiya Vidya Bhavan, Bombay, 1947), 17–18. The verses are from 'Ode to H.H. the Nizam of Hydrabad' in *The Golden Threshold*.
9. These details about 'Ode to H.H. the Nizam of Hydrabad' are contained in a letter to Edmund Gosse on 24 December 1903. Gosse had been a formative influence during her stay in England in the late 1890s. Paranjape, *Sarojini Naidu: Selected Letters*, op. cit., 41.
10. Paranjape, *Sarojini Naidu: Selected Letters*, op. cit., 64.
11. Ibid., 105–06.
12. Cited in Sengupta, *Sarojini Naidu*, op. cit., 132–33.

## 7. A Broken Engagement and Other Clouds

1. Sarojini Naidu to Syud Hossain, 8 April 1915, Syud Hossain Papers, PMML, New Delhi.
2. Hasan, *My Life: A Fragment*, op. cit., 78.
3. Hasan, *Mohamed Ali,* op. cit., 25.
4. Letters from Asaf to Syud are in the Syud Hossain Papers, PMML.
5. Asaf Ali, *Memoirs*, op. cit., 121.
6. Sarojini Naidu to Padmaja Naidu, 15 March 1917, Padmaja Naidu Papers, PMML.
7. Jugal Kishore Khanna, Oral History Transcript, PMML, 11.
8. Ibid.
9. *Bombay Chronicle*, 18 February 1918.
10. Transcript of oral history interview Aruna Asaf Ali, PMML, no. 965, 13–14. Henceforth Oral History Transcript, Aruna Asaf Ali.

## 8. A Larger Stage

1. Asaf Ali to Syud Hossain, 17 June. The year is not mentioned but it would appear to be 1916, some months before Syud Hossain returned to India.
2. A letter to the editor of the *Bombay Chronicle* sent by Asaf Ali to Syud Hossain, dated 6 October 1917. (Letters to Syud were the basis of the editorials of the *Bombay Chronicle* and the column 'Imperial Delhi'.)
3. Ibid.
4. For instance *Bombay Chronicle*, 12 June 1917; 22 December 1917; 27 October 1917.
5. *Bombay Chronicle*, 12 June 1917.
6. Ibid.
7. *Bombay Chronicle*, 18 June 1918.
8. *Bombay Chronicle*, 3 July 1917.
9. Peter Hardy, *The Muslims of British India* (Cambridge University Press, Cambridge, 1972), 167.
10. Ibid., 187.
11. Sarojini's little essay was republished independently as a little booklet, *Jinnah*, op. cit.
12. Asaf Ali to Syud Hossain, 12 December. The year is not mentioned but is almost certainly 1918.
13. Padmaja Naidu Papers, S. No. 80, PMML.

## 9. Pushing Back

1. *Bombay Chronicle*, 17 June 1918.
2. Ibid.
3. Transcript of oral history interview Jugal Kishore Sharma, S. No 177, PMML, 7. Henceforth Oral History Transcript, Jugal Kishore Sharma.
4 Asaf Ali, *Memoirs*, op. cit., 34.
5. *Bombay Chronicle*, 8 July 1918.
6. *Bombay Chronicle*, 10 July 1918.
7. *Bombay Chronicle*, 8 July 1918.
8. *Bombay Chronicle*, 20 July 1918.
9. *Bombay Chronicle*, 18 July, 22 July, 6 August, 8 August, 9 August, 17 August, 28 August, 6 September 1918.
10. For instance *Times of India*, 18 July 1918.

11. The text of the judgement is in the *Bombay Chronicle*, 6 September 1918.
12. Oral History Transcript, Jugal Kishore Khanna, 19.
13. The announcement was made by Edwin Montagu, the secretary of state for India, on 20 August 1917 in the House of Commons in London. Richard Danzig, 'The Announcement of August 20th, 1917', *Journal of Asian Studies*, Vol. 28, no. 1, 1968, 19–37.
14. F. No. 36, 1920, Home Department, Delhi Archives.
15. Ravinder Kumar (ed.), *Essays in Gandhian Politics: The Rowlatt Satyagraha of 1919* (Clarendon Press, Oxford, 1971), 'Editor's Introduction', 2.
16. Mushirul Hasan, *M.A. Ansari: Gandhi's Infallible Guide* (Manohar, New Delhi, 1987, 2010), 105.
17. T.C.A. Raghavan, *History Men: Jadunath Sarkar, G.S. Sardesai, Raghubir Sinh and Their Quest for India's Past* (HarperCollins India, Noida, 2020), 59.

## 10. In the Throes of Revolution, Piety and Hindu–Muslim Unity

1. J.T.F. Jordens, *Swami Shraddhananda: His Life and Causes* (OUP, New Delhi, 1981), 109.
2. Oral History Transcript, Jugal Kishore Khanna, 15.
3. Jordens, *Swami Shraddhananda*, op. cit., 103.
4. Padmini Sengupta, *Sarojini Naidu: A Biography* (Asia Publishing House, Bombay, 1966), 145.
5. Kumar, *Essays in Gandhian Politics*, op. cit., 4.
6. Narayani Gupta, *Delhi – Between Two Empires, 1803–1931: Society, Government and Urban Growth* (OUP, Delhi, 1981), 205–06. Another study of Delhi at that time described Asaf as 'one of the more important Muslim secondary leaders'. D.W. Ferrel, 'The Rowlatt Satyagraha in Delhi', in Kumar, *Essays in Gandhian Politics*, op. cit., 207.
7. Mushirul Hasan, *Nationalism and Communal Politics in India* (Manohar, New Delhi, 1979), 139.
8. Ibid., 140.
9. 'Speech on Khilafat', Bombay, 9 May 1919, *Collected Works of Mahatma Gandhi (CWMG)*, Vol. 15, 296.
10. CWMG (Publications Division, Government of India, Ahmedabad), Vol. 16, 320. He also referred to this in *An Autobiography*, *CWMG*, Vol. 39, 381.
11. *An Autobiography*, *CWMG*, Vol. 39, op. cit., 380–84. It details his recollection of the Delhi Khilafat Conference.

12. Letter to Asaf Ali, 27 January 1920, *CWMG*, Vol. 16, 508–09.
13. Hasan, *Mohamed Ali*, op. cit., 35.
14. Sheela Reddy, *Mr and Mrs Jinnah: The Marriage that Shook India* (Penguin Random House, Gurgaon, 2017), 235.
15. Stanley Wolpert, *Jinnah of Pakistan* (OUP, New York, 1984), 71–72.
16. Reddy, *Mr and Mrs Jinnah*, op. cit., 237.
17. *Bombay Chronicle*, 10 August 1920.
18. Cited in Hasan, *M.A. Ansari*, op. cit., 65.
19. See Gupta, *Delhi*, op. cit., 212, on the denial of a funeral to a government supporter. Gupta notes that Asaf Ali was not involved in this.
20. See the telegram from Asaf Ali to Gandhi dated 10 December 1920, *CWMG*, Vol. 19, 97.
21. *Bombay Chronicle*, 13 December 1921.
22. *CWMG*, Vol. 22, 353.

## 11. Anticlimax

1. Hasan, *Nationalism and Communal Politics in India*, op. cit., 195.
2. S. Gopal, *Nehru: A Biography*, Vol. 1 (OUP, Delhi, 1975), 85.
3. Asaf Ali to M.K. Gandhi, 28 April 1924. Cited in Ramachandra Guha, *Gandhi: The Years That Changed the World, 1914–1948* (Penguin Random House, Gurgaon, 2018), 217.
4. Cited in Gupta, *Delhi*, op. cit., 218.
5. Datta and Cleghorn, *A Nationalist Muslim and Indian Politics*, op. cit., 61.
6. Hasan, *M.A. Ansari*, op. cit., 148.
7. H.N. Mitra (ed.), *Indian Annual Register*, Vol. 2, 1925, 320. The full text of the address is at 312–23. It is pointed out that she spoke for over an hour extempore and 'her printed address no doubt covered briefly most of what she said, but she spoke at the spur of the moment without restricting to language used in the printed address. She kept the audience spell bound.'
8. B.R. Nanda, *Motilal Nehru* (Publications Division, Delhi, 1964), 196.
9. *Times of India*, 29 December 1915, 8.
10. Datta and Cleghorn, *A Nationalist Muslim and Indian Politics*, op. cit., 47.
11. Jawaharlal Nehru to Syed Mahmud, 21 March 1924, ibid., 48.
12. Ibid., 29 October 1925, 55.
13. Ibid., Syed Mahmud to Jawaharlal Nehru, 13 November 1924, 51.
14. Ibid., 5 May 1925, 53.

15. Kamala Nehru to Syed Mahmud, 6 September 1927, Syed Mahmud Papers.
16. Ibid., 15 August 1927.
17. Ibid., 20 August 1927.
18. Ibid., Undated letter.
19. Ibid., 4 May 1927.
20. Ibid., 4 May 1927.
21. Jawaharlal Nehru to Syed Mahmud, 1 December 1926, in Datta and Cleghorn, *A Nationalist Muslim and Indian Politics*, op. cit., 67.
22. *CWMG*, Vol. 67, 14.
23. Rajendra Prasad to Motilal Nehru, 11 April 1926. Cited in Datta and Cleghorn, *A Nationalist Muslim and Indian Politics*, op. cit., xvi.
24. Shankar Lal to Sarojini Naidu, 22 August 1926. Cited in . Asaf Ali, *Memoirs*, op. cit., 197. Shankar Lal was then secretary of the Delhi Congress.
25. Ibid.
26. *Bombay Chronicle*, 23 December 1926.
27. *Bombay Chronicle*, 16 November 1926, containing a report of a public meeting addressed by Motilal Nehru in Benares.
28. *Bombay Chronicle*, 23 December 1926.
29. Ibid.
30. Jordens, *Swami Shraddhananda*, op. cit., 150.
31. *Times of India*, 28 December 1926.
32. Ibid.

## 12. A Change in Status

1. Sarojini Naidu to Syud Hossain, 26 February 1928, Sarojini Naidu Papers.
2. Vinodh, *A Forgotten Ambassador in Cairo*, op. cit., 39–40.
3. *M. Asaf Ali's Memoirs*, op. cit., 143.
4. For details see Vinodh, *A Forgotten Ambassador*, op. cit., 57–76, and a brief but perceptive treatment in Reddy, *Mr and Mrs Jinnah*, op. cit., 56–57.
5. Vinodh, *A Forgotten Ambassador*, op. cit., 57–58.
6. Sarojini Naidu to Leilamani Naidu, 13 May 1921, in Paranjape, *Sarojini Naidu: Selected Letters*, op. cit., 161.
7. Vinodh, *A Forgotten Ambassador*, op. cit., 152.
8. J.N. Chakrabarti (ed.), *Dr Syud Hossain: A Glimpse of His Life, Speeches & Writings* (P. Ghosh and Company, Dhaka, 2003 [reprint]). The book was first published in Calcutta in 1960. The foreword by Asaf Ali is dated July 1950 and written when he was the governor of Orissa.

9. Vinodh, *A Forgotten Ambassador*, op. cit., 193. For the details on Syud's life in the US I have depended on this book.
10. Reddy, *Mr and Mrs Jinnah*, op. cit., a fine historical treatment of the Ruttie Petit–Jinnah courtship, marriage and final heartbreak, has these and other details.
11. Aruna Asaf Ali, Oral History Transcript, 2.
12. G.N.S. Raghavan, *Aruna Asaf Ali: A Compassionate Radical* (National Book Trust, New Delhi, 1999), 11.
13. Ibid., 13.
14. Aruna Asaf Ali, Oral History Transcript, op cit., 9.
15. *Bombay Chronicle*, 25 January 1928.
16. *Bombay Chronicle*, 26 January 1928.
17. Why both the *Times of India* and the *Bombay Chronicle* should make a mistake with the initials of Aruna's father's name remains a mystery.
18. Aruna Asaf Ali, Oral History Transcript, 9. See also Raghavan, *Aruna Asaf Ali*, op. cit., 13.
19. Aruna Asaf Ali, Oral History Transcript, 10.
20. Aruna Asaf Ali, Oral History Transcript, 11.
21. Comment inserted by G.N.S. Raghavan in Asaf Ali, *Memoirs*, op. cit., 204, possibly on the basis of what Aruna Asaf Ali told him since much the same sentiment is in her oral history interview.
22. *Times of India*, 15 February 1928, 5. The article is titled 'Through Indian Eyes' and carries a summary of different media reactions to the marriage announcement.
23. *Bombay Chronicle*, 3 February 1928.
24. *Bombay Chronicle*, 28 February 1928.
25. Ramachandra Guha, *Gandhi: The Years That Changed the World, 1914–1948* (Penguin Random House, Gurgaon, 2018), 241.
26. Ibid., 242.
27. Aruna Asaf Ali, *Private Face of a Public Person: A Study of Jawaharlal Nehru* (Radiant Publishers, New Delhi, 1989), 13.
28. Raghavan, *Aruna Asaf Ali*, op. cit., 112–13.

## 13. Domesticity and Confrontation

1. Raghavan, *Aruna Asaf Ali*, op. cit., 19–20.
2. Ibid., 20.
3. Aruna Asaf Ali, Oral History Transcript, 11.
4. 'My Discovery of Nehru', in Aruna Asaf Ali, *Fragments from the Past* (Patriot Publisher, New Delhi, 1989), 423.

5. Aruna Asaf Ali, *The Resurgence of Indian Women* (Radiant Publishers, in association with PMML, New Delhi, 1991), 97.
6. Ibid.
7. Aruna Asaf Ali, Oral History Transcript, 9.
8. Raghavan, *Aruna Asaf Ali*, op. cit., 25.
9. Ibid., 20.
10. For details see Manoranjan Jha, *Katherine Mayo and India* (Peoples Publishing House, Delhi, 1971).
11. Aruna Asaf Ali, Oral History Transcript, 25.
12. Ibid., 26.
13. Asaf Ali, 'Bhagat Singh: Hero of Independence Struggle – His Lawyer's Impressions'. This essay is included in K.L. Jauhar, *Martyr Bhagat Singh* (Sneh Prakashan, Haryana, 2007), 171–81. I am grateful to Professor Chaman Lal for this reference.
14. Chaman Lal (ed.), *The Bhagat Singh Reader* (HarperCollins, Noida, 2019), xxviii–xxix. For details of the contested consideration of these two bills see Manoranjan Jha, *Role of the Central Legislature in the Freedom Struggle* (National Book Trust, Delhi, 1972), 140–47.
15. Asaf Ali, 'Bhagat Singh: Hero of Independence Struggle – His Lawyer's Impressions', op. cit.,173.
16. A scholar of the Bhagat Singh trial has noted: 'Bhagat Singh again had a well thought out plan in place – they would not defend themselves in the British courts, but rather use the courts as platforms to spread their ideas and values by making political statements. They did not hire any lawyer for their defence, but accepted the consultancy with advocates. Nationalist lawyer Asaf Ali was made available to them for consultancy.' Lal, *The Bhagat Singh Reader*, op. cit., 22.
17. Asaf Ali, 'Bhagat Singh: Hero of Independence Struggle – His Lawyer's Impressions', op. cit., 174.
18. *Times of India*, 7 June 1929. See also Asaf Ali, 'Bhagat Singh: Hero of Independence Struggle – His Lawyer's Impressions', op. cit., 177–79.
19. Aruna Asaf Ali, Oral History Transcript, op. cit., 26.
20. *Times of India*, 8 May 1929.
21. Aruna Asaf Ali, Oral History Transcript, 26.
22. Aruna Asaf Ali, *Travel Talk* (Aundh Publishing House, Aundh, 1947), 42.
23 Asaf Ali, 'Bhagat Singh: Hero of Independence Struggle – His Lawyer's Impressions', op. cit., 172.
24. Aruna Asaf Ali, *Fragments from the Past*, op. cit., 424.
25. Gandhi to Viceroy Lord Irwin, 2 March 1930, *CWMG*, Vol. 43, 2–7.

## 14. Climbing the Political Ladder

1. Aruna Asaf Ali, Oral History Transcript, 18.
2. Raghavan, *Aruna Asaf Ali*, op. cit., 35.
3. Aruna Asaf Ali, *The Resurgence of Indian Women*, op. cit., 104–05.
4. Raghavan, *Aruna Asaf Ali*, op. cit., 35.
5. Ibid., 36.
6. *Bombay Chronicle*, 29 October 1930.
7. Raghavan, *Aruna Asaf Ali*, op. cit., 37.
8. See Ramachandra Guha, *Gandhi: The Years That Changed the World*, op. cit., 345.
9. Padmini Sengupta, *Sarojini Naidu*, op. cit., 231.
10. *Times of India*, 23 and 24 September 1930.
11. M.A. Ansari to M.K. Gandhi, February 1930. The full text of the letter and Gandhi's reply are in Mushirul Hasan, *Muslims and the Congress (Select Correspondence of Dr M.A. Ansari, 1912–1935*) (Manohar, New Delhi, 1960), 94–102.
12. Gopal, *Nehru*, op. cit., 139.
13. Cited in Mushirul Hasan, *M.A. Ansari*, op. cit., 240.
14. Satyamurti's letter of June 1931 was published by Gandhi in *Young India* along with his reply. K.V. Ramanathan (ed.), *The Satyamurti Letters: The Indian Freedom Struggle Through the Eyes of a Parliamentarian*, Vol. 1 (Pearson, Longman, New Delhi, 2000), 140.
15. Hasan, *M.A. Ansari*, op. cit., 19.
16. Cited in Ramachandra Guha, *Gandhi*, op. cit., 381.
17. The text of Asaf Ali's letter to Gandhi is in Asaf Ali, *Memoirs*, op. cit., 211–13.
18. Asaf Ali to Jawaharlal Nehru, 30 September 1933. The text of the letter is in Asaf Ali, *Memoirs*, op. cit., 215–16.
19. Jawaharlal Nehru to Asaf Ali, 12 October 1933, *Selected Works of Jawaharlal Nehru (SWJN)* (2nd Series), 43.
20. Asaf Ali's letter dated 12 July 1934 was reproduced by Chaudhury Khaliquzzaman in his book *Pathways to Pakistan* (Longmans Pakistan, Lahore, 1961), 126.
21. *Times of India*, 22 October 1934.
22. Jawaharlal Nehru prison diary entry, 14 November 1934, *SWJN* (2nd Series), Vol. 6, 303.
23. *Bombay Chronicle*, 20 November 1934.
24. Ibid.
25. Diary entry, 16 October 1942, Asaf Ali, *Memoirs*, op. cit., 227.

26. Ibid.
27. S. Gopal, *Jawaharlal Nehru,* Vol. 1, op. cit., 228–32.
28. *Harijan*, 7 August 1937, *CWMG*, Vol. 66, 16.
29. *Times of India*, 19 May 1936.
30. Ramanathan, *The Satyamurti Letters*, op. cit., Vol. 1, xv–xviii, 296–304.
31. Ibid., Vol. 1, 367.
32. Ibid., 367, 375–76. In this Satyamurti's reply is dated 20 April – clearly an error by the writer or a misprint in the volume.
33. N.G. Ranga, 'Aruna: The 1942–45 Heroine', in T.N. Kaul (ed.), *Aruna Asaf Ali: A Profile* (Lancer International, New Delhi, 1990), 20.
34. Aruna Asaf Ali, *Private Face of a Public Person*, op. cit., 54–55.
35. B.K. Nehru, 'Aruna Asaf Ali', in Kaul, *Aruna Asaf Ali*, op. cit., 23.
36. *Bombay Chronicle*, 8 October 1936.
37. Diary entry, 10 January 1943, Asaf Ali, *Memoirs*, op. cit., 293.

## 15. Ahmednagar

1. The full text of the viceroy's declaration of 17 October 1939 is in *Towards Freedom: Documents on the Movement of Independence in India 1939*, Part 1, Mushirul Hasan and S. Bhattacharya (eds.) (Indian Council of Historical Research/OUP, New Delhi, 2008) 394–98.
2. Datta and Cleghorn, *A Nationalist Muslim in Indian Politics*, op. cit., xix.
3. Ibid., 197.
4. Rajendra Prasad and Jawaharlal Nehru to Syed Mahmud, dated 26 March and 27 March 1940 respectively, ibid., 196–98.
5. B.R. Ambedkar, *Thoughts on Pakistan* (Bombay, Thacker & Co., 1941), 6.
6. Cited in Ramachandra Guha, *Gandhi*, op. cit., 626.
7. *Times of India*, 18 February 1941.
8. 'Question of Classification of Asaf Ali, Desh Bandhu Gupta, Farid ul Haq Ansari, Noor ud Din Bihari and Bahal Singh', Chief Commissioner, Delhi F. No. 3(12)XIII, General Branch, 1940, Delhi State Archives.
9. 'Supply of Western Diet to Mr Asaf Ali', Chief Commissioner, Delhi F. No. 3(38), 1941, Delhi State Archives.
10. 'Classification of Mrs Asaf Ali', Deputy Commissioner, Delhi F. No. 3(106), 1941, Delhi State Archives.
11. Diary entry, 31 August 1942, Asaf Ali, *Memoirs*, op. cit., 246.
12. Aruna Asaf Ali, Oral History Transcript, 63.

13. Diary entry, 31 August 1942, *M. Asaf Ali's Memoirs*, op. cit., 248.
14. He wrote *The History of the Indian National Congress*, published in 1935 on the party's fiftieth anniversary. Details in this para are from Asaf Ali, *Memoirs*, op. cit., 248.
15. Diary entry, 31 August 1942, Asaf Ali, *Memoirs*, op. cit., 248–49.
16. Dr Pattabhi Sitaramayya, *Feathers and Stones* (Padma Prakashan, Bombay, 1946), 7.
17. Maulana Abul Kalam Azad, *Sallies of Mind* (English translation of *Ghubar e Khatir*) (Shipra Publications, Delhi, 2003), 40.
18. Diary entry, 31 August 1942, Asaf Ali, *Memoirs*, op. cit., 245.
19. Sitaramayya, *Feathers and Stones*, op. cit., 391–92.
20. Azad, *Sallies of Mind*, op. cit., 61–62.
21. Shankarrao Deo, Interview No. 121, Centre for South Asian Studies, University of Cambridge, http://media.s-asian.cam.ac.uk/pdf/121c.pdf.
22. Sitaramayya, *Feathers and Stones*, op. cit., 10.
23. Ibid.
24. This incident is related in J.B. Kripalani, *My Times: An Autobiography* (Rupa & Co., New Delhi, 2004), 484, and also in Sitaramayya, *Feathers and Stones*, op. cit., 10–11.
25. Azad, *Sallies of Mind*, op. cit., 159.
26. Kripalani, *My Times*, op. cit., 485.
27. Sitaramayya, *Feathers and Stones*, op. cit., 22–23.
28. Ibid., 20
29. Ibid., 26.
30. Ibid., 28–29.
31. Diary entry, 24 October 1942, Asaf Ali, *Memoirs*, op. cit., 254.
32. To Indira Gandhi, 29 February 1944, *SWJN* (2nd Series), Vol. 13, 364.
33. To Indira Gandhi, 26 March 1943, 84.

## 16. The Journey to Jail and the Divides Within

1. Prison diary entry, 21 November 1943, *SWJN*, Vol. 13, 297.
2. Prison diary entry, 20 November 1942, ibid., 292.
3. Datta and Cleghorn, *A Nationalist Muslim in Indian Politics*, op. cit., 188.
4. Ibid., 219.
5. Ibid., 22.
6. Diary entry, 6 December 1943, Asaf Ali, *Memoirs*, op. cit., 272.
7. Diary entry, 20 April 1944, Asaf Ali, *Memoirs*, op. cit., 315.

8. Diary entry, 27 January 1944, Asaf Ali, *Memoirs*, op. cit., 314
9. Diary entry, 21 November 1942, *SWJN*, Vol. 13, op. cit., 296.
10. Diary entry, 20 November 1943, ibid., 292.
11. Diary entry, 8 August 1943, ibid., 211–12.

## 17. The Pain of It All

1. 'Condition of Detention of Members of the Congress Working Committee at Ahmednagar and after Transfer to their Home Provision. Release of Member of the CWC', F. No. 3/6/44, 1944, Home Political-I, National Archives of India (NAI).
2. 'Report on Health of Gandhi and Members of the Congress Working Committee. Question of Release of P Sitaramaiya, Mrs Gandhi and Sarojini Naidu', F. No. F3/56/41, 1941, Home Political-I, NAI.
3. Ibid.
4. Ibid.
5. Diary entry, 19 October 1944, *SWJN*, Vol. 13, 494.
6. Prison diary entry, 22 May 1943, *SWJN*, Vol. 13, 145.
7. Asaf Ali, *Memoirs*, op. cit., 318.
8. Diary entry, 3 June 1943, *SWJN*, Vol. 13, 158.
9. Ibid., 292.
10. Details can be found in 'Conditions of Detention of Mr Gandhi and Members of the Congress Working Committee', 1942, Home Political-I, 1942, F. No. 3/21/42, Part II, NAI.
11. Ibid.
12. 'Conditions of Detention of Mr Gandhi and Member of the Congress Working Committee', F. No. 3/21/42 PART-II, Home Political-I, NAI., op. cit.
13. *M. Asaf Ali's Memoirs*, op. cit., 246.
14. Ibid.
15 Conditions of Detention of Mr Gandhi and Member of the Congress Working Committee', F. No. 3/21/42 PART-II, Home Political-I, NAI., op. cit.
16. Raghavan, *Aruna Asaf Ali*, op. cit., 43.
17. Asaf Ali, *Memoirs*, op. cit., 287.
18. Ibid., 296.
19. The text of the viceroy's letter to Gandhi dated 5 February 1943 is in *The Transfer of Power: Constitutional Relations between Britain and India*, Vol. 3 (Her Majesty's Stationary Office, London, 1971), 587–90. Future references to the *Transfer of*

*Power* volumes will be as *TOP* followed by the volume and page numbers. See also Asaf Ali, *Memoirs*, op. cit., 295.

20. Diary entry, 17 February 1943, *SWJN* (2nd Series), Vol. 13, 68.
21. Diary entry, 25 May 1943, ibid., 150.
22. Diary entry, 17 February 1943, ibid., 69.
23. 'Condition of Detention of Members of the Congress Working Committee at Ahmednagar and after Transfer to their Home Provision. Release of Member of the CWC', F. No. 3/6/44, 1944, Home Political-I, NAI.
24. 'Report on Health of Gandhi and Members of the Congress Working Committee. Question of Release of P Sitaramaiya, Mrs Gandhi and Sarojini Naidu', F. No. F3/56/41, 1941, Home Political-I, NAI. Parts of this file are damaged.
25. Ibid.
26. 'Detention and Release of Dr Syed Mahmud A Member of Congress Working Committee', F. No. 3/34 Part I, Home Political-I, NAI.
27. Ibid.
28. Letter to Indira Gandhi, 21 October 1944, *SWJN*, Vol. 13, 497.

## 18. Preparing for the World Outside

1. Asaf Ali, *Memoirs*, op. cit., 301.
2. *CWMG*, Vol. 77, 306.
3. Raghavan, *Aruna Asaf Ali*, op. cit., 58.
4. Ibid., 50.
5. Ibid.
6. *New York Times*, 20 September 1942.
7. *CWMG*, Vol. 77, appendices XIII and XIV, 468–68.
8. Ibid.
9. G.N.S. Raghavan, *Aruna Asaf Ali*, op. cit., 60–61.
10. *CWMG*, Vol. 78, 1.
11. M.M. Shah's confessional statement dated 16 March 1943, in P.N. Chopra (ed.), *Quit India Movement: British Secret Documents* (Interprint, New Delhi, 1986), 298.
12. Intelligence Report, 28 April 1943, ibid., 306.
13. Intelligence Report, 29 October 1942, ibid., 246–47.
14. Shah's confessional statement referred to above speaks of Edatata Narayanan working with her to bring out a English newsletter at the time.
15. This recollection is in the article B.K. Nehru contributed to Kaul, *Aruna Asaf Ali*, op. cit., 23–25.

16. Asaf Ali, *Memoirs*, op. cit., 302.
17. Ibid.
18. Ibid.
19. This letter dated 21 March 1945 is in 'Condition of Detention of Members of the Congress Working Committee at Ahmednagar and after Transfer to their Home Provision. Release of Member of the CWC', F. No. 3/6/44, 1944, Home Political-I, NAI.
20. *SWJN*, Vol. 13, 547.
21. Shankarrao Deo interviewed on 27 March 1970 by the Centre for South Asian Studies of the University of Cambridge, http://media.s-asian.cam.ac.uk/pdf/121d.pdf.
22. *SWJN*, Vol 13, 521.
23. See for instance 'Question in the Council of State Regarding a Letter from Mr. Gandhi to H.E. the Viceroy Suggesting the Release of Congress Working Committee Members and Other Security Prisoners – Disallowed', F. No. 8/17, 1944, Home Political-I, NAI; 'Starred question No. 175 in the Legislative Assembly on 23.2.44 by Mr. T.T. Krishnamachari Regarding Health of Dr. Syed Mahmud and Shri Vallabhbhai Patel, Members of the Congress Working Committee', F. No. 22/24, 1944, Home Political-I, NAI; 'Sardar Mangal Singh's Starred Question No. 183 in the Legislative Assembly on 23.2.44 Regarding the Place of Detention of Members of the Working Committee on Interviews, Newspapers, Letters and Direct Allowed to Them', F. No. 22/25, 1944, Home Political-I, NAI.
24. Diary entry, 27 January 1945, *SWJN* (2nd Series), Vol. 13.
25. Diary entry, 8 March 1945, ibid., 567.
26. Ibid., 568–69.
27. Ibid., 582–86.
28. *TOP*, Vol. 5, 1039.
29. Ibid., Vol. 5, 1071.
30. *Bombay Chronicle*, 6 April, 17 April, 23 April 1945, amongst many others.
31. *Bombay Chronicle*, 29 May 1945.
32. 'First Thoughts on Coming Out of Jail', 15 June 1945, *SWJN*, Vol. 14, 2.
33. *Bombay Chronicle*, 18 June 1945.
34. Cited in Raghavan, *Aruna Asaf Ali*, op. cit., 71–72.
35. *CWMG*, Vol. 81, 109.

## 19. The World Outside

1. *Bombay Chronicle*, 2 December 1945.
2. Ibid., 25 October 1945.
3. Ibid., 18 November 1945.
4. Ibid., 2 December 1945.
5. Cited in Patrick French, *Liberty or Death; India's Journey to Independence and Division* (HarperCollins, London, 1997), 211.
6. Diary entry, 10 March 1946, Penderel Moon (ed.) *Wavell – The Viceroy's Journal*, (OUP, London, 1973), 222.
7. All-India Congress Committee Resolution, Bombay, September 1922, in Bimal Prasad (ed.), *Towards Freedom: Documents on the Movement for Independence in India, 1945* (OUP, New Delhi, 2008), 425–26.
8. B. Desai and Asaf Ali to Field Marshall Viscount Wavell, 15 October 1945, *TOP*, Vol. 6, S. No. 143, 341–44.
9. Ibid., 341–42.
10. Ibid., 387.
11. *The Hindu*, 5 January 1946, cited in Peter Ward Fay, *The Forgotten Army: India's Armed Struggle for Independence* (University of Michigan Press, Ann Arbor, 1993), 494.
12. *Bombay Chronicle*, 4 January 1946.
13 The historian S. Bhattacharya uses the term in this sense to describe the underlying spirit of 1945. Prasad, *Towards Freedom*, op. cit., General Editor's introduction, xi.
14. *Bombay Chronicle*, 5 January 1946.
15. Diary entry, 29 September 1944, Asaf Ali, *Memoirs*, op. cit., 285.
16. Prasad, *Towards Freedom*, op. cit., General Editor's introduction, xii.
17. *Hindustan Times*, 4 September 1945. Cited in Prasad (ed.), *Towards Freedom*, 1945, op. cit., 270.
18. See for instance M.C. Setalvad, *Bhulabhai Desai* (Publications Division, 2010 [1981], 340–41.

## 20. The New Radicals

1. *Bombay Sentinel*, 2 October 1945. Cited in Bimal Prasad, *Towards Freedom, 1945, Documents on the Movement for Independence in India, 1945*, (General Editor Sabyasachi Bhattacharya) op. cit., 456–58.

2. Ibid.
3. *Bombay Chronicle*, 15 February 1946.
4. The *Statesman*, 12 February 1946 in Sumit Sarkar (ed.), *Towards Freedom: Documents on the Movement for Independence in India, 1946*, Vol. 1 ( OUP, Delhi, 2009), 58.
5. *Bombay Chronicle*, 21 February, 1946.
6. Statement to the press, 23 February 1946, *CWMG*, Vol. 83, 171.
7. *Free Press Journal*, 25 February 1946, in Sarkar, *Towards Freedom*, op. cit., 60.
8. This statement is in the press statement issued by Gandhi on 23 February 1946, op. cit.
9. *Free Press Journal*, 25 February 1946 cited in Sarkar, *Towards Freedom*,1946, Vol 1, *CWMG*, Vol. 83, 60-61.
10. Statement to the press, 26 February 1946, *CWMG*, Vol. 83, 182–84.
11. Ibid.
12. Letter to Aruna Asaf Ali, 15 March 1946, *CWMG*, Vol. 83, 262.
13. Aruna Asaf Ali, *Private Face of a Public Person*, op. cit., 101–02.
14. Ibid., 13.
15. Pramod Kapoor has recently brought to life the persons and events of the naval ratings mutiny of 1946 and these details are from his book: *1946 Last War of Independence: Royal Indian Navy Mutiny* (Roli, New Delhi, 1922).
16. I am grateful to Pramod Kapoor for sharing this letter which has survived on account of its interception by the Criminal Investigation Department, Punjab, and a typed copy thereafter being preserved in the government record. R.D. Puri was then in Simla and Shaila's letter was shared by the Punjab authorities with both the Government of India and the Bombay authorities.
17. Raghavan, *Aruna Asaf Ali*, op. cit., 96.
18. Ibid.

## 21. The Necessity and Futility of High Politics

1. Lord Pethick Lawrence to Attlee, 5 May 1946, *TOP*, Vol. 7, Item 196, 431.
2. Maulana Abul Kalam Azad, *India Wins Freedom: An Autobiographical Narrative* (Orient Longman, Calcutta, 1959), 151.
3. J.B. Kripalani, *My Times: An Autobiography* (Rupa & Co., New Delhi, 2004), 425–26.
4. K.M. Munshi to Syed Mahmud, 14 July 1941, in Datta and Cleghorn, *A Nationalist Muslim and Indian Politics: Being the Selected Correspondence of the Late Dr Syed Mahmud* (Macmillan, Delhi, 1974), 210.

5. Jawaharlal Nehru to Syed Mahmud, 12 December 1939, ibid., 187.
6. Aruna Asaf Ali, *Travel Talk* (Aundh Publishing House, Aundh, 1947) 35.
7. Ibid., 136.
8. Ibid., 61.
9. Ibid., 35.
10. Wavell to George VI, 22 October 1946, *TOP*, Vol. 8, 772.
11. Aruna Asaf Ali, *Travel Talk*, op. cit., 111.
12. *Bombay Chronicle*, 8 July 1946.
13. *Times of India*, 8 July 1946.
14. *Bombay Chronicle*, 8 July 1946.
15. Aruna Asaf Ali, *Travel Talk*, op. cit., 53.
16. Ibid., 55.

## 22. A Kashmir Trial

1. Sheikh Abdullah, *Flames of the Chinar: An Autobiography*, abridged and translated by Khushwant Singh (Viking/Penguin India, New Delhi, 1993), 78.
2. Sheikh Mohammad Abdullah, *The Blazing Chinar: An Autobiography*, translated by Mohammad Amin (Gulshan Books, Srinagar, 2016), 259.
3. A.G. Noorani, *Indian Political Trials, 1775–1947* (OUP, Delhi, 2005), 291, 294.
4. Abdullah, *The Blazing Chinar*, op. cit., 262.
5. Cited in A.G. Noorani, *Indian Political Trails*, op. cit., 292–93.
6. Ibid., 294.
7. *Bombay Chronicle*, 18 August 1946.
8. Hosain Ali Khan, 'Asaf Ali: A Reminiscence', *The Statesman*, 17 January 1954. Cited in Raghavan, *M. Asaf Ali's Memoirs*, op. cit., 438–39.
9. P.S. Gill, *Up Against Odds: Autobiography of an Indian Scientist* (Allied Publishers, New Delhi, 1992), 62.
10. Sri Prakasa, *Pakistan: Birth and Early Days* (Meenakshi Prakashan, Meerut, 1961), 6.
11. Diary entry, 22 January 1945, *SWJN*, Vol. 13, 546.
12. Footnote 607, *SWJN*, Vol. 13.

## 23. Minister and then Ambassador

1. Wavell to secretary of state for India, 17 September 1946, *TOP*, Vol. 8, 534.
2. Wavell to George VI, 22 October 1946, *TOP*, Vol. 8, 772.

3. Wavell to secretary of state for India, 21 August 1946, *TOP*, Vol. 8, 272.
4. Wavell to secretary of state, 17 September 1946, *TOP*, Vol. 3, carries the text of the letter which also describes Asaf as someone who has 'always been rather a worm' (cited earlier). The editors, however, deleted the reference to the state of the Asaf–Aruna marriage as a 'personal remark'. I am grateful to Aliki-Anastasia Arkomani, Asian and African Studies Reference Specialist in the British Library, for sharing the full text of the letter.
5. *Harijan*, Vol. 10, no. 37, 20 October 1946; *CWMG*, Vol. 85, 448–49.
6. Vijaya Lakshmi Pandit, *The Scope of Happiness: A Personal Memoir* (Crown Publishers, New York, 1979), 227.
7. Wavell to George VI, 24 February 1947, *TOP*, Vol. 9, 804.
8. Nehru to Vijaya Lakshmi Pandit, 5 December 1946, *SWJN* (2nd Series), Vol. 1, 134–35.
9. Wavell to George VI, 24 February 1947, *TOP*, Vol. 9, 804.
10. Asaf Ali, *Memoirs*, op. cit., 345.
11. Jawaharlal Nehru to Asaf Ali, 21 December 1946, *SWJN* (2nd Series), Vol. 1, 557.
12. Jawaharlal Nehru to Asaf Ali, 3 February 1947, cited in Asaf Ali, *Memoirs*, op. cit., 348–49.
13. Ibid.
14. Sudhir Pant, *Asaf Ali: Patriot and Humanist* (National Book Trust, New Delhi, 1984), 59.
15. Talk with Aruna Asaf Ali, 27 June 1947, *CWMG*, Vol. 88, 222.
16. Nehru to Asaf Ali, 7 April 1947, *SWJN* (2nd Series), Vol. 2, 517.
17. Nehru to Vijaya Lakshmi Pandit, 22 May 1947, *SWJN* (2nd Series), Vol. 2 632.
18. Asaf Ali, *Memoirs*, op. cit., 389–90.
19. Jawaharlal Nehru to Asaf Ali, 18 June 1947, in Jawaharlal Nehru Papers (post 1947), 6 May 1947–30 June 1947, S. No. 3, PMML.
20. *New York Times*, 7 December 1946.
21. Inverchapel to Foreign Office, 7 December 1946, *TOP*, Vol. 9, 311.
22. Amit Das Gupta, *The Indian Civil Service and Indian Foreign Policy, 1923–1961* (Routledge, Oxon and New York, 2021), 205, 223.
23. Mohan Singh Mehta, Oral History Transcript, PMML, 308–09.
24. M.K. Gandhi to Aruna Asaf Ali, 18 December 1946, *CWMG*, Vol. 86, 241.
25. *Times of India*, 30 January 1946.
26. *Times of India*, 10 August 1952.
27. Viceroy's Personal Report, 9 April 1947, *TOP*, Vol. 10, 172,.
28. Asaf Ali, *Memoirs*, op. cit., 352.
29. Ibid., 388.

30. B.K. Nehru, *Nice Guys Finish Second* (Penguin, New Delhi, 1997), 238.
31. Nehru to Asaf Ali, 18 June 1947, *SWJN* (2nd Series), Vol. 3, 330.
32. A detailed account of this first special session on Palestine in the United Nations and India's role in it is contained in P.R. Kumaraswamy, *India's Israel Policy* (Columbia University Press, New York, 2010), 86–93.
33. Ibid., 87.
34. Jawaharlal Nehru to Asaf Ali, 14 May 1947, *SWJN* (2nd Series), Vol. 2, 497.
35. Cited in Kumaraswamy, *India's Israel Policy*, op. cit., 91.
36. Ibid., 90.
37. Jawaharlal Nehru to Asaf Ali, 1 May 1947, *SWJN* (2nd Series), Vol. 2, 494.
38. Kumaraswamy, *India's Israel Policy*, op. cit., 89, 90.

## 24. Meanings of Freedom

1. Nehru to Asaf Ali, 18 June 1947, *SWJN* (2nd Series), Vol. 3, 331. Nehru had made the same point in an earlier letter to Asaf Ali on 7 June, op. cit., 150–51.
2. *Bombay Chronicle*, 31 August 1947.
3. See for instance *Bombay Chronicle*, 2 and 3 April 1947.
4. *CWMG*, Vol. 89, 179–80, has a full account of the speech at the prayer meeting on 13 September 1947 but does not have the references to Asaf Ali that are in the *Bombay Chronicle*'s report of it. *Bombay Chronicle*, 14 September 1947.
5. Jawaharlal Nehru to Vallabhbhai Patel, 27 October 1947, *SWJN* (2nd Series), Vol. 4, 517.
6. Debate on foreign policy in the Central Legislature, 4 December 1947, *SWJN* (2nd Series), Vol. 4, 602.
7. *Bombay Chronicle*, 19 September 1947.

## 25. Closing the Circle

1. Sengupta, *Sarojini Naidu: A Biography*, op. cit., 303.
2. *Asian Relations: Report of the Proceedings and Documentation of the First Asian Relations Conference, New Delhi, March–April 1947* (Authors Press, New Delhi, 2003), 242–43.
3. *Times of India*, 20 March 1947.
4. Sarojini Naidu to Syud Hossain, 29 June 1947, Syud Hossain Papers.
5. Sengupta, *Sarojini Naidu*, op. cit., 313–14.
6. Taya Zinkin, *Reporting India* (London, Chatto & Windus, 1962), 68.

7. Vinodh, *A Forgotten Ambassador in Cairo*, op. cit., 266 and elsewhere has these details.
8. J.B. Kripalani, *My Times: An Autobiography* (Rupa, New Delhi, 2004), 498.
9. Syed Mahmud to S.K. Sinha, in Datta and Cleghorn, *A Nationalist Muslim and Indian Politics*, op, cit., 263–64.
10. Ibid., xx–xxi.
11. Telegram to Abdul Qayyum Khan dated 18 January 1948 and thereafter letter dated 29 January 1948, ibid., 265, 267.
12. Jawaharlal Nehru to Syed Mahmud, dated 26 February 1948, Datta and Cleghorn, *A Nationalist Muslim and Indian Politics*, op. cit., 268–69.
13. Jawaharlal Nehru to Asaf Ali, 10 January 1948, *SWJN* (2nd Series), Vol. 5, 567.
14. Asaf Ali to Jawaharlal Nehru, *SWJN*, vol. 7, 713. Date not given but Nehru's reply is dated 4 August in which he says that this journalist has 'a particular grouse against me'.
15. See for instance Sri Prakasa, *Pakistan*, op. cit., 31–34.
16. Jawaharlal Nehru to Vijaya Lakshmi Pandit, 21 February 1948, *SWJN* (2nd Series), Vol. 5, 570.
17. Jawaharlal Nehru to Asaf Ali, 16 February 1948, SWJN (2nd Series), Vol. 5, 493.
18. Inder Malhotra, 'Aruna Asaf Ali Obituary: Heroine of India's Freedom Struggle', *The Guardian*, 30 July 1996.
19. Details may be found in F. No. F2(119), 50 LSG, 'Purchase of Building at Darya Ganj owned by HE Shri Asaf Ali', Delhi State Archives, 1950.
20. I am grateful to Vivek Katju for sharing a copy of this letter with me.
21. *M. Asaf Ali's Memoirs*, op. cit., 313.
22. *Aruna Asaf Ali: A Compassionate Radical*, op. cit., 118.
23. Jagat S. Mehta, *The Tryst Betrayed: Reflections in Diplomacy and Development* (Penguin, New Delhi, 2010).
24. 'Letters to Chief Ministers', 8 April 1953, *SWJN* (2nd Series), Vol. 22, 534.

# Acknowledgements

In thinking about and writing this book I have benefited greatly from assistance, suggestions and advice from: Dr Abdur Razzaque Ziyadi, Prof. Adnan Farooqui, Prof. Chaman Lal, Prof. Gyanesh Kudesia, Prof. Indivar Kamtekar, Jairam Ramesh, Jyoti Luthra, Prof. Makarand Paranjape, Manini Chatterjee, M.K. Venu, Prof. Mohammad Sajjad, Navtej Sarna, Dr Pallavi Raghavan, Pankaj Pachauri, Pramod Kapoor, Dr Rakhshanda Jalil, Prof. Ravi Mishra, Prof. Salil Mishra, Dr Salima Anjum Zaidi, Dr Sanjay Kumar, Prof. Sharif Husain Qazmi, Sheela Reddy, Dr Syeda Hamid, T.C.A. Achintya and Vivek Katju. As for many others the scholarship of the late Prof. Mushirul Hasan has been for me too a compass to navigate one's way through the maze of intercommunal relations in the second and third decades of the twentieth century.

I am deeply indebted to Sohail Hashmi, master chronicler and historian of Delhi, for showing me around the Kucha Chelan locality and for providing me details about Asaf Ali that I would have otherwise not been able to access.

I am grateful to Dr Ravi Mishra, Joint Director, Nehru Memorial Museum and Library (now the Prime Minister's Museum and Library) for inviting me in March 2022 to speak on 'The Asaf Alis in the Indian National Movement'. I am similarly grateful to Dr Sanjay Kumar, Secretary, Deshkal Society, for inviting me to deliver the Dr Ravindra Kumar Memorial Lecture in November 2022 and permitting me to speak on 'Freedom in Jail: Ahmednagar Fort and the Quit India Period'. These interactions included many useful suggestions from the audience and helped me clarify my approach.

Delhi's knowledge institutions whose collections were so useful in compiling material for this book have been of immense help: The Premchand Archives and Literary Centre, Jamia Millia Islamia, the Prime Minister's Museum and Library, the National Archives of India, the Delhi State Archives and the library of the India International Centre.

My gratitude to Chiki Sarkar and Juggernaut for their commitment to this book. My editor Parth Mehrotra overcame my resistance to embark on a book on the national movement and then embraced the idea of looking at the period through relatively lesser-known individuals. I have greatly appreciated his exceptional editorial support during the course of researching and writing the book. Devangana Ojha and Arani Sinha vastly improved this book with their editorial interventions.

My wife Ranjana and daughters Pallavi and Antara have been patient, encouraging and supportive throughout the time I have worked on *Circles of Freedom*. As always they have been sounding boards, editors and clear-sighted critics.

# Index